In 1956 Russia's Communist leader Nikita Khrushchev said, *"We will take America without firing a shot. We do not have to invade the U.S. We will destroy you from within...."* Progressives are fulfilling Khrushchev's promise by making this country impotent, a socialist state controlled by amoral wealthy elites who seek to overthrow America from the inside out by redefining our rights, our institutions and ideals.

PROGRESSIVE EVIL

HOW RADICALS ARE
REDEFINING AMERICA'S RIGHTS, INSTITUTIONS AND IDEALS
MAKING HER GLOBALLY IRRELEVANT FOR THE END TIMES

LTC ROBERT L. MAGINNIS

DEFENDER

CRANE, MO

Progressive Evil: How Radicals Are Redefining America's Rights, Institutions,
and Ideals, Making Her Globally Irrelevant for the End Times
by LTC Robert L. Maginnis (USA, Retired)

Defender Publishing
Crane, MO 65633

Printed in the United States of America.

ISBN: 978-1-948014-23-6

A CIP catalog record of this book is available from the Library of
Congress.

Cover illustration and design by Jeffrey Mardis.

Dedication

To all Americans who share my love for our country, and who, like me, want to protect her from the ravages of radical progressivism.

Acknowledgments

I gratefully acknowledge…

Jan, my wife, who tolerated my taking yet another adventure into the realm of writing about a pressing issue.

My Christian brother, Don Mercer, who selflessly edited and made insightful recommendations for this effort. His wisdom, spiritual maturity, and knowledge of our culture and God's Word was most helpful.

Certainly, our founders, mostly godly men who had the biblical insight and wisdom to cobble together the documents that provided America with a unique foundation and for their tenacity to launch this nation into this challenging world 243 years ago.

The Lord Jesus Christ who gave me life, the energy, and the insight to write this important work to hopefully help others understand our present challenges and how the current circumstances are ushering in the end times.

Robert Lee Maginnis
Woodbridge, Virginia

CONTENTS

Section IV
Introduction: Progressivism's War against American Exceptionalism

PREFACE

Western humanity as we know it is on a downward spiral, thanks in part to cultural Marxism—a social and political movement that promotes unreason and irrationality through the guise of various social justice causes. That ideology deliberately deceives and disarms the malleable, unsuspecting masses. In fact, cultural Marxism is the tool of the contemporary progressivism, an evil concept that has ancient roots and apologists through the ages, like nineteenth-century German philosopher Georg Wilhelm Friedrich Hegel, Russian leader Vladimir Lenin, former US Presidents Woodrow Wilson and Franklin D. Roosevelt, and more contemporary American progressive apostles like Hillary Clinton, Barack Obama, and Bernie Sanders, among others.

The contemporary progressive left—much of the modern-day Democratic Party—has in recent years descended into sheer madness (mental illness), dragging American society down the proverbial sinkhole of slimy humanity. Consider that Democrats continue to seek to remove the constitutionally elected President Donald Trump through whatever legal or illegal means necessary, no matter the damage that campaign does to our constitutional republic. They even challenged the depths of prudence when they broke the mold set years ago on how to eject a Supreme Court nominee. Specifically, contemporary Democratic senators on the Judiciary Committee made the process to unseat President George H. W. Bush's 1991 Supreme Court nominee Clarence Thomas over sexual misconduct allegations to appear to be mere child's play compared to their radical misconduct during the 2018 confirmation process for President Trump's Supreme Court nominee, Judge Brett Kavanaugh.

Those radical progressive senators—Diane Feinstein, Richard Durbin, Patrick Leahy, Sheldon Whitehouse, Amy Klobuchar, Chris Coons, Richard Blumenthal, Mazie Hirono, Cory Booker, and Kamala Harris—savagely attacked Judge Kavanaugh and his family by disregarding all truth and they denied him both the presumption of innocence and due process. Those same Democrat senators abandoned all respect for common civility. Further, other Democrats' incivility knows no bounds, as evidenced by the madness among their ranks since the Trump election by rabid, mob-like harassment of Republican officials at restaurants, theaters, and airports—chanting insults like "racists" and "white supremacists."

These incidents, whether in the Senate chambers or on American streets and in public establishments, demonstrate a degree of incivility that goes far beyond policy differences among so-called good citizens. Both the left and right may differ about socialized medicine, gun control, the minimum wage, and abortion; however, disagreeing about policies doesn't explain why the progressive left seems to be totally, going-off-the-rails insane in terms of both behavior and perverted social views.

There is no rational explanation as to why the Democratic left embraces perverted views, such as their insistence that dozens of different genders exist, forcing young girls to share bathrooms with grown men confused about their own sexuality; eliminating voter registration requirements; or acting seemingly blind to the potential consequences of importing illegal immigrants—some of whom are violent criminals or terrorists—who come from depressed and terrorist-spewing countries by eliminating America's borders and doing away with its frontline defenders. Remember, in 2018 there was a flurry of leading Democrat lawmakers, including presidential office seekers, who called for the elimination of our frontline defense against criminal and other aliens— the US Immigration and Customs Enforcement (ICE).

The insanity seen among Democrats in 2018 and well into 2019 isn't confined to the radical left political class. No, they infected even our schools. Did you hear about the Florida middle-school physical-education teacher punished for refusing to enter the boys' locker room and shower area to observe a minor female undressing and showering? Yes, this confused girl who self-"identified" as a male was granted permission by school officials to undress and shower with boys.

The progressive left even eats its own when they refuse to fit a preordained radical stereotype. A US Marine war veteran hired as a Democratic Party leader in Pennsylvania was forced to resign when the veteran's superior saw his Facebook page that read: "I stand for the flag, I kneel at the cross."[1] The veteran's offended boss said, "We have a zero tolerance for sexual harassment or racism of any kind."[2]

This sort of behavior by the radical left is delusional, depraved, and bizarre. But there is more. Democrats in 2018 encouraged left-wing mobs to scream at Republican officials and refuse to be civil to them until they (Democrats) take control again. Remember, Hillary Clinton told CNN: "You cannot be civil with a political party [Republican] that wants to destroy what you stand for, for what you care about."[3] Clinton promised that when Democrats "win back the House and/or the Senate, that's when civility can start again." Really? That's totalitarianism like we've seen with Islamic supremacists who insist that peace only comes once they are in control. By the way, how are the Democrats doing now that they control the House?

Not all leftists agree with Clinton's promise to resurrect civility once back in power. Former Attorney General for President Barack Obama,

Eric Holder, told Democrats at a 2018 political rally to "kick" Republicans ("when they go low, we kick them"), and the new (second-time) Speaker of the House, Nancy Pelosi, told a New York political gathering in 2018 to expect "collateral damage" to fellow Americans who don't agree with her party's radical progressive agenda. Then perhaps the most outrageous and radical progressive comment came from a Minnesota Democratic Party communications official, William Davis, who threatened to "guillotine"—behead—Republicans.[4]

Thanks to these radical progressive elites; their growing chorus of contemporary protégés; and a complacent, self-absorbed, mostly godless society, the evil of cultural Marxism is succeeding at pushing America rapidly into a transitional phase of postmodern irrelevance. Yes, American society is becoming very different than it was in the past—it is far more self-focused and narcissistic, while seeking to destroy the last vestiges of true Christianity, moral principles, and everything good that once distinguished this country as a special place among the nations of the world.

The only way to understand the radical progressive left is to consider the spiritual dimension of their insanity. After all, humans are at their core spiritual beings—our thoughts, worldview, and identity.

Yes, these are cataclysmic times, especially for the spiritually discerning Christian. Evidence of America's cultural implosion is evident, and so might be Christ's promised return. After all, Jesus Christ warns in Matthew 24:37 (NIV): "As it was in the days of Noah, so it will be at the coming of the Son of Man." Foreboding times are upon us.

Contemporary America is rapidly racing down the cultural Marxist pathway, much as did the people in Noah's time—just prior to the Flood—while seemingly oblivious to the present danger satiated with their routine of "eating and drinking, marrying and giving in marriage, until the day that [Noah] entered into the ark."

Noah's contemporaries were warned about their wickedness and were told that every imagination of their thoughts was evil. They were corrupt, and violence abounded.

Christ also taught about another ancient time in Luke 17:29 (KJV): "Likewise also as it was in the days of Lot." Life moved along as normal until suddenly one day "it rained fire and brimstone from heaven, and destroyed them all. Even thus shall it be in the day when the son of man is revealed."

America's national morality—thanks to progressives using cultural Marxism—has sunk to rock bottom as did the people in the time of Noah and Lot. Ruth Graham, the wife of world-famous evangelist Billy Graham, once sounded the alarm about our national morality that should resonate loudly today as well: "If God doesn't judge America, He will need to apologize to Sodom and Gomorrah!"[5] Indeed.

God's message for America is clear. The wicked people in Noah's day who were evil and violent were destroyed by a global flood. Sexually immoral people in Lot's day were destroyed by fire. They were certainly warned of the coming destruction. Noah warned them of judgment even though they mocked him for building an ark on dry land with no sea known to man at the time. Similarly, Lot was "vexed" by the "unlawful deeds" (the sin) of Sodom, and called out their wicked ways. Yet both peoples ignored the truth, and judgment came swiftly.

Our time is very much like those insane days of Noah and Lot that were characterized by violence, wickedness, sexual immorality, and self-serving godlessness. Morally, America has abandoned the clear teachings in the Ten Commandments: "Thou shalt not kill" (abortion); "Thou shalt not commit adultery" (the sexual revolution); "Thou shalt not steal" (the socialists' wealth redistribution); and "Thou shalt not bear false witness against thy neighbor" (the defamation of their opponents like Judge Kavanaugh). Rather, our society and some of its leading institutions (government, academia, and business) have embraced a malignant, evil worldview.

God's spirit continues to strive with man, convicting him of his sin, and will continue to do so until Christ's return. As Genesis 6:3 (KJV) warns, "My spirit shall not always strive with man." Modern humanity must choose to turn to Him with all their hearts and turn away from sin, but as we know, most will not repent. The Day of Judgment will come upon them swiftly unawares.

Yes, we are ripe for judgment! Worldwide, we already see evidence of it: Our finances are constantly threatened by cyber thieves; earthquakes are routine; governments are unreliable; and man-made violence/wars know no end. There are massive, killing fires; devastating disease outbreaks; hurricanes; floods; and famines; and an epidemic of godlessness rages across the mostly amoral earth. Yet somehow man, in his secular stupor, laughs mockingly at these warnings and asserts that there will never be a judgment day. He lives as if there is no true God and lives without fear of a holy and righteous Supreme Being.

Scripture is very clear about such an affront to our Almighty God. The prophet Isaiah warned, "Woe to those who call evil good, and good evil, who put darkness for light and light for darkness, who put bitter for sweet and sweet for bitter" (Isaiah 5:20, NIV). Even the angel in the Revelation to John echoes that warning: "Woe! Woe! Woe to the inhabitants of the earth, because of the trumpet blasts about to be sounded by the other three angels!" (Revelation 8:13, NIV). Judgment is coming!

The progressive radicals aren't blind to the global chaos, however. They ignore the truth and the promised judgment. They are globalists who seek a one-world government—governed, of course, by themselves, the "elite," as prophesied in the Revelation. They seek a world stranger than that portrayed by futurist writers George Orwell in *1984* and Aldous Huxley in *Brave New World*—but on steroids. Modern cultural Marxist progressives take a figurative wrecking ball to all that's good in America while worshiping at the feet of evil. Consider some examples of their use of chaos.

Progressives use chaos to advance their revolutionary cause on America's college campuses. Any professor who dares to oppose the progressive agenda—which includes promoting abortion on demand, global warming, open borders, and more—is automatically denounced by delicate "snowflakes" (those easily offended by the statements or actions of others) who call for the professor's ouster while other baton-wielding students suited all in black destroy campus buildings in protest.

California's ruling progressive "elite" embrace chaos as well, destroying that state's formerly enviable environment. Today, San Francisco overflows with welcomed illegal immigrants and the homeless, and that once-beautiful downtown is covered with discarded hypodermic needles from tolerated illicit drug users and random piles of human feces. Meanwhile, California's "elite" progressives focus on their misguided agenda that includes such activities as banning plastic straws, debating whether to release a mass murderer (from the Charles Manson family), and celebrating their status as a sanctuary state—a finger in the eye to the Trump administration's efforts to get tough on illegal criminal aliens.

Don't expect these progressives to listen to reason and logic. Besides, they can't be bothered with reason, much less with the existential, which is why they elect to follow what the Bible calls the "broad way" that leads to destruction. For them, God's commandments aren't necessary—besides, the progressives will choose to worship other gods to include themselves and especially big, progressive government.

So, what does the remnant of God-fearing Americans do about the evil of the progressive radicals?

We need spiritual revival to sweep the land; otherwise, we are finished, doomed as a nation. We need to replace the "elite" progressives who push a cultural Marxist ideology with men and women who love God and fear Him. These replacements are humble people, given to prayer, who seek God's face and turn from their wicked ways. They are modern Esthers, Elijahs, Ezekiels, and Daniels.

Yes, the end is coming. Judgment is just around the corner, and then Jesus Christ will establish the Kingdom of God on earth. He said, "Immediately after the tribulation of those days…they shall see the Son of man coming in the clouds of heaven with power and great glory" (Matthew 24:29–30, KJV). He will "wipe away all tears from their eyes; and there shall be no more death, neither sorrow, nor crying, neither

shall there be any more pain: for the former things are passed away"
(Revelation 21:4, KJV).

While we know with 100 percent accuracy that the prophecies of the
future are certain, we cannot be complacent. Jesus told us to be about
our Father's business until He returns. Therefore, we must fight the evil
works of the progressives. In so doing, who knows how many will see
their error and turn to Christ?

Certainly, it appears that the majority of the Democratic Party
has abandoned God and His laws, which reminds me of something
Aleksandr Solzhenitsyn, the celebrated Russian author and gulag
survivor, said about why communism murdered so many innocents:
"Men have forgotten God; that's why all this has happened."[6] That's why
America is on the downward spiral, God is absent, and His judgment is
certain. God's people must double their efforts to seek spiritual revival in
our land, if it's not already too late.

SECTION I

Introduction:
Primer on Progressivism

Modern America is flushing out of its public life much of the good that God created through our Founding Fathers in exchange for the false promises of the so-called progressive left, the contemporary cultural Marxists who are thundering across our former fruited plains.

Twice before in ancient times (in the days of Noah and Lot), we saw similar developments, and in each case, the history of humanity was drastically and destructively altered. Today, America is dangerously close to being in the same predicament. Why? Because by examining the ancient precedents and comparing their similarities with today's America, we can conclude that a progressive, cultural Marxist ideology—the tenets of pure evil among mankind—is at the root of our present perilous times.

Worse, if that's possible, this volume will propose that a major reason behind America's absence in biblical prophecies of the end times is that the United States simply becomes irrelevant at some point—not because of catastrophic enemy attacks (although that is possible, especially given China's growing military prowess), natural disaster, or economic collapse. While any or all of these events could contribute to irrelevance, it is the expansive growth across America of cultural Marxism—the evil that haunts twenty-first-century mankind—that is the real danger.

Admittedly, it will take more than a mere evil philosophy to bring about the destruction of America through irrelevancy. Of course, enough people must be behind this toxic movement, committed people with means and tools. Unfortunately, such people—especially the contemporary Democratic Party controlled by leftists and socialists—with the necessary motivation and resources do exist, and their numbers and radicalism are growing. They seek a very different future for America than what I see, which is one that echoes the prophetic end times.

So, fellow Americans, the time to reverse course is now, immediately. But is that possible?

The first section of *Progressive Evil* shows how the left intends to employ cultural Marxism to destroy the good attributed to our founders. It wasn't always that way, as you will see in chapter 1, which explores the roots of the progressive movement and some of the initial good the Progressive Era (1890–1920) brought to America. However, progressives then and especially now have a dark, evil side that is self-absorbed, arrogant, and clearly anti-Christian. They seeded the evil of the Nazis, the eugenics movement (forced sterilization and abortion on demand), and racial discrimination, and brought us the morally bankrupt contemporary sexual revolution that includes the #MeToo movement and radical feminism. Next, they will destroy the remaining vestiges of American goodness, replacing it with an unrecognizable nation or perhaps something worse than the gulags of the former Soviet Russia and China's Maoist concentration camps of the 1950s.

Chapter 2 delves into the progressives' established operating principles, many of their goals for future America, the growing support they enjoy among the gullible and now mostly anti-Christian American public, and their strategy for year 2020 to recapture the White House and the US Senate, and expand their control of the House of Representatives, then remake America in their radical, self-appointed elitist image.

Chapter 3 presents a psychological profile of the progressives and their modern movement, exposing who this cabal really is and what that means for America's future. Further, Bible-believing Christians must not be duped by modern progressives whose siren song piously claims to follow Jesus Christ; no, theirs is a false, distorted, and bankrupt faith. This chapter makes clear that progressives have a total disdain for Bible-believing Christians and have every intention of forcing us to abandon our faith by fascistic coercion if necessary. They seek to excise every influence of God Almighty from the public square, replacing that goodness with humanism, evil, and worship of themselves. They are a modern anti-Christ movement.

This section is a primer, a foundation upon which to launch our journey into the damage progressives have done and are doing to our Bill of Rights (Section II), America's key institutions (Section III), and the founders' ideals that made America an exceptional country (Section IV).

Progressive Evil wraps up the progressive assault on America with a conclusion that demonstrates their mental illness and the resulting palpable evil that makes America irrelevant, therefore absent in the prophetic end times, albeit helpful to Satan in paving the way for Antichrist.

1

Roots of the American Progressive Movement

For many on the political right, progressivism brings up images of a communist, socialist, Marxist, hippie, and worse. It's a nasty label, not a flattering image, but the term at its core is simply characterized by the concept of progress. Who is against progress?

Progressive ideology is about making use of or being interested in new ideas, findings, or opportunities. It's about the advancement and adoption of social reform for the amelioration of society's ills. Progressives through the ages have come from all backgrounds, claiming they promote freedom of the individual to compete in fair conditions while championing the progress and improvement of society.

The problem for modern Americans is that progressivism is fluid, nuanced, and arguably hijacked by contemporary radicals. It has become a political ideology that divides Americans and rejects much of our founders' principled ideals.

Modern Americans tend to be ideologically liberal, conservative, or some combination of both, which is an outcome that can be traced in part to America's experience with progressivism. Those who tend to embrace a liberal ideology are likely rooted in progressivism while conservatives tend to be rooted in our founders' constitutionalism, a concept defined as "a complex of ideas, attitudes and patterns elaborating the principle that the authority of government derives from the people, and is limited by a body of fundamental law."[7]

Progressivism has come to refer to the belief that government should address social problems, a "Hamiltonian concept of positive government directing the destinies of the nation at home and abroad," according to historian William Leuchtenburg. He wrote:

> [Progressives] had little but contempt for the strict construction of the Constitution by conservative judges, who would restrict the power of the national government to act against social evils and to extend the blessings of democracy to favored lands. The real enemy was particularism, state rights, limited government.[8]

Progressivism became an umbrella label that blossomed in America 130 years ago (circa 1890) as a response to a wide range of economic, political, social, and moral issues. Those economic and social problems were associated with the country's rapid industrialization known as the "Gilded Age," a term attributed to Mark Twain and Charles Dudley Warner, who satirized the wealth inequality between society's "haves" and "have-nots" and was represented by a thin coating of gold that hid ruthless business practices and political corruption, which spawned a social movement of conscience that grew into a political movement that has profoundly impacted modern America.[9]

Regular people at the time responded to the lack of human compassion on the part of the wealthy upper class who failed to share their new prosperity, thanks to industrialization. Thus, some of the have-nots (mostly educated middle class) came together to fight for fairer wages, shorter workdays, and improved living conditions.

America's Gilded Age (1860s to 1890s) prospered the few, and as a result, saw the United States become a very different place, a growing urban culture as opposed to its early agrarian base. One scholar said that "steam and electricity replaced human muscle, iron replaced wood, and steel replaced iron. Oil could lubricate machines and light homes, streets and factories." It was a time when people and farm products could be moved by railroads in large quantities and more quickly than ever before, and the young sons and daughters from the farms came to the cities to find their fortunes.[10]

Technology changed America in the Gilded Age with the introduction of innovations like motion pictures, telegraphy, the phonograph, the safety razor, and the first plastics. The typewriter and adding machine came of age in the late 1800s. These inventions opened America to new possibilities and at the same time created a new, wealthy class of Americans.

This was the time of trusts and tycoons who built America's railroads and skyscrapers. The tycoons included the likes of Andrew Carnegie, an industrialist known for expanding America's steel production, and John D. Rockefeller's Standard Oil, which monopolized America's energy production.

The concentration of power (wealth among the few) historically was always a red flag among some of America's best leaders. Founder and later president Thomas Jefferson (1743–1826) warned long before the Gilded Age about the dangers associated with the concentration of wealth in the hands of a few. He said, "The banking establishments are more dangerous than standing armies."[11]

President Abraham Lincoln (1809–1865) said in his famous Civil War-era Gettysburg Address (November 19, 1863) that America seeks a "government of the people, by the people, for the people, shall not perish from the earth"—not one that sits on the sidelines allowing the wealthy to abuse the have-nots. Other presidents echoed that sentiment as well.[12]

President Theodore Roosevelt (1858–1919) proclaimed: "It is necessary that laws should be passed to prohibit the use of corporate funds directly or indirectly for political purposes; it is still more necessary that such laws should be thoroughly enforced." This is an obvious reference to the wealthy contributing to the corruption of the political class for their own largesse.[13]

President Franklin D. Roosevelt (1882–1945) echoed a similar view: "Government by organized money is just as dangerous as government by organized mob."[14] That's quite an indictment of the corrupting influence at the time, which explains Roosevelt's proposal of a "Second Bill of Rights" that included medical care, sustainable employment, and quality education.[15]

Even Republican President Dwight Eisenhower (1890–1969) reiterated a similar sentiment when he warned: "We must guard against the acquisition of unwarranted influence…by the military-industrial complex. The potential for the disastrous rise of misplaced power exists and will persist."[16] Clearly, contemporary America has seen this vis-à-vis the deep state that includes government bureaucrats and nongovernment, deep-pocketed influencers.

The progressive movement attacked these unpleasant byproducts of America's rapid industrialization in the Gilded Age: the exploitation of child labor, corruption in government, and ruthless business practices, for example. In light of such unpopular effects, progressives found it necessary to alter the political order to address such challenges. So they demanded that the public exercise more control over government such as through direct primaries that nominate accountable candidates for public office, direct elections of US senators as opposed to their appointment by state legislatures (as provided for in the US Constitution), the ballot initiative, the referendum, and women's suffrage (the women's right to vote in political elections).

These Progressive Era reformers were mostly urban, conservative, educated, middle-class people who used their growing influence to right social wrongs using the above tools (direct primaries, direct elections of senators, etc.) to enact redresses such as minimum wage laws for women workers, industrial accident insurance, child labor restrictions, and improved working conditions in factories.

There is a sidebar view, at least prior to World War II, that progressivism was an extension of populism, but that may be a misinterpretation of reality. Populism and progressivism are really very different. Early-twentieth-century populists revolted because of hard times on the farm, while progressives were the urbanites battling for reform in a period of prosperity attributed to industrialization. Richard Hofstadter, an American historian and professor at Columbia University in the mid twentieth century, wrote in his book, *Age of Reform*:

> Populism had been overwhelmingly rural and provincial. The ferment of the Progressive Era was urban middle-class and nationwide. Above all, progressivism differed from populism in the fact that the middle classes of the cities not only joined the trend toward protest but took over its leadership.[17]

What prompted these urbanites to protest? The statist revolution theory suggests that their zeal for reform was inspired by their "psychological maladjustment resulting from the loss of status they had formerly possessed." The Gilded Age's industrial advances moved them from being the nation's most influential families to, at the turn of the twentieth century, being surpassed or ignored in almost all walks of life. Historian Hofstadter explained, "Modern students of social psychology have suggested that certain social-psychological tensions are heightened both in social groups that are rising in the social scale and those that are falling."[18]

This view may apply to eastern progressive leaders reared in aristocratic (wealthy) homes, who lost status. However, it certainly doesn't apply to the great majority of progressive leaders from elsewhere who came from old but humble families, who became interested in reform.

Progressives did alter American politics during the era, according to Thomas G. West, who wrote the following in his book, *The Progressive Revolution in Politics and Political Science*: "It was a total rejection in theory, and a partial rejection in practice, of the principles and policies on which America had been founded and on the basis of which the Civil War [1861–1865] had been fought and won only a few years earlier."[19]

What Early American Progressives
Believed about the Role of Government

Progressives have tried and will continue to try to erase the wonderful work of our founders and replace it with something radically different, thus making average Americans far less free. Author and attorney Mark R. Levin advances this view in his book, *Rediscovering Americanism*. He writes that progressivism is thoroughly hostile to the underlying principles of the nation's founding. Levin argues:

> Progressivism is the idea of the inevitability of historical progress and the perfectibility of man—and his self-realization—through the national community or collective. While its intellectual and political advocates clothe its core in populist terminology, and despite the existence of democratic institutions and cyclical voting, progressivism's emphasis on material egalitarianism and societal engineering, and its insistence on concentrated, centralized administrative rule, lead inescapably to varying degrees of autocratic governance. Moreover, for progressives there are no absolute or permanent truths, only passing and distant historical events. Thus even values are said to be relative to time and circumstances; there is no eternal moral order—that is, what was true and good in 1776 and before is not necessarily true and good today. Consequently, the very purpose of America's founding is debased.[20]

Consider seven progressive views regarding government and the governed juxtaposed with the views of our founders.

1. Progressives Believe Government Makes You Who You Are

America's founders believed that people are created equal, with certain inalienable rights and an obligation to obey natural law. They believed that people are given by nature the ability to reason and that the moral law is discovered by reason. They acknowledged that government can be a threat, but also believed that without government, the weaker person is "not secured against the violence of the stronger." James Madison wrote the obvious about human nature: "If men were angels, no government would be necessary."[21]

The founders believed that freedom is not granted by government, but by God. Therefore, government exists to serve the individual by enforcing natural law for the political community by securing the people's natural rights. At home, it performs this duty by enforcing criminal and civil law; overseas, it does so through a strong national defense.

Progressives reject American heritage and our founding principles "if there is to be human progress," according to Levin. Further, Herbert Croly (1869–1930), a leading progressive thinker in his time and author of *The Promise of American Life*, supports Levin's conclusion by arguing: "The better future which Americans propose to build is nothing if not an idea which must in certain essential respects emancipate them from their past."[22]

To illustrate this divide, progressives labeled the founders' view of people and their flawed government as a product of benign nature. The progressive goal in government was freedom, but very different from the founders' view. The progressive insists on limits to freedom imposed by nature and necessity. Further, freedom is redefined as the fulfillment of human capacities, the primary task of government.

John Dewey, the father of American progressivism, elaborates on government's role in advancing citizen freedom: "The state has the responsibility for creating institutions under which individuals can effectively realize the potentialities that are theirs." Further, he said, government is the means of creating individuals to their fullest potential, and "individuality in a social and moral sense is something to be wrought out."[23]

2. Progressives Don't Believe People Must Consent to Be Ruled

America's founders believed mankind is naturally free; therefore, as outlined in the Massachusetts Constitution of 1780, any government must be "formed by a voluntary association of individuals." The principle is simple. Government is run based on laws that are made by elected representatives of the people, and the accountable officials are subject to removal through frequent reelection requirements.[24]

Progressives reject the founders' social compact idea. Charles E. Merriam (1874–1953), a professor of political science at the University of Chicago and a progressive, wrote:

> The individualistic ideas of the "natural right" school of political theory, indorsed in the Revolution, are discredited and repudiated.... The origin of the state is regarded, not as the result of a deliberate agreement among men, but as the result of historical development, instinctive rather than conscious; and rights are considered to have their source not in nature, but in law.[25]

Thus, according to Merriam, government does not require consent of the people just as long as it brings out the potential of individuals. He also said, "It was the idea of the state that supplanted the social contract as the ground of political right."[26]

3. Progressives Reject God and Faith

Our founders believed God is the author of liberty and of moral law, which guides us to happiness and fulfillment on earth. Further, God endows people with natural rights and "assigns them duties under the law of nature. Believers added that the God of nature is also the God of the Bible, while secular thinkers denied that God was anything more than the God of nature. Everyone saw liberty as a 'sacred cause.'"[27]

Some progressives dismiss God as a myth and redefine Him as human freedom that is realized through the right political organization (government). In fact, John Burgess (1844–1931), a prominent progressive, wrote that the purpose of the state is to realize the "perfection of humanity, the civilization of the world; the perfect development of the human reason and its attainment to universal command over individualism; the *apotheosis of man* (man becoming God)."[28]

4. Progressives Embrace Unlimited Government

America's founders sought to protect the citizens' privacy and believed that government was insufficient to direct people in terms of God, religion, and their own health. Evidently, America's religious heritage, which included persecution for one's faith, convinced the founders that liberty meant self-interested private associations—religion—had to be allowed.

America's founders refused to saddle one's private religious views and practices with government oversight, however. After all, government was merely human, not divine.

Progressives take a diametrical opposite position from the founders regarding religion. Progressives view the state as divine. They view anything private as selfishness and oppression and not to be protected by government. In fact, progressives view religion as something that deserves at a minimum some government oversight.

Therefore, people of faith should be leery of progressives. After all, Dewey, a leading progressive American leader, remarked that Plato's *Republic* presents us with the "perfect man in the perfect state," the evident obliteration of the private life by government. Further, John Burgess nails the issue with the statement that "the most fundamental and indispensable mark of statehood" was "the original, absolute, unlimited, universal power over the individual subject, and all associations of subjects." That view sounds more like Karl Marx than Thomas Jefferson. Communism makes a slave of society.[29]

5. Progressive Government Wants to Be God

Our founders created a government to promote moral conditions that encouraged values like honesty, justice, patriotism, courage, and frugality. For example, they provided for a system of personal property while making allowances for the less privileged to find a path to better lives.

An aspect of the founders' effort to promote a moral society was to protect the family—especially children. Specifically, they saw fit to regulate sexual conduct aimed at encouraging enduring marriages to protect the welfare and future of America's progeny.

The founders promoted generic Christianity because it encouraged the formation of values considered good for society. For example, the Northwest Ordinance of 1787 expressed support for education because "religion, morality, and knowledge [are] necessary to good government and the happiness of mankind."[30]

Progressivism has a contrary view. It endorses protection of the poor from capitalism through a socialistic practice of redistribution of wealth, antitrust laws, and other regulations that dictate almost every aspect of commerce.

Progressives also believe in the "spiritual" nurturing of the citizens—not by encouraging religion, but by promoting conservation, education, the arts, and culture.

6. Progressives Are Sold-out Globalists

Our founders would be appalled by America's contemporary foreign adventures and our long history of nation-building around the world—e.g., Afghanistan. For the founders, foreign entanglements were to be limited and only entered to protect our national defense. The concept of using our armed forces to spread democracy abroad was contrary to the founders' intent.

Progressives took a radically different approach to international actions and foreign policy. Their view of history that leads mankind to freedom requires modern science and elite leadership—fellow enlightened progressives—especially the sophisticates of Western Europe.

Progressives believe those educated in the latest sciences should seek opportunities to rule the less-advanced world, a colonialist view. Political scientist Charles Merriam left no doubt about their intent:

> The Teutonic races must civilize the politically uncivilized. They must have a colonial policy. Barbaric races, if incapable, may be swept away.... On the same principle, interference with the affairs of states not wholly barbaric, but nevertheless incapable of effecting political organization for themselves, is fully justified.[31]

Such heady western progressive imperialism was evident in Theodore Roosevelt's (1858–1919) book, *Expansion and Peace.* Roosevelt wrote that the best policy is global imperialism: "Every expansion of a great civilized power means a victory for law, order, and righteousness."[32] That view explains our occupation of the Philippines following the Spanish-American War (1898), which Roosevelt said was "one more fair spot of the world's surface...snatched from the forces of darkness. Fundamentally the cause of expansion is the cause of peace."[33]

Similar views were expressed by President Woodrow Wilson, who entered America in World War I to make the world safe for democracy and, without congressional approval, entered the Russian civil war in 1918 on the side of the White monarchists against the Red (communist) Bolsheviks.

7. Progressive Elites Rule the World

Our founders designed a system of government by which laws were made by officials elected by the people. The people were never to be ruled by for-life bureaucrats—an elite class of government professionals—but, as James Madison wrote, those bureaucrats should have "most wisdom to discern, and most virtue to pursue, the common good of the society."[34]

Progressives would have nothing to do with the unwashed amateurs at the helm of government. Levin said that progressive leader Croly:

> …proclaimed a new secular "science," a political and social science in which politicians, bureaucrats, academics, and experts harness the power of the state to indoctrinate and rule over the individual, and attempt to remake his nature and society in general through constant experimentation and manipulation. This is said to be progress.[35]

President Woodrow Wilson, an early progressive, endorsed Croly's view of an elite-run government. He argued that people should not be bothered with administration because they are unfit for and incapable of such government tasks. Wilson said those chores must be left to a relative handful of sensible and learned professionals, the progressive elite.[36]

Those bureaucrats must be trained in the latest science—as professional statesmen who are educated at the best universities, because politics is much too complex for simple people. In fact, as Levin quoted former President Wilson, "The federal bureaucracy will be of the noblest and most virtuous sort, with no personal, political, or ideological agenda, motivated solely and completely by its technical know-how in and public-spiritedness for the general good and welfare."[37]

Progressives didn't suggest eliminating democracy in order for the elite to ascend and rule. No, their view was to centralize power by establishing federal agencies run by neutral experts trained at the top universities and apolitical in their views. Local and state officials would be managers of highly trained staffs and would put aside the corrupting influence of politics.

Not all of today's progressives would necessarily articulate all seven views, however. Some might even express disagreement with the tenets, but whether they know it or not, all seven views form the foundation upon which they stand.

Progressive Values

Understanding progressive views about the role of government is helpful, but so is an appreciation for some more fundamental progressive values.

Founder and President Thomas Jefferson wrote that we are obliged "to respect those rights in others which we value in ourselves." Specifically, those natural rights are life and liberty of religion, association, and the possession of property. Thus, protection of life and liberty is realized through the prosecution of crimes and the associated recovery of damages from the perpetrator.[38]

Progressives reject Jefferson's claims as naïve, because men are n[ot] born free. Rather, according to early-twentieth-century progressive J[ohn] Dewey, freedom is not "something that individuals have as a ready[ly] possession."[39] He continued, saying that freedom is "somethi[ng] achieved"; it is not a gift of God or man, but a gift of g[overnment]. Therefore, explained Dewey, if man is not naturally (bo[rn free]) there are no so-called natural rights (laws). Therefore[,] and natural liberties exist only in the kingdom of m[ythical] zoology," a Darwinian view attributed to Dewey.[40]

That progressive view led the movement to conc[lude] no permanent standards of right, an obvious rejecti[on of] religions, most notably Christianity. Further, De[wey] "historical relativity," the view that humans are inde[pendent] freedom—but not by nature, rather by historical pr[ocess] according to Dewey, that right and wrong are best understood by the most enlightened because they are in conformity with history.[41]

Progressivism is grounded in the concept of progress: Mankind must move beyond the status quo and evolve into a more equal and just social construct that grants us freedom, equality, and common good. This was an ideological view especially popular in America in the late nineteenth century (circa 1890) due to a plethora of challenges associated with the Industrial Revolution: economic depression, political corruption, poverty, working conditions, child labor, unsafe consumer products, and the misuse of natural resources.

Progressivism quickly became the philosophical foundation of the American liberal tradition that spawned a "new liberalism" based on its Jeffersonian, small-government, republican origin. Initially, American progressives doubted our founders' understanding of human freedom and the necessity to check the negative powers of government. They believed that the government's task was to provide the citizenry with defenses against rising inequality, poor wages, and labor abuse.

Progressives also believed they understood the real meaning of the Preamble to the US Constitution, which begins "We the people." They believed that stronger, bigger government was necessary to advance the collective good as it affects most aspects of life. Specifically, according to progressive theorist Croly, using the nation's means to achieve the desirable liberty, equality, and opportunity for all only came with a more democratic political order that granted people the chance to flourish within the larger community of nations.

It is worth noting that progressives on both sides of the Atlantic ared a common vision for a broader global movement focused on lding a more humane, just, and economically stable world based ll opportunity for all. Of course, that view gave rise to globalism, continues today. Further, and fortunately, American progressivism a path between the radical progressive socialism prevalent in at the time and the hands-off approach of our founders.

e is also a clear set of values associated with the Progressive Era.

They embraced freedom as a value that protects the citizens from undue coercion by government that leads to a fulfilling and economically secure life for all.

The common good is a progressive value as well. It broadly means a commitment within government and society to place public needs and concerns above self-interests of the privileged—public versus private rights.

Equality is a progressive value proposed by Jefferson in our Declaration of Independence and reflected in the Universal Declaration of Human Rights (United Nations, 1948), which states: "All human beings are born free and equal in dignity and rights. They are endowed with reason and conscience and should act towards one another in a spirit of brotherhood."[42]

Social justice is a progressive value as well; it embraces the view that all people have the capacity to shape their own lives and realize their dreams.

As the reader will soon see, these progressive values are transitory and rather malleable. Progressives distort these values in a rather perverse way to marginalize all but their faithful.

History of American Progressivism

We already established that progressivism is an ideology that expresses a view of government's role and national values. It also advocates for progress—change and improvement—rather than conservative values, which preserve the status quo. With that as background, we now should consider progressivism's history beginning with the Age of Enlightenment in Europe, a subset of the eighteenth century's Age of Reason.

The Age of Reason gave Europe the idea that both knowledge and economic growth would advance civilization and the human condition. John Locke challenged the old order, the right of the people to change government that did not protect natural rights of life, liberty, and property. German philosopher Immanuel Kant joined the chorus by talking about progress from barbarism towards civilization, moving mankind toward practices and conditions that helped him prosper.[43]

These so-called enlightened ideas of liberty and progress contributed to growing doubts about the existence of an all-powerful God. Kant wrestled with the view that people's moral beliefs and practices had been based on religion, the Scriptures in the Bible or the Koran that laid out moral rules that are attributed to God, such as the Bible's Ten Commandments: Don't kill. Don't steal. Don't commit adultery. God is the authority here, not some arbitrary human opinion—and because God gave the law, man had an incentive to obey or face punishment—hell.[44]

The so-called Enlightenment was a cultural movement that coincided with the scientific revolution of the sixteenth and seventeenth centuries that attacked faith in God, the Scriptures, and organized religion in general. It killed the possibility of belief in God or any gods. It follows then that educated elite like Friedrich Nietzsche (1844–1900) declared "God is dead," and with that, he created a problem for moral philosophy. If religion was no longer the basis for moral beliefs, then what would take its place?[45]

The thinkers of the Age of Reason argued that the old way of life dictated by religion was to be replaced by a new way of thinking— enlightened thinking that championed the accomplishments of humankind. They reasoned that science and reason would introduce happiness and progress.

European enlightened thinking, as a result of the Age of Reason, influenced the nineteenth-century German Georg Wilhelm Friedrich Hegel, who is often referred to as the father of the modern progressive movement. He believed the history of mankind was the rational evolution to "perfect" humanity, but that process required a government to tame man's raw impulses. Further, Hegel's *The Philosophy of History* can be understood as man becoming god on earth.[46] That view explains the basis for progressive foreign policy as well, which is built on two central ideas from nineteenth-century German philosophy: ethical idealism and historical evolution.

Ethical idealism, according to Christopher Burkett, an associate professor of political science at Ashland University (Ashland, Ohio), "is any action motivated by a concern for one's own happiness, welfare, or interest is not moral, and accordingly, the only moral action is one undertaken purely to promote the good of others." The state's proper role, explained Burkett, is to "discourage individualistic pursuit of private interests, promoting instead cooperative moral actions that contribute to the good of the whole."[47]

Historical evolution, the second tenet of progressivism, asserts that human societies evolve from primitive origins, and over time, they become "more civilized, more ethical, and more democratic culminating in the emergence of the state." The culmination of that evolutionary process is freedom, which comes only when "a people become civilized, ethical, and democratic under the tutelage of the state."[48]

These progressive tenets are in stark contrast to the theory of our founders, who believed the laws of nature, human nature, and natural rights did not evolve; they are God-given. Further, our founders rejected the progressive notion that all self-interested actions were immoral. Burkett concluded, "Accepting human nature for what it is, [the founders] believed that the primary purpose of government was to allow individuals to exercise their liberty in pursuit of their own happiness."[49]

The progressive movement from its early days in America was always a microcosm of globalism (introduced earlier), which was predicated on the idea of elites who "knew better" than ordinary people—that's the rest of us. They (the elite progressives) know what is best for us, which gives them the moral authority to take over more functions and establish centralized government with large bureaucracies run by what Hegel, Croly, Dewey, and other progressives called "unbiased experts."

It is worth considering whether progressivism or another phenomenon really did alter America's social landscape. Thomas West argues in *Progressive Revolution in Politics and Political Science* that "few scholars...regard the progressive era as having any lasting significance in American history." West explains that there are three main explanations from those who endorse the view that progressivism did have a formative influence, however.[50]

The first argument, according to West, is that progressives "created the modern administrative state thanks to the closing of the frontier, the Gilded Age [Industrial Revolution], the rise of the modern corporation, and accidental emergencies such as wars or the Great Depression."[51]

The second argument for progressives' impact on America is the rational explanation: "Once government gets involved in providing extensive services for the public, politicians see that growth in government programs enables them to win elections. The more government does, the easier it is for congressmen to do favors for voters and donors." This explains in part the emergence of the deep state and its entrenched influencers.[52]

A third argument proposed by some scholars, according to West, is the idea that our founders are responsible for the current government overreach. Judge Robert Bork wrote in *Slouching toward Gomorrah* that the founders' devotion to the principles of liberty and equality led inexorably to the excesses of today's welfare state and cultural decay. Further, author Gordon Wood, who wrote *The American Revolution: A History*, applauds progressivism's influence by explaining that although the founders did not understand the implications of the Revolution, those ideas eventually "made possible...all our current egalitarian thinking."[53]

West agrees with the arguments that material circumstances (Industrial Revolution) and politicians' crass self-interest played a part in the transformation of American government. However, he believes today's progressivism (modern liberalism) and the associated policies arose from a conscious repudiation of the principles of the American founding rather than as a logical outgrowth, as Bork argues, of the principles of the founding. He goes on to explain that progressivism gave us a new theory of justice that significantly contributed to contemporary liberalism, the dominant view now evident in American education, media, popular culture, and politics.[54]

It would be a mistake to embrace the progressive view that their movement was America's first effort to address some of the warts that infected the young nation. In fact, there was an earlier effort, the First Reform Era, years before the American Civil War (1861–1865), that mounted social activism to reform working conditions and humanize the treatment of the mentally ill and prisoners. There was also at the same time a reform movement to abolish the great moral wrong of slavery.

The American Christian church was influenced by the "enlightened" ideas coming from Europe and progressivism at the time. Religious leaders, especially in New England, emphasized the similarities between the Anglican Church and the Puritan Congregationalists—a sort of movement to ecumenicalism. In fact, Protestant theology began questioning traditional biblical authority because of Enlightenment-rooted ideas and responded to the growing problems with a doctrine of the social gospel. Some even taught that solving social problems was a salvific necessity—works, not faith, to gain entrance to heaven.[55]

Then again on the heels of the American Civil War and lasting up to the time of the First World War, there was a Second Reform Era that overlapped the Progressive Era (1890–1920). This period, which in part enjoyed progressive support, was marked by the struggle for women's rights (the suffrage movement), the temperance movement (abstinence from alcoholic drink), and the transition from a rural economy to an urban industrial America—with an emphasis on workers' rights and conditions.

Transition to the Modern Progressive State

The contemporary progressive state owes its origins to the social and then political movement known as progressivism, or the Progressive Era. Events in that era, such as the 1911 fire that broke out at the Triangle Shirtwaist Factory in New York City, helped motivate and define the emergent progressive social movement. When the fire in that facility was announced, the workers, mostly women, ran for the exits—only to find them locked from the outside. The workers then climbed to the roof to escape the fire, but the fire engine ladders could not reach them. Many jumped to their deaths rather than face the fire, and in the end, 248 died in the senseless, preventable tragedy. Why were the doors locked?[56]

Progressives called for action in the wake of the Triangle Shirtwaist Factory fire, a cry that swept across the nation and fundamentally changed the thinking about the treatment of workers. Such disasters fueled demands for reform that eventually morphed into a political movement.

A host of progressive reformers performed important work at the time. Jane Addams (1860–1935), who grew up in Cedarville, Illinois, and received her higher education at Rockford Female Seminary, took her missionary zeal and tough rural background to found Chicago's Hull House to help immigrants adapt to American life, a typical progressive social initiative to raise the standard of living for urbanites through education and cultural enrichment programs. She is considered the founder of American social work, and in 1931 she received the Nobel Peace Prize for internationalism and peace.[57]

Reformers like Ms. Addams were helped by a cadre of like-minded journalists such as Jacob Riis, Ida Tarbell, and Upton Sinclair, who helped expose corrupt politicians and corporate greed and pressured those culprits into making reforms. These journalists, known as "muckrakers," helped inform Americans about wrongdoings and compelled them to think about what democracy really meant.

The situation of child labor in the early twentieth century was one of the muckrakers' targets. They aggressively pushed for the passage of child labor laws designed to prevent the overuse (abuse) of children in manufacturing and sought to give those working-class children the and the issue was embraced by the progressive movement. At that time, married women could not own property, make contracts, bring lawsuits, or even serve on a jury. Their husbands could legally beat them, and at that time they were required to submit to their husbands' sexual demands. All that began to change in the early 1900s, when the women's suffrage movement came into its own.

The leader of the suffrage movement was Alice Stokes Paul (1885–1977), the daughter of a Quaker businessman from New Jersey. Her mother was a suffragist who brought her young daughter with her to women's suffrage meetings long before Paul earned her PhD from the University of Pennsylvania.[58]

Paul's activism eventually led to a parade of eight thousand women in Washington, DC, on March 3, 1913, the day before President-elect Woodrow Wilson's inauguration. The women carried banners and marched down Pennsylvania Avenue from the Capitol to the White House, while maybe a half million people watched, supported, or harassed the marchers.[59]

Two weeks after that parade, Paul and other suffragists met at the White House with the newly minted president, who said it was not yet time for an amendment to the Constitution. Wilson's lack of support led to yet another demonstration and the founding of the Congressional Union for Woman Suffrage that focused exclusively on lobbying Congress for support of a constitutional amendment.[60]

The suffragists' patience was running low when, in January 1917, more than one thousand "Silent Sentinels" began eighteen months of picketing the White House, holding signs that read: "Mr. President, how long must women wait for liberty?" Some of the women protesters were arrested for obstructing traffic, and Paul herself was once jailed for seven months, where she staged a hunger strike in protest.[61]

Eventually, President Wilson gave the suffragists his support, but it was another two years before the Senate, the House, and the required thirty-six states approved the Nineteenth Amendment to the US Constitution, which granted the right of women to vote by prohibiting the states and the federal government from denying the right to vote to citizens of the United States on the basis of sex. The amendment as adopted stated: "The right of citizens of the United States to vote shall not be denied or abridged by the United States or by any State on account of sex. Congress shall have power to enforce this article by appropriate legislation."[62]

It is noteworthy that Ms. Paul and the National Women's Party soon turned their attention to the Equal Rights Amendment (ERA) to guarantee women protection from discrimination. Although Paul spent the balance of her life advocating for the ERA, the effort fell short by three states to become another constitutional amendment.[63]

On other fronts, education was a key target for progressives. John Dewey and Lester Ward put education at the top of their progressive agenda, believing that true democracy depended on a well-educated public. Thus, they pushed for compulsory education at all levels, even over the objections of parents. Their reforms led to standardized testing, equal educational opportunity for boys and girls, and discouraged corporal punishment in schools.[64]

Other progressives wanted government to become more efficient by using scientific management methods, while some wanted more democracy. Progressive leader Louis Brandeis used "scientific principles" to allegedly optimize government's performance so as to better serve people's needs. He believed that taking power out of the hands of elected officials and vesting authority in the hands of professional administrators reduced the voice of politicians. Further, centralized decision-making by expert administrators reduced corruption, a concept endorsed by Walter Lippmann, who in *Drift and Mastery* (1914) stressed the "scientific spirit" and "discipline of democracy," and issued a call for a strong central government guided by experts rather than by public opinion.[65]

State governments got into the progressive act as well. Governor Frank Lowden (1861–1943) of Illinois showed a "passion for efficiency" in efforts to streamline state government, as did others who embraced budgets to help plan their expenditures, rather than spend money haphazardly. Other state leaders like Robert M. Lafollette (1855–1925), the governor of Wisconsin at the time, called for more democracy; specifically, he advocated for the requirement that political parties hold a direct primary in order to weaken the power of machine politicians and political bosses.[66]

The progressive social movement, according to historian Alonzo Hamby, gave voice to the "issues stemming from modernization of American society. Emerging at the end of the 19th century, it established much of the tone of American politics throughout the first half of the [20th] century."[67]

Initially, progressives focused on city and state government, seeking to eliminate waste and find better ways to provide public services. The result was a more structured municipal system, with power focused at the local level—"municipal administration." Progressives put professionals, experts, and bureaucrats into positions overseeing those services.[68]

At the beginning of the progressive social movement, political parties ignored the calls for action to address the wrongs introduced by modernization and industrialization (the Gilded Age). However, in time, the progressives' direct-action campaigns and political organizing couldn't be ignored.

There were some political wins early in the era. Federal statutes attributed to President Theodore Roosevelt's intervention moved to protect public health with the passage of two laws: the Meat Inspection Act (1906), which established government inspection for meat products, and the Pure Food and Drug Act (1906), which required clear labeling of food and drug products. These acts showed progressives' growing influence on the national stage. This is no surprise to those who genuinely understand how social movements can morph into effective political movements.[69]

Dr. Martin Luther King, Jr., years later famously explained the relationship between political progressivism and the social movement phenomenon. He wrote in his famous "Letter from Birmingham Jail":

> Injustice anywhere is a threat to justice everywhere. We are caught in an inescapable network of mutuality, tied in a single garment of destiny. Whatever affects one directly, affects all indirectly. Never

again can we afford to live with the narrow, provincial "outside agitator" idea. Anyone who lives inside the United States can never be considered an outsider anywhere within its bounds.[70]

Eventually, the progressive movement's social efforts at the local and state levels to advance moral and political causes became an uncontested part of mainstream politics that defined national political parties as well.

Herbert Croly, cofounder of the *New Republic* and author of the influential book, *The Promise of American Life*, explained that most early progressives were within the Republican Party such as Theodore Roosevelt and Robert M. Lafollette. However, by the 1912 presidential campaign, all three major candidates (incumbent Howard Taft [Republican], Theodore Roosevelt [Progressive], and Woodrow Wilson [Democratic]) claimed the label "progressive" to one extent or another.[71]

Roosevelt was the first true progressive to make a national impact, however. He came to national attention under President William McKinley, first as the assistant secretary of the Navy, but more so after "Teddy" led the "Rough Riders" up San Juan Hill during the Spanish-American War (1898). He returned from that adventure and in a few short months was elected governor of New York (1898). In 1900, he became President McKinley's running mate, with the pair earning a landslide victory.

President McKinley was assassinated in September 1901, which elevated Roosevelt to become the youngest person (age forty-two) to become president (1901–1909). Roosevelt used his new position to champion progressive issues, such as his "Square Deal," which promised fairness, trust busting, regulation of railroads, control of corporations, consumer protection (pure food and drugs), and much more. In 1904, he was elected in his own right as the Republican standard-bearer, which gave him license to continue promoting progressive policies.[72]

Although Roosevelt believed corporations were good for the American economy, he closely monitored them to ensure that corporate greed did not get out of hand. That view led him to embrace antitrust laws that prohibited anticompetitive behavior (monopolies) and unfair business practices. For example, in 1902, in the midst of a coal strike by the United Mine Workers, Roosevelt intervened to create federal arbitration between the union and the owners.[73] Roosevelt took down forty-four trusts while in office.[74]

At the time, muckraker Upton Sinclair's book, *The Jungle*, compelled Roosevelt to push Congress to pass acts, as outlined above (the Meat Inspection Act, the Pure Act, and the Drug Act), and to create the Department of Commission, which became known as the Interstate Commerce Commission (ICC) that regulated railroads (and eventually trucking); eliminated rate discrimination; and much more. Further, Roosevelt's progressive views regarding the environment led to his declaration of more than fifty wildlife sanctuaries and parks.[75]

Roosevelt made great efforts to expand America's international influence, a progressive issue. The former deputy assistant secretary of the Navy built up the US Navy—not necessarily for national defense reasons, but so it would become the world's strongest naval force. Soon the US became the Northern Hemisphere's policeman, which in part prompted the construction of the Panama Canal (1903–1914), a "moon landing"-like national event at the time. The artificial, fifty-one-mile canal facilitated the movement of warships, but mostly expedited trade throughout the region.

It was a twist of fate for Roosevelt that he groomed his successor, William Howard Taft (1857–1930), who won the 1908 presidential election. Taft quietly legislated against monopoly trusts and advanced other progressive causes, yet his conservatism frustrated Roosevelt's hardened progressive ideology, prompting the former president to once again seek the Republican nomination for president. When his efforts failed to earn the 1912 nomination, Roosevelt created a third party, the Progressive Party. The nickname for the new party came from a quote attributed to Roosevelt, who, when asked whether he was fit to be president, answered that he was as fit as a "bull moose." Roosevelt's Bull Moose—Progressive—Party split the national vote, giving Woodrow

Wilson, a Democrat, the presidency (1913–1921).

Wilson was a career college professor-turned-politician, first elected as the governor of New Jersey and then soon after as the president. He abandoned his southern conservative views to embrace a national progressive ideology that eventually infected the entire Democratic Party, a legacy that extended to Franklin Roosevelt and well beyond him to the present.

Wilson showed his ideological colors when he rejected the view that "the ideal of government was for every man to be left alone and not interfered with, except when he interfered with somebody else; and that the best government was the government that did as little governing as possible."[76] Rather, he took strong exception to that view, believing that limits on government power must be abolished. At that time, fellow progressive and political scientist Theodore Woolsey opined, "The sphere of the state may reach as far as the nature and needs of man and of men reach, including intellectual and aesthetic wants of the individual, and the religious and moral nature of its citizens."[77]

Wilson's progressivism led to significant big-government advancements: a graduated income tax, the establishment of the Federal Reserve Act, the Clayton Antitrust Act, the Federal Farm Loan Act, the Federal Trade Commission Act, and the beginnings of a welfare state unmatched until Franklin Roosevelt's New Deal.

President Wilson's progressive views especially influenced his foreign policy and overseas adventures. In 1917, he told Congress, "The world must be made safe for democracy," seemingly his justification for entering the country in the First World War. But his call to spread democracy "was more urgent and pressing, more obligatory," wrote Professor Christopher Burkett.[78] That call, according to Burkett, was for a more active role in the world. It was meant to spread freedom and democracy, an ideological call for action, a new progressive foreign policy.

In his speech at the Paris Peace Conference, President Wilson proposed fourteen points for inclusion in the Treaty of Versailles, the treaty that ended the First World War. Wilson's final point was the creation of the League of Nations to maintain world peace as its primary goal, but the League was to deal with other issues as well, such as disarmament, international disputes, human and drug trafficking, and much more. For his efforts founding the League of Nations, Wilson earned a Nobel Peace Prize. However, he was unsuccessful at persuading the US Senate to embrace the treaty. In fact, the United States was never to join the League, which lasted twenty-six years and was replaced by the United Nations after the end of the Second World War.[79]

Wilson's foreign policy beliefs were widely shared among his contemporary progressives and in stark opposition to that of our founders. After all, Wilson was not a fan of the American Constitution. For example, in a 1912 campaign speech, he outlined a progressive's approach to our Constitution: "All the progressives ask or desire is permission [in an] era when 'development,' 'evolution,' is the scientific word, [to] interpret the Constitution according to the Darwinian principle; all they ask is recognition of the fact that a nation is a living thing and not a machine."[80] That view compelled his progressive view that we should use force abroad to promote freedom and welfare of other peoples, while our founders endorsed the use of force abroad first and foremost, according to Burkett, "for the sake of securing the lives and liberty of America's own citizens."[81]

President Franklin D. Roosevelt (FDR) inherited the legacy of the Progressive Era in terms of a governing philosophy and policies, as evidenced by his New Deal program to overcome the impact of the Great Depression.

The New Deal was all about big government, which Roosevelt believed was the remedy to America's Great Depression (1929–1939). He worked with Congress to pass the Emergency Banking Act, the Securities Act of 1933, and the Agriculture Adjustment Act as well as to establish the Federal Emergency Relief Administration, the Civil Works Administration, the National Recovery Administration, and other big-government programs to address employment, food, and shelter.[82]

FDR's programs were popular enough to win him reelection three times (1936, 1940, and 1944). However, like other progressives, FDR was not a constitutionalist. He tried to persuade Congress to pass the Judicial Procedures Reform Bill of 1937 to stop the Supreme Court from following a strict interpretation of the Constitution to nullify his progressive New Deal programs. That "court-packing" plan called for expanding the membership of the Supreme Court by adding one justice to the high court for each justice over the age of seventy, with a maximum of six additional justices.[83]

As an aside, bad ideas have a way of resurrecting themselves, which happened in March 2019. Congresswoman Alexandria Ocasio-Cortez, an avowed socialist, called on fellow Democrats to "pack the Supreme Court of the United States of America," an FDR-esque progressive fantasy to increase the number of justices from nine to fifteen to help kick-start their transformation of America. A number of 2020 Democratic Party presidential candidates followed Ocasio-Cortez's lead and endorsed or said they were open to "packing the court.[84]

In April 1937, two Supreme Court Justices flipped to support FDR's New Deal programs (National Labor Relations Act and the Social Security Act). Thus, FDR's high court reorganization plan became unnecessary—and by summer, the Senate struck down the court-packing legislation.[85]

With abandon, FDR and his progressive-elite supporters enormously expanded the power and size of the federal government: Social Security, welfare, unemployment programs, and much more. Most of FDR's initiatives had their intellectual base in the philosophy of fellow progressive John Dewey, who famously said "the state has the responsibility for creating institutions under which individuals can effectively realize the potentialities that are theirs."[86]

Dewey's hope in that statement was similar to that expressed in President Roosevelt's most famous words: "The only thing we have to fear is fear itself—nameless, unreasoning, unjustified terror." Then FDR masterfully played on public fear to move America closer to his progressive, big-government control.[87]

Consider Roosevelt's wordplay regarding fear and his assurances that big government will save them:

You're scared silly. You're afraid of losing your jobs, your savings, your homes. You're scared of empty pots and starving children. I will save you from hunger. I will save you from bankers. I will save you from the saber-toothed cat! Just hand over your gold and your future income, and let me plan your retirement for you.[88]

Progressivism's Impact on American Society

Arguably, the post-World War II era began a new period for progressives, which is examined in the next chapter. However, at this point, it is important to review the true impact (both positive and negative) of the Progressive Era—at least up to FDR's administration.

There are many positive results from the Progressive Era. Of course, that view depends on your governing ideology. No doubt, however, many of those "positive" outcomes are widely embraced by Americans today, such as the changes to the Constitution.

Progressives made radical changes to the US Constitution with four amendments. They pushed through the Sixteenth Amendment establishing a federal income tax, the Seventeenth Amendment allowing for the direct election of US senators, the Eighteenth Amendment prohibiting the sale of alcohol, and the Nineteenth Amendment guaranteeing women the right to vote. However, there are numerous outcomes of progressive policies that constitutionalists like me consider a violation of our founders' intent and a long-term negative impact on our freedom.

Other progressive agenda items came from people like William Jennings Bryan (1860–1925), who pushed through Prohibition against the protests of economic conservatives. Evidently, Bryan popularized the view that Prohibition would contribute to the physical health and moral improvement of the individual and, by association, the country. Of course, that effort was eventually overturned and the costs of alcohol abuse are no longer disputed, just accepted.

Progressives also promoted discriminatory policies and other intolerant ideas. President Wilson pursed a racial agenda and thus segregated the federal government, which no doubt influenced the revival of the Ku Klux Klan (early to mid-1920s), which was rooted at the time in Protestant communities that maintained white supremacy, and which, like their predecessors, opposed Catholics but also Jews. Progressives also experimented with racial zoning, a practice ended by the Supreme Court's decision in *Buchanan v. Warley, 245 U.S. 60* (1917). In that case, the city of Louisville, Kentucky, defended segregation by making it "unlawful for a white person to sell his house to anyone he pleased."[89]

Labor unions, which were very much part of the progressive political movement, tried their best to limit immigration and espoused xenophobic rhetoric about virtually anyone who wanted to immigrate to the United States. In fact, federal immigration policies during the Progressive Era, such as the Immigration Act of 1917, severely limited immigration based on nationality and excluded most Asian immigrants. It's noteworthy that today Asians are sought out for their perceived high intelligence, evidently something lost on early-twentieth-century progressives.

Progressives here and in Europe at the time pushed eugenics ("a science that deals with the improvement [as by control of human mating] of hereditary qualities of a race or breed"),[90] a favorite cause of the left that led to forced sterilization, untold numbers of abortions, and very discriminatory immigration policies.

Eugenics was championed by famous progressives and liberals alike, including President Theodore Roosevelt, H. G. Wells (British author), George Bernard Shaw (Irish playwright), John Maynard Keynes (British economist), and Margaret Sanger (the American founder of Planned Parenthood, a major abortion provider in the US even today).

Opposition to the left's pro-abortion stand was then and remains today mostly conservative Catholics and Bible-Belt Protestants who hated abortion then and rightly accused progressive elites of playing God.

The progressives' lust for eugenics is likely in part attributable to the German influence acquired by American social scientists in the post-Civil War era who studied under Professor Hegel and his protégés in German universities. Those progressives came home with elitist views about human nature that led them to advocate for selective breeding. They aimed to improve the genetic quality of the human population by encouraging the more "desirable" elements of society, a view based on racial and class hierarchy that placed white, Anglo-Saxon Protestants at the top. This was progress, in their minds' eye.

The heart of the world eugenics movement came to the United States from Europe in the early twentieth century. It captured the imagination of many, to the point of almost being spiritual in character. That religious-like draw resulted in the formulation of the Eugenics Creed, which reflects the central doctrine of the American eugenics crusade at the time. It reads:

- I believe in striving to raise the human race to the highest plane of social organization, of cooperative work and of effective endeavor.
- I believe that I am the trustee of the germ plasm that I carry; that this has been passed on to me through thousands of generations before me; and that I betray the trust if (that germ plasm being good) I so act as to jeopardize it, with its excellent possibilities, or, from motives of personal convenience, to unduly limit offspring.
- I believe that, having made our choice in marriage carefully, we, the married pair, should seek to have 4 to 6 children in order that our carefully selected germ plasm shall be reproduced in adequate degree and that this preferred stock shall not be swamped by that less carefully selected.

- I believe in such a selection of immigrants as shall not tend to adulterate our national germ plasm with socially unfit traits.
- I believe in repressing my instincts when to follow them would injure the next generation.[91]

One historian wrote that Progressive Era eugenicists' ideas were integral to "the political vocabulary of virtually every significant modernizing force between the two world wars." And the eugenicists left their mark in ways ranging from marriage laws to immigration and schooling practices—ideas right out of the Darwinist and Hegelian schools of cultivating only the "best and brightest." No wonder during that period more than thirty states adopted compulsory sterilization laws that led to more than sixty thousand forced sterilizations of those considered mentally disabled or socially disadvantaged.[92]

It's noteworthy that at the same time, German progressives influenced the National Socialist (Nazi) Party, which used compulsory sterilization as well between 1934 and 1945, contributing to the public's eventual acceptance of approximately 350,000 forced sterilizations and arguably serving as a stepping stone to the Holocaust, a horrendous anti-Semitic period best known for the genocide of nearly six million European Jews.[93]

Remember, the Nazi ideology called for preserving the master race (German: *Herrenrasse*), in which the putative Aryan races, mostly northern Europeans, were considered the highest racial hierarchy. Members of German Chancellor Adolf Hitler's master race referred to themselves as *Herrenmenschen*, meaning "master humans." Others, such as Slavs and Jews, were considered racially inferior, *Untermenschen*, and thus were thought to be a danger to the Aryan or Germanic master race's germ plasm.[94]

Meanwhile, American eugenicists-inspired laws prohibited marriages among the mentally deficient, and in fact there were statutes that required the commitment of certain people to state institutions. There was even federal law that limited immigration to protect the nation's gene pool from contamination, a view endorsed by the Eugenics Creed above.

No one should be surprised to learn that the leading progressives at the time supported eugenics. Progressive leader and future president, Woodrow Wilson, as governor of New Jersey, signed that state's forced sterilization law, and progressive Theodore Roosevelt wrote at the time that "society has no business to permit degenerates to reproduce their kind."[95]

Certainly, the eugenicists influenced federal immigration laws, which was consistent with the Eugenics Creed. They pushed for the Immigration Act of 1924, which set quotas for immigrants from Southern and Eastern Europe that remained on Washington's books until 1965. In 1928, Harry Laughlin (1880–1943), an American educator, eugenicist, and sociologist who served as the superintendent of the Eugenics Record Office, testified before Congress that immigration restrictions were necessary to defend "against the contamination of American family stocks by alien hereditary degeneracy."[96]

The only sterilization case to reach the Supreme Court was *Buck v. Bell*, *274 U.S. 200* (1927), which involved what attending physical Dr. John Bell noted "was the first case operated on under the [Virginia] sterilization law." Bell did the deed by removing a section from Carrie Buck's fallopian tubes.[97]

Ms. Carrie Buck was an unassuming girl who had a rough life. Eugenics experts testified at her hearing that she was congenitally "feeble-minded," a woman who had tainted "germ plasm" and would create generations of "socially inadequate defectives" if allowed to procreate.[98]

The high court's *Buck v. Bell* decision was written by Justice Oliver Wendell Holmes, Jr., who was devoted to eugenics as well. In 1921, Holmes told future Justice Felix Frankfurter "that he had no problem 'restricting propagation by the undesirables and putting to death infants that didn't pass the examination.'" Further, years later, Holmes said the *Buck v. Bell* case was one of his proudest moments. He told a friend, "One decision that I wrote gave me pleasure, establishing the constitutionality of a law permitting the sterilization of imbeciles."[99]

As you can see, the modern progressive state relied upon "science" (eugenics) and discriminatory immigration to protect against tainting our "germ plasm." This attitude may explain President Franklin D. Roosevelt's bias against Jews fleeing the Holocaust as well.

Dr. Rafael Medoff, the director for the David S. Wyman Institute for Holocaust Studies, published a ten-chapter study, "Distorting America's Response to the Holocaust." The 2018 report questioned a pro-FDR stance at the US Holocaust Memorial Museum's "Americans and the Holocaust" exhibit. Dr. Medoff's chapter, "Making Excuses for FDR," suggests that FDR demonstrated a clear bias against Jews fleeing Germany in the mid 1930s. That prejudice coincided with a far harsher antipathy for Jews seen in Nazi Germany that ultimately led to the Holocaust.[100]

As early as 1933, FDR's administration refused to publicly criticize Nazi Germany's obvious anti-Jewish persecution. In fact, FDR held eighty-two press conferences in 1933, and the topic of Jewish persecution only came up once. A reporter asked FDR at that press conference: "Have any organizations asked you to act in any way in connection with the reported persecution of the Jews over in Germany by the Hitler government?" The president replied: "I think a good many of these have come in. They were all sent over to the Secretary of State." The topic didn't come up again until five years later (1938) and another 348 presidential press conferences. Even then, when FDR was asked whether he had any comment on Italy's order expelling 22,000 Jews, he said: "No."[101]

FDR's administration was not only mute about the Jewish genocide that was widely known at the time, but it also suppressed Jewish immigration to this country far below the levels allowed by the quota laws. The Roosevelt administration left 190,000 quotas empty from Germany and Axis-occupied countries during the period of 1933 to 1945. In fact, although 82,787 people were on the German waiting list for US visas in 1933, only 1,241 visas were issued.[102]

Roosevelt's response to the 1938 Kristallnacht (Night of Broken

Glass) pogrom (slaughter) against Jews throughout Nazi Germany and carried out by Nazi paramilitary forces was especially telling. At a White House press conference days later, he read a prepared statement saying he "could scarcely believe that such things could occur in a twentieth century civilization." He did not mention that Jews were the victims.[103]

Let me cut to the chase regarding FDR's progressive bias against Jews, which is not that different from his progressive predecessor President Wilson's bias regarding African-Americans. Historians documented FDR's anti-Semitic bias in more than a dozen statements made privately by Roosevelt between the 1920s and the 1940s. Here I quote from Dr. Medoff's report:

> They [the statements] include him [FDR] boasting that he helped impose a quota on the admission of Jews to Harvard; claiming that Jewish domination of Poland's economy was the cause of antisemitism in that country; expressing pride that he had "no Jewish blood" in his veins; telling Winston Churchill that "the best way to settle the Jewish question...is to spread the Jews thin all over the world"; complaining (at a cabinet meeting) that there were "too many Jews among federal employees in Oregon"; and insisting (at the Casablanca conference) on quotas for Jews in professions in Allied-liberated North Africa because otherwise there would be a repeat of "the understandable complaints which the Germans bore towards the Jews in Germany."[104]

I asked Dr. Medoff via email: "Why does the Holocaust Memorial Museum evidently present a distortion of history?" He responded: "Ultimately, I think, what is most important is that they [the Holocaust Memorial Museum] are misrepresenting the historical record, regardless of their motives for doing so."[105]

Indeed, the museum hides FDR's clear anti-Semitic actions and words. It's clear to this writer that he shared a eugenicist's bias against Jews, much as did his progressive peers at the time.

Clearly, progressives used their government positions to affect social issues.

However, the progressives' principal developments at the time were economic marginalization, which led to calls for significant federal regulation, as well as concerns regarding the inequality of wealth that led to new legal policy and the domain of risk management, which contributed to the creation of Social Security, contract and tort laws, and more.

Obviously, early twentieth-century progressive thinking within the social sciences was heavily influenced by Darwinian and Hegelian theory, which, as we saw in Europe (especially in Germany) relied on genetic determinism—the elite (Aryan) rule. Perhaps surprising to some, many early American progressives were Christians (at least in name) who embraced a "social" interpretation of the Scriptures to bolster their endorsement of progressivism, a view most would eventually abandon, a change examined in chapter 3 of this volume.

Conclusion

This chapter provides a cursory review of the origins of American progressivism, their beliefs, and some of the leaders, as well as the impact of their policies. The next chapter considers the contemporary American progressive movement, their operating principles and goals, the level of support they enjoy today, and their strategy for the way ahead.

2

Modern American Progressives

If men of wisdom and knowledge, of moderation and temperance, of patience, fortitude and perseverance, of sobriety and true republican simplicity of manners, of zeal for the honour of the Supreme Being and the welfare of the commonwealth; if men possessed of these other excellent qualities are chosen to fill the seats of government, we may expect that our affairs will rest on a solid and permanent foundation.[106]

—Founding Father Samuel Adams (1780)

Progressives Have Become More Radical with Time

Samuel Adams would not be pleased with modern progressives who are a very heady, radical group believing they can end all human suffering through a divinely self-appointed mission to massively overhaul the form of government given to us by our founders. Progressives represent much that conservative Americans have come to despise and are arguably bent on some pretty evil outcomes for America—all in the name of tolerance.

No doubt modern progressives are rooted in the old progressivism outlined in the previous chapter. That century plus-old movement rooted in the European "Enlightenment" experienced change in principles, goals, and strategy through the rough-and-tumble challenges that emerged in the Gilded Age and ever since. Some of those changes were for the good, like women's suffrage and child labor laws. However, in contrast to that early-twentieth-century's movement, modern progressivism carries on the old guards' legacy but became a radicalized version of its ideological founding and now insists on transforming American society beginning with our culture in ways former progressives may never have wished.

Modern progressives smartly grasp the role of culture in a society. They evidently learned that lesson from sage Daniel Patrick Moynihan (1927–2003), a politician, sociologist, and diplomat who served in the US Senate, and although a self-identified Democrat politically, he advised Republican President Richard Nixon. Moynihan wrote about the importance of culture's influence on society: "The central conservative truth is that it is culture, not politics that determines the success of a society. The central liberal truth is that politics can change the culture and save it from itself."[107]

Evidently, contemporary progressives subscribe to Moynihan's view of culture's power over society and have therefore radicalized their politics to mold our culture into something traditionalists and especially our constitutionalist founders would never recognize, much less respect. Modern progressive politics is changing culture at every turn to emerge as a political force, arguably an evil influence that must be countered, or America is doomed to become something worse than the likes of past Marxist regimes.

What is a Marxist regime? Marxism is the antithesis of capitalism (modern America), an economic system in which the dominant feature is public (big-government) ownership of the means of production, distribution, and exchange. It reflects the socialist slogan: "From each according to his ability, to each according to his work." It even puts a horrible stamp on religion, which, according to Marx, "is the sigh of the oppressed creature, the feeling of a heartless world, and the soul of soulless circumstances."[108]

Just how dangerous and evil is modern progressivism that seeks a

Marxist-like outcome for America? Glenn Beck, a television personality and author, wrote a book about progressives, *Liars: How Progressives Exploit Our Fears for Power and Control*. In it, Beck profiled progressive goals as:

> ...the insatiable thirst for control and betterment of others; the determination to build a massive, all-controlling welfare state that holds the rest of us hostage to its preferences and whims; and the flirtation with totalitarianism masked by the guise of political correctness. Progressives regularly espouse ideas and support causes that openly involve the subjugation, murder, or mutilation of their fellow human beings, always in the name of a better world for all.[109]

The fact is that modern progressives know no limit to their radical ambition to change America. They manifest themselves in every aspect of life, and only they—society's so-called and self-appointed elite—know the answers to a bright, productive, and hopeful (socialist) future America.

Most modern progressive disciples share the view that government (politics) at every level is the necessary engine that must solve society's ills. Further, unlike many American conservatives who embrace a limited constitutional form of government, the average progressive tends to believe that America's federalist system of government based on its Constitution is outdated and must be replaced by a scientific bureaucracy and administered by elite progressives like themselves who intend to govern every aspect of our lives.

That should scare those of us who hold to traditional, biblically based values and who treasure America's founding documents. Our form of government is anathema to the average progressive.

For those of us who want to protect our form of government and traditions, it is therefore critical to gain an understanding of modern progressivism. One approach to acquiring that understanding is to study the progressives' operating principles, contemporary goals, level of national support, and strategy to reimagine America to their liking.

Modern Progressive Principles

Modern progressives believe America's societal difficulties must be resolved in their "principled" view; otherwise, this country won't survive, because the current political processes given to us by our founders are inherently flawed. After all, they—modern progressives—have run out of patience with lingering societal issues such as income disparities, sexual and racial inequities, and privileges (such as wealth) granted by accident of birth. These markers dominate the progressive, leftist agenda.

Many progressives admit that their past transformative efforts to address these ills, although perhaps well intended, didn't go far enough because they were tethered to the present dysfunctional political system. Thus, contemporary progressives are convinced of one thing: Modern America must change the current structurally oppressive system; it must undergo a top-to-bottom political transformation.

Progressives' ideological principles are a prism through which they view every problem and act as a guide to realize their necessary political transformation process ahead.

Before reviewing those principles, it is instructive to understand that many in the contemporary progressive movement, like US Senator Bernie Sanders (I-VT), a progressive and self-identified socialist and 2020 presidential contender, believes that most Americans share progressive views.

Sanders confirmed that during his 2016 presidential primary campaign:

I have never accepted this nonsense about red [Republican] states and blue [Democratic] states [party-dominated states]—in every state of the country there are people who are struggling, and they are on *our* [progressives'] side. Don't accept that division. We [progressives] are the vast majority of people.[110]

Sanders may be right, at least when it comes to certain progressive issues. He cited some examples of widely shared views: "Most Americans *do* believe that healthcare is a right, not a privilege, and want a national healthcare program." He continued, "The majority of Americans believe that the minimum wage is not enough."[111]

Sanders, much like others of his ilk, blames our form of government for failing to adequately resolve these issues (healthcare, inadequate wages), which allegedly do enjoy significant national support. Why? Because it is in fact heavily influenced by the progressives' bogeyman—big business and the wealthy, a view supported by a 2014 study by researchers at Princeton and Northwestern Universities, which found the US is not a democracy—a government system ruled by the majority—but an oligarchy, a type of government run by a small group of highly influential people and organizations.[112]

Sanders cites that study to conclude something worse than just the economic aspects of America: "I am worried that we [Americans] are moving toward an oligarchic form of society in which a handful of people are not satisfied with controlling most of the wealth. They want to control the government, too."[113] Are the wealthy capitalists really taking over America?

That may sound a bit conspiratorial—a small group of wealthy people running America.

Maybe not.

I wrote in my 2017 book, *The Deeper State*, America's government is indeed run by one elected and two unelected groupings. The national government's elected political class (president and members of Congress) are supposed to represent the interests of those who elect them. However, even though the political class is ostensibly in charge of government, they depend on the unelected, professional, administrative (bureaucratic) state, a legion of public servants who more often than not exercise great power and seldom are held accountable to the public.

Certainly, the corruption evident within the Federal Bureau of Investigation during the Obama administration and the early years of the Trump administration should be sufficient to alarm any objective American. Further, the Obama administration's reckless abuse of the Internal Revenue Service's oversight of conservative groups, the Justice Department's "Fast and Furious" gun program, and other scandals leave a sour taste in our collective mouths about our deep-state suspicions.

The second layer of the deep state, what Senator Sanders refers to above, are the nongovernment influencers of the political class (the wealthy, corporations, other countries, lobbyists, think tanks, academia). The people in this second layer were the targets of the early twentieth-century progressives, and they remain targets even today because they continue to exercise greater influence more often than not over government policy than do the majority of Americans. Why? Their influence is pervasive in Washington, because it is larded with often-biased information, money, and perks that affect what the political class and, by association, the bureaucracy sees and understands.

The third layer identified in *The Deeper State* is the unseen realm, which the mostly godless progressives dismiss. However, the evil influences of the unseen realm are evident—especially to those who are spiritual, because we see the dark spirits' everyday influence on our lives and the world around us. This influence is the substance of religion, the spirits (demons and angels) of a dimension beyond our five senses.

Arguably, those same three layers that impact our government today were active during the Gilded Age as well. After all, recall from the last chapter that the progressive movement, a grassroots social crusade, at the start rejected the immense political power at the time residing with the second layer—the wealthy few, the "robber barons" of industry who manipulated (corrupted) the political class.[114]

It is not in dispute that many of the issues that faced progressives in that era exist today as well. They exist to a large extent because of the corrupt nature of man and the third layer, the evil influences of the unseen realm within this world. Frankly, those same societal issues will remain with humankind until the end times, in spite of man's best efforts. Of course, that view is rejected by progressive theorists who believe man does evolve and will eventually escape his evil ways to become perfect. Besides, at best, progressives are agnostic (believing that the existence of God is unknowable), although many tend to be atheists.

Admittedly the progressives of the late-nineteenth and early-twentieth centuries made some headway against society's ills, as illustrated in the previous chapter. In part, those successes were due to the movement's principles, which mostly remain in place even today and provide insight into the progressives' worldview.

That brings us to consider ten enduring progressive principles that are paraphrased below for your consideration. They are replicated here in part from a 2017 article in *The Progressive Times* by Sammy Kayes, a progressive educator and activist in Chicago. They help you get into the mind of a contemporary progressive, a necessary step as you read further to consider what progressives are doing to our basic rights, our critical institutions, and the ideals that made America great.

Ten Progressive Principles

First, progressives in principle oppose corruption. They believe the concentration of wealth and power in the hands of the few—the second layer of *The Deeper State*—is wrong, and that the existence of our oligarchic or aristocratic form of government is evidence of that corruption.

Founder and former President Thomas Jefferson warned about such corruption seeping into public life: "I hope we shall crush in its birth the aristocracy of our moneyed corporations that dare already to challenge our government to a trial by strength, and bid defiance to the laws of our country."[115]

Jefferson's statement is music to progressives' ears, because it addresses a major area of concern for them. They believe the concentration of wealth in the hands of the few damages the general welfare of the country. We saw that in the previous chapter with the discussion of the Gilded Age and the associated ills brought about by modernization—child labor, urban poverty, and much more. Disallowing the few to hold so much wealth—corporations and monopolies and the like—allows for a more equal distribution of competition, according to progressive thinking.

Admittedly, modern progressive icons such as former President Bill Clinton and his wife, Hillary Clinton, literally drip with the appearance of corruption, from their time in the Arkansas governorship to the White House and, more recently, with Hillary serving in Obama's State Department. But, of course, principled progressives look aside when one of their fellow disciples violates the principle of corruption.

Second, progressives embrace the principle that it is right to stand against oppression and thus fight for the vulnerable and underprivileged—society's powerless. The powerless includes those facing discrimination for a variety of reasons. This principle is lived out in the movement's efforts to insist on government oversight of workplaces to make them safer and paying workers a living wage.

Prior to workplace regulations, workers often spent eighty to one hundred hours a week at factories earning very little an hour, which is why progressives coined this abuse as "wage slavery." As a result, progressives fought to establish a minimum wage, called for safety regulations for workers, and promoted the formation of unions to represent workers. Contemporary progressives believe much the same, but have added other requirements, such as healthcare, time off, and retirement funds to their workplace agenda.

Progressives stand by illegal aliens, another "oppressed" minority, under the guise of helping these vulnerable people. They push for "sanctuary cities" to protect those who enter America illegally while hundreds of thousands of others wait sometimes years and pay a high financial burden to enter legally. Of course, ignoring the illegality among the many is meant to fuel Democratic Party voter rolls.

The 2018 Congress conclusively demonstrates the Democrats' support of illegal immigration. Specifically, in July 2018, the House of Representatives voted on a bill that simply expressed Congress' "continued support for all United States Immigration and Customs Enforcement (ICE) officers and personnel who carry out the important mission of ICE" and "the efforts of all Federal agencies, State law enforcement, and military personnel who bring law and order to our Nation's borders."[116]

Only eighteen House Democrats voted for the resolution while thirty-five voted "no," and the balance (133) voted "present." Many Democrats complained that the vote was a political stunt. But the fact is one only has to look at progressive-dominated areas of the country for irrefutable evidence of Democratic Party support for illegal immigration.[117]

San Francisco is one such place where illegal immigrants are registered to vote in the city school board election. "We want to give immigrants the right to vote," said Norman Yee, a county supervisor. Progressives evidently refuse to hold back any citizenship rights from illegal immigrants.[118]

It is true that many, if not most, progressive Democrats support illegal immigration, as demonstrated by the designation of "sanctuary cities" and "sanctuary states" that actively protect illegals from deportation. One estimate finds that there are 564 states and municipalities that designate themselves sanctuaries for illegals, including three dark blue (Democratic Party-dominated) states: California, Illinois, and New York.[119]

Third, progressives embrace the principle of egalitarianism, a belief in the fundamental equality of all human beings. Thus, discrimination for any reason is considered a form of oppression and not to be tolerated.

Egalitarianism touches every minority, economic strata, and sexual orientation, and any other group that is marginalized or subjugated. Progressives often invoke the Preamble to the American Constitution to make their case for egalitarianism:

> We the people of the United States, in order to form "a more perfect" union, establish justice, insure domestic tranquility, provide for the common defense, promote the general welfare, and secure the blessings of liberty to ourselves and our posterity, do ordain and establish this constitution of the United States of America.

Progressives cite these words to argue for the rights of free and autonomous people of all races, ethnicities, and backgrounds. They apply this principle to other issues, such as police reform, and especially regarding the treatment of minorities; marriage rights for the homosexual, bisexual, and transsexual community; the economically disadvantaged; and, of course, the illegal immigrant.

Progressives also invoke the principle of egalitarianism to advance "moral legislation" that regulates an individual's life with respect to certain religious or personal moral standards. This is an especially interesting application of the egalitarian principle. For the progressive, legislating morality is really a matter of whether laws align with morality or one's personal sense of morality. Our Constitution does not tell us what is right or wrong; rather, it addresses governmental authority.

Consider the case of the abortion of the unborn child to understand the progressive's application of the egalitarian principle. A woman who opposes abortion on moral grounds is not compelled by the law to kill her unborn child. That decision is based on her moral view, even though under the law she could kill her child. The pro-abortion woman under current law, as progressives argue, has the same freedom of choice. Neither society nor either woman wants the government to dictate the abortion choice, so the argument goes.

An example of legislating morality is illustrated, as progressives might argue, by the Chinese law limiting a woman to bear no more than two children. Thus, a third pregnancy for a Chinese woman with two children would be tragically terminated per state law, whether the woman supports the state's decision or not.

Evidently, progressives, based on this principle, don't recognize the unborn child as having any rights. After all, some progressive politicians support late-term abortion until the very day of birth; both New York Governor Andrew Cuomo and Virginia Governor Ralph Northam have made public statements to that effect.

Fourth, progressives favor the principle of public over private property. Specifically, they tend to oppose the privatization of goods and services such as healthcare, education, and other necessities. This is the Marxist aspect of their belief system.

Progressives believe healthcare is a right for all citizens, a public trust. It should be provided to all citizens, whether or not they can afford it. Therefore, on principle, progressives oppose the privatization of healthcare for whatever reason because the less fortunate will inevitably be disadvantaged—denied healthcare because of their inability to pay.

This principle is extended to a host of other issues, and the sky is the limit for the progressive, who says that government, not the private sector, should provide citizens all the necessities of life. This explains the surge in progressive political support for a single-payer healthcare program, or what some call "Medicare for All [Life]."

In early 2019, New York City Mayor Bill de Blasio, a progressive Democrat, announced the launch of a comprehensive, universal healthcare coverage plan that guarantees benefits for every New Yorker. "Healthcare is a right, not a privilege reserved for those who can afford it," he said. And the "privilege" according to de Blasio, is extended to every New Yorker "regardless of immigration [illegals included] status or their ability to pay."[120]

Fifth, democracy is a progressive principle that is about more than voting. Progressives advocate for civic action and public engagement in society, which promotes democracy and allegedly makes the American ideals of life, liberty, and the pursuit of happiness attainable.

Earlier in this chapter, I cited a study that suggests America is really more of an oligarchy with real power that rests in just a few hands as opposed to a democracy that serves the majority. I experienced something very similar to a real democracy during my numerous trips in the 1990s to Switzerland while working with a Swiss citizen group.

Switzerland has a direct democracy form of government, a legal framework whereby all Swiss citizens over age eighteen vote on how the country is run. All Swiss citizens (illegals are not permitted to vote in Switzerland) take part in decision-making via popular votes, which are held up to four times a year. The national government, called the Federal Council, exercises executive power and is composed of federal councilors from several Swiss political parties. The councilors are elected by the Federal Assembly every four years and share the duties of a head of state.[121]

By contrast, the US Constitution established a federal system whereby we the people elect representatives who are supposed to speak for our interests in Washington. This model is opposed by modern progressives, because too often those elected representatives are more influenced by others—the second layer of *The Deeper State*—than by their constituents.

Although progressives claim to embrace this principle, they also expect common citizens to empower (elect) the elite (read "educated progressive politicians and their appointed bureaucrats") to run government, a radically different outcome than Swiss-styled direct democracy.

It's noteworthy that direct democracy in part works for Switzerland perhaps because the Swiss live in a very small geographic area and are far more homogeneous than Americans, a country with a vast geography and numerous cultures which arguably makes any meaningful comparison almost useless.

Sixth, progressives insist upon principled transparency throughout government. The people must know what their representatives are doing in order to hold them accountable, if that's even possible. This is especially important in order to keep big money out of the political process while seeking to reform the electoral system to install only the best (read "progressive elite") fit for public service.

Transparency is a hard nut to crack for contemporary America, however. Yes, Congress hosts open hearings, but only a few citizens ever attend either physically or virtually (via television or the Internet). A few citizens may read about them, thanks to our media that filters the content for the good or bad, depending on the reporters' ideological views. But the fact is that much of modern government isn't transparent, in part either by voter choice (voters neglect to pay attention) or, as some suspect, by design (feeding deep-state suspicions).

It is true that much of government's activities are beyond the reach of the citizen in spite of the Freedom of Information Act (FOIA), 5 U.S.C. § 552, which reflects the presumed commitment to open government. Those guidelines stress the importance of proactive disclosures and timely responses to inquiries, yet the veil of secrecy remains on much of the government's work, some (such as national security interests) out of true necessity, and yet others for less charitable reasons.[122] Yes, there are ways of keeping material out of the public eye either through unnecessary classification of materials or other means of categorization.

President Barack Obama came into office promising transparency. However, after eight years, he achieved only marginal improvements, such as the passage of the Digital Accountability and Transparency

(DATA) Act. The fact is most everyone agrees about the need for government transparency, which is why we have both federal and state FOIA laws that allegedly allow public access to government information. Unfortunately, and perhaps by design, FOIA requests tend to be a low priority among government bureaucrats. For example, FOIA requests at the federal level went from 77,000 in 2009 to nearly 160,000 in 2014, according to the Justice Department, yet many of those requests are never answered or take many months to years to process—and even then, they tend to be heavily redacted (censored).[123]

Seventh, modern progressives insist they are proponents of "the fourth estate," that is, they say they're advocates of the principle of freedom of the press. This principle supports their efforts regarding transparency, accountability, and education.

This is a curious principle, especially among modern progressives who tend to refuse to accept contrary views. For example, it's widely acknowledged at least among conservatives that some of the world's largest social media platforms—Facebook, Twitter, Google, and YouTube—are biased against conservatives, which violates this principle.

Newsbusters, a service of the Media Research Center, claims the problem of liberal bias with social media platforms is now reaching a "crisis level." Social media, according to Newsbusters, is plunging leftward politically as it repeatedly censors conservative organizations, even religious leaders. "Social media censorship and online restriction of conservatives and their organizations have reached a crisis level," says the statement from Newsbusters. The statement continues:

> They have skewed search results and adjusted trending topics in ways that have harmed the [political] right. Firms have restricted and deleted videos, even academic content. Conservative tech employees have found their speech limited and their careers harmed. And top tech companies have given preferential treat-

ment to anointed legacy media outlets that also lean left. These same tech titans then work with groups openly hostile to conservatives to restrict speech.[124]

Google CEO Sundar Pichai disputed the allegation of a bias against conservatives in his company's search engines and social media sites. However, "there is a very strong conviction on this side of the aisle that [Google's] algorithms are written with a bias against conservatives," said Republican Representative Steve King of Iowa at a December 2018 House Judiciary Committee hearing. Others on the committee cited studies, anecdotes, and leaked videos and emails that demonstrated the liberal bias.[125]

Predictably, progressive members of the committee rushed to Google's defense. Representative Jerry Nadler (D-NY) alleged a "fantasy, dreamed up by some conservatives, that Google and other online platforms have an anti-conservative bias." Further, and revealing, none of the Democrats on the committee alleged that Google platforms evidenced any anti-liberal partiality. Then Republican Representative Lamar Smith of Texas explained why the alleged bias mattered.[126]

"Google has revolutionized the world, though not entirely in the way I expected. Americans deserve the facts objectively reported," he said. "The muting of conservative voices by platforms has intensified, especially during the presidency of Donald Trump. More than 90 percent of all Internet searches take place on Google or its subsidiary YouTube, and they are curating what we see." But does it really matter?

Smith explained that those who write the algorithms get the liberal results they want, and a study by Dr. Robert Epstein, a Harvard-trained psychologist, authored a study that showed Google's partisanship likely swung 2.6 million votes to Hillary Clinton in the 2016 election.[127]

The progressive prejudice goes beyond our shores as well. That hypocrisy among progressives is especially evident in the case of Google's work with the Chinese government. Google reportedly cooperates with communist China's government to launch a censored version of its search engine that will blacklist websites and search terms about human rights, democracy, religion, and peaceful protest.

The Google-communist Chinese project—code named "Dragonfly"—teams Google programmers and engineers to create a custom Android app (application software that causes a computer to perform tasks for computer users) that would block information on the Internet about the communist regime's political opponents, free speech, sex, news, and academic studies. Not surprisingly, it would ban websites about the communist regime's 1989 Tiananmen Square massacre and other references to "anti-communism" and "dissidents." It also would ban books that negatively portray authoritarian governments, like George Orwell's *1984* and *Animal Farm.*[128]

Eighth, progressives claim to embrace the principle of nonviolence. They admit to past episodes of violence among their ranks, but those are allegedly aberrations, not a movement strategy.

Once again, this principle isn't rigorously displayed across modern progressives. Groups like Black Lives Matter (BLM) and the Southern Poverty Law Center (SPLC) are supported by most progressives. Yet both organizations engage in violence-promoting rhetoric through their propaganda.

In 2016, BLM protests sprung up in cities across America in the wake of the police killings of two black men in Louisiana and Minnesota. BLM held a protest in Dallas, Texas, which, although it started peacefully, ended in a gunman murdering five and injuring several on-duty police officers. Then Texas Lt. Gov. Dan Patrick blamed the violence on BLM: "I do blame people on social media, with their hatred toward police. I do blame former Black Lives Matter protests last night was peaceful, but others have not been…this has to stop."[129]

The BLM protests at the time became ugly elsewhere as well. They shut down an interstate and major thoroughfare in Miami, Florida, and vandalized a police station in Oakland, California. In St. Paul, Minneapolis, some BLM people threw water bottles, pieces of concrete, rebar, bricks, Molotov cocktails, and rocks at police.[130]

The SPLC claims to be "dedicated to fighting hate and bigotry" by using "litigation, education, and other forms of advocacy." Those may be laudable origins, but over time, the SPLC has become a political player for progressive activism using smear tactics, intimidation, ritualized defamation, and fundraising to silence its political opponents. It also has incited violence against the Family Research Council (FRC), where I serve as a nonpaid senior fellow.[131]

Floyd Lee Corkins II pleaded guilty to three federal charges, including committing an act of terrorism related to the August 15, 2012, shooting of FRC's guard. Corkins told the FBI that he wanted to kill anti-gay targets and went to the SPLC's website for ideas. At a court hearing where Corkins' comments to the FBI were revealed, he said that he intended to "kill as many as possible and smear the Chick-fil-a sandwiches [which Corkins purchased before entering FRC's headquarters in Washington, DC] in victims' faces, and kill the guard."[132]

Also, the SPLC lectures policemen on how to identify extremist organizations like white supremacists, but when questioned about groups like BLM and Antifa (a radical fascist organization), they demur. I spoke with a policeman who was directed to attend a full day of SPLC lectures for officers in Fredericksburg, Virginia, in the summer of 2018. He shared the SPLC's material with me and said when several policemen questioned the SPLC representative about these leftist, violent groups, she (a lawyer) changed the topic.

Ninth, progressives claim to represent the principle of authenticity and integrity while seeking justice for all citizens. The Obama administration proved time and again that truth was a slippery issue.

Progressive-leaning media consistently covered up for Obama, and his administration played along. Remember the attack on the US consulate in Benghazi, Libya? It was literally years before the truth emerged that the Obama administration and Hillary Clinton, then secretary of state, knew, as UN ambassador Susan Rice said, that the 2012 incident wasn't about an anti-Muslim video on YouTube. Rice went on several national television shows to describe the attack that killed four Americans, including the ambassador, as a spontaneous reaction to an anti-Muslim video when everyone, including Rice, knew at the time this was a lie.[133]

Remember the account of the US Army soldier taken captive in 2009 by the Afghan Taliban? Obama hosted Sergeant Bowe Bergdahl's parents at the White House Rose Garden to celebrate the soldier's 2014 homecoming when in fact everyone in the soldier's chain of command and certainly Obama Pentagon officials knew that Sergeant Bergdahl was a deserter, not a hero. Fake news was created to justify Obama turning over five "general officer" level Taliban leaders detained at Guantanamo Bay, Cuba, in exchange for Bergdahl, who was eventually given a dishonorable discharge in 2017 and fined $1,000 on charges of desertion and misbehavior before the enemy.[134]

Remember the billions President Obama granted Iran for the 2015 nuclear deal? He ordered the transfer of frozen Iranian assets, including an unchartered plane loaded with $1.7 billion cash secretly flown to Iran in exchange for American hostages and an ante of sorts for Obama's legacy foreign policy accomplishment, the July 2015 nuclear deal known as the Joint Comprehensive Plan of Action. The US Treasury Department confirmed that the assets related to this deal, which were returned to Iran valued at $56 billion rather than $150 billion previously alleged. In 2018, President Trump rescinded the Iran nuclear "deal" because there was insufficient evidence that Iran was keeping its end of the agreement.[135]

Finally, tenth, progressives are also for solidarity, a principle taken from the Declaration of Independence, "We the people," as a harbinger of democracy. The principle is we must stand together on issues of mutual importance, but not when there is disagreement within our ranks.

Some progressive Democrats are hypocritical in their application of this principle, such as when they discriminated against a prominent African-American defense attorney because he is a Christian with biblical convictions. An Allegheny County, Pennsylvania, attorney candidate's views on homosexuality and his affiliation with a Wilkinsburg church prompted calls for him to drop out of the race. Democratic candidate Turahn Jenkins called being homosexual or transgender a sin, a statement that drew condemnation from Democratic progressives. "We are deeply disturbed by the beliefs of Turahn Jenkins," said the progressive and pro-homosexual Stonewall Steel City Democrats in a statement.[136]

Progressives are more often than not splintered in their efforts and, as a result, seldom realize the espoused principle of solidarity. Splits among their ranks along lines of class, race, sexual orientation, and specific issues often result in competition with one another, a real political weakness called "expanded intersectionality." This means progressives' collective potential to act in solidarity is much greater than in the past, but undermined because of their internal differences. It's a good concept, but reality bodes against the movement's best interests.[137]

Obviously, certain issues trump progressives' tendency to follow their so-called defining principles.

Progressives use the above principles to guide how their movement goes about getting things done. But understanding them is not enough to equip us for a country dominated by progressives. We also need to understand progressive goals that in some, but not all cases, trace their origin back more than a century ago, to America's Progressive Era (1890–1920).

PROGRESSIVE GOALS

Progressives advocate a variety of goals for their movement. First, they characteristically seek to mitigate income inequality. They more often than not blame the upper class (wealthy) for the continued inequality (income and otherwise) much as did their early-twentieth-century protégés.

Progressives have the evidence on their side, so they claim. Since 1970, income inequality has risen as the affluent hold more and more of the nation's wealth. Specifically, 95 percent of income gains from 2009 to 2013 went to the top 1 percent of wage earners.[138]

They blame a number of factors for this income gap: lower union rates, weak federal policy, and globalization, to name a few. Their solution (goal) is to reduce income inequality through legislation such as tax reform, closing tax loopholes, and keeping domestic jobs from leaving for cheaper overseas locations.

Leading progressive and 2020 presidential contender, US Senator Elizabeth Warren (D-MA), wrote a book on the middle class, *This Fight Is Our Fight*, which focuses on income inequality. In the book, she accuses President Trump of siding with America's rich and powerful—America's real enemy, according to Warren—which disadvantages the middle class. She alleges that Americans are "angry" because our democracy "has been hijacked" by "those at the top." By that, Warren means that the wealthy who pervert our government are "making sure that day after day, decision after decision, the rich and powerful are always taken care of."[139]

The senator said:

Trump and his pals tell working people a story about what's gone [on] in their lives. …the problem is other working people. People who are black or brown. People who were born somewhere else. People who don't worship the same, dress the same, talk the same.

Warren pulled out all the stops on "identity politics" to curry favor of every group that might feel disenfranchised by Mr. Trump's "Make America Great Again" agenda.[140]

Former President Obama frequently invokes the egalitarian principle to advocate for the progressive goal of equality for various alleged disenfranchised groups and not just regarding income. In Obama's 2013 State of the Union address, the former president said:

> It is our unfinished task to restore the basic bargain that built this country—the idea that if you work hard and meet your responsibilities, you can get ahead, no matter where you come from, what you look like, or who you love.

In that speech, Mr. Obama called for reigniting the true engine of America's economic growth to help the middle class once again thrive.[141]

The progressive goal of equality means much more than rebalancing income. Mr. Obama also preached progressive propaganda, an Orwellian rewrite of American history regarding the equality issues of feminism and gay rights. He made brazen claims that the roots of modern feminism and gay rights can be traced to our founders. Not true. Modern feminism is based on *Roe v. Wade, 410 U.S. 113* (1973), the Supreme Court decision granting the constitutional right to abortion. Obama should also know better that the modern gay rights movement is traceable to a 1969 riot at a Greenwich Village gay bar, the Stonewall Inn. Police raided that bar and arrested employees and drag (homosexual men dressed as women) performers. That incident drew a large crowd of homosexual supporters who took on the police. Three days of riots ensued, and meanwhile, homosexual groups in other major cities took to the streets as well.[142]

Second, progressives seek universal healthcare reform as a major goal. They were pleased with President Obama's March 2010 Patient Protection and Affordable Care Act, aka Obamacare, which promised, according to Obama and fellow progressives, to increase healthcare affordability and efficiency. While many progressives celebrated that act, others argued that it didn't go far enough—for example, it failed to embrace single-payer healthcare, which remains a progressive goal.

While still in office, President Obama admitted that healthcare was driving up our deficit, but he argued against cutting government-funded healthcare programs such as Medicare ($705.9 billion in 2017) and Medicaid ($581.9 billion in 2017).[143] Rather, he proposed reducing payments to big pharmaceutical companies and argued that wealthier seniors should pay more for their healthcare.[144]

More recently, leading progressive, Senator Bernie Sanders, raised the single-payer healthcare system issue once again. The Vermont senator cited his belief that millions of Americans pay too much for their health insurance, while others don't receive adequate care.

The fact is Obamacare is a failed effort in cultural engineering. It was never just a healthcare law, but the progressives' way of transforming society, bringing it under big government's control. Kim Belshe, a board member of California's Health Benefit Exchange, said Obamacare's true goal was to create a "culture of coverage" in which health coverage was an "expected" (a right) of the social contract. However, as has often occurred in the past, the political process failed to deliver, thus resulted in higher deductibles and copayments and fewer doctor visits. That was the exact opposite of the law's intent.[145]

Progressives will cling to this goal, and with good reason, however. Although, according to a Gallup poll, roughly half of Americans may favor keeping Obamacare, more than half (58 percent) of all Americans want to replace it with "a federally funded healthcare system providing insurance for all Americans," which, as progressives argue, makes healthcare part of the social contract that sounds like "Medicare for All [Life]," a single-payer healthcare system.[146]

What progressives fail to mention when discussing their healthcare goal of "Medicare for All [Life]" is the high likelihood that it would bankrupt the country. That's an inconvenient detail.

One estimate of the costs associated with "Medicare for All [Life]" provided by the Mercatus Center, a George Mason University nonprofit, free-market-oriented research and education think tank, found the cost for the proposed plan is $32 trillion over ten years, yet every leading Democrat likely to seek the 2020 presidential nomination endorsed some form of "Medicare for All [Life]."[147]

Third, progressives want to raise the minimum wage. They argue that stagnating wages perpetuate income inequality, and raising the minimum wage is necessary to combat that problem. Both Senator Sanders and former representative Keith Ellison, now Minnesota's attorney general, endorsed a federally mandated wage increase to $15 an hour. They argue that had wages followed America's productivity growth over the years, the average wage today would now be $21.72 an hour, nearly three times the current $7.25 an hour.[148]

Progressives also favor labor unions (an idea that dates back to the Progressive Era), which understandably endorse a higher minimum wage and higher wages in general. That's evidently a view shared by most (58 percent) Americans, according to a 2015 Gallup survey. Almost three-fourths of Americans (72 percent) said they believe unions should have more influence than they have now.[149]

The problem with establishing ever-higher minimum wages is what it does to small businesses. Of course, every business passes on costs to the customer, but for the small business, higher minimum wages also means potentially significant numbers of layoffs for low-income personnel, something progressives won't accept.

Progressives also don't seem to embrace the concept that it is impossible to set a fair national minimum wage. Consider that if Des Moines, Iowa, for example, had a $10.10 minimum wage, that same $10.10, when translated to real buying power in New York City, would be only $4.12. Obviously, Congress wouldn't accept the political backlash if it tried to pass a law that embraced a cost-adjusted minimum wage by location. That's why such discussions are local, not national, issues.[150]

Fourth, progressives boast a goal for government to be run from the bottom up. They recognize in our modern statist environment that the real power for enforcing policy is at the state and local levels. In fact, the state is where redefining boundaries of congressional districts takes place and criminal justice reform occurs, both important issues for progressives.[151]

Author Nicco Mele writes that "our institutions have in fact failed us," in her book, *The End of Big: How the Internet Makes David the New Goliath*. Mele, the director of the Shorenstein Center on Media, Politics, and Public Policy at Harvard Kennedy School, argues that radical connectivity through social media platforms like Twitter engender a "bottom-up ethos," which means that cultural progress will come through these human grassroots networks. This "bottom-up" change, writes Mele, will impact every major institution, such as "businesses, entertainment, military, schools, media, [and] religion."[152]

Mele wants what most progressives seek: a major overhaul of our current government system, more specifically of our system's foundation, the US Constitution. However, the fault in our present form of government is not in the system but in the corrupted execution of the system. As Thomas Burke, an IT expert and contributor to *The Brenner Brief*, writes in the *American Thinker*, "If the tenets of the system are followed well, then their merits will transfer into practical living."[153]

Attorney and radio talk show host Mark Levin labels our system of government a "post-constitutional republic," by which he means contemporary American government moved far away from our original limited-government philosophy. Much of that movement is attributable to progressives and citizen neglect.[154]

After all, who gave us the alphabet soup of federal "big government" bureaucratic agencies: FDA, EPA, FCC, ACF, FEMA, FDIC, and more? Who gave us an out-of-control welfare program? Answer: Progressives like Woodrow Wilson, Teddy Roosevelt, FDR, Lyndon Johnson, and of course, Barack Obama! Our system of government would work just fine—that is, if progressive "leaders" hadn't made unwarranted modifications.[155]

Fifth, progressives seek major criminal justice reform concerning issues including gun control, police training, sentencing guidelines, privatization of prisons, and government surveillance. They seek these outcomes because of a belief that criminal violence is systemic and a result of numerous factors in American life that they intend to change in the name of progress.

One aspect of progressives' comprehensive criminal justice reform is gun control. They believe that America's "militaristic" national character leads to a pathological devotion to guns.[156] In that vein, former President Obama repeatedly called for legislation targeting American's Second Amendment right to bear arms.

Obama said in his 2013 State of the Union address:

> If you want to vote "no" [on expanding background checks on gun purchases, ban assault weapons and prohibit high-capacity ammunition magazines] that's your choice. But these proposals deserve a vote. Because in the two months since Newtown [a Connecticut elementary school where a lone gunman killed twenty-six people, including twenty young children], more than a thousand birthdays, graduations and anniversaries have been stolen from our lives by a bullet from a gun.[157]

Obama and his fellow progressives never explain how their anti-Second Amendment laws would have stopped the Newtown massacre or any other tragic gun-related violent situation. No, progressives will never be satisfied until America is just like Great Britain, where the only weapons other than those few with the police are in the hands of criminals and terrorists—and that policy isn't working out so well.

It is noteworthy that the so-called gun-free British saw, according to a 2018 government report, a 21 percent year-on-year spike in knife crime and a 20 percent rise in gun crime reported to police. "While it is possible that improved recording and more proactive policing has contributed to this rise, it is our judgment that there have also been genuine increases," a spokesperson for the British Office of National Statistics said.[158]

I will detail the progressive assault on our Second Amendment rights in the next section.

Another aspect of progressive criminal justice reform deals with illegal immigration. Leading up to the 2018 midterm elections, many rallied around the call to abolish ICE, the US Immigration and Customs Enforcement, as noted earlier. Those demands were seemingly a knee-jerk reaction to the crisis at the Mexican border, just as a thousand people (mostly young men) from Central America approached our boundary, threatening to cross without permission.

Soon progressive calls to eliminate ICE caught the attention of some of the Democratic Party's luminaries such as Senator Kirsten Gellibrand of New York. "I believe you should get rid of it, start over, reimagine it and build something that actually works." Others jumped aboard the "anti-ICE" bandwagon such as progressive New York City Mayor Bill de Blasio, and Ms. Alexandria Ocasio-Cortez, a socialist who in 2018 won a seat in the US Congress for New York's Fourteenth Congressional District.[159]

Progressive views about criminal justice reform are frightening for most law-abiding Americans.

Sixth, social justice reform is a progressive goal to help marginalized, disenfranchised, and underserved groups. Under this goal, progressives seek to alter the culture through policies that embrace immigration, require equal pay for equal work (especially for women), advance disability rights, and accept more refugees. Also, progressives use this goal to reverse "religious freedom" bills like the First Amendment Defense Act introduced in early 2018, which progressives claim legitimized discrimination, and especially which homosexual groups label as the "vilest anti-LGBT [lesbian, gay, bisexual, transgender] religious freedom bill of our time."[160]

Progressives often employ a strategy of name-calling to intimidate opponents of their social justice reform ideas. Senator Warren, used such an approach when she said:

It [opposition to progressive social justice reform] comes in all sorts of flavors: racism, sexism, homophobia, xenophobia. It comes in all sorts of forms: nasty personal attacks. Trolling on Twitter. Winking at white supremacists. It all adds up to the same thing: the politics of division.[161]

Another progressive luminary is Senator Cory Booker (D-NJ), also a 2020 Democratic presidential contender, who complained: "We are at a time where injustice has grown to become normal in our country, and it is time for us to work together to get folk woke, to help people understand their power." He said, "American history is a perpetual screaming testimony to the achievement of the impossible." For Booker, social justice includes issues like legalizing marijuana and expunging past drug-related convictions, launching a federal job guarantee pilot program, and more.[162]

Former President Obama called for social justice reforms that he hoped would result in everyone being treated equally, regardless of income, race, sex, or sexual orientation. Certainly, this opened Pandora's box regarding the advancement of homosexual rights, one of Obama's flagship issues. We have seen a notable change across the nation from 1996, when 27 percent of Americans favored legalizing same-sex marriages and now with more than six in ten favoring the issue. There is even a majority who support transgender people being allowed to use the public bathroom of the gender they identify with, a significant increase in popular support for what was once considered an obscure group.[163]

Seventh, progressives like Senator Sanders promote equal economic opportunity, a goal with a big umbrella that includes areas like early education, public school finance reform, and college affordability. Also, they push for more progressive tax structures, increased employee rights, paid parental leave, benefits for part-time workers, and a living wage for all full-time employees.

College affordability is an especially popular economic issue (goal) among progressives. Americans owe a staggering $1.5 trillion in student loans, which in part explains why Senator Sanders' idea of "debt-free" college resonated with young adult voters in 2016. However, the sticking point with his proposal is the staggering cost. The Tax Policy Center estimates that it could cost taxpayers $800 billion over a decade.[164]

Other progressives, including Representative Nancy Pelosi, campaigned in 2018 for the idea of free or debt-free college. Pelosi, now the Speaker of the House, joined fellow House Democrats to propose a bill that would provide federal grant aid to states that make an associate's degree free for every student.

Not to be outdone by House progressives, Democrats in the Senate signed on to a 2018 proposal by US Senator Brian Schatz (D-HI) who introduced a college affordability bill called the Debt-Free College Act, which aimed at providing "a dollar-for-dollar federal match to state higher education appropriations in exchange for a commitment to help students pay for the full cost of attendance without having to take on debt," according to Schatz's office.[165] The senator's plan takes into account all college-related expenses, including housing, meal plans, and books—not just tuition, like Senator Sanders' 2016 presidential campaign promise.[166]

One estimate of the government cost for Schatz's proposed bill is $80.1 billion for the first year of federal-state partnership and $95.4 billion to meet the goal of debt-free college for all students.[167] The senator failed to explain why paying for everyone's college education is the taxpayers' responsibility.

Progressives also want to alter our tax system to become a fairer and progressive tax. The concept is to require a lower tax rate for low-income earners than that of higher-income earners. That's what we already have in place, however. Further, what progressives seldom acknowledge is that nearly half (45 percent) of American households pay zero federal income tax.[168]

It is instructive to review who really pays federal taxes. The top 1 percent of Americans, those with an average income of at least $2.1 million, pay 43.6 percent of all federal individual income taxes in the United States. Further, the richest 20 percent of Americans pay 87 percent of the total federal income tax bill.[169]

Progressives' real agenda with a so-called fairer tax system is income redistribution: take from the rich and give to the poor. Progressives will never be satisfied until everyone lives at the same level—a socialist outcome.

Eighth, progressives believe many of society's ills are "systemic" and "rooted in economics, politics and discrimination," according to Steven Woolf, director of Virginia Commonwealth University's Center on Society and Health. In fact, the far left's Southern Poverty Law Center includes the following on the guidelines it provides for elementary-school teachers: "Poverty is systemic, rooted in economics, politics and discrimination." The lesson conveys to students that "poverty is caused by systemic factors, not individual shortcomings."[170]

A young woman, Maria L. Smith, expresses this view in an article titled "The Charity Band-Aid" in the *Harvard Crimson*. Her opinion-editorial addresses the need for "institutional change" by government. (Yes, progressives always call on government to fix what's wrong in society.) She argues that charitable organizations are important and rise up to "address the effects of systemic problems" in society. The number of charities has increased by 42 percent in the past decade, an indication, according to Smith, that these are just "bandages covering wounds." Her concern is that the establishment, government, is "unaccountable and unresponsive." That is, government doesn't do nearly enough—a classic progressive view.[171]

Miss Smith promotes the progressive view that government is responsible for fixing society's ills and the current government system is broken: "I am calling on government to enact serious reforms and to shape a system in which mothers have the means to feed their children without a dependence on food banks."[172]

Evidently, Miss Smith needs an American history lesson. Our

founders never envisioned the welfare state created by progressives. Charities have long existed to address the needs of the downtrodden, and we should applaud their important work. In fact, the Christian church is explicitly called out in the Scriptures to care for the needy (Matthew 25:35, James 2:14–18, Luke 3:11, 1 John 3:17–18).

The American nanny state created by progressives beginning in the late nineteenth century is true to their long-lived agenda: big government run by progressive elites who take care of all human needs must solve society's ills. That is their self-appointed destiny. Unfortunately, too many in society, including Christians, embrace this view.

Ninth, overcoming government's neglect of our environment is the *sine qua non* (that which is absolutely necessary) of climate change and a major goal for progressives. Senator Sanders writes in *The Progressive*:

> It is hard to keep track of the outrageous and destructive behavior of Donald Trump. However, the greatest long-term threat caused by his administration is that not only is it failing to take action to stop climate change, but it is actually taking steps to make the problem worse.[173]

Not only should government, according to Sanders, fix the climate problem, but in fact government is responsible for *creating* the problem. Sanders writes:

> The tragic and undisputed truth is that the Trump Administration rejects science, ignores the reality of climate change, and pursues policies that are directly leading to more carbon emissions and a major exacerbation of the crisis. On behalf of its friends in the fossil fuel industry, the administration is doing exactly the opposite of what must be done.[174]

Sanders' views reflect what former President Obama said throughout his terms in office. Obama highlighted climate change in his inaugural address and subsequent State of the Nation addresses. He called on Congress to act and directed his cabinet to come up with executive actions to reduce pollution such as: "Prepare our communities for the consequences of climate change and speed the transition to more sustainable sources of energy."[175]

The National Aeronautics and Space Administration website hosts an article, "Scientific Consensus: Earth's Climate Is Warming," that supports this view. That article states:

> Multiple studies published in peer-reviewed scientific journals show that 97 percent or more of actively publishing climate scientists agree: Climate-warming trends over the past century are extremely likely due to human activities. In addition, most of the leading scientific organizations worldwide have issued public statements endorsing this position.[176]

Not surprisingly, given the growing media clamor for the progressive perspective, many average Americans are being won over as well. Gallup polling finds that most Americans are at least "a fair amount" worried about climate change. Further, post-2016 election polling found that even among Trump supporters people want companies to reduce carbon emissions, and 78 percent support stricter air pollution regulations.[177]

The credibility of the climate change science and facts are shaping up to be a defining issue in the 2020 presidential campaign. "There are some things that started to emerge as a consensus, which is Republicans had said the climate is changing, and we're going to have to do something about it," said Douglas Holtz-Eakin, who was a top economic adviser to President George W. Bush and 2008 Republican presidential nominee John McCain. "The president's [Trump's] stance makes that harder because he denies it's even changing…. This puts us back into gridlock again," said Holtz-Eakin.[178]

The Trump administration and fellow Republicans shrug off the progressives' dire warnings about climate change, however. "Our climate always changes, and we see those ebb and flows through time," Senator Joni Ernst (R-IA) said on CNN. Fellow senator, Ben Sasse (R-NE) said while the 2018 report (by the National Climate Assessment) on climate change is important, there is too much "alarmism" around climate-change science.[179]

There is no doubt that some progressives are very serious about harnessing big government to fight climate change. Certainly, the newest initiative on climate change gained considerable attention for its grandiose goals and the political risks. The overhaul of their climate-change effort was introduced in February 2019 by Representative Alexandria Ocasio-Cortez (D-NY) and Senator Ed Markey (D-MA), the "Green New Deal," which is a takeoff from FDR's New Deal, a massive 1930s policy package that promised to rescue the US economy from the Great Depression. Similarly, the Green New Deal is an enormous measure that promises to eliminate all US carbon emissions, a major progressive goal intending to help reverse climate change. But "even the solutions that we have considered big and bold are nowhere near the scale of the actual problem that climate change presents to us," Ocasio-Cortez admitted to National Public Radio.[180]

The proposal calls for "10-year national mobilizations" to address major climate change-related goals such as the elimination of the use of all fossil fuels and transition away from nuclear energy as well. The deal specifically advocates for "meeting 100 percent of the power demand in the United States through clean, renewable, and zero-emission energy sources."[181]

Other goals associated with the Green New Deal include upgrading all existing buildings for energy efficiency; farmers eliminating pollution and greenhouse gas emissions; providing guaranteed jobs, sustaining wages, family and medical leave, paid vacations, and retirement security for all Americans; and high-quality healthcare for all Americans.[182]

The costs associated with the Green New Deal are astronomical. The American Action Forum estimated the proposal will cost up to $94.4 trillion, or about $600,000 per household. Those totals include providing every resident in the country a federal job with benefits, "adequate" housing, "healthy food," and healthcare. Further, the proposed "economic transformation" of the US would include an overhaul of transportation systems and retrofitting every single building.[183]

"The American Action Forum's analysis shows that the Green New Deal would bankrupt the nation," said Senator John Barrasso (R-WY), chairman of the Senate's Committee on Environment and Public Works. But the costs evidently don't alarm the Deal's backers because the threat is so serious to them.[184]

How dire is the danger to our climate that prompts progressives to embrace the Green New Deal? The freshman congresswoman said humans should stop reproducing because climate change will end the world in twelve years. Even Democratic 2020 hopefuls echo the alarm and throw their support behind the radical proposal.[185]

Senator Kamala Harris, one of the leading Democratic Party candidates for 2020, tweeted "I'm proud to co-sponsor @AOC and @EdMarkey's Green New Deal. We must aggressively tackle climate change which poses an existential threat to our nation." She added, "The Green New Deal is a bold plan to shift our country to 100% clean and renewable energy."[186] Also, when the senator was asked about the extreme cost, she said, "of course we can afford" the plan because climate change is "an existential threat to us."[187]

Progressive and 2020 presidential contender Sanders is one of the original backers of the proposal. "I am proud to be an original co-sponsor of the Green New Deal proposal," he wrote. "We must address the existential crisis of planetary climate change, while at the same time creating millions of good-paying jobs in our country..[188]

Just as prominent Democrats rushed to embrace the Green New Deal, Republicans were practically giddy. "I would like them to push it as far as they can. I'd like to see it on the floor. I'd like to see them actually have to vote on it," said Representative Mike Simpson (R-ID), a senior House appropriator. "It's crazy. It's loony."[189]

Senator Lindsey Graham (R-SC), agrees with Simpson. He tweeted: "Let's vote on the Green New Deal!" He added, "Americans deserve to see what kind of solutions far-left Democrats are offering to deal with climate change."[190]

What's clear is that the progressives will push for major government action to address climate change, and the Republicans, at least for now, will push back. This will no doubt become an issue in the 2020 presidential campaign and beyond.

Finally, progressives promise to cut national defense expenditures, which was $716 billion in fiscal year 2019. Progressives complain that current defense spending, which represents more than half of all discretionary spending ($1.3 trillion in 2019), is bloated and must be cut. Those savings, Democrats promise, will be redirected to medical research, environmental clean-up, and combating climate change.[191]

Thinking Americans likely heard statements from the 2018 Democrat marquee insurgent candidate, Alexandria Ocasio-Cortez, who expressed her opinion about national defense budgets. "They're like, 'We don't want another fighter jet!' They're like, 'Don't give us another nuclear bomb,' you know? They didn't even ask for it, and we gave it to them," said the young socialist from New York.[192]

In spite of such nonsensical statements, congresspersons from both sides of the aisle agree that, in the interest of "parity," there must be equal-sized increases to defense and domestic programs. "On a practical level, it's the only way you get a deal," said Emily Holubowich with the Coalition for Health Funding.[193]

Deal-making is the reality of politics on Capitol Hill, but that doesn't make sense when America's security is gravely threatened on many fronts—such as the rising near peer Chinese with a reemergent Russia. However, that notion seems to escape progressives and their Democratic Party elite.

Progressives claim their ideas (goals) are gaining more national support, which is true. So to complete the circle, consider why progressives are so energetically pursuing government legislation. Why? Because they want total control and need a majority of voters to back their issues.

How Much Support Do Modern Progressives Enjoy Across America?

Progressives enjoy considerable support among a growing cross-section of Americans. They are especially popular among the entertainment elite (Hollywood), who push progressive issues and evidently influence others.

A growing number of superstar athletes as well disrespect our national anthem by refusing to stand—they kneel or hold clenched fists in the air—and celebrities like actress Ashley Judd use their platform to address social justice issues. For example, Judd gave an endorsement of "intersectionality," a catch-all term for all prejudice against every victimized minority. The pregnant question for conservatives and libertarians, given the above pop-culture icon support for progressivism, is: Are these celebrity advocates having an impact for their progressive views?[194]

The short answer appears to be "yes," progressive views are growing in popularity. In fact, a 2017 annual Gallup poll on values and beliefs found a record number of Americans approving of progressive views regarding such issues as doctor-assisted suicide, same-sex relations, pornography, polygamy and more. The poll also found that as tolerance for these issues increased, there was also a troubling shift regarding religion in America.[195]

The often anti-God progressives appear to be gaining ground on the religious front as well. Gallup pollsters asked a random sampling of Americans: "How important would you say religion is in your own life? They found 51 percent answered "very important," while a record high minority (25 percent) said "not very important." That's quite a troubling shift in reported levels of a belief in God over the years.[196]

Gallup isn't alone in declaring this shift. Researcher Jean M. Twenge with San Diego State University found a significant decline in belief in God among Americans, a particularly significant fall from the early 1980s. Further, a 2015 Pew Research survey found that "younger millennials" are especially less likely than any previous generation to claim any religious affiliation.[197]

Progressive views about big business are gaining support, especially among young adults as well. A 2016 Harvard University survey found that 51 percent of young adults share the progressives' anti-big business view. Meanwhile, the ideology of socialism—anti-capitalism—is gaining support, even though only 16 percent of Millennials can even define the term.[198]

These surveys raise an obvious question: Do average Americans believe as do progressives that big government needs to do more heavy lifting to address society's ills? That's certainly a view we read earlier from the Harvard student. However, the problem for progressives is that nongovernment influencers—the second layer of *The Deeper State* outlined above—exert significant influence over Washington's policies than do the masses. So, it really doesn't matter what Harvard coeds and the majority think about the responsibilities of big government, because the real power brokers are the unelected, second-layer influencers.

A 2014 study identifies the "economic elites" and "business interests," rather than popular sentiment (the masses), as the true influence behind federal policies.[199] Specifically, Princeton University Professor Martin Gilens and Northwestern University Professor Benjamin I. Page wrote in *Perspectives on Politics* that almost half of the time (47 percent), Congress embraces the position of the "economic-elite" rather than the "middle class" (the voting population at large). Critics of this study claim this isn't proof of democracy's failing, but then again, the "economic-elite" evidently play a significant enough role in determining government policy. After all, the "economic-elite" really do influence lawmakers sufficiently to compel them (the lawmakers) to test the political waters before making policy decisions by asking voters to express their opinions either via public opinion polling or perhaps referenda.[200]

The Gilens and Page study illustrates why progressives are suspicious that government is "corrupt" and perhaps why average Americans are expressing similar concern about a nonresponsive government. After all, big government often does favor outcomes that the majority of Americans really don't support. Specifically, public opinion research from Data for Progress (DFP) and YouGov Blue, a progressive group, found similar results. What may surprise some readers is that some policies promoted by self-identified progressive lawmakers are in fact especially popular among mainstream Republicans.

Consider survey responses to the question: "Would you support or oppose having the government produce generic versions of life-saving drugs, even if it required revoking patents held by pharmaceutical companies?" The question earned approval from a majority of Trump voters, especially in rural zip codes.[201]

Keep in mind that the executive branch already has the legal authority to unilaterally override patent law, but it seldom does, according to scholars from Yale and Harvard universities. They wrote in the *Washington Post*:

> This is possible because existing law gives the federal government limited immunity to challenges from patent holders: Patent holders cannot stop the government from making or buying products that infringe on their patents, and can sue only for reasonable compensation.[202]

So why doesn't the federal government use this provision in the law to favor the majority's will? Further and perhaps more telling is the question: Why isn't this option even seriously considered? The answer seems to be pretty evident. The pharmaceutical lobby has great influence as opposed to the public's belief in the inviolability of intellectual property rights.[203]

Another illustration of deep-pocketed businesses trumping average consumers is the Internet-access business. Big corporations like Verizon and Comcast sell access to the Internet and protect their fat profits. DFP asked why the government hasn't created a "publicly-owned Internet company to fill coverage gaps in rural, urban, or remote areas that currently lack robust Internet access." Not surprisingly, most (56 percent) of Trump and rural American voters support publicly-owned

Internet suppliers to fill the gaps.[204] Once again, big business trumps the majority of citizens' interest in better Internet service.

A majority (55 percent) of voters across the board also support "the federal funding of community job creation for any person who can't find a job."[205] Is there a big-business reason government is kept out of the job-creation business? Probably, and the taxpayer should be concerned as well. Yet, more people are being drawn to progressive views, screaming, "Let's get government engaged in ever more aspects of our lives."

Tax policies are a common progressive target, as considered earlier regarding their goals. Progressives always seek to heavily tax the rich in order to spread (redistribute) the wealth to the less advantaged. It is interesting that DFP found reluctance by a cross-section of voters to embrace a 90 percent tax rate on all income above $1 million (40 percent versus 33 percent). Yet, a Pew Research poll in August 2017 found voters opposed to lowering taxes on corporations by a forty-nine-point margin and opposed cutting taxes on households with $250,000 incomes.

Why then did Congress spend so much time in 2017 debating regressive tax cuts amid overwhelming public opposition? The answer seems to be intuitive: wealthy Americans and corporations have a decisive advantage over ordinary Americans when it comes to influencing public policy.[206]

Progressive economic ideas enjoy considerable national support. The Center for American Progress (CAP) claims polling data shows that both college-educated and working-class people, and of all races, favor an economic agenda that protects all Americans. Further, "The polling shows that workers across race support similar views on economic policy issues," said David Madland, the coauthor of the report, entitled "The Working-Class Push for Progressive Economic Policies." "They support a higher minimum wage, higher taxes on the wealthy, and more spending on healthcare and retirement. There is broad support among workers for progressive economic policy."[207]

Some aspects of a progressive national economic policy are in fact very popular, according to CAP's study, which was conducted in 2016 and 2017. Those findings regarding progressive issues and supported by majorities include paid family leave, equal pay, and more taxpayer money for retirees, as well as increased healthcare and higher taxes for wealthiest Americans.[208]

These economic-bridging topics also help progressives leverage other matters across the American populace. Alex Rowell, a policy analyst at the CAP, said: "When you focus on these progressive issues, they are also about racial and gender equity. Women and workers of color are worse off, and when you focus on these broad economic issues, you are bringing them up."[209]

You should understand now that progressives have reason to be encouraged. Their issues are gaining widespread traction across America. But how do they overcome resistance from conservatives, libertarians, and especially a growing politically-independent section of the population who make up at least half of American voters? Progressives need a strategy to reach those people if they hope to succeed in 2020 and beyond.

Just What Is the Progressives' Strategy to Reach Their Goals?

Past progressive strategies to persuade voters to embrace their views are not necessarily a prologue for future efforts. However, they do provide some insight as that movement anticipates the 2020 presidential election and beyond.

Understand that progressives are beside themselves regarding the setbacks experienced thanks to President Trump's outright reversal of many of former President Obama's policies while other Obama-era agenda initiatives failed to deliver results without any Republican help. Progressive hope was trashed in 2016, made somewhat of a tepid recovery with the 2018 midterm elections, and now, in 2019 and beyond, they are out to recover lost ground and continue their revolution to take over and radically transform America.

Just how are they planning the political way ahead? Arguably, the resurrection of their hopes began in early 2018, when many of the leading progressives gathered at the Netroots Nation conference to hear from their ideological luminaries and to begin charting a path to victory in the 2020 presidential election and beyond. They weren't disappointed by the stable of speakers who screamed the progressive agenda in one speech after another: single-payer healthcare, abolishing immigration and the customs enforcement agency, and more.[210]

A Democrat midterm (2018) darling and now member of Congress spoke at the Netroots Nation conference, Alexandria Ocasio-Cortez. The twenty-eight-year-old Latina shocked the political establishment by defeating the No. 4 House Democrat, New York Representative Joe Crowley. Oscasio-Cortez, a devoted socialist, urged fellow Democrats at the Netroots conference to "come home" to ideas that she claims were first proposed by progressive icon President Franklin D. Roosevelt. "We are picking up where we left off when we were at our most powerful, when we were at our greatest," she said.[211]

Democratic Party progressives like Ms. Oscasio-Cortez used the forum to outline their platform to win big in 2020. Her leading progressive issues include a "Medicare-for-All [Life]" healthcare system; tuition-free college and a student debt bailout; a $15-an-hour minimum wage; a federal jobs guarantee; a major overhaul of the nation's immigration enforcement; and action to address inaccessibly high housing costs," and much more, such as the Green New Deal," which wasn't fully announced until early 2019.[212]

Other conference speakers nearly screamed their true ideological bent. "Republicans are going to call us socialists no matter what we do. So we might as well give them the real thing," said Cynthia Nixon, the actress and activist who lost in her challenge to New York Governor Andrew Cuomo in the September 2018 Democratic primary.[213] They are really socialists and happy to be.

The Democratic Party's drift toward socialism is almost complete, and it suits their progressive ambitions. After all, socialism is gaining in popularity, according to a 2018 Gallup poll, which found 37 percent of Americans of all stripes say they now have a positive view of socialism, with 58 percent holding a negative view. But among Democrats and Democratic-leaning independents, 57 percent have a positive view of socialism.[214]

New York City Mayor Bill de Blasio is another significant progressive voice who spoke at the Netroots conference. He compared the political environment in 2018 to that of 1974, after then President Richard Nixon resigned amid the Watergate scandal. "This is an extraordinary moment," de Blasio said. "We can't think of it as, we're just filling a niche. We have to see ourselves as authors of an emerging majority…[which] requires telling the voices of false pragmatism and phony moderation that we don't believe their lies," blasted de Blasio. Then he proclaimed, "Progressives, it's our time."[215]

Ohio Democrat and US Congressman Tim Rayan, a new member of the progressive left, once opposed abortion but flipped to pro-abortion. Now, at the Netroots conference, Rayan called for a host of other progressive agenda initiatives: national marijuana legalization, a student debt bailout, an expansion of Social Security, and efforts to reverse the effects of global warming. "Every now and then, you've got to get in a fight," Ryan said.[216]

Kamala Harris is a progressive US senator from California and a Democratic presidential hopeful for 2020. Senator Harris said at the Netroots conference: "Race, gender, sexual orientation are defining issues for America."[217] She complained that the ideological right has weaponized "identity politics" and they "try to shut us up."[218]

Harris, a former California attorney general, told the gathering of national progressives: "It's a pejorative. That phrase [identity politics] is used to divide and used to distract. Its purpose is to minimize and marginalize issues that impact all of us."[219]

Ms. Harris identified the issues that matter to her progressive way of thinking: civil rights, women's reproductive rights (abortion on demand), criminal justice reform, and immigrant rights (sanctuary cities and legal rights for illegals), and she said, "We won't be silent" on these issues. She said these are the very things "that will define our identity as Americans [and].... This is about American identity."[220]

Harris' comments were meant not just for moderate Democrats who hoped to reverse the party's far left direction to a more centralist agenda. Her comments preview what could become her campaign agenda for 2020 and beyond.

She called on Democrats to give credit to those "who have been the backbone of the Democratic Party," in particular, women of color like her who elected progressive leaders in the past. She then called for "electing women of color as those leaders" of the Democratic Party in the future. She never claimed to be shy about promoting herself.[221]

Other rising stars among Democrat stalwarts at the Netroots Nation conference included Massachusetts Senator Elizabeth Warren and New Jersey Senator Cory Booker, both presidential candidates. They addressed many of the same issues as the others above, confirming the progressive agenda for 2020.

Yes, progressives are upset and are rallying around their issues. But what is their likely strategy for 2020 to take back both the presidency and the Senate and expand their slim majority in the House?

Below are a number of actions, some associated with specific issues that will inevitably become the core of the progressives' 2020 strategy.

Progressives' 2020 Strategic Issues

First, progressives intend to rally support across their broad movement. That begins by reassuring discouraged and disenfranchised communities uncertain and worried about what the Trump administration has done and might do in the future.

The day after the 2016 election, the homosexual group, Human Rights Campaign (HRC), reported receiving more website hits than it did the day the Supreme Court made same-sex marriage legal, said

HRC communications director Jay Brown. "Our folks are scared. They are worried, and they are coming to us for answers—do I need to get married now? Do I need to shore up my parenting rights?" Brown said.[222]

Second, progressives will look to the federal courts and state and localities to hold fast to their past policy advances. It is true that lower courts made President Trump's attempt to enforce immigration laws problematic. But there are enough progressives at the local level, they hope, to slow his efforts. For example, Los Angeles Police Chief Charlie Beck said after the 2016 presidential election that Trump's victory would not change his plans to ignore federal immigration enforcement, despite the president's pledge to toughen federal immigration laws. The LAPD prohibits officers from initiating contact with someone to determine whether they are in the country legally.[223]

There is a political bias in the federal judiciary, in spite of Chief Justice John G. Roberts' protestations otherwise. In November 2018, Justice Roberts responded to President Trump's criticism of an "Obama judge" who ruled against the administration. In a rare public statement, Roberts said, "We do not have Obama judges or Trump judges, Bush judges or Clinton judges. What we have is an extraordinary group of dedicated judges doing their level best to do equal right to those appearing before them."[224]

Roberts' surprising public statement didn't sit well with President Trump, who quickly tweeted: "Sorry Chief Justice John Roberts, but you do indeed have 'Obama judges,' and they have a much different point of view than the people who are charged with the safety of our country. It would be great if the 9th Circuit was indeed an 'independent judiciary.'"[225]

The American people agree with President Trump. Seventy percent of Americans believe Supreme Court appointments are either the most important or an important factor in deciding who to elect as president and evidently Democrats agree. If not true, how might any objective person justify the Democrats' brutal character assassination campaign against Judge Brent Kavanaugh?[226]

Nearly six in ten current federal judges were appointed by Democratic presidents, according to the Pew Research Center.[227] Does the party affiliation of the president who appoints a judge really matter? It seems as if campaigns are an indicator. After all, presidential campaigns promise to appoint judges who support their views. Then presidential candidate Donald Trump promised in 2016: "I am looking to appoint judges very much in the mold of Justice Scalia. I'm looking for judges—and I've actually picked 20 of them so that people would see." Justice Scalia was a conservative, constitutional constructionist.[228]

The reality of presidential politics demonstrates that conservative presidents tend to nominate judges who exercise a philosophy of judicial restraint, thus they follow our laws as written. Liberal presidents like Obama tend to nominate judicial activists who legislate from the bench to shape the law to reach progressive outcomes. After all, as established earlier, progressives believe in a "living [malleable] Constitution," which can be interpreted to mean whatever they choose.

Progressives know that the longer Trump is in office appointing strict constitutionalist judges, the more difficult it will be to change the direction of America. Keep in mind that FDR, the left's favorite progressive president, understood the judicial branch's role. FDR desperately tried to get the Judicial Procedures Reform Bill of 1937 (the so-called court-packing plan) through Congress to add more justices to the US Supreme Court. Why? He needed more like-minded justices to help neutralize the high court's hostility toward many of FDR's progressive New Deal programs.[229]

Courts matter and progressives understand how to use them to get their way. Of course, in fairness, each side understands the value of selecting the "right" type of judges and justices.

Third, Democrat lawmakers will continue to push their progressive agenda to the limits. New York Governor Cuomo directed state police to create a new hate crimes unit to counter what he called an "explosion" in hate crimes. That's clearly a message to the Trump administration that progressive America is not going to roll over. At the same time,

Connecticut Governor Daniel Malloy, another progressive Democrat, said his state would continue to accept Syrian refugees in spite of the Trump administration's contrary policy.[230]

Expect the progressive push to continue, because more Democrats are now openly progressive and thus will back that agenda. Also, Democrats are more likely to associate themselves with the label "progressive" than at any time in recent memory, according to Elaine Kamarck at the Brookings Institution. She found a "huge increase" in the number of Democrats self-identifying as "progressive" in 2018—44 percent in 2018, compared to 29 percent in 2016 and 26 percent in 2014.[231]

Fourth, progressives will refocus their efforts on the white, working class and rural voters who abandoned the Democratic Party's 2016 presidential candidate Hillary Clinton, who labeled these people as "deplorables," who then abandoned Clinton to cast ballots for Mr. Trump. "As long as you try to win by mobilizing a minority of the electorate, which was [GOP strategist] Karl Rove's specialty, you risk creating a monster like we have," said Scott Lilly, senior fellow at the left-leaning CAP and a former longtime senior Capitol Hill staffer. "The truth is here, an awful lot of people who voted the other way last week [2016 presidential election] ought to be on our side. We have [lost them] by not maintaining a dialogue with them," Lilly adds.[232]

Progressives believe their path to victory in 2020 requires winning back Trump voters by "taking Trump on right where it hurts for him." Specifically, a *USA Today* poll found that healthcare will be the most important issue for midwestern Trump-to-Democrat voters likely to decide the 2020 election. This group will also be sympathetic to Democrats' argument that Trump's tax cuts hurt the federal deficit and therefore directly impact entitlement programs like Medicare and Social Security.[233]

Fifth, progressives will target the "rising American electorate" of African-Americans, Latinos, Millennials, Asian-Americans, unmarried women, and LGBT people. Whit Ayres, a Republican pollster, notes that if a relatively small group of votes had gone the other way in parts of Pennsylvania and Michigan, the national pundit class would be discussing the debacle facing the Republican Party. After all, Ayres said, the election was not a "wave" election endorsing Trump's approach, but rather "two waves going in different directions."[234]

The new American electorate is a target Democrats hope to attract. Steve Phillips, cofounder of the Progressive Group Democracy in Color, said Democrats in the past were too concerned about alienating their old base of working-class white voters, which explains their failure to attract more people of color. He continued, "Trump's message was, white people, let's take our country back. The Democrats responded by saying, Trump had a bad personality," Phillips complained.[235]

Phillips is trying to target a new progressive Democrat base. He claims Democrats (progressives) need to identify their diverse base—and own it. "The culture of the Democratic Party lies in Georgia, Arizona, Texas and places that are going through this demographic revolution. It does not lie in places such as rural Wisconsin"—all states, notably, that Clinton lost in 2016.[236]

Sixth, progressives insist the Democratic Party must keep tracking left to win. They claim to be scoring historic victories in communities the Democratic Party's establishment has traditionally ignored. For example, a Pennsylvania group of Democrat socialists claim their candidates must run unapologetically progressive in order to win.

"Buying into this polarizing narrative of us and them, but thinking success is mimicking everything the Republicans do has definitely been the heart of the problem in my district," said Kristin Seale, the Democratic Party candidate for state representative in a suburb of Philadelphia where Republicans typically dominate.[237]

Evidently, at the time, Seale was one of twenty-six candidates in the United States formally endorsed by the national chapter of Democratic Socialists of America. Seale joined the socialists because of shared values and ties to the labor movement.

Progressives bet their leftist ideas will continue to grow and are part of a winning formula for future elections.

Seventh, run against Trump. The level of dissatisfaction with him is a palpable factor that progressives won't ignore when seeking to win in 2020. Exit polling during the 2018 midterm elections found that 39 percent of voters said they cast ballots to express their opposition to Trump, while 26 percent said they wanted to show support for him.[238]

Finally, make a moral argument for progressive issues like healthcare, which will pull at the voters' heartstrings. Jean Ross with the National Nurses United said: "The only thing that stands in the way of 'Medicare for All [Life]' in the United States is a lack of political and moral will. The moral argument is the only argument strong enough to create the political will necessary."[239]

Nina Turner, a former Ohio state senator and president of Our Revolution, called the ongoing US healthcare crisis "a sin and a shame." She pointed out that eight years after the passage of Obamacare, millions of Americans are still without health insurance.[240]

Progressives will claim the moral high ground to persuade voters to favor their candidate.

The emerging progressive strategy to win back control over the levers of America's government may work. They have significant and growing support across the electorate and a smart way ahead.

Conclusion

Progressives have a clear set of operating principles, enduring goals, and a new emergent strategy to win control over our future. The challenge for those who do not support the progressive agenda is to persuade the American electorate, who are malleable to progressive arguments and issues, to turn in a different direction to recapture the founders' true purpose and direction for this great country.

Their message is based on deception and lies, but convincing the electorate that this is so will be THE challenge of the century. Many are already deceived, as we can see by the Clinton victory in the popular vote. While popularity of the socialist ideology appears to be on the increase, conservatives must find a way of presenting the counter facts. The evil must be brought into the light. Conservative victory in 2020 and beyond will depend heavily on presenting the truth in a manner that the people, especially Millennials, can digest.

3

Psychological and Biblical Considerations of Modern Progressivism

ox News host Tucker Carlson suggested that progressives have gone crazy. "Their new position is that it is immoral to restrict any kind of immigration, from any country, in any amount, for any reason ever," he said.[241] No, Mr. Carlson, progressives aren't crazy *per se*, but they may be delusional (a symptom of mental illness), an issue addressed later in this volume. Many simply believe in things that many other Americans find wrong and/or distasteful, especially Americans who believe in the foundational documents of this republic and biblical values.

This chapter won't establish whether progressives are crazy, but it will consider a psychological and biblical profile of this ideologically driven group. Let's begin with a bit of progressive mind exploring.

A 1960 study published by the Johns Hopkins University Press, "Psychiatry, Psychology and the Progressive Movement," examined the movement's impact on the human psyche, psychiatry, and psychology before World War I. The author of that study suggested the progressive movement of the late nineteenth and early twentieth centuries was "not limited to politics, economics and social philosophy, but pervaded all of the endeavors of middle-class Americans."[242]

The study, which appeared in the *American Quarterly*, outlined the parameters of progressivism. Specifically, as we saw earlier, at least in the late nineteenth and early twentieth centuries, the movement's essence was based on the "firm belief that to a considerable degree man could make and remake his own world." Progressives believed (and perhaps continue to believe today) that the human being is malleable, although not necessarily inherently good. Further, the responsibility for addressing the ills of society rested mostly on the social environment and "progressives believed that man could change his own environment and so reconstruct both societies and individuals."[243]

The study's author opined that "progressives themselves were to be the self-appointed arbiters of man's destiny. They were able, literate and largely professional groups, accustomed to the role of leadership and, like Theodore Roosevelt, unafraid of it."[244]

They were motivated by altruism. Direction in life came from the man of goodwill who "had transcended his own interests; he governed by right of his moral superiority." The author continued: "Social responsibility inspired in many progressives a feeling of guilt for all of the evil that a faulty society had caused, and the sophisticated with New England consciences equated righteousness with social reform."[245]

The author concluded with a list of progressivism's psychological attributes: "optimism, environmentalism, moral fervor, and leadership by enlightened elite."[246] Further, he admitted that more needs to be done to understand the impact of the Progressive Era's social reform movement.

"The historian will discover the full dynamics of progressivism only when he examines not just politics, economics and social philosophy, but all aspects of American life," wrote the study's author.[247] Of course, a major aspect of American life is religion, a belief in God that progressives mostly reject.

This chapter considers three questions to help the reader explore progressivism: What makes progressives tick (translation: "behave in a certain way")? What does the Bible say about the issues important to progressives? What do many progressives think about Bible-believing Christians?

What Makes Progressives Tick?

Two authors provide invaluable insight into progressive thinking. The first is a late professor who claims progressivism is a religion. The second is a Progressive Era Baptist pastor who indicates that progressive thinking during his time was rooted in well-known "science" and "philosophy," which helps the reader understand what made those progressives tick and may provide insights about modern progressives as well.

Progressivism is a religion, and anyone who follows another faith is delusional, according to a leading progressive scholar, Richard Dworkin, a former law and philosophy professor at New York University. Dworkin, now deceased, was considered one of the leading intellectuals of modern times.[248]

Peter Berkowitz, a political scientist at Stanford University's Hoover Institution, wrote an analysis of Dworkin's final book, *Religion Without God.* In it, Berkowitz wrote that Dworkin claims "that traditional religious faith is not only devoid of truth but politically harmful." Further, America's leading universities have fallen in line with that view, which explains why modern faculties have "been largely conservative-ideas-free-zones," Berkowitz observed. The rejection of traditional religions at most institutes of higher learning made room to advance the "smug conviction that progressivism is the truth, truth is progressivism, and that is all that students really need to know," he said.[249]

Dworkin appears to break with progressive orthodoxy in his posthumously published book, however. Berkowitz explained that Dworkin promotes conciliation in the cultural and political wars by focusing on religion. But don't be misled, Berkowitz cautioned, because

Dworkin never abandoned progressivism's foundational issues such as abortion, affirmative action, assisted suicide, same-sex marriage, and a malleable US Constitution.[250]

The mind-blowing aspect of his final book, which is based on the Albert Einstein lectures, is Dworkin's claim that "we can separate God from religion." He then argues, "If we can come to understand what the religious point of view really is and why it does not require or assume a supernatural person—then we may be able to lower, at least, the temperature of these [contemporary] battles by separating questions of science from questions of value."[251]

It's not surprising that Dworkin redefines religion to conform to his progressive sensibilities. Berkowitz explained that Dworkin suggests "a hostile takeover attempt" of people of traditional religions by contemporary progressives. Berkowitz said Dworkin's "hostile takeover" takes place when the progressive appropriates "the religious label for his own left-liberal and atheistic outlook…in how the progressive mind, under the guise of conciliation, seeks to command the moral high ground exclusively and discredit that which differs from it."[252]

Dworkin formulates his god-free religion when he "denies that belief in gods or God is essential to the religious perspective." For Dworkin, religion consists of "two central judgments about value," which Dworkin "believes religious people—theists and some atheists—regard as objectively true."[253]

Those truths include first, "each person has an innate and inescapable responsibility to try to make his life a successful one which 'means living well, accepting ethical responsibilities to oneself as well as moral responsibilities to others, not just if we happen to think this important but because it is in itself important whether we think so or not.'"[254]

The second truth is "what we call 'nature'—the universe as a whole and in all its parts—is not just a matter of fact but is itself sublime: something of intrinsic value and wonder."[255]

Berkowitz concluded that Dworkin "reveals his conviction that one of progressivism's bedrock assumptions is a matter of faith [a religion] and not a truth of reason." Although Dworkin disparaged traditional biblical faith, he "makes clear that the religious attitude as he understands it compels protection of abortion and also leads inexorably to progressive views about affirmative action, assisted suicide, same-sex marriage, and right on down the line."[256]

Dworkin also believes that "Americans who believe in God are an angry and intolerant lot," wrote Berkowitz. But as Harvard political scientist Robert Putnam writes in *American Grace*, the "men and women of faith in contemporary America are more engaged in civic life, more tolerant, and tend to make better friends and neighbors than secular Americans."[257] That's a clear rejection of Dworkin's view of "Americans who believe in God."[258]

It is a twist of logic that Dworkin's characterization of progressivism as a "religion" without God represents "an establishment of religion in violation of the First Amendment," observed Berkowitz. That's quite juxtaposition for a philosopher who seeks elite-run big government.[259]

A Baptist preacher who lived and worked during the entire Progressive Era provides further insights into that movement's ideology and answers the question in part: What makes progressives tick? A. C. Dixon (1854–1925) was an author and evangelist known as one of America's original fundamentalists, an organizer and editor of the *Fundamentals: A Testimony of the Truth*, a collection of essays from the fundamentalist movement.[260] One of Dixon's sermons is especially helpful, because it contrasted progressive thinking with traditional biblical and Christian thinking, which he entitled "The Bible at the Center of the Modern University" (1920). Dixon's aim with the sermon was to refute the popular progressive view at the time that progressivism's scientific thinking "would have no serious effect on [societal] morality." Dixon rebuts that notion to claim there "was an eternal natural order in which men lived, created by God and ordered to the good of man, which was portrayed in Genesis [first book of the Bible]."[261]

Dixon rightly attributes progressivism's reliance on "scientific thinking" to Charles Darwin (1809–1882), who indirectly is credited with the rise of German militarism. Darwinism "taught that life was a struggle and that those who won the struggle were by that fact proved better than those who lost"—might makes right, a theory embraced by German despots, arguably by German philosopher Georg Wilhelm Friedrich Hegel (the father of modern progressivism), and some progressives today.[262]

Pastor Dixon traces Darwin's views about the evolution of life to an Anglican clergyman. Darwin wrote in his autobiography that he received from an Anglican priest the suggestion of the "hypothesis that everything was evolved from beneath; that life originated with germinal, embryonic beginnings; that in nature there is perpetual war, which is called 'the struggle for existence,' the strong and fit destroying the weak and unfit, and thus causing everything to move upward."[263]

Reverend Thomas Robert Malthus, an Anglican priest and Darwin's source of evolution thinking, taught that "man increases with geometrical ratio, while food supply increases with only arithmetical ratio. Therefore wars and pestilences are necessary, that the surplus population may be killed off, in order that the remainder may survive."[264]

Dixon concludes that "Darwin was deceived by the plausible reasoning of Malthus, and made this mistake [assuming wars and pestilences are necessary] one of the foundation-stones of his scientific system."[265]

Dixon's point in declaring the nexus between progressivism and Darwinism was to criticize the eugenics movement that was pressed vigorously by progressive reformists at his time. Dixon said the American eugenics movement and the writings of Adolf Hitler's Nazis used similar reasoning to develop their racial and eugenic policies, based on the presumed supremacy of the Aryan race, a topic explored later in this volume.[266]

Pastor Dixon also exposed Friedrich Wilhelm Nietzsche (1844–1900), a student of Darwin's theory that "humankind had evolved from remote ape-like ancestors, in a completely naturalistic way, through a process of chance and necessity (fortuitous random variations appearing in and inevitable natural selection acting on, individuals within a changing environment). Even the mental faculties of human beings, including love and reason, were acquired during the course of evolutionary ascent from earlier primate forms."[267]

The neurotic Nietzsche "hypnotized the German mind with his pagan brute philosophy," said Dixon. Nietzsche said the "weak and the botched shall perish; the first principle of humanity. And they ought to be helped to perish. What is more harmful than any vice?"[268] Obviously that's an idea that promotes the Nazi's eugenics policies and one embraced by some twentieth-century American eugenicists as well.

Nietzsche also targeted Christianity for elimination. He said, "Christianity is the greatest of all conceivable corruptions, the one immortal blemish of mankind." He hated Christianity because it stood for the weak and "botched," while he glorified the Aryan race: German "blond beast," one-third brute, one-third devil, and one-third philosopher.[269]

Nietzsche's philosophy of beastliness has its roots in the evolutionary assumption that the strong and fit in the struggle for existence "have the scientific right to destroy the weak and unfit." That philosophy infected the brain of the German Kaiser, who embraced the alleged scientific right "to destroy all weaker nations and erect his throne upon their ruins."[270]

Dixon spoke of the impact of Nietzsche on the German Kaiser, and eventually on Hitler's Third Reich, which encouraged the First World War, "The War to End All Wars," which killed at least fifteen million and wounded another twenty million, as well as the Second World War, with the Holocaust that claimed six million innocent Jewish lives.[271]

The pastor spoke that sermon, which included much of the above content, on a Sunday morning four months after World War I began. A man came up to Pastor Dixon after the service and said the following:

> I am a German, brought into London on a captured ship; and why I have not been interned I do not know; but I have an intimation that I shall be interned next week, and before I go I would like to give you a piece of my mind. You have said that

this terrible war was due to Darwinian evolution, and I believe it. I hope I am a Christian. I love Jesus Christ and believe the Bible, but my wife and daughter have had their faith wrecked by Nietzsche and his pagan gang. But what I want to say to you is that we Germans got Darwinism from England. We took it from you and worked it out to its legitimate consequences. So, when you mention it again, speak softly, for you are really getting back what you sent.[272]

Dixon said he could not deny the German's claim. "Back of this war and responsibility for it is Darwin's pagan teaching that the strong and fit have the scientific right to destroy the weak and unfit," he wrote.[273]

What makes progressives tick? We saw that Dworkin espoused a godless religion known as progressivism that infects that movement even today, and by association, many who call themselves members of the modern Democratic Party if for no reason than by relationship. It is pretty obvious that the roots of the modern progressive movement are also linked to the types of radical and anti-God philosophies espoused by the likes of Darwin and the brutish Nietzsche, who are widely embraced by modern progressives, albeit naïve dupes of that anti-God worldview today.

What Does the Bible Say about the Issues Important to Progressives?

Progressives who pay any attention to Christianity and/or other faiths pick and choose religious Scriptures that support their worldview and then tend to discard the balance as fairy tales. In the case of Christianity, don't forget that progressivism is about change, and that applies to so-called progressive Christians and their view of God's Word. They seek change for the sake of progress, a view that man must keep moving forward to a better future. As one progressive pastor said: "To not move forward is to resist God."[274]

Progressives cite a number of New Testament Scriptures to demonstrate the necessity of progress for the contemporary Christian. For example, some applaud the Apostle Peter's statement (2 Peter 3:18, NIV) that we must "grow in…knowledge of our Lord and Savior Jesus Christ." Luke asks Jesus in Luke 11:1 (NIV), "Lord, teach us to pray." Paul allegedly progresses in his Christian maturity regarding resisting sin in 1 Corinthians 9:27 (NLT): "I discipline my body like an athlete, training it to do what it should. Otherwise, I fear that after preaching to others I myself might be disqualified." These Scriptures are pleasing to the progressive mind because they interpret them to call for "progress."

Progressives tend to handle the Bible in a very self-serving manner that allows them to dismiss much of scriptural teaching as outdated while endorsing other selected passages that support their radical agenda. The following examples illustrate the point.

First, consider how some deal with the Scriptures. Reverend Roger Wolsey, a United Methodist pastor in Boulder, Colorado, offers a progressive's view of the Bible. Progressives, according to Wolsey, select a few verses to interpret literally, and the balance of the Holy Scriptures are just stories. Further, Wolsey's message to Christian fundamentalists is that progressives take the Bible seriously, though with the aforementioned caveat.[275]

Wolsey continues to explain that he can't speak for all "progressive Christians," an oxymoron to fundamentalist Christians. However, he states that Christian progressives take the Bible seriously, but not literally, unless it fits their worldview. Why? Perhaps, according to Wolsey, they doubt that God actually wrote the Bible. Progressives believe that fallible men who were inspired by the Holy Spirit wrote the Bible, which makes the text error-prone and led to inconsistencies and contradictions, which, he argues, "endear" progressives to the Bible, because "we agree with those passages, but because we recognize that they are fully human they're authentic, they're down to earth." The "flawed" passages encourage the progressive because "mature people who realize that it's best not to hide our dirty laundry or to deny our very real human feelings and passions."[276]

Progressives often seek to modernize the Scriptures, a dangerous and anti-God undertaking. Revelation 22:18–19 (ESV) warns against "modernization." The Apostle John wrote:

> I warn everyone who hears the words of the prophecy of this book: if anyone adds to them, God will add to him the plagues described in this book, and if anyone takes away from the words of the book of this prophecy, God will take away his share in the tree of life and in the holy city, which are described in this book.

The fact is that all truth is available in God's Word, and neither time nor circumstance alters God's instructions. Peter wrote in 1 Peter 1:25 (NIV): "But the word of the Lord endures forever." Of course, the progressive seeks change even in terms of updating truth. But Romans 12:2 (KJV) is clear about divining the truth: We must "not be conformed to this world: but be ye transformed by the renewing of your mind, that ye may prove what is that good, and acceptable, and perfect, will of God."

Progressives also believe that modern enlightenment grants us a new truth—a new revelation. That's a false premise, because as 1 Peter 1:25 states, the Word of God does not change. Neither progressives nor anyone else is at liberty to break the Scriptures (John 10:35).

Progressives tend to embrace many sins, a red flag for true Bible-believing Christians. Progressives pick and choose the Scriptures to embrace antibiblical sins like homosexuality and abortion, which places them beyond God's rules for fellowship (1 Corinthians 5:1–2).

Progressives reject the teaching about a real hell. They tend to be religious pluralists who reject the scriptural teaching that hell is the destination for those who reject Jesus' salvation. They equate God's love (John 3:16) with salvation (Matthew 7:13–14). Yet, the Apostle Peter clearly wrote: "Salvation is found in no one else [other than Jesus

Christ], for there is no other name under heaven given to mankind by which we must be saved" (Acts 4:12, NIV).

Progressives reject the unchanging nature of truth in God's Word. Christians must be on guard to reject progressivism as destructive of God's Word and be watchful of new "truth" seeping into our churches. What God calls sin in His Word is not changed by time, context, or modern revelation.

Some progressive Christians claim to rely on "the Holy Spirit" to help them interpret the Scriptures, but they add to that "interpretation" the influences of secular tradition, reason, experience, and "insights of contemporary science." No wonder they believe there is no "objective, one, right way" to interpret a passage.

Some progressives rationalize that each person interprets the Scriptures via his or her own personal experiences, education, upbringing, sociopolitical context, and more. This view can be particularly dangerous for Christians because it leads to arrogance. Any people who think they are more enlightened than other Christians are dangerous. That happens when we supplement God's Word with nonbiblical information (experiences, education, and politics), which leads some to claim to be more "enlightened" than others.

The progressives' urge to "progress" and their reliance on modern science for answers to life's most daunting problems may in their mind necessitate a move beyond biblical teaching as well. However, Jesus is clear about following the Word of God. Our Lord instructed His apostles to teach the disciples "to obey everything I have commanded you" (Matthew 28:20, NIV). Our worldly experiences do not alter God's Word.

Some Scriptures are even more important than others, according to Wolsey. Progressives employ a "canon within the canon" lens, which means some Scriptures receive greater weight than others. Although the context and language of the Old Testament are perhaps more difficult to discern than, say, the rather straightforward Gospels, the sixty-six books of God's Word are an entire message creating a complete scriptural tapestry.

Progressives even equate human tradition and understanding with Scripture. They do this by pointing out human failings to justify progressing beyond God's Word. The classic progressive illustration of past human failings is that in earlier times, Christians owned and abused slaves, a clear wrong. That's a misunderstanding of the Scriptures. The Bible never teaches that Christians may own, much less abuse, slaves. Past human failings are not justification for ignoring the scriptural teachings about slavery or any other wrong (sin).

Wolsey explains his cherry-picking approach to Scripture by stating that he gives "greatest weight to Mark, Luke, Matthew, John (in that order), certain letters that Paul actually wrote…the prophets, and the Psalms." The balance of the Bible is interpreted as to how "they jibe and are in sync with these primary texts." Wolsey also illustrates that "many progressive Christians refer to themselves as 'Matthew 25 Christians,'" which refers to the test that Jesus uses to identify those who are in or not in the kingdom based on what they do. Other progressives refer to themselves as "Sermon on the Mount Christians," those who prioritize this portion of the gospel as central. There are also "Red Letter [progressive] Christians" who give greatest weight to Jesus' words, identified by red typeface in the modern translations.[277]

In fact, progressives tend to see an endorsement of their views throughout the Bible, especially when it comes to homosexuality. Wolsey illustrates this view regarding "the sin of Sodom" in Ezekiel 16:49–50 (NIV): "Now this was the sin of your sister Sodom: She and her daughters were arrogant, overfed and unconcerned; they did not help the poor and needy. They were haughty and did detestable things before me."

Wolsey argues that Jesus supports the view that "the sin of Sodom" was their lack of hospitality, not homosexuality. He illustrates with Jesus' words in Matthew 10:9–15 (NIV):

Do not get any gold or silver or copper to take with you in your belts—no bag for the journey or extra shirt or sandals or a staff, for the worker is worth his keep. Whatever town or village you enter, search there for some worthy person and stay at their house until you leave. As you enter the home, give it your greeting. If the home is deserving, let your peace rest on it; if it is not, let your peace return to you. If anyone will not welcome you or listen to your words, leave that home or town and shake the dust off your feet. Truly I tell you, it will be more bearable for Sodom and Gomorrah on the Day of Judgment than for that town.

Evidently, Wolsey believes Jesus' words here endorse contemporary homosexuality. He concludes: "Employing this approach leaves me with no question in my mind that homosexuality between consenting adults in a committed, monogamous relationship is not sinful."[278]

Wolsey is joined by other progressives who see tolerance for homosexuality elsewhere in God's Word. A writer for listverse.com interprets Jesus' healing of the Roman centurion's servant as an endorsement of homosexuality as well (Matthew 8:5–13). He argues that the Greek word used for the centurion's boy is *pias*, which he believes could mean "girl" and "young gay lover" as well. The author cites Kenneth Dover, an ancient Greek scholar, to make his case that Jesus "indirectly gave his blessing to a gay relationship."[279]

Some claim the story of Ruth and Naomi is about a lesbian relationship. Ruth, according to that author, tells the older Naomi that she'll never leave her, even in death, and "clings" to her; allegedly the Hebrew word here translates to "clinging," in the way that a husband becomes one with his wife. The author concludes: "It's almost as if God himself sees nothing wrong with being LGBT."[280]

Even the alleged "gay" love in the account of King David and King Saul's son Jonathan is part of the progressive Christian's view. The first thing David and Jonathan do when they meet, according to the author, is to "get naked." David says Jonathan's love is "more wonderful than that of women" (2 Samuel 1:26), and David claims to love Saul more than his own soul (1 Samuel 18:1–4).[281]

At this point, allow me to take a slight diversion to explain why progressives will never convince Bible-believing Christians to embrace homosexuality. The answer is simple: Biblical Christians "are bound to their idea of human sexuality because it is fundamentally inseparable from their understanding of God," a view expressed by freelance author Kyle Cupp.[282]

The impasse between progressive and Bible-believing Christians on this divisive issue is the fact that the "sexual difference is woven into all of scripture," according to Matthew Schmitz's writing in *First Things*. The fact is, biblical Christianity orders sexual differences towards procreation and serves as a foundational principle. "Tug on the strand of sexual difference," Schmitz writes, "and you risk unraveling the whole" of Christianity.[283]

Thus, the broader culture's acceptance of homosexuality and self-defined gender identities is more than nuance for Bible-believing Christians. "It threatens more than the Christian notion of sexual difference and complementarity," writes Cupp. "If this traditional Christian understanding of human sexuality is wrong, then the biblical authors were misguided in building their conceptions of God and the church on the foundations of sexual difference. The Bible would call that building a house on the sand."[284]

Let me be very clear about homosexuality, a contentious issue pushed by most progressives. The Bible is absolutely unambiguous that homosexual behavior is a sin (Genesis 19:1–13; Leviticus 18:22, 20:13; Romans 1:26–27; 1 Corinthians 6:9). Those passages identify homosexual behavior as sinful, not as a struggle with temptation. Specifically, Romans 1:26–27 states that homosexual behavior is a result of denying and disobeying God, so when someone continues to sin, God then "gives them over" to more wicked and depraved sin.

Bible-believing Christians understand that all people are sinful, and the world lures us through enticements to practice sin; for some, that may include homosexual behavior. Although homosexual attraction is very real for some, 1 Peter 1:5–8 tells us that we can control what we do with those feelings and we have a responsibility to resist those temptations (Ephesians 6:13). The Apostle Paul encourages us to "walk by the spirit" so as not to "gratify the desires of the flesh" (Galatians 5:16).

Now, back to progressive heresy regarding their proclivity to pick and choose Scriptures. To illustrate the view that the Bible supports many classic progressive issues, the author of listverse.com claims the three Abrahamic religions don't like women, which he demonstrates with the case of Deborah in Judges 4.[285]

Deborah was Israel's first female judge, who destroyed the Canaanites that attacked the Israelites. However, once victorious, she was shoved to the side, never to be heard from again. The progressive opines that there is a presumed antifeminist outcome that marks the Bible and all the descendants of Abraham as misogynous.[286]

Racism, the listverse.com author argues, is not encouraged by the Bible. Yet he claims that "extreme Christianity" (read "Bible-believing contemporary Christian church") is racist. However, ancient Greek, Roman, and Hebrew societies were almost color blind, according to the progressive. He explains that slavery in the biblical times always refers to people (no matter their skin color) as spoils of war. Therefore, ancients weren't racist, just slave holders. Then he cites Galatians 3:28 (KJV) to supposedly illustrate his point: "There is neither Jew nor Greek, there is neither bond nor free, there is neither male nor female: for ye are all one in Christ Jesus."[287]

Jesus is a socialist, according to the progressive article writer. That's music to the ears of contemporary progressives, especially the left wing of the Democratic Party that promotes the redistribution of wealth, aka socialism. After all, the listverse.com author argues, Jesus, an established poor carpenter, once told a wealthy follower that the only way to salvation was to sell all his possessions and give it to the poor (Matthew 19:16–30). So, the writer paraphrases, rich people today are doomed to hell, according to Jesus—that is unless they engage in "some serious wealth distribution."[288]

Progressives take great liberties with biblical content...to the point of heresy. Bible-believing Christians must understand the rationale and techniques progressives use to protect themselves and to bend God's Word to their liking.

What Do Many Progressives Think about Bible-Believing Christians?

The previous material exposed numerous dangers to biblical Christianity attributed to progressives and their ideology. The bottom line is that progressive ideology is nonbiblical about the nature of truth (everything is relative), the nature of man (he is basically good), and the nature of God's Word (it is changeable).

Progressives see Bible-believing Christians as pawns in their world to manipulate in order to form a future that fits their radical, anti-God agenda.

Justin Steckbauer is a Christian author who works for the Salvation Army and is the founder of lifestyleofpeace.com. On his blog, he provides a thoughtful article, "Biblical Christianity vs. Progressive Ideology: A Threat to Western Christianity," which makes a compelling case as to why progressives are a threat to our way of life, especially our Christian faith. Some of his points are outlined below with my elaboration to answer the question: What do many progressives think about Bible-believing Christians?[289]

Steckbauer begins by reiterating that progressivism lowers the truth of Scripture to "the realm of philosophical relativism." We saw that in the examples outlined in the previous section of this chapter. Progressives dismiss Bible verses about homosexuality being a sin and excuse abortion—both clear sins in God's Word.[290]

We learned previously that progressives believe the Scriptures are mostly stories—fairy tales—without any truth; thus, they are free to interpret God's Word to fit their own beliefs and ideas. That's dangerous for Christians, because it reverses the role of the Bible as the guide and puts man in the driver's seat to judge the Bible. No wonder, as illustrated above, progressives see God's Word as endorsing many societal evils.

The prior chapters also demonstrated the rabid influence of progressive ideology's impact on Western societies, thanks to leading progressives such as Darwin, Marx, Hegel, Kant, and other atheist thinkers. American progressives embraced those foreign ideological thinkers and brought their views into American society in order to alter our previously Christian-influenced culture. And their effect is likely permanent. After all, does anyone seriously believe that, this side of Christ's Second Coming, we will ever restore morality in America concerning issues like abortion and homosexuality?

The major challenge and threat to Christians going forward is the progressives' intent to manipulate big government through political action to gain leverage over an ever-expanding litany of societal issues: large administrative bureaucracies, "democratic" socialism, redistribution of wealth, unlimited welfare, abortion on demand paid for by others, free healthcare for all, free college, and unlimited and unbridled immigration irrespective of national laws, and every other progressive issue mentioned in chapter 2.

Yes, the Christian church was and will continue to be victimized by progressive political ideology. That's a fact. The more progressive the American culture becomes, the more those in Christian church pews will themselves become radicalized and distant from God's Word.

Do you doubt that's where we are heading? Progressives have every intention of compelling secularists, agnostics, atheists, and people of all faiths to change (progress) by surrendering to the views and demands on antibiblical "gay" marriage, transgender rights, abortion, and many more aberrant and sinful worldly paths. Further, progressives will use a future big government controlled by them to force even Bible-believing Christian pastors to ignore God's Word to perform homosexual marriages or face jail—or worse.

Do you believe a pro-life Christian church will ever be forced to host an abortion clinic? I believe that will happen once America is under a progressive, big-government rule that defines intolerance as anyone who holds to a biblical view about social issues like abortion and homosexuality. Progressives will use the like-minded judiciary to enforce their radical views about right and wrong. And they won't stop with abortion and homosexuality.

Progressives aim to force their will on all people by using the strong arm of big government to impose all the strictures of climate change, gun control, socialism (redistribution of wealth), and removal of a church's tax-exempt status. Then they will take our religious freedom, our liberty to live out our Christian faith in a radically secularized world.

Progressives will use politics and big government to attack our rights and values using cultural Marxism that promotes political correctness, gender ideology, and a broad homosexual dogma. I explore this assault in the next three sections of this volume.

The only good news here is that Christians shouldn't be concerned that so-called progressive churches backed by progressive government is about to replace fundamentalist, conservative, Bible-believing congregations. No. People want real truth found in God's Word, not relative truth found in half-baked scientific ideas pushed by wishy-washy "love above all else" ideology, as Steckbauer states in his article.[291]

On the other hand, there is evidence of a growing apostasy within the Christian church. It is a sign of the end times, and Europe is a prime example. Many wonder whether the Muslim invasion of Europe is a punishment for drifting away from the faith. America is drifting as well.

Is this outlook too dire? Study history to see how previous empires and civilizations fell. America in the hands of progressives will be no less vulnerable to willingly jump over a cliff, and Christians in particular may face a future like early believers in ancient Rome's coliseum.

Conclusion

Progressives are classically crazy—what many Christians call evil and delusional, as explored later in this volume—especially when juxaposed with a biblical world view. They seek the polar opposite of the Word of God and intend to impose their cultural, Marxist ways on the balance of mankind using the arm of big government run by progressive elitists.

These "perilous times" are spoken of in 2 Timothy 3:1 (NJKV), and they can be translated as "raging insanity." The Apostle Paul describes that condition: "For men will be lovers of themselves, lovers of money, boasters, proud, blashemers, disobedient to parents, unthankful, unholy, unloving, inforgiving, slanderers, without self-control, brutal, despisers of good, traitors, headstrong, haughty, lovers of pleausre rather than lovers of God, having a form of godliness but denying its power. And from such people turn away!" (2 Timothy 3:2–5, NJKV).

Is there any doubt this Scripture passage fits the contemporary progressive?

SECTION II

Introduction:
Progressivism and Our Basic Rights

The liberties of our country, the freedom of our civil constitution, are worth defending against all hazards: And it is our duty to defend them against all attacks.[292]

—Samuel Adams, American founder and signer of the
United States Declaration of Independence

America's founders created a remarkable Constitution that limits the power of the federal government with three branches and protects individual rights through the Bill of Rights. In 1789, James Madison—the chief architect of the Constitution and an initial opponent of the Bill of Rights—persuaded Thomas Jefferson to draft a slate of amendments to satisfy critics who felt the Constitution was incomplete without human rights protections.

Our founders fought over whether a Bill of Rights—ten amendments to the proposed Constitution—was necessary to limit governmental power, a response to calls from the states for greater constitutional protection for individual liberties.

The battle over the proposed Bill of Rights was between federalists and antifederalists. The federalists wanted to preserve a strong national, federal government, while the antifederalists favored strong state governments and believed the national government created by the proposed Constitution was too strong.

The federalists sound like modern-day progressives who seek a strong central government run by elites. The antifederalists are better aligned with modern-day conservatives who tend to favor strong state (local) governments rather than a strong federal government. They also believed in the reliability of average citizens as opposed to elites, whom they distrusted and thought were corrupt. Further, the antifederalists held that a Bill of Rights was necessary against future federal government infringement on individual liberty, much like the monarchy shed by the American Revolution (1775–1783).

The federalists' arguments against the proposed Bill of Rights included their soured association with the British crown. They feared any Bill of Rights would be linked to the British concept dating back to the Coronation Charter of King Henry I, the Magna Carta, and the English Bill of Rights of 1689. Those documents were the British king's promise that he would not abuse his power. Thus, federalists argued that the people had nothing to fear from an unaccountable monarch any longer. Rather, the proposed Constitution put in place a means to hold government representatives accountable on a regular basis via popular vote for congressional representatives.[293]

Founder Alexander Hamilton also dismissed the Bill of Rights as "volumes of those aphorisms," which had no practical power and no means by which the legislature could have been forced to adhere to it. Other federalists argued that the Constitution already included statements in defense of specific rights that limited federal jurisdiction.[294]

The antifederalists countered that the Bill of Rights was directly linked to the charges made against King George III in the Declaration of Independence. They wanted protection from the twenty-seven grievances against the king identified in the Declaration of Independence, such as "repeated injuries and usurpations, all having in direct object the establishment of an absolute tyranny over these states."[295]

The first clause of the Constitution's Preamble to the Bill of Rights states why it is necessary to prevent such abuses in the future:

> The Conventions of a number of the States, having at the time of their adopting the Constitution, expressed a desire, in order to prevent the misconstruction or abuse of its powers, that further declaratory and restrictive clauses should be added: And as extending the ground of public confidence in the Government, will best ensure the beneficent ends of its institution.[296]

Thus, the Bill of Rights was written in response to a warning in the Preamble of the Declaration of Independence: "In order to prevent the misconstruction or abuse of its powers." Our founders (at least the antifederalists) feared the possibility of anyone incorrectly interpreting ("misconstruction") the Constitution, thus abusing the limits of government.

The Bill of Rights was ratified on December 15, 1791, a political necessity to satisfy antifederalist objections (perhaps like modern conservatives). Our Bill of Rights protects our freedoms of religion, speech, press, assembly, and petition; our rights to keep and bear arms and to be entitled due process of law; and our freedoms from self-incrimination and double jeopardy.

There is no surprise that modern progressives try to supplement our current lot of constitutional rights to fit their radical ideology. In fact, their favorite icon and former president, Franklin D. Roosevelt, created his own bill of rights, which he announced during his State of the Union Address on January 11, 1944. In that address, Roosevelt said the following:

> It is our duty now to begin to lay the plans and determine the strategy for the winning of a lasting peace and the establishment

of an American standard of living higher than ever before known. We cannot be content, no matter how high that general standard of living may be, if some fraction of our people—whether it be one-third or one-fifth or one-tenth—is ill-fed, ill-clothed, ill-housed, and insecure.[297]

"We have come to a clear realization of the fact that true individual freedom cannot exist without economic security and independence," said the former president. Then he explained, "In our day these economic truths have become accepted as self-evident. We have accepted, so to speak, a second Bill of Rights under which a new basis of security and prosperity can be established for all—regardless of station, race, or creed."[298]

Roosevelt's second Bill of Rights was a litany of progressive, big government, nanny-state programs: guaranteed jobs, a minimum wage, the right to sell, control over competition, guaranteed housing, and full access to medical care, education, and more. Don't these "rights" sound strangely similar to the issues listed in the Green New Deal, outlined in the previous section?

Progressives are also dead set on altering the current constitutional rights to fit their ideology, which is the primary focus of this section

Here we will explore six of the ten rights (amendments) in the Bill of Rights and outline how progressives sought and continue to seek to alter them to their favor. Those rights include: freedom of speech and religion; the right to bear arms; freedom from unreasonable search and seizure; the right to due process; the presumption of innocence, and power vested in the states.

4

First Amendment

Congress shall make no law respecting an establishment of religion, or prohibiting the free exercise thereof; or abridging the freedom of speech, or of the press; or the right of the people peacefully to assemble, and to petition the government for a redress of grievances.[299]

—First Amendment, US Constitution

Progressives abuse our First Amendment to fit their radical agenda. We will explore here the structure of the amendment, its history, how it evolved in the courts and culture, and how progressives intend to mold it to fit their agenda.

America's early history made freedom of speech and religion important issues for all citizens, because it was the very absence of those freedoms that brought this country together. Founder Thomas Jefferson understood our religious heritage and wrote the first of ten amendments to our Constitution to address concerns that emanated from the colonies' early years while under the iron thumb of the British monarchy.[300]

First Amendment's Six Rights

The First Amendment includes six "rights" or clauses, freedoms for every citizen.

First, it states that "congress shall make no law respecting an establishment of religion." That clause is often referred to as the "establishment clause." It grants "separation of church and state" as a freedom enjoyed by all citizens—preventing past issues our ancestors experienced in Europe with the government-funded, government-sanctioned churches.[301]

The second clause, "or prohibiting the free exercise thereof," protects the citizens' freedom of religion. Our ancestors came from countries where many were persecuted for their faith. Our founders wanted to guarantee that big government would never again require uniformity of belief (religion). There will be no Church of the United States like there was a Church of England. Further, freedom of religion is not just freedom to worship, but it's also the right to follow the tenets and precepts of our faith within every private and public aspect of our lives.[302]

The third clause, "abridging the freedom of speech," is the very essence of free speech, which means that someone's right to say whatever he or she wants is protected within limits. Those exceptions are defined by the judiciary, and some limits are addressed in the following pages.[303]

The fourth clause guarantees freedom of the press: "or abridging the freedom of speech, or of the press." Thomas Paine, an English-born, American political activist, philosopher, political theorist, and revolutionary, published pamphlets titled "Common Sense" during the American Revolution in which he expressed opposition to the British crown and, as a result, rallied support for the colonies. This clause is about the freedom to publish and distribute "speech" in the written form.[304]

The fifth clause addresses the "right of the people to peaceably assemble." That's the custom of Americans across this great land: to meet in community and town assemblies to debate and to chart their collective futures. That was not always our freedom while we were under British colonial rule, which suppressed Americans and fomented our revolutionary movement. This clause was intended to prevent government from restricting social movements, such as the one that is the subject of this volume.[305]

The final clause grants the citizens the means to resolve problems: "and to petition the government for a redress of grievances." Under the British Crown, there was no opportunity to pursue lawsuits against the crown's tyranny. The right to petition government became essential for a free people and our accountable, constitutional government. Otherwise, the citizens have no recourse other than armed rebellion—the very reason that led to the American Revolution.[306]

Two Special Clauses

Although each of the six clauses of the First Amendment is important, two have earned special attention over the life of our country: freedom of speech and freedom of religion. Both experienced significant reinterpretation, thanks to the Supreme Court and our culture.

It is important to appreciate that the First Amendment only restricts actions by the federal government as opposed to requiring government to actually and proactively protect practitioners of speech and faith. That is an important distinction as we explore these freedoms, the right to express oneself in both speech and faith without having to worry about government interference.

First, consider the freedom of speech.

Over time, the US Supreme Court interpreted that right to exclude certain speech, such as shouting "fire" in a crowded theater or distributing obscene materials (pornography). There are also limits to speech that are disallowed when it obstructs the government's effort to defend itself.

The *Schenck v. United States 249 U.S. 47* (1919) Supreme Court case upheld the conviction of Socialist Party activist Charles Schenck for distributing fliers urging young men to dodge the World War I draft. That decision defined the limits of speech, creating a "clear and present danger" standard.[307]

The high court's record indicates that in June of 1917, soon after the US entered World War I, Congress passed the Espionage Act, which made it illegal to:

> ...willfully make or convey false reports or false statements with intent to interfere with the operation or success of the military or naval forces of the United States or to promote the success of its enemies...[or] willfully cause or attempt to cause insubordination, disloyalty, mutiny, or refusal of duty, in the military or naval forces of the United States, or shall willfully obstruct the recruiting or enlistment service of the United States, to the injury of the service or of the United States.[308]

The plaintiff in the Supreme Court case, Mr. Schenck, was the general secretary of the US Socialist Party at the time he opposed the military draft. His party printed and distributed fifteen thousand leaflets calling for men to resist the government's military conscription. Subsequently, Schenck was arrested and charged with violating the Espionage Act, Public Law 65-24 (1917). He was convicted and then sentenced to ten years in prison for each of three counts. On appeal to the high court, the lower court's decision was upheld because it was determined that the leaflets encouraging men to resist conscription were dangerous to national security, a violation of the Espionage Act.[309]

Another case that further defined freedom of speech was the 1971 Supreme Court case, *New York Times Company v. United States 403 U.S. 713*. That decision granted public media like the *Times* and the *Washington Post* the constitutional freedom to publish the *Pentagon Papers* without risk of government censorship. Those top-secret documents were leaked to the newspapers, exposing unseemly aspects of America's involvement in the Vietnam War (1955–1975) and how the public was misled.[310]

In that case, Daniel Ellsberg, a military analyst employed by the RAND Corporation (a nonprofit, global policy think tank) at the time, copied more than seven thousand pages of the Pentagon Papers revealing the history of the government's actions in the Vietnam War. Ellsberg gave the *Times* and the *Post* the classified documents that exposed government knowledge that the war would cost more lives than the public was told.[311]

Mr. Ellsberg was charged with theft, conspiracy, and violations of the Espionage Act for leaking the papers. Meanwhile, the government obtained a court order preventing the *Times* from printing the documents, arguing that their publication would threaten national security. This was the first case in which the government successfully ordered a prior restraint on national security grounds.[312]

The case against Ellsberg was eventually dismissed as a mistrial when evidence surfaced about government-ordered wiretappings and break-ins associated with the case.[313]

Another freedom of speech Supreme Court case addressed the burning of the American flag. The *Texas v. Johnson, 491 U.S. 397* (1990) case involved Gregory Lee Johnson, a self-identified communist who burned the American flag during the 1984 Republican National Convention in Dallas, Texas, in protest of President Ronald Reagan. In that case, the high court reversed a Texas court's decision that Johnson broke the law by desecrating the flag.[314]

As demonstrated above, the Supreme Court put limits on freedom of speech. However, over the course of the country's history, our culture has also influenced the meaning of freedom of speech.

Culture's impact on free speech is evidenced among our youth. A 2018 national survey by the Constitution Center of high school students and teachers provides some insight into the next generation's views about our constitutional freedom of speech guaranteed by the

First Amendment. Specifically, an overwhelming number (90 percent) of high school students surveyed said people should have the right to express unpopular opinions. In fact, students are more likely than their teachers to support public speech, even threatening speech. That includes strong support for the right of school newspapers to report controversial stories (60 percent) as compared to less than half of teachers who do (45 percent).[315]

Students strongly disagree with the First Amendment right to burn the American flag (73 percent) as opposed to only 61 percent for teachers. Further, regarding athletes protesting the national anthem, like former National Football League player Colin Kaepernick, 60 percent of students believe that's a free speech right, compared with 63 percent of teachers and 81 percent of college students.[316]

On another front, and as many readers will likely agree, the Internet earns high marks for propagating "hate speech," a view shared by most teachers (85 percent), as do most (70 percent) students.[317]

What free speech means will continue to evolve with changes in our culture and with future high court decisions as well.

The second significant clause of the First Amendment concerns freedom of religion. Although the "establishment clause" prohibits any state religion, as our ancestors experienced in Europe, it has gone much too far in drawing a line between church and state.

The First Amendment addresses religious freedom with the clauses "no law respecting an establishment or religion, or prohibiting the free exercise thereof." Keep in mind the United States was formed in large part by groups of people who escaped religious persecution in Europe. Our Founding Fathers wanted to avoid the mistakes inherent with the establishment of an official state religion. That was the genesis of the clauses and a view reinforced by our first four presidents, who expressed their views regarding this important liberty and government's role.

Those American presidents articulated an aversion to mixing religion and politics, believing the best way to protect religious liberty was to keep the government out of religion. For example, President George Washington said: "In this enlightened Age and in this Land of equal liberty it is our boast, that a man's religious tenets will not forfeit the protection of the laws, nor deprive him of the right of attaining and holding the highest offices that are known in the United States."[318]

President Thomas Jefferson explained his understanding of the First Amendment's religion clauses in an 1802 letter to the Danbury Baptist Association in Connecticut. He reflected on the view of "the whole American people which declared that their legislature should 'make no law respecting an establishment of religion, or prohibiting the free exercise thereof,' thus building a wall between church and State."[319]

The early presidents' views about the separation of church and state explains why America has no official religion and thus has managed to avoid religious conflicts the likes of which tore countries apart elsewhere. However, the founders never intended America's government to be antireligion as it has become, especially in recent years and to a large extent attributable to progressives.

Most recently, former President Barack Obama soiled the government-religion association during his eight-year tenure. He accomplished this antireligion feat mostly through informal statements and some actions.

Obama and his administration breathlessly attacked Catholics and Protestants alike, but he was especially disrespectful of religious Jews and Israel in particular. So, it is more accurate, perhaps, to say he was antibiblical in part because of his preferential treatment of Muslims and Islamic nations. Wallbuilders, a Christian organization dedicated to presenting America's forgotten history, compiled a list of progressive President Obama's antibiblical track record in four groupings:

(1) numerous records of his attacks on biblical persons or organizations; (2) examples of the hostility toward biblical faith that have become evident in the past three years in the Obama-led

military; (3) a listing of his open attacks on biblical values; and finally (4) a listing of numerous incidents of his preferential deference for Islam's activities and positions, including letting his Islamic advisors guide and influence his hostility toward people of biblical faith.[320]

Obama's antibiblical activities influenced the broader culture, as demonstrated by many incidents documented by the Washington, DC-based Family Research Council (FRC). For example, consider the case of Hampton High School in Tennessee, where the principal issued a no-prayer edict for graduation. He threatened to stop and escort out of the graduation ceremony anyone who even tried to pray.[321]

Unfortunately, that sort of hysteria was evident and continues to be seen across the nation, according to the Family Research Council, which documented, like Homebuilders, a significant upsurge in government hostility to religion under President Obama's time in the White House.

FRC's report, "Hostility to Religion: The Growing Threat to Religious Liberty in America," stated that since 2014 there has been a 76 percent increase in religious freedom violations.[322]

FRC president, Tony Perkins, said "The recent spike in government driven religious hostility is sad, but not surprising, especially considering the Obama administration's antagonism toward biblical Christianity." He said the sixty-six-page report underscores the legitimacy of the actions taken by President Trump to end polices in federal agencies that "fan the flames of this religious intolerance."[323]

Freedom of religion is a precious right that must be preserved. Progressives would redefine it as freedom to worship, to say our prayers, and to study God's Word inside our churches are permissible, but would not allow our faith to motivate our public actions. However, from the very first day at Plymouth Rock among the early Puritans and throughout our rich history, Americans have allowed and must continue to allow the tenets and precepts of their faith to guide their civic and personal actions.

Progressive Plans for First Amendment

Progressives and their cadre of leftists won't be satisfied with past efforts to take a wrecking ball to the First Amendment. No, they have plans to take it completely captive and make it subservient to their radical agenda.

What is it that progressives want to do with the First Amendment, especially regarding the two most important clauses: freedom of speech and religion?

We established in the previous chapter the progressive view of Christians. They are willing to tolerate Christians' right to worship (keep our faith in a box) but not our right to allow that faith to influence public discourse.

The reality is that progressivism is a competing "religion," as established earlier, and it seeks to replace other faith groups. Therefore, it presents itself accordingly and expects equal treatment at the least while denigrating other faiths as illegitimate.

Progressives are just as obnoxious regarding free speech. Too often, they literally push the envelope of civility when it comes to free speech— as seen by what's happening on many college campuses today.

Consider a recent example of progressive tyranny in the name of freedom of speech on a publicly funded college campus.

In November 2016, a student group at the University of Wisconsin-Madison brought Ben Shapiro, a conservative commentator, to deliver a speech entitled "Dismantling Safe Spaces: Facts Don't Care About Your Feelings." A small group of students tried to shout Shapiro off the stage.[324]

The exchange between Shapiro and the student protestors was pretty typical of many campus protests today. The protestors chanted "Shame!" and "Safety" before Shapiro said a single word. Shapiro said at the start of his speech: "At least wait until I say something that offends you before being offended."[325]

For another fifteen minutes, Shapiro silently watched the protest that took place in front of the auditorium's stage before he moved to the blackboard to write in giant letters "Morons." Eventually, campus police moved the protesters to the exits and Shapiro delivered his talk.[326]

Shapiro, who edits *The Daily Wire* and contributes to *National Review*, is a provocateur who argues that "the political left [arguably progressives] is a bunch of crybabies—eager, for instance, to blame white privilege for all 'inequality of outcomes.'"[327]

The fact is modern speech in our pluralistic, democratic culture is more complex because of the diversity of venues and nuances in public life. Current platforms for speech are wide open today: There's Internet speech (social media), student speech and privacy, employee speech and whistleblowers, intellectual property, right of protestors, and many others.

No matter the forum, progressives tend to believe that First Amendment law should be unequal when it comes to speech with which they disagree. Consider the case of campaign-finance law that carved out an exception for media corporations so they can speak freely about politics. Media and their progressive friends, however, disagree with the high court's decision on the issue (*Citizens United v. Federal Election Commission, 558 U.S. 310*), which allows unions and nonmedia corporations to speak freely about politics.

Once again, the progressives' bogeymen are the wealthy and corporations. Their mouthpiece, the *New York Times*, intoned on the issue by stating that "the corrupting influence of money is not limited to bribery...[when] outside spending is unlimited, and political speech depends heavily on access to costly technology and ads, the wealthy can distort this fundamental element of democracy by drowning out those who lack financial resources."[328] The problem, according to the *Times* and progressives, is the conservative, establishment rich!

Of course, progressives never complain about undue political influence on the left when George Soros uses his billionaire deep pockets to fund leftist social programs. No, only right-leaning political action groups should stay out of politics and be quiet.

Senator Bernie Sanders and former Secretary of State Hillary Clinton are predictably hostile to the First Amendment. They favor amending the First Amendment to permit government regulation of political speech. Their logic is explained by *Washington Post* columnist George Will: "There is no reason the regulatory, redistributive state should distinguish among various markets. So, government that is competent and duty-bound to regulate markets for goods and services to promote social justice is competent and duty-bound to regulate the marketplace of ideas for the same purpose." Understand? Government should regulate our politics, our ideology, and maybe our religious views as well.[329]

It follows that Sanders and Clinton detest the high court's 2010 decision in *Citizens United v. Federal Election Commission* (cited above). That decision held that unions and corporations—particularly advocacy groups like the National Rifle Association—can engage in unregulated spending on political advocacy (ideas) not coordinated with any particular candidate, political party, or campaign. At its base, the ruling means that Americans do not forfeit their First Amendment rights when they come together in incorporated entities—advocacy groups—to magnify their speech.

Progressives like Massachusetts Senator Elizabeth Warren—as noted earlier, a 2020 Democratic Party presidential contender—responded to the Supreme Court's *Citizens United* decision by name calling: "Corporations are not people." She expressed her view when she said: "People have hearts. They have kids. They get jobs. They get sick. They cry. They dance. They live. They love. And they die." Thus by association, corporations are not like people with the aforementioned characteristics. But Warren should know from her law school classes at Harvard that corporations have rights like people. The corporate personhood persona derives from English common law and is "deeply rooted in our legal and constitutional tradition."[330]

In fact, English jurist William Blackstone influenced our founders' thinking on the topic of corporations, which he called "artificial persons," created to encourage the cooperation among individuals. Therefore, corporations are granted certain rights to hold property and have lives, identities, and missions.[331]

Corporations without the rights of personhood outlined above would have no constitutional protection against arbitrary search and seizure. Besides, and as an example of the too common hypocrisy among progressives, Bernie Sanders once voted to exempt for-profit media corporations from government regulation. Why? Sanders found those media corporations supported his social agenda.

There is yet another vulnerability related to free speech that affects what we think, our ideas. US Court of Appeals Judge Janice Rogers Brown warned about the danger to society and the First Amendment should we weaken the protection of "private property" in order to enable government to redistribute wealth—a progressive goal linked to their First Amendment manipulation agenda. The suspect proclivity, explained Judge Brown, would be to weaken constitutional protections of free speech in order to empower government to redistribute our ideas, evidently considered "private property" just as much as one might seize and redistribute our house or a boat. In other words, the First Amendment also protects our ideas from big government seizure.[332]

Unfortunately, our ideas are under attack—especially on college campuses and more broadly across the culture. For example, some idea-related "private property" attacks are camouflaged in the name of so-called campaign finance reform whereby progressives like Sanders and Clinton would expand government's regulatory reach to political speech to shut down those with contrary views. Therefore, the argument for economic equality—campaign finance reform—easily becomes an argument for equalizing political influence (ideas) all intended to influence election outcomes.

Conclusion

The First Amendment has been adulterated by culture and our Supreme Court. Now progressives are seizing the reins of big government to distort the application of the First Amendment to their radical point of view by not only controlling what our lips say but what our minds think and the ideas we seek to broadcast for political and public information purposes. Worse, they want to closet our religion and then compel us to embrace what our forefathers sought to prevent—a state-sanctioned religion: progressivism.

Clearly the foundation of progressivism includes a psychological need for control—overwhelming, oppressive government control going so far as to rewrite our Constitution. We shall see this same need manifested in the remaining chapters. Is this not another indicator of the "raging insanity" mentioned earlier?

5

Second Amendment

A well-regulated Militia, being necessary to the security of a free State, the right of the people to keep and bear Arms, shall not be infringed.[333]

—Second Amendment, US Constitution

Our Second Amendment is rooted in English law, our Revolutionary War experience, and European political thought. It's a simple concept: People have the right to defend themselves against tyranny, whether at the hands of government or a criminal.[334]

Our forefathers were the grandchildren of Europeans who knew about oppressive government. Those with French ancestors knew of the monarchy's persecution of Protestants in the seventeenth century. At the time, French soldiers were billeted in Protestant homes until the inhabitants converted to state-sanctioned Catholicism or left, like some Huguenot forefathers who found new homes in America.[335]

England wasn't much better, with its Whig political class constantly on guard against royal encroachments such as pro-Catholic King James II's attempt to disarm Protestants.[336]

As a result of King James II, the British commoners sought their own bill of rights the year after the so-called Glorious Revolution of 1688–1689, which replaced King James II with the joint monarchy of his Protestant daughter Mary and her Dutch husband, William of Orange. One of the rights derived from that era was the right to keep and bear arms, which came to America as well.[337]

American founder James Madison originally proposed the Second Amendment to provide more power to state militias, a compromise with antifederalists who supported state power as opposed to power concentrated at the federal level, a byproduct of the Whig tradition. Also, the thinking at the time was that having guns in the hands of citizens was necessary to give them the opportunity to fight back against a tyrannical federal government, an idea found in our Declaration of Independence.[338]

The concept of a right of revolution against government is found in British political theory and especially in the struggle against a tyrannical king. It is noteworthy that although founders like James Madison and Thomas Jefferson were inspired by fresh memories against British King George III's oppressive rule, they constructed in our Constitution a new nation that was expected to govern itself more by the ballot box than the musket. However, those founders recognized historical precedent and the nature of man—evil to the core—when casting the Bill of Rights with the Second Amendment.

The Second Amendment clause, "a well-regulated Militia," refers to groups of men who banded together during our Revolutionary War to protect their communities and eventually the colonies—to wit, the new United States, once independence was declared from Great Britain in 1776.[339] Our founders understood that "well-regulated" militias were necessary to defend the United States against foreign aggressors, but when peace returned, so they thought at the time, part-time militia fighters would revert back into ordinary civilians.[340]

The early antifederalists (those who opposed a strong central government) feared a regular standing army as opposed to state volunteer militias, forces that would defend them against big government oppression. Further, the antifederalists feared that Congress might consolidate state militias under its wing into a regular army (like the British army with which they were all too familiar). They also feared it might abuse its legislative power ("organizing, arming and disciplining the militia") by failing to properly equip (arm) the militia and then deny the states access to those forces. The impact would be to neuter their usefulness to the states by removing them from state authority or by compromising their ability to fight.[341]

James Madison considered these and other antifederalist objections and proposed the Second Amendment as a means to empower state militias and buy the antifederalists' support for the Constitution. The founders' intent was to establish a principle that government did not have the authority to disarm citizens.[342]

Ever since the ink dried on the Constitution's parchment, the crux of the debate over the Second Amendment has been over whether it protects the right of private citizens to keep and bear arms, not over the establishment of a militia.[343]

The faction that argued for the collective right to raise a "well-regulated Militia" saw the amendment really as a means to organize groups of citizen soldiers, like a national guard, a reserve force that replaced the state militias such as those that formed after the American Civil War.[344]

The opposing view gives all citizens, not just militias, the right to own and bear firearms. Certainly, the emergence of the National Rifle Association after the American Civil War brought national visibility to the issue by pursuing a vigorous campaign against gun-control measures.[345]

Thus the Second Amendment was from the beginning, at least in the thinking of the antifederalists, intended to permit the citizen's right to bear arms as well as to endorse the necessity of a militia—primarily to protect against federal tyranny and foreign aggression. That's a concept that tracks back at least to Blackstone's commentaries on the laws of England.[346]

Molding Current-Day Second Amendment

There are two classic interpretations of the founders' original intent regarding the Second Amendment, as enumerated above. First, those who sided with the federalists believed the amendment was primarily about the right of each state to maintain and train militia units to provide protection against an oppressive federal government. Therefore, a "well-regulated Militia" grants the right to bear arms for only those in the official militia to carry guns legally.[347]

The other classic view finds the amendment granting every citizen the right to own guns, free of federal regulations, because the amendment's militia clause was never intended to restrict the citizen's right to bear arms.[348]

The history of the Supreme Court's testing of the constitutionality of each view is significant. The government's right to a militia has never really been seriously challenged. However, the individual's right to bear arms has seen many disputes.

One of the first high court rulings came in 1876 in *U.S. v. Cruikshank, 92 U.S. 542,* a case that involved the Ku Klux Klan's efforts to disallow black Americans the right to assemble and bear arms. The court found in that case the right of each individual to bear arms was not granted under the Constitution. However, a decade later, the *Presser v. Illinois, 116 U.S. 252,* ruling said the Second Amendment only limited the federal government from prohibiting gun ownership, not states.[349]

Later, in 1894, the case of *Miller v. Texas, 153 U.S. 535,* the Supreme Court found that Dallas' Franklin Miller indeed had a Second Amendment right to carry a concealed weapon. Here the court found the Second Amendment does not apply to states, so it struck down for the time Texas' restrictions on carrying firearms.[350]

American gun-control advocates—mostly progressives—long argued that limits are necessary to keep firearms out of hands that might endanger society. Congress passed legislation supportive of that view in the 1990s. The legislation was called the Brady Handgun Violence

Prevention Act, largely due to former White House Press Secretary James S. Brady, who was wounded during an assassination attempt on President Ronald Reagan in 1981. That act mandated federal background checks on those purchasing firearms and imposed a five-day waiting period—that is, until the National Instant Criminal Background Check System was implemented in 1998.[351]

Gun-control advocates suffered a significant setback over the past couple decades thanks to a series of Supreme Court rulings such as *District of Columbia, v. Heller 554 U.S. 570* (2008) and *McDonald v. Chicago, 561 U.S. 742* (2010).[352]

The high court narrowly (five to four) decided the *District of Columbia v. Heller* case that invalidated a federal law barring most civilians from possessing guns in the District of Columbia. The case centered on Dick Heller, a licensed special police officer in Washington, DC, who challenged the city's handgun ban. The court found that individuals who were not part of a state militia in fact had the right to bear arms. Justice Antonin Scalia's decision states, "The Second Amendment protects an individual right to possess a firearm unconnected with service in a militia, and to use that arm for traditionally lawful purposes, such as self-defense within the home."[353]

That decision delineated constraints on firearm possession, such as ownership of firearms by felons and the mentally ill; bans on carrying arms in schools and government buildings; restrictions on gun sales; bans on the concealed carrying of weapons; and generally bans on weapons "not typically possessed by law-abiding citizens for lawful purposes."[354]

The *McDonald v. Chicago* case brought further clarity to the Second Amendment. That narrow decision (five to four) found that Chicago's citywide handgun ban was unconstitutional. Justice Samuel Alito wrote for the majority: "Self-defense is a basic right, recognized by many legal systems from ancient times to the present day, and in *Heller*, we held that individual self-defense is 'the central component' of the Second Amendment right."[355] Further, the court affirmed that the Second Amendment "applies equally to the federal government and the states."[356]

The Supreme Court ruled again in 2016 to clarify the right to bear arms. In this case, *Casetano v. Massachusetts, 577,* the court unanimously reversed a Massachusetts court's decision that upheld the state's stun-gun ban. *Casetano* involved a woman who was in possession of a stun gun for self-defense against an abusive ex-boyfriend. The high court found that her possession of a stun gun, an instrument that qualified as a "bearable" arm, is protected under the Second Amendment.[357]

Meanwhile, the debate over controlling gun possession remained a heated topic in part due to a series of mass shootings. The 2013 Sandy Hook shooting in Newtown, Connecticut, which claimed the lives of twenty children and six adults, led progressive President Obama at the time to seek tighter background checks and a further ban on assault weapons.[358]

A few years later, the Las Vegas, Nevada, mass shooting at a country music concert claimed fifty-eight lives, and the 2016 attack on a Orlando, Florida, nightclub inspired renewed efforts to restrict the sale of devices known as "bump stocks," an attachment to a weapon to help increase the rate of fire.[359]

Progressive Plans for the Second Amendment

Expect progressives to continue their efforts to limit the rights of individual citizens to bear arms. Although the high court's recent decisions reinforce that right, progressives are ideologically fixated on denying law-abiding Americans their Second Amendment rights.

Consider one perspective on progressives' hatred for firearms. Jim Ostrowski, a New York-based libertarian activist and attorney, gave a speech at a Second Amendment rally. That 2013 speech vividly outlines the progressives' threat to our right to bear arms. Ostrowski said:

> Progressives don't hate guns; they love guns. They love them so much they want to be the only ones who have any. They want a gun monopoly.

Again, a progressive is a person who has this fantastic dream of creating a utopia on earth by threatening people with government guns if they don't comply with their utopian schemes. The difference between progressives and us is this. They want to use guns aggressively, to make peaceful people do things they don't want to do. We wish to use them only defensively, to stop a government that gets out of control and engages in mass murder, or systemically tramples the Bill of Rights. The progressive state uses guns against us on a daily basis to impose their will on us. Yet, to my knowledge, not a single Patriot has fired a gun back. We have exercised remarkable restraint. So, again, the government schools, the politicians and the mainstream media lie. The truly violent gun fanatics and gun lovers are the progressive gun grabbers, not us.[360]

Progressives have to accept the fact that, at least for now, taking our guns away in view of recent high court decisions is an uphill challenge. Further, they need to recognize how daunting that task is, because there are a lot of guns in the United States. At least 42 percent of American households have guns, and there are perhaps more than three hundred million privately owned firearms in this country.[361]

So, what are progressives likely to do in light of these facts? They will seek to redefine what the right to bear arms really means for society.

Let there be no doubt that progressives prefer to have no guns in civilian hands, as well articulated by Ostrowski above. So, their strategy is to incrementally restrict gun ownership by making guns less necessary for the purpose of personal security and safety, the basis for recent favorable Supreme Court decisions. That's quite a challenge in this permissive culture.

Let me be clear about progressives and their view of guns. First, understand that they really believe only "experts" should rule society. As illustrated earlier, this means that the average citizen is completely incapable of knowing his or her own best interest—and that extends to bearing and using firearms. Further, progressives really believe the Second Amendment—and, by extension, the Supreme Court—is simply wrong. "They do not believe in natural law or individual rights. The Second Amendment is simply a political inconvenience," a view expressed by Dean Weingarten, a policeman and retired military officer.[362]

Weingarten rightly states that "progressives generally view the state as god," and they align themselves with their ideological forefather, progressive President Woodrow Wilson, who believed that "limits on government power should be abolished." Therefore, and logically, if you believe the state is god, that unlimited government power is good, that (progressive-thinking) experts are far better at determining what is good for you than you are for yourself, then, as Weingarten argues, "it is intuitively obvious the Second Amendment was a historical mistake."[363]

There are plenty of progressive "leaders" who voice that view. Former President Obama used his bully pulpit to redefine the right to bear arms.

In 2013, Obama used his State of the Union address to propose new gun restrictions and unapologetically invoked the memory of the victims of the Newtown, Connecticut, school shooting to make his point. He urged lawmakers to pass legislation on universal background checks that would make it more difficult for criminals to possess a firearm.

With the victims' families in the Capitol Hill chamber to hear his address, Obama said: "If you want to vote 'no,' that's your choice. But these proposals deserve a vote. Because in the two months since Newtown, more than a thousand birthdays, graduations and anniversaries have been stolen from our lives by a bullet from a gun."[364]

Obama piled on by reminding lawmakers of former congresswoman Gabby Giffords, who was shot in the head during a 2011 mass shooting in her home state of Arizona. "Gabby Giffords deserves a vote," Obama added. "The families of Newtown deserve a vote. The families of Aurora [Colorado's Columbine High School] deserve a vote."[365]

When sympathy for the crime victims doesn't work, progressives revert to fake facts. In 2016, the National Rifle Association aired an advertisement claiming that presidential candidate at the time Hillary

Clinton "doesn't believe in your right to keep a gun at home for self-defense." The *Washington Post*, a progressive mouthpiece, rushed to Clinton's defense, asserting the allegation was "false." Glenn Kessler wrote for the *Post*:

> Clinton has said that she disagreed with the Supreme Court's decision in *Heller*, but she has made no proposals that would strip Americans of the right to keep a gun at home for self-defense. Clinton is certainly in favor of more gun regulations and tougher background checks, and a more nuanced ad could have made this case. Conjuring up a hypothetical Supreme Court justice ruling in a hypothetical case is simply not enough for such a sweeping claim. That tips the ad's claim into the Four-Pinocchio category.[366]

What a travesty. Clinton's disagreement with *Heller* is a clear rejection of "the right to keep a gun at home for self-defense," as Kessler argues. Clinton and her ilk are against the individual right to own firearms, and make no mistake: If Clinton were ever in the position of authority, she would take your guns away.

Progressives inevitably lead the charge against guns in the wake of unfortunate gun-related violence (Newtown, Las Vegas, and Orlando). Consider the campaign in the wake of the terrible 2018 high school shooting crimes in Parkland, Florida. At the time, progressive social justice warriors targeted the NRA as the bogeyman. Media outlets like CNN praised the activism and the passion of those who marched in Washington that winter against gun violence and at the same time put on display their agenda via placards carried at the Washington, DC, demonstration and in their speeches, such as:[367]

- "When they give us that inch…we will take a mile!"
- "I have a dream that enough is enough. And that this should be a gun-free world. Period!"

- "Welcome to the revolution…. The people demand a law banning the sale of assault weapons. The people demand we prohibit the sale of high capacity magazines."

There is no ambiguity here: They want to ban guns.

At the same time, that view was shared on the op-ed page of the *New York Times* by former Supreme Court Justice John Paul Stevens, the same man who was once a single vote away from writing the individual right to bear arms out of the Bill of Rights in the *Heller* case. Stevens wrote to "demand a repeal of the Second Amendment." He continued by saying that move would bring progressives "closer to their objective than any other possible reform."[368]

Progressive and CNN "journalist" Chris Cuomo, the brother of New York Governor Andrew Cuomo, tweeted the day after Stevens' *Times* editorial was published: "No one calling for a 2a repeal." He continued, "Stop with the bogeymen," to which Adam Winkler, a progressive law professor, said, "There's not a snowflakes chance in hell we are going to repeal the Second Amendment." Then he added, "Anytime soon."[369]

Classically, progressives argue that gun supporters are angry white guys in leather jackets while gun-control advocates are hippies with peace signs. Those stereotypes may play well in media soundbites, but they muddy an issue that, frankly, ought to be championed by progressives as well as gun advocates.

Progressives ought to oppose gun control, argues one author in UWIRE, because the issue is really about individual liberty. That writer makes the point that "progressives champion equality while supporting gun laws with consistently discriminatory enforcement." That is hypocrisy.[370]

The contemporary gun-control laws result in a high percent of arrests among ethnic minorities, the very demographic progressives insist they are protecting. For example, nine out of ten of those in stop-and-frisk situations are black or Latino.[371]

Isn't it ironic that progressives support a movement—efforts to control guns—that law enforcement uses to target the very groups the liberals say their efforts are intended to protect? Progressives ought to oppose gun control simply because it is about preserving individual freedom. This is an issue not about guns, but about state-sponsored, systemic discrimination. What a twist of fate.

Conclusion

Progressives hate the Second Amendment for a number of reasons. They believe their "god," big government, ought to regulate every aspect of human life—including controlling who bears arms. Further, they want progressive-run big government to be the exclusive bearer of arms so as to use those weapons to compel the rest of us to conform to their agenda. But in a real catharsis, progressives fail the logic test, because while insisting on gun control, the very segment of society they claim to want to help, minorities, has the largest numbers of victims of systemic, gun-related discrimination.

6

Fourth Amendment

The right of the people to be secure in their persons, houses, papers, and effects, against unreasonable searches and seizures, shall not be violated, and no Warrants shall issue, but upon probable cause, supported by Oath or affirmation, and particularly describing the place to be searched, and the persons or things to be seized.[372]

—Fourth Amendment, US Constitution

At our founding, the British used general search warrants indiscriminately; the warrants did not specify what would be searched and which items would be seized. Those "writs of assistance" did not need justification, nor were they supported by sworn information presented to a magistrate. No wonder the warrants were subject to abuse.[373]

Understandably, the American colonists were hostile to indiscriminate searches and seizures, which were widespread throughout New England. Further, the founders believed citizens should be protected from such government intrusions, an idea that dated to Sir Edward Coke, who in 1604 said that "the house of every one is to him as his castle and fortress, as well for his defense against injury and violence as for his repose."[374]

Colonist James Otis, Jr., a Boston attorney, challenged the writs of assistance as a violation of American liberties before the Massachusetts Superior Court in a five-hour speech. Otis called for "greater restrictions on the writ, such as limiting them to a single search, requiring that they be based on particularized information and mandating judicial oversight." He vowed to oppose the writs "to [his] dying day," and labeled them the "worst instrument of arbitrary power, the most destructive of English liberty and the fundamental principles of law, that was ever found in an English law book."[375]

The Otis writs of assistance case of 1761 failed to persuade the Massachusetts Superior Court. Perhaps the outcome was preordained, because Lieutenant Governor Thomas Hutchinson, "a man pliable to the wishes of the monarchy," was a monarchy-appointed chief justice who convinced his fellow judges of the writs' legality, thus protecting his position and salary.[376]

The pressure on colonial courts mounted against the writs, however. In 1767, the British Parliament enacted the Townshend Act authorizing custom officials to use writs of assistance to search and seize smuggled goods. After all, the king of England saw the American colonies as simply a financial investment, so he used revenue collection bills like the Townshend Act to extract as much money from the colonists as possible.

Those revenue acts fueled popular resentment among Americans and encouraged smuggling operations to circumvent those egregious custom taxes. Historian O. M. Dickerson wrote: "It took courage for judges to refuse writs of assistance when demanded by the customs officers, since they held their commissions at the will of the crown and were dependent for their salaries upon the revenues collected by customs commissioners."[377]

The colonialists reacted to the opposition to writs of assistance by adopting in their state constitutions prohibitions against searches and seizures in the declarations of rights. Virginia, the first colony to write such a provision, banned all general warrants. It declared:

...that general warrants, whereby any officer or messenger may be commanded to search suspected places without evidence of a fact committed or to seize any person or persons not named, or whose offense is not particularly described and support by evidenced, are grievous and oppressive, and ought not be granted.

Other colonies followed with similar provisions in their declaration of rights.[378]

Founder James Madison drafted the Fourth Amendment to our Constitution, which was similar to the provision in the colonial constitutions. That early version stated:

The rights of the people to be secure in their persons, their houses, their papers, and their other property, from all unreasonable searches and seizures, shall not be violated by warrants issued without probable cause, supported by oath or affirmation, or not particularly describing the places to be searched or the persons of things to be seized.[379]

Madison's original version of the amendment underwent a number of modifications. A major change created what Yale Kamisar, a Fourth Amendment scholar, labeled a "double-barreled form" that gave the amendment a broader scope that granted the citizen a substantive right to security against government intrusion and, as a result, the Amendment's second clause specified what is required by a warrant.[380]

The final version of the Fourth Amendment created a dilemma for future generations regarding the proper relationship between the two clauses: the first clause, which protects against unreasonable searches and seizures, and the second clause, which specifies what is required by a warrant. The question became whether the clauses are to be interpreted separately, meaning that "all searches without a warrant must only be 'reasonable' and those with a warrant must meet the particularity and specificity requirements, or does the warrant clause somehow explicate or give meaning to the reasonableness clause by announcing that searches without a warrant are assumed to be unreasonable?"[381]

Changes to the Fourth Amendment

Originally, the Fourth Amendment applied only to the federal government and its jurisdictions. However, it was eventually applied to the states through the due process clause of the Fourteenth Amendment.[382] Further, over the next two centuries, the Supreme Court brought clarity to the Fourth Amendment and the nation adjusted to new technologies.

The early Fourth Amendment cases were pretty typical. The 1914 *Weeks v. United States, 232 U.S. 383* Supreme Court case involved police officers in Kansas City, Missouri, who used a hidden key to enter Mr. Fremont Weeks' home to conduct a warrantless search. That search took documents later used in court to charge and then find Mr. Weeks guilty of sending lottery tickets through the U S Mail. Upon appeal, the Supreme Court found the evidence collected during the illegal search of Mr. Weeks' home was in violation of the Fourth Amendment and was thus inadmissible at the trial. The high court wrote that in order for a search to be legal, there must be probable cause to gain a search warrant.[383]

Another common Fourth Amendment example was the 1968 *Terry v. Ohio, 392 U.S. 1* case that involved a police officer stopping a suspect on the street to frisk without probable cause to arrest. The high court favored such actions "if the officer has reasonable suspicion the person has committed, is committing, or is about to commit a crime and the peace officer has a reasonable belief that the person 'may be armed and presently dangerous.'"[384]

The 1973 *United States v. Mara, 410 U.S. 19* case involved the compelled production of handwriting samples. The high court found the requirement to produce handwriting samples was not an unreasonable search or seizure under the Fourth Amendment, because "handwriting, like speech, is repeatedly shown to the public, and there is no more expectation of privacy in the physical characteristics of a person's script than there is in the tone of his voice."[385]

Eventually, technology became a factor in Fourth Amendment cases such as the 1928 *Olmstead v. United States, 277 U.S. 438,* which "reviewed whether the use of wiretapped private telephone conversations, obtained by federal agents without judicial approval and subsequently used as evidence, constituted a violation of the defendant's rights provided by the Fourth and Fifth Amendments." In a narrow (five to four) decision, the high court held that neither the defendant's Fourth nor Fifth Amendment rights were violated. However, that decision was later overturned by *Katz v. United States, 389 U.S. 347* (1967).[386]

Katz v. United States considered the nature of privacy and the legal definition of a "search," such as electronic-based communications like telephone calls. The court refined interpretations of unreasonable search and seizure to count as "immaterial intrusion with technology as a search," thus overruling *Olmstead.* That decision established the "Katz test" to determine when a person has a "reasonable expectation of privacy."

That case involved a government wiretap. Here, the Supreme Court ruled that the Fourth Amendment's protections "cannot be extended and expanded to include telephone wires reaching to the whole world." That was an ugly precedent for government's use of modern technologies.[387]

Other modern technologies were considered by the high court as they apply to the Fourth Amendment, such as the 1995 *Vernonia School District v. Acton, 515 U.S. 646* case that considered the constitutionality of a school district policy authorizing random drug testing of student athletes. The school district had a known drug problem, and student athletes were among the users and dealers. By 1989, the drug problem created serious student behavior issues, which prompted the school district to introduce the student athlete drug policy. James Acton, a seventh grader, refused to participate in a random drug test, and his parents refused to consent to the testing. As a result, Acton was not allowed to participate in football and sued the school district for violating his rights. Upon appeal, the high court found the drug-testing policy was reasonable and did not violate the Fourth Amendment rights of the student. Although students have rights at school, the court held, they must be balanced with the school's responsibility to provide a safe environment.[388]

The 2013 *Maryland v. King, 569 U.S. 435* case involved police taking an arrestee's DNA sample. The court found that it did not violate the Fourth Amendment. "Taking and analyzing a cheek swab of the arrestee's DNA is, like fingerprinting and photographing, a legitimate police booking procedure that is reasonable under the Fourth Amendment," wrote Justice Anthony Kennedy for the five-justice majority.[389]

Then again, in 1965, *Griswold v. Connecticut, 381 U.S. 479* found that married people had the right to use contraception, considered a privacy issue by the high court. The case concerned a Connecticut law that criminalized the encouragement of or use of birth control. Justice William O. Douglas wrote for the majority to dismiss the Fourth Amendment as applicable; however, the decision did find a constitutional guarantee of privacy among the "vague 'penumbras' and 'emanations' of the other constitutional protections," wrote Kevin Bleyer in the *Daily Beast*.[390]

Clearly, traditional Fourth Amendment authority is now being pushed into new horizons, thanks to modern technologies. Before there were telecommunication systems, we had no need of laws to protect the integrity of conversations, but new electronic devices created a concern with the government's use of those tools to find, identify, acquire, analyze, and store information about citizens. What are the limits on law enforcement's use of modern techniques and the privacy rights of citizens?

Those limits are important to establish "because of the public nature of criminal trials and the constitutional evidentiary rules of governing the government's use of evidence acquired by modern surveillance technology." The citizen's argument must insist that the government's use of evidence derived from its reliance on advanced technologies demands that the courts review the legality of government conduct.[391]

Paul J. Larkin Jr., a senior legal research fellow with the Heritage Foundation, presents a cautionary conclusion to a monograph on the Fourth Amendment and new technologies:

> How will the Supreme Court make that trade-off with regard to technologies unheard of two decades ago, to say nothing of two centuries ago? Nothing is certain. We will learn the answer only as specific cases push the Court to balance the still critical needs for security and liberty.[392]

The intent here is to outline the maturation of the high court's interpretation of the application of the Fourth Amendment over time. However, what's hard to anticipate is how the Fourth Amendment might fare under progressive justices and a progressive future administration.

What Progressives Want to Do With the Fourth Amendment

We gain insights about the dangers to the Fourth Amendment based upon views expressed by self-identified progressives. Those views will no doubt influence the vetting of future judge/justice candidates by progressives, as well as how they will insist the Department of Justice applies the law.

Edward Snowden, the former National Security Agency (NSA) contractor who decided that the US government was peering into too many private phone calls, exposed the government's intrusion into privacy by leaking a trove of secrets. He then fled to China and Russia, all the time claiming justification for his actions in the name of protecting Americans' Fourth Amendment right against unreasonable search and seizure. Snowden, a modern self-proclaimed Robin Hood (legendary heroic outlaw originally depicted in English folklore), was praised by the *New York Times*, which called for clemency, insisting that Snowden has "done his country a great service."[393]

Politics blocked congressional efforts to protect the Fourth Amendment in light of Snowden's revelations, and that included efforts by self-identified progressives. In 2013, Congressman Justin Amash (R-MI) began a debate on the House floor vowing to defend the Fourth Amendment. The bottom line for Amash was requiring that any government surveillance, no matter the technology, be warranted. But once Amash's amendment received a vote, it was rejected by both Republicans and Democrats, 271 to 205. Both top Republicans and top Democrats sank the amendment with the support of the Obama White House and eight Democrat progressive caucus members.[394]

Senator Bernie Sanders spoke for many progressives when he expressed alarm at the NSA, which refused to rule out collecting intelligence on members of Congress. Sanders responded to the NSA's announcement:

> The NSA is collecting enormous amounts of information. They know about the phone calls made by every person in this country, where they're calling, who they're calling and how long they're on the phone. Let us not forget that a mere 40 years ago we had a president of the United States who completely disregarded the law in an effort to destroy his political opponents. In my view, the information collected by the NSA has the potential to give an unscrupulous administration enormous power over elected officials.[395]

Those are nice words, but progressive history demonstrates why liberty-loving Americans need to view the likes of Sanders and his ilk skeptically. After all, Benjamin Franklin cautioned, "They, who can give up essential liberty to obtain a little temporary safety, deserve neither liberty nor safety."[396]

Columnist Thomas Sowell also warned about this threat in his essay, "Dismantling America," that:

> It was the Progressives of a hundred years ago who began saying that the Constitution needed to be subordinated to whatever they chose to call 'the needs of the times'… The agenda then, as now, has been for our betters to decide among themselves which Constitutional safeguards against arbitrary government power should be disregarded, in the name of meeting 'the needs of the times'—as they choose to define those needs."[397]

If government data-mining such as that done by the NSA can be justified on national security grounds, then big government acting as "god," as many progressives advocate, all overseen by progressive "experts," can threaten our Fourth Amendment rights. That is exactly what President Obama's Internal Revenue Service did in the case of government bureaucrat Lois Lerner, who evidently used the IRS' power to target conservative groups, and so did the Justice Department under Obama's Attorney General Eric Holder, which abused its authority to conduct the Fast and Furious program allowing criminals to purchase guns in Phoenix-based gun shops in order to track them into Mexico, but resulted in the loss of life of US border agents and many civilians.

The danger comes with a progressive-run government's (deep state) manipulation of our Justice Department and the government's sophisticated means of scooping up all sorts of data that is then used to control the population with the help of liberal-biased social media platforms like Facebook and Twitter.

Don't think progressive-run government at the helm of big government won't totally abuse our Fourth Amendment rights. Please review what happened with the Justice Department's use of the Foreign Intelligence Surveillance Act (FISA) Court in 2016 to create a fake scenario to attack then presidential candidate Donald Trump.

The evidence is compelling that the FBI abused a FISA warrant. In 2016, the FISA court issued a warrant to wiretap then presidential candidate Donald Trump's former foreign policy adviser Carter Page as part of its Russia investigation. The House Intelligence Committee declared that the Department of Justice and the FBI participated in a fraud on the FISA court in order to surveil Mr. Page, a US citizen. The committee concluded the FBI and DOJ deliberately and intentionally advanced unverified opposition research—the infamous Christopher Steele dossier—paid for by the Democratic National Committee and designed to harm Mr. Trump by creating a fictional Russian collusion story as reliable fact.

Conclusion

Our Fourth Amendment is in grave danger should progressives continue to have the means to whittle away further its intent to protect our privacy. Their obvious abuse of the FISA court should be a clarion call to every freedom-loving American. And, as I have said before, it is all about gaining and maintaining control.

7

Fifth Amendment

No person shall be held to answer for a capital, or otherwise infamous crime, unless on a presentment or indictment of a grand Jury, except in cases arising in the land or naval forces, or in the Militia, when in actual service in time of War or public danger; nor shall any person be subject for the same offence to be twice put in jeopardy of life or limb; nor shall be compelled in any criminal case to be a witness against himself, nor be deprived of life, liberty, or property, without due process of law; nor shall private property be taken for public use without just compensation.[398]

—Fifth Amendment, US Constitution

What do Michaele and Tareq Salahis, Mark McGwire, Monica Goodling, Jack Abramoff, and Kenneth Lay have in common? They refused to answer questions by invoking their Fifth Amendment right against self-incrimination.[399]

- The Salahis snuck into a White House party uninvited and even met the president. The incident led to multiple investigations, including a hearing in Congress during which the couple invoked their Fifth Amendment rights.

- Mark McGwire, a former St. Louis Cardinals slugger, pleaded the Fifth Amendment in 2005 when testifying before a House committee while being questioned about steroid use in baseball.
- Monica Goodling was the senior counsel to former Attorney General Alberto Gonzales, who was called before the Senate Judiciary Committee in 2007 regarding her role in the firing of eight US attorneys. She invoked her Fifth Amendment rights instead of answering questions about whether the attorneys were fired for political reasons.
- In 2004 Jack Abramoff, a lobbyist, invoked his Fifth Amendment rights when hauled before the Senate Indian Affairs Committee and asked about his lobbying on behalf of American Indian tribes and casinos.
- Kenneth Lay, the former CEO and chairman of Enron Corporation, told Congress in 2002 he wanted to "tell his story" about his company's collapse, but once before the Senate Commerce Committee, he pleaded the Fifth Amendment.

The Fifth Amendment clause that protects against self-incrimination is the best known of the amendment's five clauses. The other four are also intended to protect citizens suspected of crimes: protection from prosecution unless legally indicated by a grand jury; protection from double jeopardy; protection without due process of law; and protection of private property without just compensation for public use, known as the "takings clause."

This chapter will explain each of the Fifth Amendment's clauses, along with a brief history, and will conclude with what progressives have done to those rights and suggestions about what they might do regarding the amendment's freedoms in the future.

Each of the Fifth Amendment's clauses is developed below.

First, no person can be forced to stand trial for "a capital, or infamous crime" without having been first indicted, charged, by a grand jury.

This provision applies only to felony charges in a federal court. The sole exception is a corollary to the Constitution's Article 1, Section 8 (rules governing the armed forces): "except in cases arising in the land or naval forces or in the militia, when in actual service in time of war or public danger."[400]

The grand jury (which tracks its history back to the British Magna Carta) clause requires an *ex parte* (Latin "for one party") hearing to determine if the government has sufficient evidence to try the accused person of committing a federal crime. Should there be found sufficient evidence for an indictment, only then may the government proceed to trial.

The original grand jury was the British king's instrument obliging citizens to help enforce the law. This is one of the few provisions in the Bill of Rights not applied to the states, such as the Third Amendment's protection against quartering of soldiers.

Second, the "double jeopardy" clause protects citizens against being tried for the same offense a second time after being acquitted. The principle of double jeopardy is found in the *Digest of Justinian* as the precept that "the governor should not permit the same person to be again accused of a crime of which he had been acquitted."[401] At that time, criminal procedure was quite different, since "after a public acquittal a defendant could again be prosecuted by his informer within thirty days, but after that time this cannot be done," according to the Roman jurist Paulus.[402]

The clause prohibits the government from forcing a citizen to undergo repeated trials for the same offense, a concept explained by Justice Hugo Black in *Green v. United States, 355 U.S. 184* (1957): "The underlying idea...is that the state with all its resources and power should not be allowed to make repeated attempts to convict an individual for an alleged offense."[403]

There are caveats that permit reprosecution, however. One such case involves when the government seeks a retrial after a mistrial—

the termination of a trial prior to final judgment—or if the defendant consents to the mistrial. However, retrial is forbidden after an acquittal, a finding of not guilty as charged.[404]

Third, as illustrated above, "self-incrimination" is the best-known Fifth Amendment clause. It protects suspects from being forced to testify against themselves, thus to remain silent—colloquially known as "taking the Fifth." Judges instruct jurors in such situations to not take the plea (remain silent) as a sign or admission of guilt.

Our judicial system grants the accused the presumption of innocence, which puts the burden on the state to prove guilt. The concern about not compelling the accused to testify against themselves is that words can be manipulated like any evidence, and therefore pleading the Fifth protects the accused from themselves—that is, it protects them from how their words might be used against them.

Over the centuries, the Supreme Court has read into this clause many additional rights, however. The 1965 *Griffin v. California 380 U.S. 609* case struck down a California rule of evidence that permitted a jury to consider as evidence the defendant's failure to testify—silence is not necessarily indicative of guilt.

The most controversial high court decision regarding the Fifth Amendment's third clause is the case of *Miranda v. Arizona 384 U.S. 436* (1966). The court, in order to protect criminal suspects from "physical brutality" and "informal compulsion," devised a set of warnings that police must provide before questioning. Further, the individuals must be told that they have the right to remain silent; that any statements they do make may be used against them;, and that they have the right to have an attorney present during questioning. The court went even further to fashion an exclusionary rule to enforce the right of Miranda warnings: "Unless and until such warnings and waiver are demonstrated by the prosecution at trial, no evidence obtained as a result of interrogation can be used against" the defendant at trial.[405]

Fourth, the "due process" clause protects life, liberty, and property without procedural safeguards. The origin of this dates back to the British Magna Carta, a statement of the subjects' rights issued by King John of England in 1215: "No free man shall be arrested or imprisoned… except by lawful judgment of his peers or by the law of the land." Similarly, in the seventeenth century, the American colonies insisted on the observance of regular legal order, which meant that government must function in accordance with law.

This clause outlines the principle of the rule of law: government must act in accordance with legal rules, which calls for a "procedural due process" that provides for fairness and lawfulness of decision-making used by courts and the executive.[406]

There are procedural and substantive considerations with due process. Procedural due process pertains to rules, elements, or methods of enforcement. The government must follow those measures before citizens can be deprived of life, liberty, or property. Substantive due process means there are limits on government authority, a provision that enjoys different opinions within the judiciary.

Finally, the Fifth Amendment identifies the "takings clause," which bans government from seizing private property for public use—rights of eminent domain—without offering the owner "just compensation."[407]

The high court found in *Armstrong v. United States 364 U.S. 40* (1960) that the "Fifth Amendment's [takings clause]…was designed to bar Government from forcing some people alone to bear public burdens which, in all fairness and justice, should be borne by the public as a whole." The principle is that government should not single out an individual to bear excessive burdens for the public good.[408]

This clause calls for fairness to apply to government's authority to acquire private property against the will of the owner, because it was understood that individual rights sometimes must yield to societal rights. Therefore, this empowers government to exercise eminent domain to take private property. However, the amendment also requires adequate compensation to the private owner with such action.[409]

What Progressives Want to Do to the Fifth Amendment

Progressives have used Fifth Amendment "due process" language to create an array of "rights" not found in the Constitution—including privacy, birth control, abortion, and same-sex "marriage." Specifically, those "rights" came about as a result of progressive high-court appointees who curtailed the authority of states to pass laws protecting innocent human life, the traditional family, and religious liberty.[410]

Consider a few contemporary examples of progressive manipulation and abuse of our Fifth Amendment "due process" clause.

Manipulation of the Fifth Amendment is especially notable when it comes to the progressives' political opponents. There are some obvious examples, such as the #MeToo movement, the bane of men's rights groups.

One glaring example is the progressive Obama administration's set of rules regarding campus sexual-assault cases that promoted biases and procedures that favored accusers and led to hundreds of lawsuits by male students found guilty after being afforded no reasonable opportunities to defend themselves—denial of due process.[411]

The Foundation for Individual Rights in Education reports that under President Obama's rules, "approximately 117 federal courts, and many state courts, have raised concerns about the lack of meaningful procedural protections in campus adjudications" of sex-based cases.[412] The Obama administration fueled this "believe the victim" movement with its interpretation of Title IX of the Education Amendments of 1972, the primary federal law prohibiting sex discrimination in education regarding harassment and assault cases on US college campuses. But the #MeToo movement influenced the progressive Obama administration to presume the guilt of accused students (read "male students") and denied them basic rights to defend themselves.[413]

Those same Fifth Amendment-denying progressives wildly reacted to President Trump's Department of Education's revisions of the Title

IX rules to grant the accused his due process in lieu of the Obama administration's immediate presumption of guilt. Even the self-declaring arbiters of justice, the American Civil Liberties Union, condemned Trump's proposal for "promot[ing] an unfair process, inappropriately favoring the accused," and making "schools less safe for survivors of sexual harassment and assault." Really?[414]

It wasn't a surprise that the Democratic Party joined the #MeToo movement and the ACLU to accuse the Republicans of "shield[ing] the accused and turn[ing] its back on victims." Further, 2020 presidential candidate and former Vice President, Joe Biden, wagged his accusing finger at Trump's due process-granting regulations, saying they would sweep "rape and assault under the rug" and shame "survivors into silence." Then the height of hypocrisy emanated from the ever-shrill Speaker of the House Nancy Pelosi (D-CA), who accused President Trump's secretary of education, Betsy Devos, of an "anti-women and anti-equality agenda."[415]

Mrs. Devos fully supports due process and free-speech protections for all (including male) students accused of harassment and assault. Further, she embraces the Supreme Court's definition of sexual harassment as so "severe, pervasive, and objectively offensive" that it denies equal educational access. Not surprisingly, that judicially tested definition is radically different than the one Obama dictated: the subjective standard of harassment as "unwelcome conduct of a sexual nature, including verbal conduct." Obama's definition was so stilted that it could include telling a joke that another heard while eavesdropping on a conversation and then ran to college administrators alleging abuse.[416]

Devos' rewritten Title IX regulations do not require institutions of higher learning to punish or prohibit speech that would be constitutionally protected in public institutions; therefore, administrators are not obliged to restrict speech that some students may find offensive. Further, the new language requires due process in assault cases. Specifically, it requires that colleges "objectively evaluate all evidence" to provide live hearings affording both parties equal opportunities to present evidence. It recommends schools use a "preponderance of evidence" standard of proof and, more importantly, the regulations reject the practice of categorically believing accusers (women) and presuming the guilt of the accused (almost always men).

The new regulations grant both parties (accuser and accused) the rights of cross-examination, a cornerstone of our system of justice. The cross-examination would be conducted by student advisers, with limits involving the accuser's sexual history.

On a very different front, progressives once again are guilty of denying due process and the presumption of innocence even in the most highly visible circumstances, the national confirmation case for the Supreme Court. The nomination of Judge Brett Kavanaugh for a seat on the high court was a raw display of progressive politics turning a confirmation process into a circus.

The circus atmosphere that encompassed the October 2018 Kavanaugh Supreme Court nomination process was over the top compared to any prior judicial confirmation, and that includes the hearings that featured sex-related accusations against then-Judge Clarence Thomas. The Kavanaugh hearings featured disruptive protestors; multiple salacious, uncorroborated sexual charges; and preplanned delaying tactics against the nominee.

Progressive Democrats led the charge on the Senate Judiciary Committee and made it clear from the start that a "no" vote for Judge Kavanaugh was the only option for them—that is, if they failed to derail his nomination.

Progressives low-crawled through the confirmation process, displaying some of the most despicable behavior ever seen in the US Senate. There was absolutely no balance or dignity to the process, and the lowest point came when unknown persons leaked a letter presumably hidden for months by Senator Dianne Feinstein (D-CA) that generated last-minute chaos and delay. The accusations in the letter were uncorroborated and remained so even after a hurry-up FBI investigation and a very public judiciary committee hearing.

Progressives not only used incredible arguments during the anti-Kavanaugh campaign, but their behavior invited other clowns to their circus, such as pile-on accusations made against the judge—including some by a porn-star lawyer's client. Once again, the alleged sexual abuse charges were void of corroboration, but that fact didn't stop the no-due-process-progressives who uniformly embraced the phony and salacious allegations.

On yet another front, consider how progressives tried to use the Fifth Amendment to target their hatred for citizens' gun rights. In 2016, House Democrats staged a sit-in to demand a vote on a gun-control bill that would deny anyone on the government's "no fly" list the right to purchase a firearm. The problem with this issue is that the government's "no fly" list is plagued with serious problems; it is based on the flimsiest of evidence. Therefore, denying a citizen the right to buy a weapon would jeopardize his or her right to due process, which evidently doesn't bother progressives—after all, they would ban all citizens' Second Amendment rights, and denying them "due process" is just another back-door means of accomplishing one of their agenda items.

Even the hard-left ACLU admits that the watch list is "error-prone and unreliable," and would "place individuals on blacklists without a meaningful process to correct government error and clear their names."[417]

Truth and facts won't stop progressives from pursuing their target. After all, their true motives were made clear by West Virginia Senator Joe Manchin (D), who complained on MSNBC during the 2016 presidential campaign that "due process is what's killing us right now" when it comes to denying gun purchases to people suspected of having ties to terrorism.[418] I suspect the good senator wasn't as concerned about terrorists with guns as his progressive colleagues are about disarming every law-abiding American in order to push their radical agenda.

Conclusion

Progressives are not respecters of the Fifth Amendment. Ignoring or altering due process is another tool the progressives wield to ensure compliance with their goals. They use it to fit their political purposes— more often than not to the detriment of society and our constitutional rights. Expect worse abuses of this "right" should progressives gain more control of government in the future.

8

Sixth Amendment

In all criminal prosecutions, the accused shall enjoy the right to a speedy and public trial, by an impartial jury of the state and district wherein the crime shall have been committed, which district shall have been previously ascertained by law, and to be informed of the nature and cause of the accusation; to be confronted with the witnesses against him; to have compulsory process for obtaining witnesses in his favor, and to have the assistance of counsel for his defense.[419]

—Sixth Amendment, US Constitution

The presumption of innocence is a fundamental principle in our criminal justice system, so declares the Supreme Court. But jurors are inclined to believe that those who are arrested are guilty as charged, and the media frenzy—especially in high-profile cases—makes having a fair trial very difficult. In fact, research suggests that the presumption of innocence exists mostly in theory because, as studies suggest, half of all jurors are ready to convict before hearing any evidence.[420]

The 1985 murder case of Teresa Halbach was horrific, and the public's "lust for retribution was palpable," according to Keith Findley, codirector of the Wisconsin Innocence Project and the defense attorney in the case. Findley said, "The presumption of innocence had no chance."[421]

The local prosecutor in the case hosted a press conference that detailed the grisly crime and outlined his evidence "as if guilt was a given and a trial was unnecessary." It was nearly impossible, said Findley, for his client Steven Avery to prevail. "The presumption of guilt was on full display," said Findley.[422]

Findley did prevail against great odds, and the case became a documentary, *Making a Murderer*, that followed the trial's proceedings, which produced DNA evidence to prove Avery's innocence and exonerate him of the crime.[423]

This chapter addresses a cluster of Sixth Amendment rights that delineate criminal prosecutions, with the best known not explicitly stated: the presumption of innocence, as illustrated above. Below are brief explanations of the roots of the Sixth Amendment's clauses and their evolution up to the present. The chapter closes with a summary of what progressives have done with and their aim for the Sixth Amendment in the future.

History and Clauses

The Sixth Amendment creates a collection of rights that should make criminal prosecutions more accurate, fair, and legitimate. The textbook, *American Government: Roots and Reform*, states that the Sixth Amendment is "the centerpiece of the constitutional guarantees afforded to individuals facing criminal prosecution…[and] sets out…specific rights, more than any other provision of the Bill of Rights."[424]

This amendment, much like the others in our Bill of Rights, was specifically designed to rectify the unjust, legacy judicial system of colonial-era Great Britain.

Courts during the colonial times were controlled by the British appointees who decided when and how a person was tried. Colonial juries were seldom impartial with many commoners tried by lords and landowners who often happened to be the accuser; more often than not, that meant a certain conviction followed by a draconian punishment.

Colonial criminal cases were also frequently brought to trial by victims, not by trained prosecutors. Thus, trials seldom included qualified lawyers, which meant that both victim and defendant represented themselves, argued their case, and brought witnesses to bolster their argument.[425] Further, those early trials were public and heard by juries of ordinary men, local citizens who typically knew both the victims and defendants. The jurors decided issues of guilt and tended to check early government's power to punish by applying the conscience of the community—leniency.[426]

America's founders wanted to create a fair judicial system and used the Sixth Amendment to create our adversarial judicial process by requiring both sides to conduct investigations, present their findings, and argue their cases in open court. This approach was dissimilar to the British court system described above, which was little more than an inquisitorial system: state-run investigations and court-run presentations by appointed presiding officials.[427]

Over time and by virtue of the Sixth Amendment, American court proceedings did modernize with professional police forces investigating crimes and arresting suspects. Then state prosecutors displaced victims representing themselves by confronting suspects in court while defendants hired lawyers to level the playing field. Meanwhile, judges made rules of evidence and procedures for lawyer conduct regarding juries, trials, evidence, and even plea bargaining.[428]

These changes came about partly due to Supreme Court decisions, and others are due to the legal profession's own house cleaning.

Consider the Sixth Amendment's six clauses (rights) and a seventh, an unstated although implied right that formed the basis of our contemporary criminal justice system.

First, the Sixth Amendment grants the accused the right to "a speedy and public trial"; otherwise, the case can be dismissed. Of course, trial dates are subject to state statutes and court dockets. However, the accused will always be notified of a court date.

The concept of a public trial dates back to early England when justice was executed by the tribe or the community. When a member committed an infraction against another local citizen, he was considered as having committed the wrong against the entire community. Therefore, the individual was tried and judged by communal law.[429]

In 1166, King Henry II of England oversaw the passage of the Assise of Clarenden, an act that transformed English law and led to trial by jury in common law. The Assise courts required that every criminal trial include a full court of at least twelve freemen who could charge the accused with a specific offense. Attending the trial was a duty, which understandably became a burden. Those who failed to show could be fined.[430]

Our founders embraced the British concept of a public trial in the Sixth Amendment, using some of the same motives as their forefathers. Specifically, they believed:

> In a nation which was to be governed by a rule of law, formulated by the people, the public trial was essential in order to assure the accused a fair trial. Further, it is not unsound to assume that the concept had a dual purpose in the United States as it did in England, maintaining judicial integrity and assuring the people as well as the accused a fair trial.[431]

The words "public trial" in the Sixth Amendment are meant to protect the accused from being tried in secret, out of the view of the public. There are a few recognized, overriding reasons for denying a public trial, such as national security and serious privacy interests, however.

Second, the Sixth Amendment calls for an "impartial jury" to hear a criminal case. Founder Alexander Hamilton wrote about the importance of a jury trial in the "Federalist 83":

The friends and adversaries of the plan of the convention, if they agree on nothing else, concur at least in the value they set upon the trial by jury; or if there is any difference between them it consists of this: the former argued it as a valuable safeguard to liberty; the latter represent it as the very palladium of free government.[432]

A jury-based trial supported by the due process clause in the Fifth Amendment and by the Fourteenth Amendment require conviction on all counts beyond a reasonable doubt, and the verdict must be unanimous.[433] The importance of such a jury trial was addressed by the late Justice Antonin Scalia, who wrote for the majority in *Blakely v. Washington, 542 U.S. 296* (2004) to reinforce the importance of the Sixth Amendment's guarantee that a criminal defendant shall have an impartial jury, rather than a judge, decide his fate. Scalia concluded:

The framers would not have thought it too much to demand that, before depriving a man of three years of his liberty, the state should suffer the modest inconvenience of submitting its accusation to the unanimous suffrage of twelve of his equals and neighbors…rather than a lone employee of the state.[434]

Unfortunately, modern juries tend to be little more than fact finders, thanks to the Supreme Court. Further, contemporary judges instruct the jury that it must find defendants guilty if the prosecution provides the factual elements of the crime, and then the judge awards the punishment, relieving the jury of that often-weighty decision.

Third, the accused must be "informed of the nature and cause of the accusation." Of course, although this clause appears in the middle of the Sixth Amendment, the step is routinely the court's first action in the judicial process. It means the accused have the right to be informed of the nature and cause of any accusation against them. Further, those accused of a crime must be informed not just of the charges, but of their rights when arrested or confronted by law enforcement officials.

Our last chapter reviewed the historic case of *Miranda v. Arizona*, which declared that whenever people are taken into police custody, and before questioning, they must be told of their Fifth Amendment right to avoid making self-incriminating statements. Although "Mirandizing" someone—reading their rights (telling them they have the right to remain silent, warning that anything said could be used against them in court, and informing them of their right to an attorney—even if they can't afford one)—is often the first thing a law enforcement officer says to the accused, it is then immediately followed by an explanation of the nature of the charges.

Fourth, the Sixth Amendment requires the accused to be "confronted with the witnesses against him." The aim here is to ensure transparency and fairness. As mentioned above, suspects are informed of the alleged crimes and have the right to confront their accuser and to cross-examine the accusers' witnesses at a trial.[435]

Restrictions on the defendant's right to cross-examine witnesses gradually became accepted as a result of the use of the Fourteenth Amendment's due process clause and cases like *Smith v. Illinois, 390 U.S. 129* (1968). The issue in *Smith* was whether the state could introduce as evidence statements obtained from an undercover informant, against a defendant charged with illegal drug distribution. The state wanted to protect the identity of the witness, but the high court found that the right to confront the witness had been violated and the conviction was thrown out. The right to cross-examine is an absolute right.[436]

There are exceptions to the right to cross-examine a witness based upon another high court ruling. In *Maryland v. Craig, 497 U.S. 836* (1990), the state used a closed-circuit television in the trial to allow an allegedly abused child to testify because the prosecutor convinced the court that additional trauma would occur to the alleged victim if forced to testify in the presence of the defendant. The Supreme Court ruled that the defendant's Sixth Amendment confrontation right had not been violated due to extraordinary circumstances.[437]

Fifth, the clause "compulsory process for obtaining witnesses in his favor" grants the defendant the right to obtain subpoenas to call witnesses, documents, and evidence to help his defense. The possible origin of this right may track back to the 1603 trial for treason of Sir Walter Raleigh, an English landed gentleman, writer, soldier, politician, and explorer. Raleigh was charged with conspiracy to overthrow and kill the king of England.

The history of the trial indicates Raleigh was allegedly a coconspirator with Lord Baron Cobham, who previously confessed to the conspiracy and implicated Raleigh. Cobham was convicted in a separate trial and then his confession was the only evidence used against Raleigh in his trial.[438]

Raleigh understandably claimed at his trial that Cobham implicated him only to save his own life. Thus, Raleigh asked to cross-examine Cobham about the confession because Raleigh argued Cobham would not lie on cross-examination about Raleigh's involvement in the alleged conspiracy. Therefore, Raleigh argued that Cobham's confession was unreliable hearsay. Unfortunately for Raleigh, seventeenth-century English law allowed hearsay evidence, and as a result, he was convicted and later beheaded.[439] But that outcome may have influenced future jurisprudence regarding the reliance of hearsay evidence and certainly the inclusion of the clause in the Sixth Amendment.

The compulsory process clause allows modern defendants to subpoena witnesses to force them to testify and permits defendants to testify in their own defense, as they may wish.[440]

The sixth clause, "assistance of counsel for his defense," grants the accused the right of counsel. Prior to 1932, this was understood to mean the accused could hire an attorney to represent them in court if they could afford to do so. That view changed over the years, beginning with the *Powell v. Alabama 287 U.S. 45* (1932) decision, which involved black youths charged for and convicted of raping white women. Upon appeal, the high court threw out the convictions because the defendants had not been able to obtain legal assistance during the trial.[441]

Supreme Court Justice George Sutherland delivered the Court's opinion in *Powell v. Alabama* to affirm the right to obtain counsel:

> In a capital case, where the defendant is unable to employ counsel and is incapable of making his own defense adequately because of ignorance, feeble-mindedness, illiteracy or the like, it is the duty of the court, whether requested or not, to assign counsel for him as a necessary requisite of due process of law, and that duty is not discharged by an assignment at such a time and under such circumstances as to preclude the giving of effective aid in the preparation and trial of the case.[442]

The right to counsel even at the state level became the law of the land in 1963 with the high court's decision in *Gideon v. Wainwright, 372 U.S. 335*. The Supreme Court held in that case that defendants facing prison time are entitled to court-appointed lawyers paid for by the government. Further, the court insisted those appointed attorneys (public defenders) must effectively represent their clients, which meant they were to explain to the suspect the consequences of pleading guilty and provide a competent defense if the case goes to trial.[443]

Finally, the missing clause but an implied right is the presumption of innocence. Although neither the Constitution nor the Sixth Amendment explicitly cite the presumption of innocence as a right, it is a general principle taken from English common law and backed by an 1895 Supreme Court case, *Coffin v. United States 156 U.S. 432*.[444]

The plaintiffs, F. A. Coffin and Percival B. Coffin, were charged with aiding and abetting the former president of the Indianapolis National Bank in misdemeanor bank fraud. The high court's decision established the presumption of innocence by stating:

> The principle that there is a presumption of innocence in favor of the accused is the undoubted law, axiomatic and elementary, and its enforcement lies at the foundation of the administration

of our criminal law.… Concluding, then, that the presumption of innocence is evidence in favor of the accused, introduced by the law in his behalf, let us consider what is "reasonable doubt." It is, of necessity, the condition of mind produced by the proof resulting from the evidence in the cause. It is the result of the proof, not the proof itself, whereas the presumption of innocence is one of the instruments of proof, going to bring about the proof from which reasonable doubt arises; thus one is a cause, the other an effect. To say that the one is the equivalent of the other is therefore to say that legal evidence can be excluded from the jury, and that such exclusion may be cured by instructing them correctly in regard to the method by which they are required to reach their conclusion upon the proof actually before them; in other words, that the exclusion of an important element of proof can be justified by correctly instructing as to the proof admitted. The evolution of the principle of the presumption of innocence, and its resultant, the doctrine of reasonable doubt, make more apparent the correctness of these views, and indicate the necessity of enforcing the one in order that the other may continue to exist.[445]

The founders provide these rights to the criminally accused to promote trust in the justice system. Unfortunately, it appears that some progressives are not fans of the Sixth Amendment rights, at least when they are applied to their political opponents and when pushing their radical social agenda.

What Progressives Did and Might Do to Our Sixth Amendment Rights

Progressives have always favored leftist judges who legislate from the bench driven by their Darwinian and atheistic ideology, and favor a "living constitution" which they contort to fit their radical agenda.

For more than a century, progressives used their control of government to promote their radical agenda. Consider that then presidential candidate Senator Barack Obama said in a 2007 speech that, once president, he intended "to fundamentally transform America." To some, that promise was aimed at the destruction of all of America's Judeo-Christian traditions. How? President Obama went about "transforming" America by using executive orders, relying on cherry-picked liberal judges and sometimes advocating for totally partisan legislation (such as Obamacare), when he should have tried to persuade a bipartisan congressional majority to act.

Obama's view of the high court put on display his progressive agenda, which he exposed when outlining his ideal appointments for the Supreme Court in a radio interview:

> The Supreme Court never ventured into the issues of redistribution of wealth, and of more basic issues such as political and economic justice in society. To that extent, as radical as I think people try to characterize the Warren Court, it wasn't that radical. It didn't break free from the essential constraints that were placed by the Founding Fathers in the Constitution.[446]

Obama showed his contempt for the Constitution by appointing Sonia Sotomayor (2009) and Elena Kagan (2010) to the high court. Both women are progressives—in the tradition of Presidents Wilson, Roosevelt, and Obama—who evidenced their firm belief in our Constitution as a dead letter. Progressives of their ilk will continue to use their positions on the high court and elsewhere across the judiciary to advance a radical agenda, ignoring the tenets of the Constitution.

Let's now be specific about progressives and the Sixth Amendment. They have abandoned all pretense about the "presumption of innocence" in favor of the politically expedient "ends justify the means." This basic concept, "presumption of innocence,"—affirmed by the high court as outlined above—forms the foundation of our legal system, which means the accused don't have to prove their innocence; rather they have to prove the defendant's guilt.

That bedrock concept of American law informs everything that transpires in our nations' courtrooms and should permeate our cultural thinking as well. However, progressives evidently don't believe in this concept, especially when it comes to unwelcomed Supreme Court nominees.

We saw evidence of this disdain and the lack of respect for the presumption of innocence dating back to the Supreme Court confirmation hearings of Robert Bork (1987) and Clarence Thomas (1991). Progressives were at the time more than willing to destroy both men over baseless allegations. More recently, as discussed earlier, progressives attacked President Trump's nominee for the high court, Brett Kavanaugh (2018) by demonstrating that anything goes—even the presumption of innocence—in their efforts to destroy a good man.

On background, two women accused Judge Kavanaugh of sexual misconduct thirty years earlier, one while the judge was a high school student and the other while he was a freshman at Yale University. The judge repeatedly, categorically, and unequivocally denied their accusations both to the FBI and to the Senate Judiciary Committee, all while under oath and under the threat of committing a federal felony for lying.[447]

Neither woman could present any evidence to support the accusations. Meanwhile, hundreds of people, including many women, who have known the judge for decades offered strong descriptions of Kavanaugh as a respectful, honorable person. But the lack of corroboration and overwhelming contradictory evidence didn't derail progressives in their effort to create a circus atmosphere surrounding their public roast of a good man.

Hawaii Senator Maize Horono, a far-left progressive, demonstrated her true colors regarding Judge Kavanaugh when she said:

I put his denial in the context of everything that I know about him in terms of how he approaches his cases.... When I say that he is very outcome driven, he has an ideological agenda, very outcome driven, and I could sit here and talk to you about some of the cases that exemplifies his, in my view, inability to be fair.[448]

Evidently, Horono believes that Judge Kavanaugh's denials were irrelevant because she disagrees with his politics—and besides, she believed the accusers' stories, even though there was absolutely no corroboration. The obvious conclusion is that if presumption of innocence is subject to one's personal political views, then nothing is off the table for progressives. What's next? No doubt, every one of our freedoms (freedom of speech, the right to due process, and the right to bear arms) is fair game to progressives.

Senator Chris Coons (D-DE) spouted the same nonsense: "It is Judge Kavanaugh who is seeking a lifetime appointment to the Supreme Court, and who I think now bears the burden of disproving these allegations." He proclaimed, "This isn't a criminal proceeding," so presumption of innocence doesn't matter.[449]

Senate minority leader Chuck Schumer (D-NY) got the same talking points as Coons: "No, it's not a legal proceeding. It's fact-finding proceeding."[450]

"What I believe is we ought to get to the bottom and find the facts in the way that the FBI has always done," Schumer said. "There's no presumption of innocence or guilt when you have a nominee before you. There is, rather—find the facts...and then let the Senate and let the American people make their judgment, not whether they're guilty or innocent, but whether the person deserves to have the office for which he or she is chosen. Plain and simple."[451]

Progressives apply the same contorted thinking elsewhere, as evidenced in the preceding chapter when it applies to the Fifth Amendment's due process, especially regarding Title IX sexual harassment and assault allegations on college campuses. But it really is somewhat worse than just the denial of due process, because progressives on many campuses ignore all the clauses in the Sixth Amendment to advance their agenda.

We see evidence of that abuse in a book by K. C. Johnson and Stuart Taylor, Jr., *The Campus Rape Frenzy: The Attack on Due Process at America's Universities*. The authors explain that because the country's higher education institutions with few exceptions accept big government grants and scholarships, they evidently feel obligated to become an arm of the state to ram through a pro-feminist agenda. Therefore, as an arm of the state, many of these institutions apply so-called campus justice that makes trash of the tenets of the Sixth Amendment.

The issue isn't just due process denied, it's an abrogation of virtually the entire Sixth Amendment as a result of Obama's 2011 Department of Education Title IX laws barring sex discrimination in education, which were tethered to the progressive feminist agenda. The Obama Department of Education issued guidelines that imposed limits on the questioning or cross-examination of complaining students, restrictions on the introduction of evidence, and mandatory use of the "preponderance of the evidence." What resulted was a process that affected thousands of young college men caught in a vortex of questionable allegations, sloppy investigations, arbitrary and inadequate procedures, and penalties with life-changing consequences. Obviously, this was a progressive's dream legal system to advance an agenda.

Sexual assault and harassment are wrong, but more often than not, justice on campus—thanks to Obama's Title IX regulations—favor the alleged victims and trash the alleged perpetrators' Sixth Amendment rights. Although campus justice isn't bound by the same rules as are our courts, they at least ought to be consistent, which most are not. Too often, allegations of sexual matters enter a labyrinth overseen by a cadre of university officials who act as prosecutor, legislator, judge, and jury—much like the British monarchs who imposed their will over American colonists.

The campus Title IX officer, who is often steeped in progressive rape-culture rhetoric and "the woman is always right" ideology, investigates the charges, drafts a report, and makes recommendations on disposition and penalty. Those outcomes are then routinely rubber-stamped by campus officials.

These outcomes are also shrouded in secrecy under the guise of "privacy," which leaves the accused (almost always a man) little opportunity to correct the facts and no opportunity to confront the accuser. The result is predictable. Many young male lives and reputations are ruined, and there is no recourse to remove the blemish.

A defense lawyer explained to a federal appeals court the result of campus justice abuses:

> The result of their ignorance is a failure to appreciate the hard-won principles of guilt and innocence that have emerged through centuries of political struggle and legal development. Instead, these have been swept away in a storm of campus zealotry, replaced by a dysfunctional culture that fosters sexual recklessness and simultaneously encourages women to feel traumatized at men's expense.[452]

Conclusion

Progressives have shown their colors regarding the tenets of the Sixth Amendment. Besides, as we've seen time and again with leading progressives like the Obamas and the Clintons, they escape any serious criminal prosecution, so I suppose manipulating the judicial system—tenets of the Sixth Amendment—is something they take for granted, and "Katy, bar the door!" regarding what they might do in the future when our high court is stacked with progressives and the White House and Congress are led by similarly minded radicals. In short, if you can control the judicial system through an infusion of progressive thought, you can eliminate all forms of legal opposition and eventually change the thought patterns of the people. George Orwell's *1984* is then a reality.

9

Tenth Amendment

The powers not delegated to the United States by the Constitution, nor prohibited by it to the states, are reserved to the states respectively, or to the people.[453]

—Tenth Amendment, US Constitution

Our founders intended the Tenth Amendment to settle the great debate over federalism, a compromise to persuade all colonies to approve America's Constitution. That amendment remains the subject of both debate and compromise even at the present.

Early in the young nation's history, Chief Justice John Marshall explained the substance of the great debate regarding the Tenth Amendment in the Supreme Court case, *McCulloch v. Maryland, 7 U.S. 316* (1819). Justice Marshall wrote:

The United States Constitution was an experiment for a new form of government, a system where powers were no longer centralized but distributed between the central government and the states. The framers believed that the separation of powers would have contributed to the preservation of individual liberty.[454]

Indeed, the founders came together at the Continental Convention with the goal of forming a "more perfect" union to provide military security and better trade relationships, all without threatening state sovereignty. "It was not the job of the federal constitution to create states or to give them power," explained Ernest Young, a law professor and federalism expert at Duke University. Rather, "It [the Convention] was trying to elbow out a little space for the federal government to exist too."[455]

The product of that great debate among our founders was the creation of a "rough balance" between the new federal government and the states, an algorithm that mutually shares a range of government powers among the federal government and the various states. Further, the founders constructed in our Constitution the means to adjust those powers when one or the other oversteps its authority, and that means is the allegedly apolitical federal judiciary.[456]

The debate over federalism wasn't ended by the ratification of the Constitution, but continues to this day, especially as our federal government increases into areas previously left to the domain of local governments: healthcare, gun laws, abortion, immigration, education, and drug control.

This chapter will review the history of the Tenth Amendment, how our government system of shared powers evolved over the past two centuries, the damage progressives brought to our system of shared government, and plans modern progressives have for the amendment's future.

History of the Tenth Amendment: Great Debate over Federalism

Our Constitution created a federalism type of government with a single, central government that shares equal status and responsibilities with the states.[457] Arriving at that delicate balance of power was a time-consuming process for our founders that required tradeoffs at the Constitutional Convention. That session convened in May 1787 with the aim of revising the Articles of Confederation and Perpetual Union, which was adopted by the thirteen original states, served as an interim constitution, and was used by the Continental Congress to conduct business, mostly business that involved fighting the American Revolutionary War.[458]

The Articles of Confederation purposely created a weak central government with limits such as one vote per state and one chamber of Congress. Laws required a supermajority to pass Congress, and there was no executive branch or supreme court. These weaknesses resulted in conflicts among the states, something the delegates to the Constitutional Convention hoped to overcome with a new agreement (a lasting constitution).[459]

The Articles granted the Continental Congress the power to declare wars, but denied it the means to tax the colonies in order to pay for an army—a significant vulnerability. That failing became a weapon for federalist advocates—those who favored a strong central government—especially in the wake of the 1786 Shays' Rebellion, an armed uprising by Massachusetts farmers attributed in part to the federal government's failure to pay war debts.

At the Constitutional Convention, federalists proposed the federalization of the colonies as opposed to the system of government many of those same founders experienced with Great Britain, a monarchy that granted local government's limited power.

Understandably, many of the delegates came to the Convention distrustful of a strong central government. This misgiving was the genesis of the great debate that pitted federalists against those who favored a weaker federal government (antifederalists) much like the one created by the Articles of Confederation.[460]

Antifederalists like Patrick Henry of Virginia argued that federalism promoted a corrupt government that would inevitably battle among the proposed three branches of government that were part of the draft constitution (executive, legislative, and judicial). Worse, the antifederalists feared the chief executive, a president, would become a virtual king, something they had fought the Revolutionary War to escape.[461]

Federalist James Madison dismissed Henry's concern about corruption and a king-like presidency. Madison argued that the proposed government would be "neither wholly national nor wholly federal," but would share powers with the states, such as the power allotted the colonies in the Articles of Confederation. Madison promised: "Each state retains its sovereignty, freedom, and independence, and every power, jurisdiction, and right, which is not by this Confederation expressly delegated to the United States, in Congress assembled."[462]

Ultimately, the proposed Constitution provided for a federalist government structure and won the favor of thirty-nine of the fifty-five delegates, and then went to the thirteen original states for approval.

The great debate at the Convention over federalism was a concern for citizens' rights, which the British system had denied the colonialists. So, in order to address those concerns and to ensure the Constitution's ratification, the Bill of Rights (as mentioned earlier in this volume) was included in the document. Of course, the Tenth Amendment specifically addressed the issue of power sharing between the central government and the states.[463]

The US Constitution became effective March 4, 1789, with New Hampshire's ratification, but it was more than a year later before Rhode Island, the thirteenth state, ratified the document on May 29, 1790.[464]

Nineteenth and Twentieth Centuries' Progressives Trashed the Tenth Amendment to Create a Post-Constitutional Republic

The Tenth Amendment has waxed and waned in how it has been interpreted and in measuring the influence it has enjoyed over America's history by reason of the Congress, the executive branch, the Supreme Court, and progressives.

Legal scholars are pretty sanguine about this amendment. Kenneth Mack, a legal historian at Harvard Law School, said: "There isn't much consensus on what the 10th Amendment means," then and now.

Understandably, "people who like states' rights [also] like the 10th Amendment. People who don't like states' rights tend to be dismissive of the 10th Amendment," said Sanford Levinson, a professor of law and government at the University of Texas. Thus, the default rule for states over the centuries is explained by Ernest Young, a law professor and federalism expert at Duke University, who said, "If they [the states] are not forbidden from doing things then presumptively they can."[465]

The whole notion of federalism was supposed to lead to shared power, but American history demonstrates that progressives long ago trashed the concept and have been doing so ever since. In part, as Cato Institute's Roger Pilon explained, the reality of human affairs in government is that "politics is about who gets what," a crass but true statement. Pilon argues that the "purpose of government is to solve our every problem, and then all is politics." Then of course, he continued, eventually it all ends up in the courts, politicizing the allegedly nonpolitical branch in the process.[466]

Over time, the elephant in the federalists' living room has become an explosively large, overwhelmingly progressive federal government, and damn be the sharing of power with the states. That's properly why Pilon concluded, "We're living today in a post-constitutional republic."[467]

"The vast redistributive and regulatory powers Congress now indulges are nowhere among the 'few and defined' constitutionally authorized powers that James Madison outlined in Federalist 45," said Pilon. He's right, of course. For decades, Congress has legislated well beyond its authority, along with the executive branch creating new powers from whole cloth, despite the limiting words in our Constitution—and all at the expense of the states and the trusting (read "naïve") citizens.[468]

Our founders expected accountability, but Congress today uses broadly worded measures that direct unaccountable executive bureaucrats and an alphabet soup of federal agencies to fill in the micromanaging details of governing with regulations, guidance as if they are enforcing constitutionally legitimate laws.

Worse, the federal judiciary either does the bidding of Congress and the executive branch or legislates from the bench, a clear absurdity for our founders. Gone are many of the checks and balances Madison promised the antifederalists.

Arguably, since FDR's New Deal in the 1930s, the Supreme Court countenanced an expansion of federal power far beyond that intended by our founders. In fact, the high court embraced the deference doctrines that grant Congress to act beyond its authority, enabling it to delegate legislative-like powers to the executive branch, and gave its numerous agencies the authority to act with minimal oversight.

The high court's affirmation of those new powers radically altered the Tenth Amendment's role in modern jurisprudence and significantly diminished the states' rights.

The consequences of this *ex parte* power are frightening. Big government created from whole cloth the authority to squander our financial future. Today, our federal debt exceeds $21 trillion and is growing, having more than doubled over the past decade—thanks in part to President Obama and a spendthrift, compliant, Democratic Party-controlled Congress. (To be fair the Republican Party hasn't done much better.) Our unfunded liabilities vastly exceed that, with our debt-to-GDP ratio having more than doubled and expected to reach 100 percent in ten years.[469] Meanwhile, the states are left holding much of the debt and citizen expectations of future benefits.

Where is the discipline our founders expected? Early on in our nation's history, the political class obeyed the constitutional rules, but that began to change during the Progressive Era (1890–1920) and considering the growing popularity of President Woodrow Wilson's view of our founding document: "The Constitution was not made to fit us like a straitjacket. In its elasticity lies its chief greatness." That concept got completely out of hand by the time President Franklin D. Roosevelt introduced his New Deal, however.[470]

One of FDR's principal New Deal architects explained the ideological objective: "Fundamental changes of attitude, new disciplines, revised legal structures, unaccustomed limitations on activity, are all necessary if we are to plan. This amounts, in fact, to the abandonment, finally, of laissez-faire. It amounts, practically, to the abolition of 'business.'"[471]

The result of the New Deal and FDR's push for reform was a rewritten US Constitution to socially reengineer the direction of the country to their liking. They embraced redistribution of wealth and big government with widespread planning by elite government bureaucrats—the epitome of what the father of modern progressivism, German philosopher Hegel, envisioned.

Decades later, Rexford Tugwell, one of the architects of FDR's New Deal, confessed: "To the extent that these new social virtues [i.e., New Deal policies] developed, they were tortured interpretations of a document [i.e., the Constitution] intended to prevent them."[472]

Initially in the early 1930s, progressives ran into significant resistance from the Supreme Court. But then FDR threatened his infamous court-packing scheme following his 1936 landslide reelection. That threat brought the high court in line, transforming it into a compliant partner in the progressive conspiracy to rewrite the Constitution to fit the progressive agenda.

Soon the floodgates of the redistribution of wealth and regulatory big government sank its teeth into the country. By 1943, big government took off into the stratosphere, by virtue of the abandonment of the nondelegation doctrine that allowed Congress to pass more of its powers to federal bureaucrats and accept a growing mountain of debt to fuel government expansion.

Federal programs soon overtook state programs, replacing the intent of the Tenth Amendment, competitive federalism, with "cooperative federalism." Congress reached far beyond the Constitution's division of powers to expand the executive branch agencies, granting them legislative, executive, and judicial functions. Today we have executive agencies that seem to be laws unto themselves.

The result is that states adjusted to the new, more powerful, central government model known as "cooperative federalism," a tool that robs states of power and trashes the Tenth Amendment. The concept is simple: big government runs up big deficits ($21 trillion plus) and then transfers the borrowed money to the states in the form of grants, albeit with conditions. This scheme mandates that the states match the federal contributions (which overstretches state budgets), such as in the case of Medicaid, while acting as the federal government's agent and at the ever-growing state's expense.

Pilon points out that this constitutional inversion led to ever more "free goods" known as "entitlements"—Social Security, Medicare, etc.—that are considered politically "untouchable." Further, the inversion encumbered state governments that soon found no escape from the claws of big government. And Congress refuses to address those "entitlement" programs, even though they are rapidly becoming fiscally unsustainable.

Yes, we are in a post-constitutional republic, having trashed the Tenth Amendment and created enormous debt, which is saddled on the states—and much of the blame rightly goes to progressives.

Modern Progressives Have Plans for the Tenth Amendment

President Barack Obama famously used his pen and phone to expand his power unilaterally, arguably unconstitutionally, to change immigration, healthcare, and energy and tax laws. Other progressive presidents from Roosevelt to Clinton favored the power of the "imperial presidency" as well to champion by fiat their agenda—and, in many cases, powers that should belong to the states.

Progressives routinely run roughshod over laws that don't fit their agenda. For example, Obama bureaucrats at the Department of Health and Human Services worked with legal abortion absolutists to mandate that every business provide coverage for "morning after"-type (abortifacient) drugs, and Obama's Justice Department argued their own views trumped the Religious Freedom and Restoration Act of 1993, an attempt to force the Little Sisters of the Poor (a Roman Catholic charity) to provide abortion services against their faith.

The arrogance of progressives knows no end. They willy-nilly and unilaterally modify laws to their liking, and they reject constitutional limits on Congress' legislative jurisdiction as well. Remember then Speaker of the House Nancy Pelosi's response to a question about the source of power that authorized Obamacare?

Pelosi was speaking at the National Association of Counties' 2010 annual Legislative Conference in Washington, DC. at the time. She said in response to an Obamacare question: "But we have to pass the bill so that you can find out what is in it, away from the fog of the controversy."[473] That's palpable arrogance.

Progressives have rejected and will in the future reject limits on their power. What's clear is that progressive government is a serious threat to our liberties, the Constitution, and our security—and that's true, even when they are momentarily out of power.

Progressives' hypocrisy knows no end as well. They bounce back and forth between advocating federalism and states' rights. Since the election of President Trump, they have suddenly embraced local rights. Professor Sanford Levinson, a law professor at the University of Texas, opined about that odd turn of events: "What is so interesting about the present moment is that the ideology has become completely and utterly mixed up." The fact is progressive federalism tends to be opportunistic and, as historian Mack said, whether someone embraces federalism often depends on "whose ox is being gored." People call for federalism solutions when "they think it is going to do something that they prefer to have done." In other words, it is "simply, completely, opportunistic," said Levinson[474]

Once progressives are out of power, they embrace what Yale law professor, Heather Gerken, calls "uncooperative federalism." That means progressives at the local level influence policy by refusing to work with the federal government.

Herbert Croly, an adviser to President Theodore Roosevelt, urged fellow progressives with no political leverage in Washington to employ "uncooperative federalism," which he defined at the time as the use of Hamiltonian (local) means to achieve Jeffersonian (national federalist) ends, thus drawing on federal power to defend their progressive rights.

There are numerous examples of the exiled progressives' "uncooperative federalism" today. Probably the best example is the "sanctuary city." President Trump insists that state and local authorities help federal law enforcement to carry out immigration policy, but progressives at many state and municipal locations refuse. This standoff, says Professor Levinson, has "overtones of the fugitive slave issue in 1850...psychologically we are in a pre-Civil War situation."[475]

Sanctuary cities are a hot topic among progressives, especially since President Trump took office. Cities lined up in opposition after Trump called for cooperation enforcing federal immigration laws. New York Governor Andrew Cuomo said, "We won't allow a federal government that attacks immigrants to do so in our state." Los Angeles Police Chief Charlie Beck said his department was "not going to work in conjunction with Homeland Security on deportation efforts."[476]

There are other examples of progressive-fueled "uncooperative federalism" across the country on issues such as climate change, healthcare, and the legalization of marijuana, just to name a few.

What's especially interesting with "uncooperative federalism" is that it brings modern progressives into radical agreement with arch conservative and former Supreme Court Justice Antonin Scalia. Progressives were upset in 1997 with Justice Scalia's majority opinion that found the federal government could not legally direct states to enforce the provisions of the 1993 Brady Handgun Violence Prevention Act. Justice Scalia wrote in *Printz v. United States (95-1478), 521 U.S. 898* (1997): "The Federal Government may neither issue directives requiring the States to address particular problems, nor command the States' officers, or those of their political subdivisions, to administer or enforce a federal regulatory program."[477]

At the time, progressives criticized *Printz* as a "conservative" decision that promoted states' rights at the expense of duly enacted national reforms, a Tenth Amendment example run amok. How time and circumstances can turn perspectives on their head.

Today, progressives should celebrate Scalia's handiwork because it is the single best legal precedent they have in support of the constitutionality of sanctuary cities. Scalia wrote in *Printz* that the "federal commandeering of state governments" goes against the Constitution and "such commands are fundamentally incompatible with our system of dual sovereignty [federalism]."[478]

Conclusion

Don't be fooled by progressive "uncooperative federalism" or their momentary local orientation. They desperately thirst for the opportunity to return to big-government power. Upon returning, they will pick up where Obama left off, transforming America into a giant big-brother state run by progressive elites (bureaucrats) who worship government and hate our Constitution. By now it is obvious that the alteration, even elimination, of the amendments is directed at one purpose: control over every aspect of American life.

SECTION III

Introduction: Progressivism's Influence on American Institutions

This country, with its institutions, belongs to the people who inhabit it. Whenever they shall grow weary of the existing government, they can exercise their constitutional right of amending it, or exercise their revolutionary right to overthrow it.[479]

—Abraham Lincoln, sixteenth president (1861–1865)

A society is held together by key institutions that provide the structure upon which people chart and conduct their lives together. Five institutions are especially critical to binding a society together: family, education, religion, government, and economy. Destroy any one and society begins to implode; destroy all five and you no longer have a country.

This section will explore each of these five critical institutions as they were intended by our founders. Then we explore the influence early progressives had for each institution, especially beginning with the Progressive Era (1880–1920) and up to the recent past. Finally, we consider what progressives might do to each institution in the future and the danger that presents for the United States.

10

Progressivism's Impact on Family

This chapter will define the family, a critical institution to society, and outline what progressives did in the past—both the good and the bad—that impacted the family. We will consider the current state of the American family (thanks in part to progressivism's malfeasance) and suggest what progressives plan to do with/for/to future American families.

What Is the Family, and Why Is It An Important Institution?

Family: A social unit where the father is concerned with parking space, the children with outer space, and the mother with closet space.

—Evan Esar, American humorist[480]

Humorist Evan Esar's definition of the family is tongue-in-cheek, but given our cultural implosion, family has come to mean quite a diversity of groups, ideas, and circumstances: a variety of gender combinations; differing numbers of members; and a cross section of generations, races/

ethnic groups, and birth backgrounds. We see this family diversity on full view within pop culture, especially depicted on television shows like *Modern Family* (ABC), *Raising Hope* (USA Network), *Baby Daddy* (ABC), and many more.

The US Census Bureau uses a fixed, limited definition of family as a "householder and one or more other people living in the same household who are related to the householder by birth, marriage, or adoption."[481]

The Bible defines family in a narrow sense "as the union of one man and one woman in matrimony which is normally blessed with one or several natural or adopted children."[482] The concept of family is found in the Book of Genesis, beginning with the creation of man (Adam) and subsequently a woman (Eve) as man's helper (Genesis 2:18, 20). The Scripture passage reads: "Therefore a man shall leave his father and his mother and hold fast to his wife, and they shall become one flesh" (Genesis 2:24, ESV). This text establishes the natural family that "become[s] one flesh" and then obeys God's command to "be fruitful and increase in number; fill the earth and subdue it. Rule over the fish in the sea and the birds in the sky and over every living creature that moves on the ground" (Genesis 1:28, NIV).

This is the original order of creation: male and female reproducing the human race within marriage at the heart of civil law defining and regulating the relationship. This affiliation is the nucleus of civilization, the basic social unit of society (a building block), and part of all past and present cultures and religions.

The ancient Greek philosopher Aristotle wrote that the family is nature's way of supplying mankind's basic needs—food, water, shelter, and much more. Those needs are what American sociologist Dr. Abraham Maslow called the "Hierarchy of Needs," which are the elements crucial to human life. But the typical family provides much more than the basic needs from the time a child enters this world helpless.[483]

Family members meet one another's psychological needs for affection, appreciation, sense of belonging, and love. They prepare offspring for the future by teaching social graces, sharing burdens, and role modeling through life's challenges.

Children tend to thrive best when parents help promote positive growth and development. Family typically provides financial security for the household, and parents teach children how to manage resources to help them grow into responsible, productive adults ready to nurture their own families.

Families are also an important source of happiness and satisfaction as members interact, recreate together, and live under the same roof. They are always looking for new ways to spend time together that fosters a healthy relationship and provide a foundation for stability. They have one another's backs, and their love is unconditional.

Family knows when a member is under stress, struggling with a challenge. That is when other members support and encourage the ill, injured, or emotionally discouraged.

Healthy families benefit their communities by relieving the burdens of their members, thus sparing their community the associated costs. Further, healthy families make positive contributions to their communities by modeling good citizenship and teaching their children the importance of contributing to the welfare of others through selfless service.

Good parents see to the education of their children to help them better assimilate into society and become productive citizens. They teach their children values like love, respect, honesty, and courage—all of which help form a worldview. They discipline the children to help them understand the consequences of their actions as well.

Families vary in their structure, as explained above. However, insular families with both parents and children living together (as described in the Bible) tend to live healthier lives to a large degree because they form good habits: they eat healthier, avoid abuse of alcohol and drugs, and are active, supportive, and good citizens.

Yes, family structure matters, and even some progressives agree. The left-of-center, Washington, DC,-based Brookings Institution admits in a study that children raised by two biological parents in a stable marriage do better than children in other family structures.[484]

Another study found that states with more married parents do better "on a broad range of economic indicators, including upward mobility for poor children and lower rates of child poverty." Even the liberal *Washington Post* reports that "the share of parents who are married in a state is a better predictor of that state's economic health than the racial composition and educational attainment of the state's residents."[485]

Society benefits especially greatly when boys are raised in traditional families. Sociologist Daniel Patrick Moynihan warned in 1965:

> From the wild Irish slums of the 19th century Eastern seaboard, to the riot-torn suburbs of Los Angeles, there is one unmistakable lesson in American history: a community that allows a large number of men to grow up in broken families, dominated by women, never acquiring any stable relationship to male authority, never acquiring any set of rational expectations about the future—that community asks for and gets chaos.[486]

The aforementioned provides a foundation to understand the importance of family. Now consider America's early family and how progressives altered the environment to impact those families arguably for both the good and bad.

How Have Progressives Impacted the Early-American Family?

There is no average American family, according to former Supreme Court Justice Sandra Day O'Connor. She wrote in *Troxel v. Granville*, *530 U.S. 57* (2000) that "the demographic changes of the past century make it difficult to speak of an average American family." Indeed, the American family radically changed from the early days of this country to the present.[487]

Consider the structure, laws and cultural dynamics surrounding the early American family leading up to and through the Progressive Era (1890–1920).

At our founding, the "average" American family consisted of a husband, a wife, and their biological children. Most everyone at the time married and stayed married until death, because divorce was rare. When it was available, such as in parts of the South, legally ending a marriage was only possible through a special act of a state legislature. In the northern states, some divorces were granted by judges but only on fault-based grounds.[488]

Marriage in early America was limited as well to heterosexual couples who shared distinctive roles. Women lost their legal identity once married, essentially becoming the property of their husbands. William Blackstone explained the English common law that prescribed the marriage of a man and women as a contract that created "one person in law: that is, the very being or legal existence of the woman [wa]s suspended during the marriage, or at least [wa]s incorporated and consolidated into that of the husband."[489]

Early-American women were wholly dependent upon and subordinate to men, and their role as wives in the marriage was to serve their husbands at home. Women at the time could not own property, enter contracts, or sue anyone.

Husbands were the providers for their families and had a duty to meet their wives' needs. Further, in "exchange" for such provision, the husbands had the right to expect the wives' "services," which included sex, whether they consented or not. In fact, the Louisiana Supreme Court explained the husband's right to sex: "The husband of a woman cannot himself be guilty of an actual rape upon his wife, on account of the matrimonial consent which she has given, and which she cannot retract," *State v. Haines, 25 So. 372, 372* (La. 1899).[490]

Husbands were responsible for their wives' behavior and had the right and the responsibility to correct them for disobedience—albeit without inflicting permanent injury. Further, if a wife had an affair with another man, her husband could sue that man for damages (tort—a wrongful act or an infringement of a right) because the other man had taken the husband's "property."[491]

Family law at the time regulated relationships between the races as well, and in the South, blacks were not even permitted to marry because they were slaves (another person's property) and lacked the legal capacity to consent. Further, the female slave (whether coupled with another slave or not) belonged to the white master who could sell her, thus breaking up any slave couple ("marriage"). Further, the separation of the races continued under miscegenation ("the interbreeding of people considered to be of different racial types"[492]) laws for many years, even after the Emancipation Proclamation, the 1863 declaration by the US Congress "that all persons held as slaves…are, and henceforward shall be free."[493]

Early-American law and culture mostly kept sex within marriage. State laws criminalized sex outside of marriage (fornication), living together outside marriage (cohabitation), and having children outside of marriage (bastardy). Children born outside of marriage were treated harshly and were considered the children of no one (*filius nullius*). The mother of a nonmarital offspring was required to support the child, but there was no such expectation of the sperm donor (father).[494]

The marital relationship and especially the rights of women began to change in the nineteenth century, when states granted married women more rights, such as through the Married Women's Property Acts (1870). These laws gave women the right to inherit property and maintain ownership and control of their estates. However, a woman's place still remained at home under her husband's control well into the twentieth century. That relationship included a husband's right to chastise his wife, which legally and culturally lasted well into the middle of the twentieth century.[495]

These legal and cultural relationships that affected the marriage and family are a necessary background for appreciating the Progressive Era's impact on the institution of the family, especially regarding women within American society.

It was the coincidence of the early family culture described above and the Gilded Age (1870–1900) that contributed to the cultural explosion during the Progressive Era and especially the impact on the family. That transformation took place in behalf of coalitions of interests and fiercely contrasting ideologies in the late nineteenth century.

Social changes began to take shape much earlier, however. Through the rise of American Protestantism that followed the revival movement of the 1830s, a new doctrine known as "pietism" took hold, casting aside many traditional Christian rituals and liturgies and calling for genuine rebirth among believers (people to be born again vis-à-vis John 3:7).[496]

The "pietism" movement among Protestants was two pronged, with one in the South and the other in the northern tier of the United States. Southern "pietists" tended to be more reserved about their faith, which they segregated from their lives within the broader culture. The northern group tended to be evangelical in their actions, not only regarding personal salvation but even calling for evangelizing all of society "to spread holiness,"—the creation of an American Christian commonwealth by introducing all to Christ's salvation. They saw their mandate (calling) was "to transform the world into the image of Christ."[497]

Evangelical pietism took root especially in New England and accompanied disciples who emigrated to western New York State and throughout the Midwest. These people tended to be "cultural imperialists" for Christ, seeking to impose their Protestant (biblical) values and morality on others, even by using the coercive power of the state.[498] For example, some pietists clashed with the growing community of new religious immigrants, which were mostly Catholics and Lutherans.

Catholics and Lutherans, known at the time as the "liturgicals," were quite different from the Protestants. The liturgicals saw salvation not as a personal decision for Christ but as an act of joining their church, obeying rituals, and following the church's sacraments. Unlike the pietists, the liturgicals were far less evangelical—culturally imperialistic—about their faith and values, and far more accepting of "sinful" behaviors like alcohol consumption, a practice brought from their homelands mostly in Ireland and Germany.

These church-based pietists and liturgicals soon affiliated with nineteenth-century political parties. The Whigs, Republicans, aligned themselves with the Protestant pietists, and the Democratic Party associated with the Catholic and Lutheran liturgicals. That explains in part why Republicans became known for trying to stamp out liquor—the Progressive Era's prohibition movement that led to the Eighteenth Amendment to the US Constitution—and limiting Sunday activities except church attendance, as well as efforts to restrict or abolish immigration aimed at keeping liturgicals (read "Catholics and Lutherans") out of the country.[499]

The pietists also concentrated on spiritually saving Catholic and Lutheran youth by trying to eliminate their parochial schools. The object was to "Christianize the Catholics" by forcing them into public schools, which promoted Protestantism. But the liturgicals fought back, objecting to efforts by pietists to outlaw their parochial schools as well as their habit of beer consumption.

It was widely understood that early progressives and their pietist allies believed that society's ills could be resolved by better education, safe workplaces, and honest government.[500] In fact, scholars like John Dewey believed in the importance of applied knowledge and thus asserted that schools were ideal platforms for social change—a view supported by pietists, but for different reasons, as we saw in the first section of this book.[501]

Following this line of thinking, the Republicans with their pietist allies sought to use public schools to "unify and make homogeneous the society." Of course, at that time, there was no concern for separating religion and the public school system, which was often a fount of religious instruction: daily Bible reading, prayers, hymns, and textbooks were rife with anti-Catholic information. It is noteworthy that around the turn of the nineteenth century, New York City school textbooks spoke of "the deceitful Catholics" and pounded into the children, Catholic and

Protestant alike, the message that "Catholics are necessarily, morally, intellectually, infallibly, a stupid race."[502]

The purpose of the public schools was to produce "a morally and politically homogeneous people." As Paul Kleppner explained in his book, *The Third Electoral System, 1853–1892: Parties, Voters, and Political Culture*:

> When they [the pietists] spoke of "moral education," they had in mind principles of morality shared in common by the adherents of gospel religion, for in the public school all children, even those whose parents were enslaved by "Lutheran formalism or Romish superstition," would be exposed to the Bible. That alone was cause for righteous optimism, for they believed the Bible to be "the agent in converting the soul," "the volume that makes human beings men."[503]

The progressive vision for American children was homogenization, and the public school was the instrument of the state to make that happen. President Theodore Roosevelt's (a Republican) favorite social scientist, Edward Alsworth Ross, summarized the purpose of the public school at that time. He explained that the role of the public school is "to collect little plastic lumps of human dough from private households and shape them on the social kneadingboard."[504]

The progressive view was to empower government schools to take up the task of control and inculcation of moral values previously performed by parents and church. That fight was evidenced across the country at the time, pitting middle- and upper-class, urban, progressive Protestants against working-class Catholics and Lutherans.

Early in the twentieth century in San Francisco, we saw upper-class progressives transforming that city's public school system by installing an all-powerful school superintendent. The public purpose of that installation was to take the schools out of politics per se, but the real reason was to push through a progressive program of social control, to impose upper-class control over a working-class population, and to impose pietists' Protestant control over Catholic ethnics.[505]

On another social front, the women's suffrage movement was dominated by pietist progressives as well. Evidently, the purpose of the suffrage movement was more sinister than just seeking equal opportunity for women regarding the right to vote. Rather, it was a means to create an electoral majority for pietist measures to better control the lives of American families. Specifically, the pietists used government to pierce family privacy to determine what families drank (alcohol), when and where they drank alcohol, how they spent their Sundays (in church or not), and how their children should be educated.

At the time, women became very socially and politically active, not just on suffrage and Nineteenth Amendment (women's right to vote) issues, but on the creation of public kindergartens, daycare for children of working mothers, and facilities to support children in need. This was the beginning of government's involvement in the childcare industry and encouragement of mothers leaving the home for paid jobs.[506]

The women's suffrage movement was also closely associated with the promotion of "science" (eugenics), an especially popular doctrine among progressives. At the time, eugenics was understood as encouraging the breeding of the "fit" and discouraging the breeding of the "unfit." The "fitness" for "breeding" coincided with native, white Protestants; the "unfit" were the foreign born, Catholics, and Lutherans.[507]

The founder of the American eugenics movement, biologist Charles Benedict Davenport of New York, saw the growing feminist (suffrage) movement as the means to maintain the number of biologically superior persons—white, Protestants—as opposed to the "unfit."[508]

Biologist Harry H. Laughlin, an aide to Davenport and the associate editor of the *Eugenical News*, was very influential at the time on immigration policy as well. He was an expert witness before the House Committee on Immigration and Naturalization, where he stressed the importance of cutting the immigration of the biologically "inferior" Southern Europeans, allegedly to protect Anglo-Saxon women and the nation's blood supply.[509]

Laughlin said American women must keep the nation's blood pure by not marrying what he called the "colored races." To Laughlin, the moral was clear: "The perpetuity of the American race and consequently of American institutions depends upon the virtue and fecundity of American women." But there was a problem with the fecundity of American women, according to University of California eugenicist Samuel J. Holmes. He said, "The trouble with birth control is that it is practiced least where it should be practiced most [among the 'unfit']."[510]

The eugenics movement and the birth-control movement were closely linked. Progressive leader Margaret Higgins Sanger, author, founder, and editor of *Birth Control Review*, called for the emancipation of women through birth control as the latest in applied science and "efficiency." She wrote in her autobiography:

In an age which has developed science and industry and economic efficiency to their highest points, so little thought has been given to the development of a science of parenthood, a science [stopping of breeding of the unfit] of maternity which could prevent this appalling and unestimated waste of womankind and maternal effort.[511]

Sanger also wrote:

The eugenicists wanted to shift the birth control emphasis from less children for the poor to more children for the rich. We went back of that and sought first to stop the multiplication of the unfit. This appeared the most important and greatest step toward race betterment.[512]

On other fronts, progressives and pietist Protestants formed a coalition that urged regulation of every aspect of American family life for the spread of Christianity. It combined the technocratic drive for government regulation, an obvious progressive aim, supported by the pietist religious impulse to save the country—all by state coercion if necessary.[513]

Prohibition is one such issue that satisfied the coalition of the progressives and their religious pietist allies. Not surprisingly, the social gospel movement that combined political collectivism with pietist Protestant Christianity fueled the progressive movement and hit its high point in the Progressive Era in 1912.

That effort coincided with the Progressive Party's national convention that was an assemblage of a broad coalition of groups: middle- and upper-class businessmen, intellectuals, academics, technocrats, efficiency experts, and social engineers—all urban, highly educated, and, of course, white Protestants, mostly pietists.

The social engineers at the convention included well-known social work leaders such as Jane Addams and Lillian Wald, as well as social gospel leaders like Lyman Abbott, the Reverend R. Heber Newton, and progressive candidate for governor of Vermont Reverend Fraser Metzger, leader of the inter-church federation of Vermont.[514]

At the convention, the Progressive Party labeled itself the "recrudescence of the religious spirit in American political life." To evidence that view, former President Theodore Roosevelt's nomination (for the presidency as the Progressive Party's candidate) acceptance address was entitled "A Confession of Faith." The convention participants sang a host of Protestant hymns and patriotic songs: "Onward, Christian Soldiers," "The Battle Hymn of the Republic," and "Follow, Follow, We Will Follow Jesus," but "Jesus" was replaced with "Roosevelt."[515]

The *New York Times* reported at the time that the assemblage was "a convention of fanatics," "religious fanatics....a Methodist camp following done over into political terms."[516]

Indeed, progressives and Protestant pietists united in a political movement to attack social issues that impacted the country and especially the family. They sought to control the sexual choices of the American people, their drinking preferences, the nurture of children, and their education, all overseen by the elite technocrats informed by the pietists using the power of the state to stipulate the details of American family life.

This coalition pushed government into statism, a significant reach of government into every aspect of American life. It recreated an old alliance of big government, business, and the intellectual—not that different from the relationship between the old European monarchies and the mercantilist system of centuries past.

Progressives at that time also used the media (muckrackers), the intellectuals, and the elite business leaders to centralize power in the hands of the few. Elected officials were replaced by bureaucrats (experts) who knew better, according to progressive doctrine.

Indeed, the Progressive Era reforms were mostly fueled at the time by Republicans and northern Protestant pietists, who used government to influence many aspects of American family life, such as changing the law regarding women's rights, worker rights, and education, eugenics, and immigration policies.

Progressives politically began to transition from the Republican to the Democratic Party after Theodore Roosevelt lost to Woodrow Wilson in the 1912 presidential election. Soon, Wilson took up the mantel of progressivism by embracing big-government policies that accelerated through time to President Franklin Roosevelt's New Deal and President Johnson's War Against Poverty, to President Obama's Obamacare, up until the present time, with progressives dominating the House of Representatives and pushing radical ideas like the earlier addressed Green New Deal, which threatens to bankrupt the country.

What Is the Current State of the American Family?

The family must succeed if civilization is to succeed; right now, the American family is failing. Consider that 40 percent of American births are to unmarried women, and 89 percent of those unmarried women are teen mothers. The problem is especially bad among non-Hispanic black children: almost three of every four are born outside of marriage.[517]

In 1995, the sage sociologist and Democratic politician Daniel Patrick Moynihan was asked about the biggest change he had seen during his four decades in politics. Moynihan said: "The biggest change, in my judgment, is that the family structure has come apart all over the North Atlantic world."[518] The problem only got worse over the past quarter of a century.

Although both major political parties decry the family breakdown, nothing they do seems to be working. Well-known sociologist Charles Murray writes in his book, *Coming Apart,* that at least one segment of society succeeds. The upper class knows the secret of family prosperity: traditional family values. Simply put, men and women who get married, stay married, and have children within marriage are more likely to be in, and stay in, the middle or upper classes.[519]

Why is the contemporary American family in trouble with that one exception? Evidently, most "families" don't embrace traditional family values, according to Murray. After all, the symptoms of the troubled contemporary American family are represented by a picture of a battlefield strewn with damaged lives: abortions, more sex outside of marriage, more cohabitation, less marriage, and more "families" headed by unmarried parents, and the list goes on.

These tragic symptoms of a failed family culture were contrasted very publicly beginning in 1984 with NBC's *Cosby Show* starring the now-disgraced actor Bill Cosby, who was depicted as a middle-class, black obstetrician living with his wife and five children in Brooklyn, New York. The show was a huge success, perhaps because it presented a picture of the ideal American family of the past, which viewers wanted to affirm but knew just how far things had digressed.

What viewers wanted was to resurrect the nuclear family of the 1950s. At that time, most married women walked the church aisle by age twenty, and only 16 percent worked outside the home—in part, because they were pregnant within the first seven months of marriage.

The man was the breadwinner and returned each evening to his wife, who kept the home fires burning, an iconic 1950s lifestyle profiled by nostalgic television sitcoms like *The Cosby Show, Leave It to Beaver, and Father Knows Best.*

The perfect nuclear family-era housewife was profiled in a 1955 article in *Housekeeping Monthly.* Perfection entailed:

> Your goal: To try and make sure your home is a place of peace, order, and tranquility where your husband can renew himself in body and spirit.... Make him comfortable. Have him lean back in a comfortable chair or have him lie down in the bedroom.... Arrange his pillow and offer to take off his shoes. Speak in a low, soothing and pleasant voice.... Remember, he is the master of the house and as such will always exercise his will with fairness and truthfulness. You have no right to question him. A good wife always knows her place.

America's 1950s nuclear family was but a blip in history, owing to unique economic and political circumstances. Soon that ideal was ruptured by the social revolution in the 1960s, and, thanks in a large part to progressives like Betty Friedan, the American family's world was turned upside down.

Friedan described herself at the time as a housewife and mother from the New York suburbs. That characterization was misleading because she was an active socialist and worked as a journalist for a union for many years after her marriage. Her claim to fame came with the publication of her book.

Friedan surveyed her former Smith College (Northampton, Massachusetts) classmates and then claimed that 1960s women lacked any way to express themselves beyond cooking or sex, what Friedan called *The Feminine Mystique,* the title of her bestselling book and the platform upon which she launched a progressive women's-rights movement that seeded among American women ill feelings for motherhood and men.

Friedan used her popularity to build the National Organization for Women (NOW) to advance awareness about a proposed Equal Rights' Amendment, which failed but not without first raising awareness that led to significant reforms in the women's rights arena. Her agenda was clear: She wanted women to take control, and the shortcuts to that end were contraception (abortion mostly) and employment outside the home—which meant liberation from men.

The feminist revolution coincided with the Vietnam War protests and the civil rights movement, a troubled time that, thanks to progressives, took its toll on the 1950s-era nuclear family. With encouragement from Friedan and others, the feminist revolution contributed to growing family dysfunction, and their solution was a typical progressive answer: Create more government programs to advance women's rights—free women from the bondage of staying at home raising children.

It was during this period that the American family began to take a nose dive. We saw the rate of cohabiting couples increase from maybe half a million different-sex couples in 1960 to 59.8 million households headed by an unmarried person by the year 2016. That's a sad figure, and both children and society paid the heavy toll.[520]

The black family is on life support as a result of this plunge. In the mid 1960s, sociologist Daniel Moynihan published *The Negro Family: The Case for National Action*, which argued that the underlying cause of inequality between the races was not economics or race, but family structure. He cited the alarming incidence of single motherhood and the lack of male influences in the home. Moynihan advised Democrat President Lyndon Johnson to create job and education programs to empower black fathers to marry the mother of their children and raise their families—a real boost to big-government welfare programs.

Progressives were tone deaf to Moynihan's family-based solutions. Rather President Johnson declared a "War on Poverty" that led to more big-government programs, such as the 1962 Food Stamp Act (today known as the Supplemental Nutrition Assistance Program [SNAP]). Recipients of food stamps increased from a half million in 1965 to more than ten million by 1971, and the effect was the fall of Americans living in poverty, which declined from 19 percent in 1964 to 11.1 percent in 1973. Today, more than forty-two million Americans receive SNAP benefits at an annual cost of $79 billion in 2016.[521] However, big-government programs like SNAP did not stop the decline in the nuclear family in spite of such significant largesse. In fact, as some conservatives argued then and now, Johnson's War on Poverty actually undermined the family by subsidizing absentee fathers.

Why are most households now headed by unmarried persons? Several forces are at play. Certainly, the advent of birth-control pills, which became widely available in the 1960s, made nonmarital relationships (sex) more attractive to some. Should the pill fail, tragically, abortion on demand was and is considered a woman's "right" (due to *Roe v. Wade 410 U.S. 113* [1973]), which results in millions of young lives being tossed in the trash annually. Further, states decriminalized sex outside of marriage (fornication) and the pop culture promoted extramarital liaisons. America has become awash in an amoral sewer of anything goes.

Cohabitation rates grew greatest among African-Americans and Latinos, as did the percent of children born to unmarried women. Not surprisingly, those unmarried females with children at home tended to be poor, and the numbers of children in those situations grew significantly.

The rate of marriages ending in divorce increased throughout the twentieth century as well. Further, the growing cohort of divorcees were more likely to cohabit prior to or in lieu of remarriage. This outcome is in part attributable to "no fault" divorce laws—a feminist agenda item—beginning with the state of California in 1969. The impact for the culture was more acceptance of divorce.

Starting in the 1980s, marriage as an institution took a nosedive into political correctness as same-sex (homosexual) "marriage" became an agenda item for progressives. Hawaii was the first state to establish a statewide alternative legal status for homosexual couples; Vermont soon followed with civil unions. The 2003 *Lawrence v. Texas, 539 U.S. 538*

Supreme Court case struck down laws that prohibited the criminalization of the defining behavior of homosexuals (sodomy). Soon, same-sex couples were allowed to legally marry and thus have "families."

It wasn't long before the high court case *Obergefell v. Hodges, 576 U.S.* (2015) ruled that the fundamental right to marry is guaranteed to same-sex couples by the due process clause and the equal protection clause of the Fourteenth Amendment. That five-to-four ruling required all fifty states to perform and recognize the marriages of same-sex couples on the same terms and conditions as the marriages of opposite-sex couples, with all the accompanying rights and responsibilities.[522]

The contemporary American family is devastated today, as a result of progressive initiatives: leftist cultural influences, radical feminism, homosexuality, and abortion on demand, the so-called War on Poverty, and a host of other big-government programs that encourage single parenthood and fail to hold fathers accountable.

What Are Progressives' Plans for Future American Families?

Progressives have big plans for America's families once they retake both chambers of the Congress and the presidency. Unfortunately, those plans will inevitably follow the same paths their misguided ideological forefathers took that gave us today's dysfunctional family.

One view of progressives' ongoing impact on the American family is through the promotion of cultural themes, about which one progressive observed: "If this relationship doesn't feel good, don't hassle with it—just go on to another one," or "Sexuality should be divorced from emotions—it's just another kind of fun. Enjoy it like good food."[523]

Those of us on the political right—especially on the religious right—are accustomed to such amoral messages from Hollywood liberals and other progressives who routinely denigrate the family and the beauty of sex within marriage. But the Center for American Progress (CAP), a progressive organization, claims these views don't represent most progressives either; rather, they claim that most support marriage and policies that advance the family.[524]

The CAP claims it endorses policies based on research by Paul Amato, a professor at Pennsylvania State University in the Department of Sociology and Criminology. Amato writes in his book, *Alone Together: How Marriage in America Is Changing*, that inadequate resources and financial stress contribute to family conflict and instability. Specifically, Amato writes that "lower levels of income, educational attainment, and occupational prestige were associated with higher rates of marital problems, less marital happiness, and greater instability."[525]

The CAP cites four progressive policies that are supported by Professor Amato's work that, if followed, will make families stronger. However, each of CAP's policies requires more big-government programs and a nation willing to keep throwing good money after bad.

First, CAP claims that "fairly compensated work provides a solid foundation for the creation and maintenance of strong and healthy family relationships." Therefore, progressives like Amato argue for a higher minimum wage believing that more money in the workers' pockets will keep families together.[526]

The problem for families is that, according to University of California economist Hilary Hoynes, the research "suggests that marriage decisions are not sensitive to financial decisions. The literature on the effect of welfare on out-of-wedlock births is also quite conclusive.... overall these effects are often insignificant and when they are not, they are small."[527]

Juxtapose CAP's claims with a ream of research literature that addresses the minimum wage debate. Progressives prefer to have the federal government mandate a high national minimum wage, but wages fit for New York City ought to be very different than those in Waco, Texas. After all, the cost of living is very different in those two places. Any debate about minimum wages ought to be done locally and keep the federal government out of the picture, but that doesn't correspond with progressives' federalist agenda.

Second, progressives argue for strengthening collective bargaining for labor. CAP states research finds that "controlling for many factors, union membership is positively and significantly associated with marriage." The benefit of the nexus of labor unions and marriage is explained by "the increased income, regularity and stability of employment, and fringe benefits that come with union membership."[528]

Progressives typically favor strengthening labor markets, higher minimum wages, and collective bargaining. Do these measures really increase the incidents of marriage and, by association, family stability? Not really. They may in fact provide disincentives to marry and increase the incentives to divorce or separate.

Third, progressives argue that expanding Medicaid is part of a secure foundation for families. CAP states that when a family member lacks health insurance, it can lead to financial burdens, more stress, poor health outcomes, and family instability.[529]

Medicaid is a government program that provides health coverage for "low-asset people" wherein the costs are shared by the federal and state governments, and those costs are increasing exponentially. In fact, what progressives like Senators Bernie Sanders and Elizabeth Warren call for is "Medicare for All [Life]," which, according to congressional Republicans, would cost the federal government $33 trillion by 2031 and quickly bankrupt the country.[530]

Let there be no doubt about progressive enthusiasm for this program. The first hearing hosted by the new Democratic Party majority in the House of Representatives (January 4, 2019) was on "Medicare-for-All [Life]." "It's a huge step forward to have the Speaker's [Nancy Pelosi] support," said Representative Pramila Jayapal (D-WA), the bill's sponsor. "We have to push on the inside while continuing to build support for this on the outside."[531]

Fourth, CAP calls for supporting reproductive rights (read "abortion") to support families. It claims that "the failure to expand Medicaid, combined with overly restrictive abortion legislation and other barriers to reproductive care, harms families' economic security by reducing their ability to plan their childbearing." Therefore, better reproductive rights, according to CAP, strengthens families.[532]

"Reproductive rights," the progressives' code for "abortion," is a flagship issue for progressives, as demonstrated earlier in this chapter. In fact, progressive Democrats wasted no time upon taking back the US House of Representatives on January 3, 2019, to propose pro-abortion legislation that would repeal the Mexico City Policy (which Democrats named Protecting Life in Global Health Assistance), but which President Trump reinstated upon taking office. The Democrats' fresh bill would make foreign abortion providers once again eligible for American foreign aid.[533]

Progressives even push to reform work-family policies that ensure all workers have access to benefits that allegedly improve family stability. However, once again, these policies require big government and more often than not congressional legislation and more taxpayer money, as well as dramatic increases in costs for businesses. These programs include subsidized higher levels of educational attainment and lower levels of incarceration (perhaps more crime), earned sick days (more costs for employers), flexible work schedules (with potential impact on employers), paid family leave (more costs for employers), pre-K (kindergarten), and affordable (read "subsidized by business or government"], high-quality childcare.

Conclusion

Progressives haven't changed much since a century ago. They love big government, imposing their ideological wills on the masses, and believe elite bureaucrats can solve man's every problem. Further, the modern welfare state, if given enough money and regulation, promises to vanquish the problems facing the modern American family. Their predecessors made similar claims, and the situation for the American family has only gotten worse. Progressives need to keep their hands off our families.

Yes, progressives have big plans for the American family, which inevitably requires more big-government programs, lots of new regulations, and increased redistribution of wealth.

11

Progressivism's Impact on Education

Far from failing in its intended task, our educational system is in fact succeeding magnificently, because its aim is to keep the American people thoughtless enough to go on supporting the system.[534]

—Richard Mitchell, American author and educator (1929–2002)

America's education system is a catastrophe, and we can blame progressives. They took over America's once very sound academic education system during the late nineteenth and early twentieth centuries and then transformed it into a social engineering charade that should anger every patriot.

No wonder today's homeschooling network is growing by leaps and bounds as our public education system dives into the globe's backcountry. But worse, modern progressives who may be worse than their forefathers are ready to further damage what is left of our educational establishment with their radical ideas.

This chapter explains why our educational establishment trails other advanced nations and concludes with suggestions on what can be done to reverse that tragic situation. However, before we discuss that dismal state of affairs, we need to explore where our educational establishment was in early America as a point of comparison and then look at how progressives turned that great academic system on its head into something like a social reengineering system more akin to the education establishment in the former Soviet Union. Then we will explore options to reverse the current trend as opposed to what contemporary progressives plan for America's future schools.

How Bad Is Our Education System?

United States fifteen-year-old students place near the bottom among the leading thirty-five industrialized nations on math, according to an international student test. That result should alarm every American, because China, our primary global adversary, tops the charts when it comes to math and science; even America's best students tend to significantly trail Chinese students in most academic subjects. Why?[535]

A 2016 *Atlantic* article reports that American teenagers placed "near the bottom" on math in the 2015 Programme for International Student Assessment Test, worse than their showing in 2012. Another troubling indicator of our failing education system is the fact that at least forty-four million American adults are functionally illiterate. Yet, America's federal and state governments spend an estimated $620 billion annually on K–12 education, or $12,296 for every student in public school. Something is very wrong with this picture.[536]

Unfortunately, our education system's poor performance isn't a new phenomenon. Consider that in 1988, only 5 percent of American high school seniors could read well enough to comprehend our historical documents (e.g., the US Constitution), college textbooks, and literary essays.[537]

Alarm over our education system prompted President Ronald Reagan to commission a study about the decline in American education. The final report from that 1983 study begins: "We are a nation at risk." The report detailed the dismal state of our nation's educational institution and concluded: "If an unfriendly foreign power had attempted to impose on America the mediocre educational performance that exists today, we might well have viewed it as an act of war. As it stands, we have allowed this to happen to ourselves."[538]

How did this happen to the world's richest nation? Believe it or not, America once had an education system that was the envy of the world—but that was two centuries ago.

Early American Education

The early-American colonialists emphasized education, which resulted in a remarkably high literacy level. Not surprisingly, their interest in education spawned a system of learning that initially started at home, but in time branched out to grammar schools and later colleges that produced brilliant American scientists, writers, and statesmen.

These Americans who left Europe for the new world were "people of the book [Bible]," a label given them by historians who understood the reason for migrating to the new world was their Christian faith. Many of these "people of the book" came from places where they were taught how to reason from God's Word in civil society, an idea Reformation-era Protestant John Calvin matured in Geneva, Switzerland, and a practice the immigrants brought to America.[539]

The Calvinist tradition understandably influenced the education of American children first at home, where parents taught them to read, write, and cipher (do arithmetic), all with a careful eye on the cultivation of a virtuous character and a Christian conscience.

Those settlers—especially the Puritans, who arrived at the northern tip of Cape Cod in 1620 aboard the Mayflower—quickly put their mark on their new home. They left Europe for the new world seeking religious liberty and, in the case of the Puritans, agreed before stepping ashore in New England to the Mayflower Compact, which spelled out the establishment of a Christian government based on biblical law.

The Mayflower Compact also guided their pursuit of a Christian education for their children, which explains the importance of every settler learning to read the Bible. That Christian heritage also resulted in children being named after biblical characters and explains why every aspect of the local New England cultural life revolved around the Sabbath worship service and Christian holidays.[540]

The first American education law was enacted by Puritans in the Massachusetts Bay Colony legislature in 1642, which reflected the colonists' concerns for their children:

> Forasmuch as the good education of children is of singular behoof and benefit to any commonwealth and whereas many parents and masters are too indulgent and negligent of their duty in this kind.[541]

> It is therefore ordered by this Court and the authority thereof, That the selectmen of every town, in the several precincts and quarters where they dwell, shall have a vigilant eye over their brethren and neighbors, to see, first that none of them shall suffer so much barbarism in any of their families, as not to endeavor to teach, by themselves or others, their children and apprentices as much learning as may enable them perfectly to read the English tongue, and knowledge of the capital laws, upon penalty of twenty shillings for each neglect therein.[542]

The injunction to teach (educate) was soon followed by the drafting of the first school-focused law in Massachusetts, which read:

It is therefore ordered by this Court and authority thereof, That every township within this jurisdiction, after the Lord hath increased them to the number of fifty householders, shall then forthwith appoint one within their town to teach all such children as shall resort to him, to write and read, whose wages shall be paid, either by the parents or masters of such children or by the inhabitants in general, by way of supply.... [And it is further ordered] That where any town shall increase to the number of one hundred families or householders, they shall set up a grammar school, the masters thereof being able to instruct youths so far as they may be fitted for the university.[543]

There was already a model for a grammar school at the time of this new law. Puritans founded the first grammar school in 1635, the Boston Latin School. It was modeled after the European Latin schools, which emphasized religion, Latin, and classical literature. The school's masters considered speaking more than one language important; therefore, learning Latin was a priority, much as it was in English grammar schools at the time. Latin proficiency also became a requirement for admission to Harvard Seminary, which was founded the year after the Boston Latin School.[544]

Most of the original colonists in New England were conservative Christians who, like the Massachusetts Puritans, sought to educate their children in the Calvinist view of life. They used the *New England Primer*, the first reading primer designed for the American colonies, to catechize their children in Calvinist precepts. The book also was used to teach the English alphabet using biblical illustrations such as "a," "in Adam's fall we sinned all"; "b," "heaven to find, the Bible mind"; and "c," "Christ crucif'd for sinners dy'd." Young children learned their alphabet along with Christian principles and Bible stories owing to the *Primer*.[545]

Much later, American educator Noah Webster, a devout Christian born in West Hartford, Connecticut, helped with the publication of the *Blue-Backed Speller*, an American English book, first published in 1783, that sold twenty million copies and, along with other published materials, helped turn America into the most literate nation on earth.[546]

America's high literacy rate at the time created a giant market for books, a boon for citizens such as Webster, who, by age forty-two, compiled the *Dictionary of the American Language* as well.[547] It is noteworthy that by the time America turned thirty years old, numerous millions of books were sold to a very literate general population, and challenging reading materials were even found in the hands of grammar school-aged children.

Reading levels among young children at that time far exceeded that of today's average elementary students. At that time, the fourth-grade reader included writings from Nathaniel Hawthorne, a nineteenth-century novelist, and the fifth-grade readings included William Shakespeare, a sixteenth-century English poet and playwright. Contemporary columnist Thomas Sowell observed about the reading materials used by late eighteenth- and early nineteenth-century young Americans: "These were not the textbooks of the elite but of the masses."[548]

Indeed, America's literacy was significant and noted by two renowned Frenchmen. Pierre DuPont de Nemours, a French writer, economist, publisher and government official, wrote at the time that "most young Americans can read, write, and cipher [do arithmetic]. Not more than four in a thousand are unable to write legibly." Later, during an extended tour of the new republic, Alexis de Tocqueville, a French diplomat, political scientist, and historian best known for his work, *Democracy in America*, claimed that Americans were the most educated people in history.[549]

The American education system these Frenchmen celebrated reflected the spirit and tenacity of the colonialists. In fact, it is noteworthy that none of the colonialists educated in England participated in drafting the Declaration of Independence, the US Constitution, and the Bill of Rights. Rather, the drafters of these founding documents were exclusively educated in the colonies, and many, like James Madison, were educated at American seminaries like the College of New Jersey, Harvard, and Yale.[550]

George Washington, our first president and the leader of the Constitutional Convention, was homeschooled in northern Virginia by his father. His only formal education was in surveying. Yet, he was considered an educated man who became known as the "Father of Our country" and the "Moses of America." He wrote more than forty volumes of personal correspondence and his "Farewell Address" to the nation remains a lesson on the importance of religion and morality in politics, and is still considered one of the most important of our historical documents.[551]

As the country grew, so did our education system. The grammar school, also known as the common school, which began in Boston, became part of every community's landscape. These were typically one-room affairs with a lone teacher. The students' parents initially paid tuition and provided housing for the teacher, but in time, costs were paid by local taxes. Like the schools that began in New England, common schools popped up in communities small and large alike and followed the Puritan model of institutionalizing religion into the curriculum in order to instill good morals and obedience, besides instructing young minds in reading, writing, and ciphering.

America's early educational system endured mostly unscathed by reformers until after the Civil War (1861–1865). However, radical changes began with the Progressive Era in the late nineteenth century and were especially widespread by the 1930s. Many of those more radical changes came as a result of progressives like John Dewey, the founder of the progressive education movement, who had a very different view of the purpose of educating America's youth than our founders, much less our Puritan forefathers.

Progressives' Impact on American Education in the Late-Nineteenth and Early-Twentieth Centuries

Progressives beginning in the late-nineteenth century trashed America's education system by adopting a philosophy and methods that moved young minds away from studying literature, history, science, and math and put more emphasis on learning nonacademic life skills. These "educators," who came to dominate America's education establishment, purposed among themselves to agree that a "narrow focus" on academic training like that of our forefathers was insufficient for a progressive country. Rather, these public educators wanted to focus on what they called the "whole child." This mindset dominates our education system still today, and the data above shows that we are regressive and paying a huge price globally.

That in itself should alarm every parent and taxpayer, even today. However, the history of the progressive takeover of the American school system and what they did is frankly frightening and unforgiveable, and their assault on our future is far from over.

I attribute much of the following material to Dr. Andrew Bernstein with the graduate school of the City University of New York, who documented the progressives' war on learning in his 2018 article, "Heroes and Villains in American Education." Below is a summary of Bernstein's much longer case exposing progressive malfeasance regarding our educational system.[552]

Early progressives pushed to distance public education from academics. They sought to replace academics and Christian character building with activities better suited to prepare them to work on farms or in factories. Jane Addams, an educational reformer introduced earlier in this volume, wrote, "We are impatient with the schools which lay all stress on reading and writing, suspecting them to rest upon the assumption that all knowledge and interest must be brought to the children through the medium of books." Lawrence Cremin, a leading scholar of progressive education, wrote of Addams' theory, "Industry… would have to be seized upon and conquered by the educators." This emphasis on group work was a theme that would be sounded over and again by progressives and their intellectual descendants.[553]

Naturally, like progressives today, those educators claimed their approach was based on science. Specifically, at that time, they embraced the Stanford-Binet intelligence test (intelligence quotient [IQ] test) to measure a student's intellectual ability. The results were then used to "facilitate progressive reforms in education, especially identification of the feebleminded and the gifted, curricular differentiation, vocational guidance and grouping based on students' ability."[554]

It shouldn't be surprising that many of those advocating widespread IQ testing were eugenicists who, as explained in the previous chapter, called for limiting the "breeding" of the "unfit." Lewis Terman, a psychology professor at Stanford University, another advocate for IQ testing, and a eugenicist, wrote, "There is no possibility at present of convincing society that they [so-called feebleminded persons] should not be allowed to reproduce." So, eugenicists like Terman did the next best thing: They segregated the intellectually gifted from the less intelligent using IQ tests.[555]

Starting in the mid-1920s, psychologists used seventy-five different IQ tests to annually gauge the intellectual ability of some four million students. Historian Diane Ravitch wrote of this development: "The public schools employed the tests to predict which students were likely to go to college and which should be guided into vocational programs." Ravitch continued: "The decision became a self-fulfilling prophecy, since only those in the college track took the courses that would prepare them for college."[556]

Once IQ testing was under the progressives' belt, they sought to create a new field of education, "curriculum studies." Proponents argued that only true education experts could harness science to determine a school's best curriculum. What this really meant was that no longer would local school boards and parents dictate that their children learn reading, writing, arithmetic, history, geography, sciences, and much more. No. What children learned in school was to be left up to the new science of "curriculum studies," and of course, this was influenced by IQ testing that determined the child's future. Evidently, parents and local teachers no longer knew best.

Historian Ravitch wrote:

The invention of the scientific curriculum expert represented an extraordinary shift in power away from teachers, parents, and local communities to professional experts.... In modern school districts, control over curriculum was transferred from educators who had majored in English, history, or mathematics to trained curriculum specialists.[557]

This was a real coup for professional educators. They conceived the new field of curriculum design under the auspices of an educational engineer who would establish the criteria for a child's preparation for a particular profession, and society would benefit. After all, this utilitarian approach prepared young people to reach their intellectual potential while satisfying what society demanded—more agricultural education if farming production lagged, or industrial education to help factory production.

Progressive John F. Bobbitt at the University of Chicago, a proponent of the new field of curriculum design, defended the social engineering approach by rhetorically asking:

How would a 20th-century plumber's knowledge of Shakespeare's drama or poetry benefit society? Beyond the basic science training necessary to help a farmer grow crops, how would his understanding of physics or mathematics aid society? For what social purpose should we teach a future factory worker ancient history?[558]

Bobbit's 1918 book, *Curriculum*, became the standard textbook on curriculum development in teachers' colleges for many years. His disdain for the study of the classics by low-IQ students was shared with W. W. Charters at the Carnegie Institute of Technology, who said "brilliant products of genius," like the classics, were of little value to most Americans. Rather, Charters argued that schools should discover what was "most useful to the young in coping with the humble problems of their lives." Translation: Schools must identify the students' potential and limits and then train them accordingly.[559]

The next progressive agenda item for America's education system was the adoption of "cardinal principles," a new, "scientific" approach to schooling. Naturally, the source of these "principles" was big government and the professional educational establishment, beginning with the US Bureau of Education and the National Education Association (NEA).[560]

The Bureau called for revamping American schooling in partnership with the NEA, which resulted in the creation of the Commission on the Reorganization of Secondary Education (CRSE). That commission issued "cardinal principles of secondary education" in 1918, which remains with modern American education today.

The CRSE directed schools to "concern themselves less with academic matters than with the preparation for effective living." Yes, that's a clear message to educators to get involved in scientifically reengineering society. Translation: Stop teaching students to reason independently and focus on pursuing the "common good."[561]

Evidently, the new focus on pursuing the "common good" included the "cardinal principles" of teaching personal hygiene, "a love for clean sport," "command of fundamental processes" (evidently a reference to academics), "worthy home-membership" (rules of proper family management), "vocation" (teaching blue-collar employment skills), "civics" (to replace history—no need to study about the US Constitution and the ideas of the founding fathers; rather, focus on group projects), "worthy use of leisure" (training in leisure activities), and "ethical character" (government-run moral training on "collective thinking").[562]

Historian Ravitch explained: "The driving purpose behind the seven objectives [cardinal principles] was socialization, teaching students to fit into society…. The overriding goal was social efficiency, not the realization of individual desire for self-improvement."[563]

What happened here? The US government, in cahoots with the NEA, stripped academic training from the core of the nation's schooling. Bernstein concludes from the CRSE's report that academics (reading, writing, and arithmetic) were to become "an afterthought," a view that became entrenched within American colleges of education.[564]

Prior to the CRSE's report, the NEA had already endorsed the necessity of academic training, which made the NEA look hypocritical with the release of the CRSE report. Specifically, in 1893, the NEA's own Commission of Ten, then headed by Harvard's Charles Eliot, declared:

> As studies in language and in the natural sciences are best adapted to cultivate the habits of observation; as mathematics are the traditional training of the reasoning faculties...so history and its allied branches are better adapted than any other studies to promote the invaluable mental power which we call judgment.[565]

CRSE shuttered most of the study of history in American schools as well. Prior to its report, most American high schools offered four years of history: ancient, European, English, and American. But CRSE created from whole cloth a new field, "social studies," which focused on "social efficiency, or teaching students the skills and attitudes necessary to fit into the social order."[566]

Further, and thanks to CRSE's views about civics, the study of government, became part of the new social activism field. Instead of studying the typical topics associated with civics, such as Congress, the presidency, and the founding documents, the emphasis on government was dumbed down to local-level government functions. The CRSE's "social studies" chairman explained:

> The old chronicler who recorded the deeds of kings and warriors and neglected the labors of the common man is dead. The great palaces and cathedrals and pyramids are often but the empty shells of a parasitic growth on the working group. The elaborate descriptions of these old tombs are but sounding brass and tinkling cymbals compared to the record of the joys and sorrows,

the hopes and disappointments of the masses, who are infinitely more important than any arrangement of wood and stone and iron.[567]

Professor Bernstein concludes that the above statement echoes Marxist ideology. He explains that the emphasis is on the masses and rejects the need for knowledge of past kings and rulers and their achievements. The progressive promise is to focus on little guys, not the past great achievers like founders George Washington and Thomas Jefferson. Thus, the educator was expected to socialize children, not nurture them with a love for learning and thinking.[568]

The cardinal principle of progressive faith was, concludes Bernstein, that "independent thinking is useless to society, even dangerous." And as regards rote learning, John Dewey, the founder of progressive education who wrote his PhD dissertation on German philosopher Immanuel Kant, said: "The mere absorbing of facts and truths is so exclusively individual an affair that it tends very naturally to pass into selfishness. There is no obvious social motive for the acquirement of mere learning, there is no clear social gain in success thereat."[569]

Dewey believed that children learn best by experience and should engage in real-life activities. Further, he saw the value of academic training, to an extent. After all, he and his wife, Alice, founded the Laboratory School at the University of Chicago, where "they continually experimented with different ways of [teaching] young students about primitive life in the Bronze Age...early Greek civilization...Prince Henry of Portugal, Columbus, and other explorers...Shakespeare's plays; science; mathematics; algebra and geometry; English, French, and even Latin."[570]

As laudatory as Dewey's statements about learning might be, it was his practice to lecture at the Laboratory School rather than focus on experience and real-life activities that speaks the loudest. Further, Dewey's view of the purpose of learning was not about acquiring knowledge, but about "saturating [students] with the spirit of service." He believed the purpose of education was to prime students for "social cooperation and community life," not to teach them "science, nor literature, nor history, nor geography."[571]

Bernstein writes that Dewey was "a brilliant mind trained in academic study," and he gave progressives the sanction of "lofty philosophy." Yet, Dewey's influence was "catastrophic," because he gave credibility to virulent opponents to academic training like William Heard Kilpatrick, a Dewey disciple.[572]

Kilpatrick held the philosophy of education chair at Columbia University's Teachers College (1918–1940), where he trained "a substantial percentage of the articulate leaders of American education." Kilpatrick, according to E. D. Hirsch, author of the *Schools We Need and Why We Don't Have Them*, writes that Kilpatrick, not Dewey, was "the most influential introducer of progressive ideas into American schools of education."[573]

Kilpatrick chaired the CRSE committee on mathematics and there argued for severely curtailing math instruction for all but future scientists and engineers. The balance of the students only need basic arithmetic in high school, according to Kilpatrick.[574]

Bernstein writes that Kilpatrick "was interested not in encouraging independence but in engineering social conformity." Once again, the aim of progressive educators was reengineering society. Historian Ravitch quotes Kilpatrick to explain his education aim:

> In contrast to the "customary set-task sit-alone-at-your-own-desk procedure" which promotes "selfish individualism," the project method [involves] the pressure of social approval [which] would encourage conformity to "the ideals necessary for approved social life."[575]

I suggest in the introduction of this chapter that what progressives are doing with American education is very much like the social reengineering seen in the former Soviet Union. It might not surprise some readers that leading progressive educators like Kilpatrick and Dewey in fact visited the former Soviet Union and boasted about that murderous regime's successful education system.

In 1929, Kilpatrick visited the Soviet Union, where he indicated that he was delighted to see his project method in action. While in Russia, he witnessed groups of students "disposing of disintegrating carcasses of animals left frozen by the roadside." Kilpatrick reported, "No school system in history has been more thoroughly and consistently made to work into the social and political program of the state."[576]

Dewey traveled to the Soviet Union in 1929 as well, and said he "was deeply moved by what he saw." He reported that Soviet educators "realized that the goals of the progressive school were undermined by 'the egoistic and private ideals and methods inculcated by the institution of private property, profit and acquisition possession.'" He even praised the communists for their efforts to target the institution of the family, which he considered individualistic and pernicious to communal living.[577]

Columbia University professor and progressive educator, George Counts, twice visited the Soviet Union to become convinced American schools must help America transform from a capitalist into a socialist nation. His aim was to transform progressive education into political activism to support that aim.[578]

Professor Counts was serious about harnessing education to promote socialism. In his book, *Dare the Schools Build a New Social Order?*, explained Ravitch, Counts "forthrightly called for elimination of capitalism, property rights, private profits, and competition, and establishment of collective ownership of natural resources, capital, and the means of production and distribution."[579]

Evidently, Counts' promotion of socialism was welcomed by other progressives. Ravitch explained, "Virtually every prominent progressive in the 1930s agreed that the traditional academic curriculum reflected the failed capitalist economic order."[580]

This pro-socialist education establishment agenda continues even today. Bernstein observes: "Intelligent Americans often note two seemingly distinct aspects of America's schools: (1) The teaching of academic subjects is poorly done (if done at all), and (2) the educational system is a hotbed of anti-capitalist propaganda. The fact is that the two observations are intimately related."[581]

Thus, as Bernstein notes, "Progressives and their intellectual heirs severely dumbed down the schools as a necessary means of inculcating conformity, dependency, and obedience."[582]

A few prominent American intellectuals rejected the progressive educational establishment's proposed academic-free curriculum, however. That group included Robert Maynard Hutchins, president of the University of Chicago, and Mortimer J. Adler, who campaigned on behalf of a "Great Books" program by maintaining that "a liberal education was unthinkable without a grounding in the great books."[583]

Adler proposed that a solid academic foundation was necessary for life. He wrote *The Paideia Program: An Educational Syllabus*, which called for terminating the progressive educational approach. He said:

> A single elementary and secondary school program for all students would ensure the upgrading of the curriculum and the quality of instruction to serve the needs of the brightest and to [education-ally] lift the...least advantaged. He proposed that...vocational... training be given only after students had completed a full course of basic education in the humanities, arts, sciences, and language.[584]

Predictably, progressives like Kilpatrick totally rejected Hutchins' and Adler's Great Books program. Ravitch wrote:

> William Heard Kilpatrick was...horrified by Hutchins' views. He fulminated that Hutchins was an authoritarian whose ideas were out of step with "every intellectual advance of the last 300 years." Worse, "Dr. Hutchins stands near to Hitler. When you have a professed absolute, then you have to have some authority to give it content, and there the dictator comes in."[585]

Dewey's criticism of the Great Books view was classic progressivism. He rejected Hutchins' view that there are absolute principles, eternal truths. Rather, like other progressives, Dewey insisted every belief was subject to scientific experimentation and progress—evolution. Further, and classically progressive in ideology, Dewey argued that truth in ancient or medieval times was not necessarily applicable for the modern world. That's when Dewey compared Hutchins to Hitler. Ravitch wrote:

> Astonishingly, Dewey went so far as to imply that Hutchins was ideologically linked with the jackbooted thugs who were then brutalizing Europe. "I would not intimate that the author [Hutchins] has any sympathy with fascism. But basically, his idea as to the proper course to be taken is akin to the distrust of freedom and the consequent appeal to some fixed authority that is now over-running the world."[586]

The educational system battle lines were drawn. Progressives sought to saturate students in the spirit of service and to prepare for community life. The Great Books educators sought to teach students to think, learn, and understand their world.

Given that challenge, progressives formed a new strategy to target the pro-academic crowd: "Cripple their [students'] ability to read."

Rudolf Flesch, an Austrian immigrant and Columbia University PhD, wrote a book, *Why Johnny Can't Read* (1955), to address America's rampant reading problems. Flesch wrote to American parents:

> There are no remedial reading cases in Austrian schools.... There are no remedial reading cases in Germany, in France, in Italy, in Norway, in Spain—practically anywhere in the world except in the United States.... Did you know that there was no such thing as remedial reading in this country either until about thirty years ago?[587]

Flesch discovered that, starting early in the twentieth century, the progressive educational establishment quit teaching the phonics method of instructing reading. Of course, phonics makes good use of the Roman alphabet to sound out words. Bernstein explains, "Children between the ages of five and six can master the written alphabet and begin to sound out words."[588]

Progressive educators favored some variant of the "whole word" method to teach children. The theory, explained Bernstein, was that "students need only master a core group of commonly used words and then employ context cues to decipher the rest." Then each year, children are introduced to new words until they have a complete vocabulary.[589]

The problem with this approach is that it relies on the student's ability to guess. Martin Gross explains in *The Conspiracy of Ignorance: The Failure of American Public Schools* that proponents of the whole-word or "look-say" method claim that "reading is 'a psycholinguistic guessing game.' Students are encouraged to 'create' and are not marked wrong for guessing wrong."[590]

Bernstein quotes Leonard Peikoff, a philosopher, who writes about this method of teaching students to read:

How would you like to see, at the head of our army, a general with this kind of schooling? He receives a telegram [today an instant message, if not a tweet] from the president during a crisis ordering him to "reject nuclear option," proceeds to make a good guess, and reads it as "release nuclear option." Linguistically, the two are as close as "carrots" and "cake."[591]

Fortunately, Flesch's book on reading set off a national debate that gained significant popularity and motivated publishers to issue new reading textbooks focused on the use of phonics.[592]

Predictably, the progressive educational establishment clung to the whole-word method of teaching reading. By the 1980s, they embraced a "whole-language" method, which retained the whole-word approach and continued to stiff-arm phonics.

What's the impact? A large segment of our population can't read. Progressive California public schools used the whole-language method and then, in 1992, the National Assessment of Educational Progress tested those students. The NAEP found that more than half (53 percent) of California fourth graders were reading below the baseline established for that grade. Two years later, the same test was administered and the number of semiliterate children in California rose to 56 percent.[593]

Schools that dropped whole language and reintroduced phonics found exceptional results. For example, a Texas school that switched to intensive phonics after decades of using whole language found that 98 percent of students from the school scored at or above grade level.[594]

Why can't American students read? Progressive educators don't want them to read.

Progressives (socialists) are all about control. These "elites" will ensure that their offspring are educated well, but if no one else is so educated, that's just fine. That means the odds of rebellion are reduced and the odds of controlling them increase. Of course, there is a certain arrogance about progressive thinkers that they always know what's best. In short, they are deceivers and know exactly what they are doing.

The progressive-created problems in public schools aren't limited to reading, however. The entire public-school curriculum is in trouble. After all, the same principles used by curriculum designers for reading also target math, science, and other subjects as well.

Bernstein reports that by the late 1990s, "only three states required more than two years of math to graduate from a public high school." Those graduates more often than not never took a full course in basic algebra, much less trigonometry, which means they don't learn enough math to prepare for college.[595]

Science is falling out of many public-school curricula. Although most (93 percent) high school students study biology, only half (54 percent) take chemistry and even fewer (24 percent) ever study physics. Author Martin Gross wrote, "Only 20 percent of public high school graduates—one in five—take all three basic science courses."[596]

Social studies replaced history, which pushes political activism rather than an examination of the founding of America and our rich history. Of course, this dumbing down is partly due to the diminishment of student reading levels.

Consider an illustration of the reading problem used by Bernstein.

"The 1922 Texas high school reading list for the ninth grade included such works as [James F.] Cooper's *The Last of the Mohicans* and [Walter] Scott's *Ivanhoe*; the estimated grade levels for the list ranged from 8.0 to 12.9. By contrast, the 2015–16 ninth grade reading list includes Sandra Cisneros's *The House on Mango Street* and Rodman Philbrick's *Freak the Mighty*; the estimated grade levels for this list range from 4.5 to 6.7."[597] It is, therefore, appalling but not surprising that, as eminent scholar Richard Pipes reports, applicants for his freshman seminar at Harvard University are 'almost totally unfamiliar with the world's great literature.'"[598]

The problem is deeper because we now have public teachers who are no longer masters of their subject. Yes, they took plenty of "education" courses in college, but very few courses on the very topics which they are hired to teach: English, math, reading, and science. Bernstein wrote, "English teachers…had taken few literature courses, had never read the books they were now teaching, and were ill-equipped to interpret them."[599]

Progressives ruined America's public schools. They dumbed down academics in order to push their social reengineering agenda that suits their overall progressive philosophy of life. The ramifications are very serious, have already impacted our nation's competitiveness, and likely could contribute to making America globally irrelevant in the coming decades.

What Are Progressives' Plans for Our Educational Institution in the Future?

Progressive disciples promise to fix the educational system their ideological forefathers broke in order to make America more competitive. This is an empty promise but as seen in prior chapters progressives will use big government, lots of regulation and the public trough to fuel their dead-end agenda.

Below are progressive education policy proposals likely to be pushed by 2020 progressive (read "Democratic Party") presidential candidates.

Contemporary progressives argue that educational opportunity is one of their defining values—especially now, because the economic benefits of education are so obvious. Evidently, they perceive the need to better educate future workers because job creation appears to trend toward a larger portion of jobs requiring some postsecondary training or college degrees. Meanwhile, the share of jobs in industries that require no postsecondary training are shrinking and will continue to do so in the future.

Therefore, pathways leading to high-wage jobs and careers are important goals for our education system. That is why the Center for American Progress (CAP) espouses the following seven progressive education policies "to revitalize the American dream." Anticipate 2020 progressive candidates to embrace each.

First, CAP recommends that the taxpayer "provide a tutor for every child performing below grade level." The US education system must "scale up" tutoring through a variety of mechanisms to provide a high-quality tutoring experience for students performing below grade level. This proposal would be at taxpayer expense.[600]

This is another big progressive government program. In fact, the No Child Left Behind Act of 2001 included a tutoring program known as Supplemental Education Services (SES). While perhaps good in concept, it has problems, such as low participation rates and lack of quality control. There are scandals involving tutoring providers who overcharge, hire tutors with criminal records, or violate regulations. Tutoring services were phased out of Department of Education programs, and have now been totally scrapped under the Every Student Succeeds Act.

At what point should parents of low-performing students be expected to step in to provide for supplemental help for their children? That seems to be lost on progressives who believe big government is the failsafe solution when the burden ought to fall squarely on the parents' shoulders.

Second, CAP recommends our school systems "offer free breakfast and lunch for all students, regardless of income." Yes, there is already a school lunch program, but progressives argue that a low-income student program creates a stigma and shames many students from participating, especially at the high school level. So, progressives want free breakfast and lunch—including in the summer months—for all students, regardless of income. CAP argues that forty-one million Americans, including thirteen million children, have insufficient food to eat. Meeting student nutritional needs is important for learning and the taxpayer ought to pay.[601]

Why is the taxpayer burdened with providing free meals for children from all economic sectors? This is an example of an out-of-control system that fails to understand any constraints on the taxpayers' willingness to subsidize a poorly run institution.

Third, CAP recommends a policy that ensures "opportunities to combine college preparatory academics with technical training and workplace experience." This recommendation reflects the progressive idea that tailors the education experience to the student's intellectual capabilities. On the surface that's appropriate, but isn't that already what public schools are supposed to do? Why do we need yet another big government program?[602]

At what point should students, with their parents' counsel, chart their own academic future? Certainly by high school, most students know their proclivities and likely whether they will excel academically or are better suited for job-related technical training.

Fourth, CAP recommends transitioning "to a 9-to-5 school day to better fit parents' needs." That sounds logical, because parents working outside the home—both two-income and one-income/one parent households—are the norm today, and their work hours seldom coincide with the median school day that ends at 2:50 PM. But that puts the public school and by association the taxpayer in the business of providing childcare—before and after school—which is already a significant drain on the taxpayer. Further, progressives want children at school, at taxpayers' expense, longer to increase the economic productivity of parents by reducing the time they take off from work to accommodate their children's schedules. That means the schools are mostly responsible for raising tomorrow's children, more so than their parents. That may please progressives who dislike the family and believe government can do a better job.[603]

Fifth, CAP calls for more resources to "support, train, and pay teachers like professionals." It is true that teachers are not paid as well as many other professionals. The average pay for a new teacher is $38,617, while the average gross salary of all American teachers is $58,950.[604] That is only 60 percent of the average salary of similarly trained educational professionals in other Western countries. No wonder many young people avoid the teaching profession.

Granted, the teacher isn't paid as well as other professions. But the problem isn't necessarily that school systems lack sufficient taxpayer investments. Too much of the education pie goes to overhead and administration and not enough goes to those doing the actual teaching. Cut some of that overhead and pay the actual teachers more.

Sixth, CAP calls for creating "a safe and healthy environment in every school." What parent wouldn't endorse that recommendation? However, this is another progressive agenda issue. CAP wants a cadre of specialists—counselors, social workers, and psychologists—to help socially reengineer the next generation. For the progressive, the school, as opposed to the family, is the center for addressing every issue, such as mental health, violence, poverty, drug use, sex, delinquency, and more.

It's all about Big Brother superintending every aspect of the children's lives and socializing them to fit the progressives' ideal, compliant citizens.[605]

Seventh, CAP calls for a school infrastructure program. CAP states that nearly fourteen million American students attend schools that need extensive repairs or complete replacement. No doubt school infrastructure is an ongoing concern, and like any other public buildings, schools must be maintained. One estimate claims that addressing deferred maintenance and repairs for our public schools would cost about $200 billion.[606]

CAP's seven public school-related proposals are evidently insufficient for some progressive political leaders. Consider what two leading progressives have in mind beyond CAP's education proposals.

US Senator Elizabeth Warren has a host of recommendations regarding education, beginning with student loans. She said the federal government is making too much money on the student-loan portfolio and proposed in April 2019 a plan to cancel the majority of student loan debt. She also wants to improve and support education from pre-K to college, preserve Head Start and the school lunch programs, promote comprehensive sex education, improve mentoring programs, and invest in education, infrastructure, and research at public schools.[607]

In early 2019 Senator Warren urged that "affordable and high-quality child care and early education should be a right, not a privilege reserved for the rich." She proposed to tax the "ultra-millionaires—those with a net worth of more than $50 million—" to pay for this new "right."[608]

The problem with Warren's proposal is not just the cost but the fact that high-quality daycare is both rare and can be harmful, particularly for boys. A Tennessee study found that children enrolled in "quality day care" fell behind their peers by third grade. "You have school systems that are pushing pre-K when they have demonstrably failing K-12 systems," Dale Farran, one of the authors of the FiveThirtyEight study. "It makes me cringe."[609]

Socialist presidential candidate Senator Bernie Sanders seeks to create the best-educated workforce in the world and intends to fight to make sure that every American who studies hard in school can go to college, regardless of how much money their parents make and without going into debt. That's a worthy goal, but the problem is in the details. Who pays?

Sanders agrees with Warren that the federal government should be out of the profit-making business on student loans. He claims it is morally wrong and bad economics.[610] That's why he calls for free tuition for all, a view he evidently shares with Senator Warren.

Sanders points out that other countries like Germany and Finland fund college tuition so as not to discourage would-be students from going to college. Of course, as Sanders knows, the Germans have a progressive school system that early on directs students to trade schools, college, or nowhere. This is much like how early twentieth-century progressive American education officials used the IQ test to redirect students.[611]

It is noteworthy that the British Eleven-Plus examination system is similar to what Sanders recommends, a sort of IQ test to get ahead. The British administer a test to students that governs their admission to grammar schools and other secondary schools. The British "grammar school" is a secondary school that offers an academic course in preparation for university entrance and for the professions."[612]

Critics of the British Eleven-Plus system claim there is a strong class bias in the examination to become eligible for "grammar school." One study found that "children on the borderline of passing were more likely to get grammar school places if they came from middle-class families," according to David Kynaston, a British historian.[613] Another critic, Richard Hoggart, a British sociologist, claims that "what happens in thousands of homes is that the Eleven-Plus examination is identified in the minds of parents, not with 'our Jimmy is a clever lad and he's going to have his talents trained,' but 'our Jimmy is going to move into another class, he's going to get a white-collar job' or something like that."[614]

What Can Be Done?

Henry Louis Mencken was an American journalist, essayist, satirist, and scholar known for his work, *The American Language*, a study of the English language. Mencken concluded "that a startling and dramatic improvement in American education required only that we hang all the professors and burn down the schools."[615]

Richard Mitchell wrote in 1981 that Mencken's "moderate proposal" was "nothing more than cosmetic and would in fact provide only an outward appearance of improvement. Those who knew less, on the other hand, had somewhat more elaborate plans of their own, and they just happened to be in charge of the schools."[616]

There is no shortage of critics of our educational establishment, and every new presidential administration promises to do something about the mess but never does. Arthur Bestor, an American historian and noted critic of American public education, labeled the colleges of education and the federal and state departments of education an "interlocking directorate" that champions a vision and philosophy "they will never renounce."[617]

Predictably, the education establishment rejects outside help. Bernstein cites the example of three Nobel laureates in science who offered to design at no charge California's K-12 science curriculum. California's progressive state education officials turned down the gratis offer and then hired "professional educators" with no science training for $178,000 to develop a science curriculum.[618]

It's obvious that the educational establishment is a brick wall, impenetrable to contrary ideas or advice. So, as parents across America have discovered, their only recourse is to circumvent the education "Nazis" with alternatives like home schooling and private schooling.

It isn't surprising that as our nation's public schools continue to fail, the number of homeschoolers is skyrocketing.

US Department of Education researchers reviewed data from the 2016 National Household Education Survey and then mailed printed questionnaires to 206,000 households. They used that survey to estimate the US homeschool population size and demographic characteristics of those parents. The researchers estimated there were 1,689,726 students ages 5–17 in homeschools in 2016, which represented 3.3 percent of all school-age children that year.[619]

That figure may be under reported. But homeschooling and private schooling for those who can afford it or have the patience is a growth industry. Meanwhile, public education gobbles up an ever-increasing portion of our local taxes and then squanders it on a failing, top-heavy, inefficient system.

Parents need to tackle this problem head on. They must insist, for example, that public schools use phonics to teach young children to read and tap into full-time graduate students working on degrees in real subjects like math and science—not education—to tutor their children as well. Parents should call on politicians at the local level to champion intellectual training and rigorous academic curriculum as opposed to progressive social reengineering curricula. Then, parents must go to local school board meetings, talk with the teachers, get elected to the school boards, and make a real difference.

Conclusion

Progressivism ruined our public education system. It will continue the same malfeasance, given the opportunity, as well as drain our coffers—all in the name of "educating" our children. For the sake of our children and America's future, this catastrophe must be stopped, and now. Remember, centralized government control over the education system is the same as thought control. In other words, if you can control the input, the output is preordained.

12

Progressivism's Impact on Religion

Ultimately, America's answer to the intolerant man is diversity, the very diversity which our heritage of religious freedom has inspired.[620]

—Robert F. Kennedy, Sixty-fourth US Attorney General and US Senator from New York

The reader will recall in chapter 10 that Protestant "pietists" aligned themselves with progressives to undermine Catholics and Lutherans in the late nineteenth and early twentieth centuries. That alliance faded soon after the 1912 Progressive Party's convention. However, progressivism's ideology, which revolves around the assumption that human beings are by nature free and equal, also demotes freedom while expanding the domain of equality—especially in the realm of religion. Progressives are a true threat to religious freedom and specifically to the First Amendment.

Progressives' god is big government (and their religion is politics), and they view our constitutional rights (Bill of Rights) as totally malleable, subservient to "science," equality, and the modern times. Thus, the right to publicly live out our faith, which our founders tried to protect via our Constitution, is today the target of progressivism. That is why Christians—and, for that matter, those of all genuine faiths—rightly perceive that progressives embrace policies that tend to be antireligion— that is, except for their own blind obedience to progress and their god, i.e., big government.

This chapter explores the condition of religion in America today and then, especially over the past decade, outlines what progressives have done to our precious religious liberties. Finally, the chapter explores what plans progressives have for America's future regarding the institution of religion with special attention to the First Amendment's guarantee of religious freedom.

Overview of Religion in America Today: Under Siege by Progressives

Progressives reject religion and the protections accorded to people of faith in our Constitution. This is illustrated by their fixed view of God and religion within American society as well as by their nonbiblical view of Christianity.

Progressives redefine God as human freedom achieved through the right political organization or as simply a myth, a view expressed by Dr. Thomas G. West in his book, *The Progressive Revolution in Politics and Political Science*. West, a professor at Hillsdale College, indicates, as noted earlier in this book, that Hegel, whose philosophy strongly influenced early progressives, said: "The state is the divine idea as it exists on earth." John Burgess, a progressive pioneer at Columbia University regarded as "the most influential political scientist of the period (1844–1931)," wrote that the purpose of the state is the "perfection of humanity, the civilization of the world; the perfect development of the human reason and its attainment to universal command over individualism; the apotheosis of man" (man becoming god). Even Walter Rauschenbusch, a Progressive Era theologian, said Christianity is the social gospel of progress.[621]

Juxtapose these progressive views about religion with what French philosopher and observer of the new American republic, Alexis de Tocqueville, said about the anticipated demise of religion at the hands of societal progress. Specifically, de Tocqueville opined that secular prophecies like progressivism (my words) regard "the gradual decay of religious faith" inevitable in society because it "must necessarily fail, the more generally liberty is established and knowledge is diffused."[622]

Contemporary progressives would agree that the religious community will fail, as de Tocqueville said, and they are contributing to that failure. This becomes self-evident as the tension mounts between the religious community at large that adheres to their faith's teachings while rejecting public moral standards pushed by the progressive culture with the help of big government.

This phenomenon is especially evident among our youth. Specifically, we see progressivism clouding the discernment about moral issues among the Millennial generation, those born in 1977 through 1994. It is no secret that the importance of religion has diminished among Millennials, an outcome that pleases progressives and bolsters de Tocqueville's dire prediction.

Typically, children follow their parents' choice of religion, but when that faith is not reinforced by the culture and the school—which is generally the case today—then religion's value for the young person fades with time. Of course, students educated in private, faith-based schools or taught at home by religious parents tend to maintain and understand the relevance of faith for their lives. They are then more likely to live out that faith in the public eye. Arguably, they are what Jesus said: "You are the salt of the earth.... You are the light of the world" (Matthew 5:13–14, NIV).

It isn't surprising, given today's amoral culture that Millennials tend to create their own path in life, seeking what makes them happy and doing what they want, a drastic departure from their parents' generation. The older generations tended to embrace tradition, making themselves good citizens by emulating their parents. That's not the course taken by many Millennials, especially regarding their religious heritage.

"And more than any other group, Millennials have been and are still being formed in this cultural context," Michael Hout, a sociology professor at New York University said. "As a result, they are more likely to have a 'do-it-yourself' attitude toward religion."[623]

"Do-it-yourself" Millennials accept different communities, such as homosexuals, likely opposed by their parents. That's an example of the influence progressivism brings to the culture. They may ask: If a religion discriminates instead of loving all, how can Millennials support that view? The accepting attitude of the Millennial generation tends on the whole to differ from many mainline religious teachings on a number of significant issues beyond homosexuality.

A twenty-year-old English literature college junior explained this view of religion in *UWIRE:*

> Millennials are finding religion in their own way. Some find it in music by attending music festivals and dressing freely. Some find it in knowledge, becoming well-read individuals and striving to obtain higher levels of education. Spirituality is attractive for all ages, though the definition of spirituality differs. If the older generations want religion to remain important for the millennial generation, then it should be progressive and change with the times.[624]

Indeed, Millennials and other young Americans are changing with the times. The Barna Group, a research organization that tracks the role of faith in America, confirms progressivism's impact on America's youth, particularly regarding faith. Over time, reports Barna, the consensus on key moral principles is that young Americans are moving to religious apathy. In fact, Barna states, "The leading edge of Gen Z (those born in the mid-1990s to mid-2000s), along with Millennials, appear to hold notably different views about morality than earlier generations."[625]

Barna details that generational shift in the moral compass of young Americans. One-quarter of Gen Z (24 percent) strongly agree that what is morally right and wrong changes over time based on society, a true progressive view. Not surprisingly, there is a wide generational divide on this view; twice as many Gen Z than Boomers (those born 1946 to 1964) embrace this view. In fact, 21 percent of Gen Z and 23 percent of Millennials believe each individual is his or her own moral authority. One teen in a Barna focus group said, "Society changes, and what's good or bad changes as well. It is all relative to what's happening in the world." We have the likes of progressive education leader John Dewey and his disciples to thank for promoting that view across the contemporary academy.[626]

Predictably, Barna found progressive views among Gen Z regarding specific moral issues. Gen Z is the most progressive on abortion; almost three in ten believe it is wrong while four in ten feel a strong conviction that marriage ought to be a lifelong commitment between a man and woman. On other issues such as sex before marriage, only one-fifth of Gen Z believe it is wrong. Further, they are least likely to take issue with same-sex sexual activity; only one-fifth (20 percent) is strongly opposed to it.[627]

Thankfully, religious faith continues to have a significant impact on moral beliefs. Barna found belief that lying is wrong is the most commonly shared moral sentiment among faith segments, next to marriage as a lifelong commitment between a man and a woman. However, the greatest differences were over sexuality. More than three-quarters of engaged Christians believe sex before marriage (76 percent) and homosexual behavior are morally wrong (77 percent), compared to only fractions of those with no faith (5 percent and 4 percent respectively) and one-quarter of churched Christians (25 percent and 24 percent respectively).[628]

Progressives' impact on American culture is on full display as outlined above. Our next generation has in large numbers bought into a progressive worldview that is troubling, especially with regard to our freedom of religion, which is under assault.

What Have Progressives Done in the Past That
Impacted the Institution of Religion?

Religious freedom is under attack, and Christians, at least for now, are bearing the brunt of that fight. However, progressives' aim, Peter Berkowitz, a scholar at the Hoover Institute, wrote in the *Hoover Digest*, is to "supplant respect for the diversity of religious belief with a homogenizing doctrine that punishes the expression of traditional faith and compels the practice of a secular faith."[629]

Evidence of this serious challenge is too familiar within contemporary culture such as a wedding photographer fined for declining to photograph a same-sex commitment ceremony; a baker refusing to make a cake for a gay wedding; a pharmacist sanctioned for refusing to fill "emergency" abortifacient prescriptions; a faith-based adoption agency threatened with losing its license for declining to place a child with a homosexual couple; and Hobby Lobby and other Christian-owned companies facing sanctions for refusing to cover contraception in employee health insurance.

These clashes between mostly Bible-believing Christians and big government backed by progressives are right now mostly limited to issues of sex and morality. However, the faith community verses progressive conflict is likely to get much deeper and has very significant implications for America's religious community and all our constitutionally guaranteed rights.

You see, progressivism's assault on people with biblical faith brings to this ideological battle an alliance of many likeminded partners: media, the entertainment industry, universities, many major city governments, and the Democratic Party which promote equality, demanding social justice and using big government to enforce their views. They look down their collective noses to label people with biblical world views as bigoted, racist, and homophobic.[630]

Progressives assume all human beings are naturally free and equal, but they allow equality to trump freedom, and that's a problem when it comes to the First Amendment's guarantee of religious freedom.[631] Equality is the dictating principle with religious behavior codes taking a backseat under all situations.

They also view the US Constitution as antiquated, antidemocratic and unjust. Therefore big government must use its might to do all that is good in progressive eyes which means take sides when equality and religious freedom are at loggerheads.[632]

So the question for the faithful should not be whether equality is good, but which form or forms of equality are morally relevant and which should government protect. That's critical for Bible-believing people who are awake to what is happening in modern America.[633]

Scholar Douglas Laycock, a professor at the University of Virginia School of Law, suggests what is at stake here. He explains that many progressives are really aiming much deeper, beyond particular religious-based objections to "question the free exercise of religion in principle—suggesting that [it] maybe a bad idea, or at least, a right to be minimized."[634]

For now, the progressives are focused on redefining religious freedom but that's just the beginning and given the opportunity they will "minimize" our religious liberty as well. Bruce Abramson, director of policy at the Iron Dome Alliance and a senior fellow with the London Center, wrote an outstanding article for the magazine *Mosiac*, "The Decline—and Fall?—of Religious Freedom in America." Abramson argues that Christians are presently bearing the brunt of the religious liberty fight. However, "if freedom falls for those Christians, it will likely fall for all." Mr. Abramson is Jewish.[635]

Abramson acknowledges America's form of government, which is steeped in classical liberalism, due to our Constitution, which established religion with the individual's freedom to choose and follow his faith. That was intentional because some of our founders and their ancestors migrated from Europe to escape state religious monopolies, where there was no religious liberty. America, as a result of our founders, therefore became a competitive religious marketplace where one can select from competing churches, synagogues, mosques or any variety of spiritual offerings or none at all. Religious liberty was very important to our founders.[636]

A competitive religious marketplace is good for all Americans even today because traditional and nontraditional religions thrive side-by-side, protected by our First Amendment. Each person is free to live according to the teachings of his faith. Naturally our founders anticipated people would have conflicting opinions about ultimate questions—life, death, salvation—and therefore they sought to protect minority views and their associated behaviors from headstrong majorities. However, that Constitutional safeguard depends on a fundamental countrywide unity: "Only a citizenry in the habit of tolerating a multiplicity of outlooks and ways of life—and in the habit of recognizing one another as equal in freedom—will be capable of honoring constitutional imperatives and effectively operating the organs of constitutional government," explained Berkowitz.[637]

Thus our founders created an environment where we are free to follow our faith-based convictions within the culture, and government is not to intrude. But that freedom is now under attack from progressives.[638]

Progressives are leading the charge at every turn to force big government and by association the larger popular culture to rethink America's relationship between church and state. Evidence of that rethinking is heard over the airwaves and read in print from people like Wisconsin Senator Tammy Baldwin (D) who threatens our religious freedom. She opined: "The First Amendment says that in institutions of faith there is absolute power to, you know, observe deeply held religious beliefs. But I don't think it extends far beyond that."[639]

The good senator missed the mark and certainly her statement is not congruent with our founders' intent. The First Amendment makes no such narrow guarantee—freedom of worship. No, it's much broader and guarantees, as Abramson argues, the free exercise of religion which "explicitly includes the right to lead a faith-based life and to behave in a manner that faith dictates and eschew choices that faith prohibits. The distinction between the two concepts is profound."[640]

This profound distinction is clear when contemporary mores and religious precepts are at odds. Under those circumstances, it is then appropriate to ask: When should secular law tolerate individual behavior motivated by contradictory religious teachings? Abramson correctly responds: "The right to exercise our faith freely means the right to follow a minority moral code…or it means nothing."[641]

Until recently the First Amendment recognized that right but no longer. Today, the right to exercise our faith freely is moving rapidly to mean "nothing." The change started to come about with the Supreme Court case *Oregon v. Smith, 494 U.S. 872* (1990). That case is about two members of a Native American church who lost their jobs for ingesting the sacramental hallucinogenic peyote, a banned substance in Oregon.[642]

The question before the high court was "Does the free exercise clause of the First Amendment protect a person's participation in a religious ceremony that violates an individual state's general criminal laws?" Justice Antonin Scalia wrote for the court's majority that Oregon could have created a religious exemption for religiously-based peyote use, but he concluded, the state was under no constitutional obligation to do so and further, even though the free exercise clause prevents states from targeting religious practices, the Constitution does not exempt the faithful (the native church members) from following the law. The court ruled against the Native Americans.[643]

Justice Harry Blackmun dissented from the majority in *Smith* to argue:

This Court over the years painstakingly has developed a consistent and exacting standard to test the constitutionality of a state statute that burdens the free exercise of religion. Such a statute may stand only if the law in general and the state's refusal to allow a religious exemption in particular, are justified by a compelling interest that cannot be served by less restrictive means.[644]

Justice Blackmun's dissent triggered Congress to draft the 1993 Religious Freedom Restoration Act (RFRA), which prevents state law from infringing on religious practice except as a last resort. The bill passed both chambers of Congress and President Bill Clinton signed RFRA into law.[645]

Clinton said at the RFRA signing ceremony:

> We all have a shared desire here to protect perhaps the most precious of all American liberties, religious freedom…. The free exercise of religion has been called the first freedom, that which originally sparked the development of the full range of the Bill of Rights. Our founders cared a lot about religion…. They knew that there needed to be a space of freedom between government and people of faith that otherwise government might usurp…. Let us…respect one another's faiths, fight to the death to preserve the right of every American to practice whatever convictions he or she has, but bring our values back to the table of American discourse to heal our troubled land.[646]

Until this decade (2010–2019), the consensus was that government should "carve narrow exemptions for religious believers from any but the most critical of our laws." That narrow exemption began to crumble in 2010 with the passage of President Obama's legacy healthcare policy, the Affordable Care Act, aka Obamacare.[647]

Obamacare created a fight between religious rights and the progressives' abortion rights. The Obama administration mandated that employers provide employees the full range of contraceptives, including abortifacients (abortion inducing drugs). Christian employers like Hobby Lobby complained that the government's mandate violated their religious views, forcing them to condone the murder of innocent unborn children. Hobby Lobby sought an exemption from the law and, on appeal to the high court, Justice Samuel Alito wrote for the majority that there were ways to meet the government's interest while also satisfying the religious objections. Hobby Lobby's requested waiver was granted.[648]

Predictably, Justice Ruth Bader Ginsburg dissented with a classic progressive interpretation of the dispute. She argued that RFRA only applies to individuals, not to businesses (corporations). "Accommodations to religious beliefs or observances…must not significantly impinge on the interests of third parties," Ginsburg wrote. Her view was that government—the progressive Obama administration at the time— had determined that abortifacients were important for women's health, therefore employers had an obligation to make them available, and religious accommodations were inappropriate.[649]

The progressive elite jumped on the bandwagon to echo Justice Ginsburg's view, thus jeopardizing RFRA's future. Meanwhile, numerous states passed their own version of RFRA and progressives like Tim Cook, CEO of Apple, complained about the states' rush to protect the religious. Cook wrote in the *Washington Post*:

> There's something very dangerous happening in states across the country. A wave of legislation…would allow people to discriminate against their neighbors. Some…say individuals can cite their personal religious beliefs to refuse service to a customer or resist a state nondiscrimination law.[650]

Cook's alleged discrimination complaint became the bogyman that fueled the progressives' anti-RFRA movement. But the truth of the matter was that RFRA created a simple test in order to prevail against big government's infringement on a citizen's religious liberty: "Either a law does not serve a compelling government interest or a narrow waiver would not harm government interest," explained Abramson.[651]

Cook's caricature of RFRA laws as "allow[ing] people to discriminate against their neighbors" energized the progressives. This anti-RFRA rabble claimed the federal and state laws allow religious believers to follow their own moral codes, which progressive opponents said was immoral because it abused equality, the more important societal principle.[652]

Homosexuality is a progressive test-bed for the anti-RFRA cabal as well. Progressives attacked the RFRA law as it applied to Christians seeking protection from support for so-called gay marriage, a political issue as incendiary as abortion.

The reader will recall a number of high-profile Christian bakers and photographers were caught in progressives' crosshairs because the faithful declined on religious grounds to support homosexual marriage. When they made that claim regarding homosexual marriage (e.g., photographing, making a cake for), they faced human-rights, discrimination charges—and some were even driven out of business.[653]

One of the targets of the anti-RFRA, pro-homosexual cadre was Memories Pizza, a Christian shop in northern Indiana that boasted a sign that read: "Every day before we open the store, we gather and pray together. If there is something you would like us to pray for, just write it down and drop it in the box and we will pray for you." The proprietor had never been asked to cater any wedding and had never refused to serve any customer. However, when a reporter explicitly asked whether she would participate in a gay marriage, she said: "We don't like gay marriages, so we won't go to them."[654]

The proprietor's answer was used as proof of her bias, and soon venomous attacks landed on Memories Pizza, forcing it to close. The attackers followed Tim Cook's prescriptive argument against RFRA, claiming they "have great reverence for religious freedom," but it is the Christians who regarded "their feelings by persisting in an immoral preference for the dictates of their creed."[655]

The Memories Pizza episode drew considerable attention and certainly contributed to drawing the battle lines leading up to the Supreme Court's *Obergefell v. Hodges, 576 US* (2015) decision that found a constitutional right to marry that includes homosexual couples. Even the deputy director of the American Civil Liberties Union, which previously campaigned for the federal RFRA, called for Congress "to amend the RFRA so that it cannot be used as a defense for discrimination."[656]

Anti-RFRA rabble even invoked a parallel between bakers who refuse to make a wedding cake for a homosexual couple and cafes that once refused to serve blacks. Abramson dismissed the alleged comparison, saying there is a clear difference between a public business and a client who seeks a personalized, customized service. But the silliness of such arguments may no longer be a factor in our upside-down culture.[657]

Abramson warns:

> We have reached a watershed moment in American law, society, and culture: for the first time, avoiding participation in a given event or activity [refusing to make a cake or photograph a wedding] can now be construed as violating someone else's civil (or human) rights—and can be actionable as such—even when the avoidance has been dictated by a religious conviction.[658]

This outcome represents a major shift, especially for people of faith. No longer is it an argument about equal rights, but the offended now seek to "curtail the rights of those deemed responsible for that lack of hospitality." Religious accommodation in a hostile, poison-filled secular culture is becoming more difficult to obtain than ever.[659]

Abramson argues that this shift is really an attack on RFRA, "an explicit, intentional attack on religious freedom." Progressives aim to remove "a safeguard that balances the critical liberal goal of religious freedom with the potentially competing and contradictory critical needs of a liberal society." It creates a quandary for those who are committed to classical American liberalism.[660]

He warns that those attempting to roll back religious freedom want to confine religious conviction—faith-motivated behavior—to "little more than an opinion due no particular deference." Further, citing a religious concern becomes no more than an attempt to escape one's obligations to the broader society, as progressives argue.[661]

Our constitutionally guaranteed freedom of religion crumbles when we refuse people the right to align their lives with the dictates of their faith. Once that falls, then our other rights will follow as well.

What Do Progressives Plan to Do with/to/for
Religion in the Future?

Progressives are gaining power across the nation and once they have the leverage we should expect the worse especially for the mounting assault on the institution of religion. Progressives will use government's power, the courts and their coalition of cultural "elites" to strip away the remaining vestiges of religious freedom for all except their own.

Progressive political power is growing. The left-leaning Brookings Institution announced that nearly half (44 percent) of House primary candidates in 2018 identified themselves as progressives, up from about 29 percent in 2016. That surge of progressive credentials even dominates the Democratic Party's upper rungs of the growing 2020 presidential field, which includes Senators Bernie Sanders (VT), Elizabeth Warren (MA), Kamala Harris (CA), and Cory Booker (NJ), South Bend, Indiana, Mayor Pete Buttigieg, and Representative Beto O'Rourke of Texas, among others.[662]

We should expect the growing cadre of progressives who might eventually gain access to the nation's levers of government to continue pushing their agenda as seen above, especially their radical, anti-religious freedom aim of labeling all discrimination immoral even if it is based on a religious code associated with morally contentious issues such as abortion, homosexuality, and illegal immigration. Unless public behavior satisfies the progressives' litmus of "true equality" for all, then it's immoral in their eyes.

Expect progressives to also call for the impeachment of conservative Supreme Court such as Brett Kavanaugh and replace them with like-minded, socialist-leaning judges to the high court who will consider our Constitution outmoded, a malleable document that must be updated to fit their radical views, and then expect anti-First Amendment religious liberty decisions to completely void the remaining vestiges of our religious freedom.

Worse, progressives will insist that everyone worship their god—

the all-powerful state. Big government is the progressives' god that determines right and wrong and what is moral and immoral, tramples on religious freedom in the name of equality, and destroys anyone or entity that may disagree.

Dr. Roger Taylor, a private practice medical doctor, writes in *First Things* a compelling case that progressivism is indeed a religion that seeks to push all others to the sidelines. Progressivism, he says, has sacred texts (like the Communist Manifesto); a clergy at left-leaning universities, in Hollywood, and a growing political cabal; a heaven— perfect man building a utopia on earth; a doctrine (that includes same-sex marriage, many genders, abortion on demand, and euthanasia); and follows the long tradition of Islam believing that the whole world should be converted to their religion or die.[663]

Conclusion

Converting America to the "religion" of progressivism requires the destruction of our Constitution and calls for principled people of faith to sit on the sidelines and do nothing. That's what progressives expect. If you want to regulate every aspect of individual lives, you must gain control over religious thought and practice. Communist regimes learned that they cannot totally wipe out religion, but they can levy requirements to deter its practice and denigrate its effectiveness.

13

Progressivism's Impact on Government

If men were angels, no government would be necessary.
—American Founding Father James Madison[664]

Government is an institution represented by a community of people who agree to a purpose, a set of organizational policies, a mechanism for forming new policies, and a means of enforcement. Government outlines those ingredients in a kind of constitution, a statement of governing principles, and a philosophy that balances those ingredients with individual freedoms.

The purpose of the United States government is found in the Preamble of its Constitution, which states that its goals are to "establish justice, insure domestic tranquility, provide for the common defense, promote the general welfare, and secure the blessings of liberty to ourselves and our posterity." Translation: Government's primary duty is to secure our freedom.

Thus, our founders drafted the Constitution to recognize, as founder James Madison warns above, that men are not angels; rather, they live in "a state of nature, where the weaker individual is not secured against the violence of the stronger." That is why government helps regulate men's behavior to fulfill the purpose outlined in the Preamble.[665]

Indeed, the US Constitution provides the form and structure of our government. It establishes a federal democratic republic, an indivisible union of sovereign states. It is democratic because people govern themselves by electing representatives. The founders also established three principles on which to govern: inherent rights, self-government, and separation of powers.

Our founders, especially the antifederalists, distrusted strong central governments because they tend to turn oppressive. Therefore, the founders designed a set of checks and balances with enough power for government to govern, while containing its urge to trample on the rights of the citizens.

The original American philosophy of governing was captured by the French historian Alexis de Tocqueville in his book, *Democracy in America*. He wrote:

> I think that in no country in the civilized world is less atten-
> tion paid to philosophy than in the United States…. Neverthe-
> less it is easy to perceive that almost all the inhabitants of the
> United States conduct their understanding in the same manner,
> and govern it by the same rules; that is to say, that without ever
> having taken the trouble to define the rules of a philosophical
> method, they are in possession of one, common to the whole
> people. To evade the bondage of system and habit, of family
> maxims, class opinions, and, in some degree, of national preju-
> dices; to accept tradition only as a means of information, and
> existing facts only as a lesson used in doing otherwise, and doing
> better; to seek the reason of things for one's self, and in one's self
> alone; to tend to results without being bound to means, and to
> aim at the substance through the form; —such are the principal
> characteristics of what I shall call the philosophical method of
> the Americans…. [In] most of the operations of the mind, each

American appeals to the individual exercise of his own under-standing alone.[666]

This framework and philosophy of governing is where the American government started in the late eighteenth century, but it changed over the coming century as a result of progressives, as outlined in the first section of this book. Those people, for a variety of reasons (some good), ignored founder Thomas Jefferson's warning to George Washington that "to take a single step beyond the boundaries [of the Constitution]…is to take possession of a boundless field of power."[667] Madison also cautioned that government must "keep close to our chartered authorities."[668]

Both Jefferson and Madison were strict constructionists who believed our Constitution is a contract between the citizens and their government. Any authority assumed by government beyond the enumerated powers is a usurpation of power, unless properly amended. Our Constitution has twenty-seven amendments, of which the first ten are the Bill of Rights and the last one, the Twenty-seventh Amendment, added in 1992 after a long delay, regulates congressional pay rates.

Unfortunately, progressives took great liberties with our Constitution, which they consider a living contract. And, as history shows, they trashed the founders' intent and made a new government out of whole cloth.

This chapter will review the progressives' ideological view of government, the impact they had on our government over the past two centuries plus, the blowback results of their manipulation of our current government, and what they might do given the opportunity with and to government in the future.

What Is the Progressive Ideology Regarding Government?

As a reminder, progressivism is a philosophy based on the idea of progress, the fulfillment of human capacities, which asserts that advancements of science, technology, economic development, and social organization are vital for the improvement of the human condition, which, progressives argue, is the primary task of government.

American progressivism began to take hold in the late nineteenth century as a social movement, but then quickly morphed into a political movement that embraced the view that government was the primary tool for change. As progressive John Dewey wrote, "The state has the responsibility for creating institutions under which individuals can effectively realize the potentialities that are theirs." That means government must address societal ills that hold men back from their potentialities such as corruption, economic inequality, unregulated capitalism and monopolistic corporations, insufficient worker rights, and much more, as illustrated earlier in this volume.[669]

Historian Alonzo Hamby defined American progressivism as the "political movement that addresses ideas, impulses, and issues stemming from modernization of American society [the Industrial Revolution]. Emerging at the end of the nineteenth century, it established much of the tone of American politics throughout the first half of the [twentieth] century."[670]

Early twentieth-century progressives generally shared the view that the existing constitutional system must change into a dynamic instrument aided by science and an administrative bureaucracy. President Woodrow Wilson explained that view: "All that progressives ask or desire is permission—in an era when development, evolution, is a scientific word—to interpret the Constitution according to the Darwinian principle; all they ask is recognition of the fact that a nation is a living thing and not a machine."[671]

Wilson's view was echoed by historian William Leuchtenburg, who observed that progressives had "contempt for the strict construction of the Constitution by conservative judges, who would restrict the power of the national government to act against social evils...the real enemy [according to progressives then and now] was particularism, state rights, limited government."[672]

Progressive icon Louis Brandeis, an associate justice on the Supreme

Court (1916–1939), argued that to make American government better able to serve the peoples' needs, society must make governmental operations and services more efficient and rational. He advocated using "scientific principles" and data produced by social scientists to realize efficiency, even at the expense of democracy, by placing power in the hands of professional bureaucrats. Further, he favored centralized decision-making by those same trained government bureaucrats anticipating more efficiency and less corruption would result.[673]

Walter Lippmann, a twentieth-century American political commentator and reporter, noted that progressives stressed the "scientific spirit" and "discipline of democracy," which inevitably led to a strong central government guided by experts rather than public opinion.[674]

Thus, the political progressive movement created our present government: giant with a bloated bureaucracy armed with innumerable regulations, an alphabet soup of agencies, and an out-of-control deficit ($21 trillion and growing), as well as a host of public ills now burdening our founders' vision of limited government of the people.

What Did Progressives Do to Our Founders' Vision for American Government?

Post-Civil War Americans tended to share a common set of beliefs about the purpose of government, much as outlined above. However, that view began to change, albeit gradually, and by the late nineteenth century, progressive views increased. Then, by the mid twentieth century, contemporary liberalism (progressivism) dominated American politics.

That transformation was accompanied by a litany of progressive government interventions such as trust busting, Constitutional amendments, and the introduction of big social programs like Social Security. The result was the installation of big government that became an agent for transferring wealth and dabbling into every aspect of the citizens' lives.

By the mid-1960s, President Lyndon B. Johnson's Great Society initiative became a true national-level social re-engineering experiment, far more than was FDR's Social Security program. In fact, LBJ's Great Society was created to reshape the behavior of the poor with the objective of moving them off the welfare rolls, another progressive initiative that failed in time.[675]

Decades later, another progressive president showed similar social reengineering plans. President Obama's promised "transformation of America" initiatives like Obamacare were made possible by progressive advances that came well before him, such as LBJ's Great Society, FDR's New Deal, and Wilson's achievements such as the national income tax, the Federal Reserve Act, and the Federal Trade Commission Act.

These big-government initiatives earned more attention, but progressives really had much more impact at the state and local government level, especially in the movement's early years.

Progressive structural changes to state and local governments came under the banner of direct democracy. Those early progressives opposed founder James Madison's concern about the tyranny of the majority, an issue mentioned in the last chapter especially regarding freedom of religion. Our founders were aware of passionate majorities in history that made decisions that adversely impacted minorities. Even founder Thomas Jefferson warned that "elective despotism was not the government we fought for."[676]

Madison also warned that the majority might use the democratic process to expropriate the minority's wealth. The consequence he feared would lead to the demise of government because it failed to protect all citizens, both majority and minority.

The founders believed our Constitution, with its checks and balances and an independent judiciary, were enough of a firewall against the tyranny of either the majority or the minority to protect against a rising abusive government. However, President Theodore Roosevelt took issue with that view when he said: "I have scant patience with this talk of the tyranny of the majority.... We are today suffering from the tyranny of minorities." He insisted the citizens were calling on government to protect them by regulating corporations and propertied interests. But the government, Roosevelt believed, was too displaced by the founders' design from what the people needed to protect their interests.[677]

That view fueled early progressive efforts, especially at the state and local levels, to go around institutions that stood between popular opinion and government action.

Herbert Croly, editor of the *New Republic*, influenced Roosevelt to rejoin national politics in 1912 to become the Progressive Party's presidential candidate because of his belief that genuine democracy had to be achieved by going around political institutions. After all, late nineteenth- and early twentieth-century politics were dominated by corrupt bosses and political machines, which forced the public to seek alternative routes to political justice against abusive minorities with influence over the levers of government.[678]

Croly had faith in voters to govern directly, and he rejected Madison's view that representative government was sufficient to mitigate their interests. Croly wrote in *Progressive Democracy*:

> Public opinion has a thousand methods of seeking information and obtaining definite and effective expression which it did not have four generations ago.... Under such conditions the discussions which take place in a congress or a parliament no longer possess their former function. They no longer create and guide what public opinion there is. Their purpose rather is to provide a mirror for public opinion.[679]

Thus, Croly and other progressive luminaries called on state legislatures and local governments to listen to popular opinion rather than moneyed special interests. That popular clamor led to the enactment of the ballot initiative, popular referendum by which a measure approved by the state legislature could be rejected by the voters, and the recall, by which officeholders could be ousted before the end of their terms.

Another issue that bothered citizens was lawmaker allegiance to their unelected political party leaders and not to the voters. Progressives won the right to have party primaries to reduce the power of political parties and tie political candidates more closely to the voters.[680]

Theodore Roosevelt was genuinely concerned at the time about the minority thwarting the majority's will. He expressed concern particularly about special interests:

> No sane man who has been familiar with the government of this country for the last twenty years will complain that we have had too much of the rule of the majority. The trouble has been a far different one—that, at many times and in many localities, there have held public office in the States and in the Nation men who have, in fact, served not the whole people but some special class or special interest.[681]

Roosevelt also called for popular referenda on key state judicial decisions. He argued that the courts were not carrying out the will of the people as he saw it, and he argued that meant the institutions—courts—had to give way.[682]

Woodrow Wilson agreed with Roosevelt and Croly regarding direct democracy, especially the direct primary, the initiative, the referendum, the recall, and the direct election of senators. Further, Wilson believed that a minority was pushing for a strict interpretation of the Constitution that disadvantaged the majority. He argued that the state legislatures had become corrupt and needed to be fixed.

"You must admit," Wilson said, "that it is a little inconvenient sometimes to have what has been called an astronomical system of government, in which you can't change anything until there has been a certain number of revolutions of the seasons."[683] Wilson and many other progressives saw these direct democracy measures as necessary to make public institutions accountable to the voters.

These state and local progressive successes brought more accountability, but with the exception of the direct election of senators, none of these measures was to hold the federal government to account.

So the federal government, to the pleasure of progressives, became their tool that eventually came to violate the very concerns that motivated them to link state and local government to voters—recall, referendum, and initiatives. Unfortunately, there remains no such mechanism at the federal level, which explains perhaps the expansive federal government we have today.

The Blowback of Progressivism

Progressive national government administrations created a monstrous federal system that reflects the very things early progressives opposed. Those early progressives promised to fight corruption, seek democratic reforms, and make government more efficient and accountable. Today's US federal government is just the opposite.

The contemporary American federal government is corrupt, seized by political correctness; fiscally irresponsible; overregulated by a cadre of elite, very powerful and arguably unaccountable bureaucrats; and terribly bloated.

Even though today's federal government violates the very principles espoused by early progressives, contemporary progressives are guilty of using the current federal system to pursue their ends in stark contrast to our rights and in violation of the founding principles: inherent rights, self-government and separation of powers.

Consider some of the symptoms of our out of control government that serve progressive ambitions today.

GOVERNMENT CORRUPTION

Progressives long claimed to oppose government corruption, especially those in the late nineteenth and early twentieth centuries. They called out political machines that were led by corrupt organizations like New York City's William Magear Tweed, widely known as "Boss" Tweed, who controlled the political machine called Tammany Hall. Tweed's control of the Democratic Party's political machine in New York ultimately landed him in jail after he was convicted of stealing up to $45 million from the city's coffers through political corruption. Tammany Hall, under the "Boss," controlled the outcome of elections by his ability to ensure voter loyalty through jobs created on city projects.[684]

Understandably early progressives worked to end such misconduct, which was chronicled by writers such as Lincoln Steffens, who wrote in *Shame of the Cities* about the goings-on in cities like New York.

Unfortunately, fraud in government at all levels is not a new phenomenon, in spite of progressive calls to end practices that contribute to the problem. Consider the record of the administration of the most recent progressive president, Barack Obama.

President Obama claimed, "We're probably the first administration in modern history that hasn't had a major scandal in the White House." He must be blind.[685] His presidency will be remembered for the IRS scandal that targeted pro-life and Tea Party groups (and even the kingpin Lois Lerner, who escaped any accountability by "taking the Fifth" and running off to her taxpayer-funded retirement); the Veteran Administration's deadly medical appointment waiting list for veterans; Hillary Clinton's illegal use of an unsecured, hackable, home-brewed server for her official duties as secretary of state; and, of course, Attorney General Eric Holder's "Fast and Furious" gun-running program.

Attorney General Holder fought Congress over his illegal gun-running disgrace, and in the end, he was found to be in "contempt of Congress." That operation contributed to the murder of hundreds of Mexican citizens and some US Border Patrol officers with weapons supplied by the US government.

Indeed, some of Obama's deputies were terribly corrupt. After all, Clinton's State Department enjoyed a *quid pro quo* relationship with the family business, the Clinton Foundation, via a "pay to play" arrangement. Specifically, according to Republicans on the House Oversight Committee in December 2018, the Clinton Foundation enjoyed sky-high donations while Ms. Clinton was in office and then the contribution amounts plunged once she left the Department of State. Tax documents show that the Clinton Foundation took in $26.6 million in 2017, a 58 percent drop from the $62.9 million the prior year.

North Carolina Republican Representative Mark Meadows, then chairman of the House Oversight and Government Reform Subcommittee on Government Operations, said at a hearing: "Now several reports suggest that the decrease in donations [to the Clinton Foundation] could reflect a 'pay to play' activity in the years prior to the decline in donations."[686]

Tom Fitton, president of Judicial Watch, testified that the Clinton Foundation received "staggering sums" of money from Saudi benefactors, estimated between $18 million and $50 million. He added: "While Mrs. Clinton was secretary of state, [former president] Bill Clinton gave two speeches in Saudi Arabia earning a total of $600,000."[687]

Also don't forget the Clinton Foundation's relationship with a mysterious Russian billionaire with close ties to Russian President Vladimir Putin. Viktor Vekselberg at the time was in charge of Secretary Clinton's "Russian reset," and as part of that "reset," Clinton helped create "a major technology transfer initiative" that undermined our nation's security, according to Peter Schweizer, the president of the Government Accountability Institute and author of *Clinton Cash*.[688]

Clinton's "reset" created "Skolkovo," Russia's copycat Silicon Valley, which encouraged US firms to help Moscow with technology and investment and in spite of both the FBI and State Department warnings that Russia was getting access through Clinton's initiative to sensitive military technologies.[689]

Just as the "Skolkovo" project got off the ground, former President Bill Clinton traveled to Russia to deliver a speech for a cool $500,000, a fee paid by a mysterious source known as "Renaissance Capital." While in Moscow delivering the speech, Clinton met with Vekselberg, among other Russian movers and shakers.[690]

Unfortunately, the mainstream media and the Democratic Party ignored these scandals because they seem to be joined at the hip when it comes to ignoring progressives' corruption, even when exposed to clear manipulations of the truth.

The Obama administration had a track record of lying to the public as well. Recall the news accounts that fifty intelligence analysts claimed their reports about the Islamic State threat were watered down by Obama officials to mislead the public about the danger posed by the terrorist group?[691]

Also remember the Benghazi scandal, whereby Obama officials—especially then US Ambassador to the United Nations Susan Rice—misled the public on Sunday talk shows to claim the Libya operation was a big success? Even Hillary Clinton, secretary of state at that time, abandoned our ambassador, his staff, and CIA personnel to their death and later lied about what happened. In congressional testimony, Clinton excused the manipulation of the facts: "Was it [the attack that killed Americans in Benghazi] because of a protest [which Rice and Clinton claimed] or was it because of guys out for a walk one night who decided that they'd go kill some Americans? What difference at this point does it make?"[692]

No one can forget how sore loser Clinton and her progressive friends and deeply embedded federal government bureaucrats targeted Donald Trump, the duly elected president. During the campaign, Clinton created and paid for the infamous fictitious "Steele dossier," which claimed that Trump committed collusion with the Russians (never proven even though thoroughly investigated by Congress and a special counsel). Of course, the mainstream media licked their chops to continue the attacks against Trump in spite of contrary evidence. Even the deep state's corrupt FBI officials rushed to Clinton's side with spin and cover-ups, and worse.

Former FBI Deputy Director Andrew McCabe admitted that after

President Trump fired his boss, FBI Director James Comey, agency senior officials actually discussed invoking the Twenty-fifth Amendment to remove Mr. Trump from office. That amendment deals with issues related to presidential succession and disability, and clarifies that the vice president becomes president should the president die, resign, or be removed from office.

McCabe told CBS' *60 Minutes*, "There were meetings at the Justice Department at which it was discussed whether the vice president and a majority of the Cabinet could be brought together to remove the president of the United States under the Twenty-fifth Amendment," according to the program's host.[693]

Those discussions allegedly took place in May 2017, just prior to the appointment of Special Counsel Robert Mueller to oversee the probe into Russian interference in the 2016 election. In fact, Deputy Attorney General Rod Rosenstein at the time even suggested he might secretly record Mr. Trump by wearing a hidden microphone while at a White House meeting.[694]

Then there is the seldom-mentioned case of Hillary Clinton and her replacement at State, John Kerry, who evidently used their positions to enrich members of their own families at taxpayer expense.

Secretary Kerry's daughter enjoyed insider treatment for her nonprofit group. The *Daily Caller* found that more than $9 million of State Department money made its way through Peace Corps funding mechanisms into the hands of Dr. Vanessa Kerry's nonprofit, and all without competition.[695]

Dr. Kerry's nonprofit, Seed Global Health, received her first contract in 2012, while Clinton was still at the helm of State and Senator John Kerry was the head of the US Senate's Committee on Foreign Relations, the congressional overseer of the State Department and the Peace Corps. That's a conflict of interest.

That certainly smells like crony capitalism, but then once John Kerry assumed duties as the new Secretary of State, his daughter got a four-year extension to the noncompetitive contract. "Kerry and government officials colluded to launch the program and ensure that Seed would get the contract," wrote *The Daily Caller.*[696]

Unfortunately, corruption is part of our modern government, and both major political parties are guilty. As mentioned earlier, I wrote an entire book, *The Deeper State*, that profiles just how bad the corruption is within our system of government.

No, we shouldn't put all the blame on progressives. There is plenty of guilt for both major political parties. But the fact is progressives (mostly Democrats) aggressively fought to build big government starting with President Theodore Roosevelt (a Republican), continued to do so under Woodrow Wilson (a Democrat), reached warp speed with Franklin D. Roosevelt (a Democrat), and picked up momentum once again with John F. Kennedy (a Democrat), Lyndon B. Johnson (a Democrat), Jimmy Carter (a Democrat), and, more recently, Barack Obama (a Democrat). Corruption followed as government grew in breadth and girth.

POLITICAL CORRECTNESS

Good government requires effective communication even among those with opposing opinions. When we can't speak openly about our true differences, democracy suffers—and that's a problem that progressives brought to our current government.

"Political correctness" is a barrier that threatens to strangle the public conversation that nurtures democracy, yet few really know the origin. The term "political correctness" is "used to refer to language that seems intended to give the least amount of offense, especially when describing groups identified by external markers such as race, gender, culture, or sexual orientation."[697]

The phrase was coined in the late 1920s by the Soviets and their allies to describe why the views of certain Communist Party faithful needed correction to the party line.[698] Specifically, the concept dates to the Spanish-French abstract artist Pablo Picasso, who supported communist causes albeit without being in the Soviet Union and directly subject to the dictates of the regime.[699]

Soviet dictator Joseph Stalin was not a fan of Picasso's abstract art. Rather, Stalin favored "Soviet realism," photographic-like art that portrayed real people in realistic settings, sort of the Norman Rockwell style, albeit with a hammer and sickle and of poor and boring quality.[700]

Evidently, the Soviets wanted to make use of Picasso's public alignment with communism, so they created the phrase "politically correct," which was introduced by the conjunction "but," to explain why a Soviet public figure could be considered a loyal and faithful member of the Communist Party while straying to applaud Picasso. Thus, because Picasso was useful to the communists, he and his abstract art were regarded as correct for politics' sake: "politically correct."[701]

The term as originally used by the Soviets was meant to camouflage their real views, and similarly today, it is just as abusive to honest dialogue, especially useful to progressives.

Progressives as a group embrace "political correctness" more than other demographic tribes, according to More in Common, a British nonprofit that conducted a poll of eight thousand Americans, thirty one-hour interviews, and six focus groups from December 2017 to September 2018. More in Common's report based on those efforts, "Hidden Tribes: A Study of America's Polarized Landscape," found that progressives are the only group among those examined who strongly (70 percent) back the use of political correctness.[702]

Who are these progressives? More in Common indicates they are "much more likely to be rich, highly educated—and white. They are nearly twice as likely as the average to make more than $100,000 a year. They are nearly three times as likely to have a postgraduate degree."[703]

This helps us understand our current government because the new (2018) cohort of Democratic Party members of the House of Representatives and virtually all of the Democrats now vying to become the next president (twenty strong at this writing) are mostly self-identified progressives. They fit the above profile and likely will use the double-speak of political correctness in their messaging in government, to the people, and in the media.

Conservatives and many Republican members of Congress mock instances in which political correctness goes awry in order to win the license to spew hatred, a typical progressive trick. After all, for the progressive, anyone who dares criticize political correctness is automatically classified as a tool of the right and therefore a purveyor of hate speech.

Political correctness is mostly a tool of the progressives to marginalize their opponents—mostly those on the political right—by discounting their views as irrelevant. This tool is dysfunctional, especially in government, where differences of policy need to be found without injecting *ad hominem* attacks often associated with political correctness.

GIANT DEFICIT

The US government carries a giant ($21 trillion) deficit, and progressives want to throw caution to the wind to radically push our accounts payable to new heights.

We will consider where the US government is now regarding our fiscal house before addressing what progressives say about government spending now and the future.

The US federal budget deficit for fiscal year 2019 is expected to reach $985 billion. That occurs because the US government plans to spend $4.407 trillion, which is more than the projected revenue, $3.422 trillion.[704]

Unfortunately, the deficit compared with last year will grow 18 percent for fiscal year 2019. Why is our deficit growing?[705]

First, the US government has steadily increased spending for security since the attacks on September 11, 2001, in total, about $2 trillion more debt just for defense. Yes, military spending more than doubled, which includes funds to fight the global war on terror, ongoing operations in Afghanistan, the Islamic State fight that is winding down in Iraq and Syria, as well as military operations to contest near-peer adversaries China and Russia—a growing, very credible threat.[706]

Consider the following sidebar on defense spending. I always encourage readers to be careful about comparing the Pentagon's budget with those of other countries like China. Read my 2018 book, *Alliance of Evil*, to appreciate the competition with China and Russia as well as to better understand the comparisons that are often made between the US military and the Chinese. What few analysts ever mention is that half of the US military's budget goes to personnel costs (a necessity in a capitalist economy where quality people come for a premium), compared with a small fraction of the Chinese budget for personnel. In fact, in some areas of importance, the Chinese outspend the Pentagon—and besides, Beijing has always hidden a significant portion of its defense spending in other government programs.[707]

Second, President Trump's tax cuts (Tax Cuts and Jobs Act in December 2017) do impact our deficit in the short term. Obviously, tax cuts reduce government revenue, but supply-side economists tell us that the government will in time recoup those losses because of economic growth and the tax base. Of course, the National Bureau of Economic Research finds that only 17 percent of all revenue from income tax cuts is ever regained, and worse, only half of the revenue from corporate taxes is recaptured.[708]

Third, we add to the growing deficit due to mandatory spending. Most readers will point out the $1 trillion annual cost of Social Security, but keep in mind payroll taxes and the Social Security Trust Fund, at least until 2035, will keep the dollars flowing.[709]

Meanwhile, Medicare will cost $625 billion in fiscal year 2019, but about half (49 percent) is added to the deficit while payroll taxes and premiums buy the balance.[710]

The rest of the mandatory budget includes Medicaid ($412 billion in fiscal year 2019), welfare programs, unemployment benefits, student loans, and retirement and disability programs.[711]

Finally, the government always overspends and on purpose. Government spending stimulates the economy, and besides, politicians use that money to reward voters by creating jobs. Also, need I remind you that few politicians ever get reelected because they raise taxes and feed unemployment? Thus there is real incentive to spend, spend, spend.[712]

Then again there might come a time, perhaps soon, when buyers of America's debt like China begin to wonder whether we can pay them back. That's when they start demanding higher interest rates, which then slows our economic growth, a vicious cycle.

So, you may ask: Should we be worried about our deficit? We are not at a crisis point as yet. But there may come a time when our debt-to-gross domestic product (GDP) ratio exceeds a to-be-determined tipping point, then our economy will slow and those holding our debt will begin calling for repayment.

Yes, you should be concerned about the deficit. We should be reducing the deficit and trying to keep our economy healthy by keeping our government on an appetite suppressant when it comes to spending.

We should consider warnings about debt from our experts. The Committee for a Responsible Federal Budget warns that our annual deficit could reach $1 trillion next year, which must remind us that the debt clock on social programs is ticking louder[713].

Maya MacGuineas, president for the Committee, said: "Those elected to Congress this year [2018] will face stark and difficult choices to put the debt on a downward path and protect our nation's social programs from insolvency." She continued, "It's no longer a problem for the future."[714]

Mick Mulvaney, Trump's then-budget director, a known debt hawk, underscored the need to be fiscally responsible: "America's booming economy will create increased government revenues—an important step toward long-term fiscal sustainability. But this fiscal picture is a blunt warning to Congress of the dire consequences of irresponsible and unnecessary spending."[715]

Treasury Secretary Steven Mnuchin echoed Mulvaney's warning suggesting that Democrats now running the House of Representatives and holding the nation's purse strings must cut government spending on discretionary programs or face even higher deficits.[716]

Unfortunately, progressives (many Democrats in the House) are unlikely to listen to warnings about spending. They have big spending in mind. After all, many of those same Democrats won their 2018 elections promising to promote transformative policies like free college, guaranteed jobs, and the "Green New Deal"—all giant-ticket items for a future bloated federal budget.

A popular progressive agenda item is a single-payer healthcare plan ("Medicare for All [Life])," which, according to the left-leaning Urban Institute and the libertarian-leaning Mercatus Center, would cost the federal government $32 trillion over ten years. Of course, progressives argue the plan could reduce overall healthcare spending by trimming overhead, but it would still require a massive tax increase.[717]

Other progressive spending increases for education and jobs add trillions in new spending or tax credits. Speaker of the House Nancy Pelosi (D-CA) and Majority Whip Steny Hoyer (D-MD) argue for a "pay as you go" rule. But that doesn't work for progressives.[718]

"We need infrastructure, we need debt-free college, we need universal child care—all of these are items that pay dividends to our society and require upfront investment," Rep. Raul Grijalva (D-AZ), the co-chair of the Congressional Progressive Caucus. Representative Grijalva continued, "Pay-go stifles any idea about smart investments."

Then again, Stephanie Kelton, a professor at Stony Brook University and former Bernie Sanders economic adviser, makes the case that government needs not worry about deficits. She recommends printing more money. "I have a strong sense the American people would care very little about the government's budget outcome if the government was delivering a good economy,"said Kelton, a prominent supporter of the Modern Monetary Theory that deemphasizes deficits and favors government taking on far more debt.[719]

Unfortunately, Democratic Party politicians seem to embrace the Modern Monetary Theory to a fault. Senators Cory Booker (D-NJ) and Kirsten Gillibrand (D-NY) and of course Bernie Sanders welcome a pilot version of the approach for select areas in order to push private employers to raise wages. One estimate of such a limited program that brings salaries up to $15 an hour could cost about $400 billion a year.[720] But, as economic adviser Kelton said, it's just money.

I recognize all these figures are very much in the weeds for the average citizen. However, progressives have big and expensive plans for our future. Once they get their hands on the government levers, they will have the means to increase our taxes to push through even more goodies for the masses while running up the government's tab with our debt holders like China until such time as those investors call for repayment. That can't be too far down the line.

BLOATED GOVERNMENT

We do have a bloated government workforce, but it's not what most people think. The problem isn't the total number of civil servants, but the army of proxies and duplication of effort. Our federal bureaucracy suffers from fragmentation of authority, duplication of labor, overlapping responsibility with much of the work contracted outside the Beltway—a veritable Rube Goldberg albatross.

Let's begin with a few facts. The federal government has exploded in size over the past half century. Just since 1960, Washington increased inflation-adjusted spending fivefold and doubled outlays since the year 2000 alone. We've added dozens of bureaucracies, each manned by new thousands of workers. But there is something that escapes most Americans. The number of federal bureaucrats is fewer today (2.085 million excluding postal workers) than when Ronald Reagan won reelection in 1984 (2.2 million).[721]

Washington's dirty secret is that much of government's size is hidden from the public and administered by outsiders. After about 1960, our federal government grew a bloated leviathan by proxy, enlisting state and local government workers, for-profit contractors, and nonprofit grant enterprises to perform a vast portion of federal responsibilities.

Much of this new work came about by cause of progressive programs like the War on Poverty, healthcare, and environmental protection. Consider that we've seen a ten fold increase in federal funds spent on state and local grants, and as a result, that workforce is now north of eighteen million strong.

The federal government is also attached at the hip to an army of for-profit firms. One estimate indicates that just the Pentagon alone obligates more than $300 billion each year to private contractors via more than one hundred thousand single-bid contracts. Those contractors deliver a vast array of services and almost match the government bureaucrats man for man. Even the relatively new Department of Homeland Security is tethered to contractors; it has more contract employees (almost two hundred thousand) compared to federal bureaucrats (about 188,000).[722]

Many of these contractors work side by side with government bureaucrats, but millions of others are fueled by government grants and fees to deliver services and goods across the world such, as the US Agency for International Development (foreign aid), which pumps most of its annual budget ($20+ billion) into nonprofits via grants. Then there was the American Recovery and Reinvestment Act of 2009, which allocated $800 billion in "stimulus" that included eighty thousand federal grants, contracts, or loans to state and local governments for various for-profit businesses and nonprofit groups.[723]

Relying on proxies to perform government work is a difficult task, as we've seen in some high-profile cases. Remember the debacle in 2013 with the launch of Obamacare health exchanges? The government hired contractors supposedly supervised by federal bureaucrats. That didn't work very well. Then there was the scandal at Veterans Affairs hospitals, once again run by contractors overseen by "contract officer representatives." There were too few government people to properly monitor those contracts.

So, what we really have is big government masquerading through proxies. This form of bloated government is hard to constrain and its performance is more difficult to diagnose, much less keep moving in an effective, efficient manner.

Another federal government inefficiency that contributes to our inflated government is duplication of effort. A 2017 Government Accountability Office (GAO) report identified 395 examples of duplication of effort, such as the roles performed by the US Department of Agriculture's food safety and inspection service and the Food and Drug Administration. The FDA inspects shelled eggs and the USDA inspects liquid, frozen, and dehydrated eggs. Why?[724]

Why does the FDA inspect all fish except catfish? Why does the USDA have oversight for closed-faced sandwiches and bagel dogs and the FDA monitors corndogs?[725]

Duplication of effort cost the taxpayer tens of billions of dollars, says the GAO.[726]

How then does one fix the problem of duplication of effort and government bloating through contracts and grants?

We need a comprehensive reorganization that improves efficiency, effectiveness, and accountability. Most everyone agrees to those aspirational goals, but such ambitions run into opposition when congressmen and senators face job loss in their districts and states, and besides, progressives love big government and seldom have the appetite for cuts.

There is a way to trim the excess to help realize those goals, however. Simply ask members of Congress to commit to a plan up front that promises to make needed adjustments based on a bipartisan expert commission's plan no matter whose ox gets gored.

This approach worked in the past with Congress' creation of the Base Realignment and Closure Commission. In the wake of the Cold War, our military needed to scale back its infrastructure. The president appointed independent experts with the advice of congressional leaders from both parties, who then identified unneeded military facilities for closure. Between 1998 and 2005, the Commission closed 130 major bases and other installations, saving $3.8 billion annually.[727]

This test case demonstrates that cutting federal holdings can work if devised by a panel of experts and earns congressional approval before the cuts are announced.

The big question is whether progressives now flooding into Congress and seeking the presidency are willing to cut the ballooning of proxies and duplication of effort. After all, a central goal of progressive politics is using government as a powerful agent for improving American life, and that means lots of big government programs and no limit on spending.

TOO MANY REGULATIONS

Progressives more often than not favor government regulation of the public sector because they believe public institutions and officials are likely to spend money more wisely and at a lower cost to deliver services than the private sector. The problem, according to progressives, is the private sector's profit motive trumps quality services for the public. Thus, progressives call on government to regulate the private sector for the public's good.[728]

Our founders faced a similar problem and chose a better way when it comes to regulations. They complained that King George III "erected a multitude of new offices, and sent hither swarms of officers to harness our people, and eat out their substance." That objection fueled our Declaration of Independence and the popular desire at the time to make government leave us alone.[729]

Unfortunately, modern progressive government doesn't leave us alone. Rather, it peers into virtually every aspect of our lives—our bedrooms, our wallets, our medicine cabinets, our refrigerators, and even our morals—it has become Big Brother.[730]

It seems today we can hardly breathe without first filling out some government form in triplicate. Government regulations are suffocating us with micromanagement of every aspect of our lives.

Government shuts down children's lemonade stands for lack of a business permit, regulates the size of sodas, and even determines whether we can buy our kids a McDonald's Happy Meal.[731]

Former President Ronald Reagan wisely said, "Government exists to protect us from each other. Where government has gone beyond its limits is in deciding to protect us from ourselves." That is precisely what big government does today—and with great zeal, owing to progressives.[732]

Progressives argue that regulation is necessary in certain areas such as our water system and our food supply. They caution that the private sector will cut corners if given oversight of protecting our water supply. The same goes for consumer protection and product safety. Does anyone doubt that some manufacturers would sell us dangerous products if it meant more profit?[733]

But most Americans believe there is too much government regulation of business and industry, according to a Gallup poll. Each year for more than a decade, Americans told Gallup there is "too much" government regulation. Not surprisingly, 68 percent of Republicans believe regulation is too high; only 20 percent of Democrats (probably the non-progressive remnant) do.[734]

Government over-regulation of our lives comes at a high cost to America's economy as well. A 2016 study from the Mercatus Institute estimated that since 1980, federal regulations have slowed our economy by 25 percent or about $13,000 in per capita income.[735]

Local government shares much of the blame for the cost drag created by overregulation. State and local laws and land-use controls may cost the US GDP as much as 8.9 percent in terms of growth.[736]

Let's put the use of federal government regulation into perspective. Our government diverts private resources to achieve policy goals through spending programs and regulation. Federal spending is very public and is always subject to congressional and public debate. Federal regulation is rather hidden, more of a clandestine drain on our economy.

Federal regulation drains the national economy in the name of enforcing standards ranging from environmental quality, consumer protection, business and banking practices, and employment nondiscrimination, to Internet privacy and disclosure and safe food, drugs, and workplaces.[737]

Although most regulatory programs enjoy broad public support, they create a heavy burden for businesses. Those businesses must comply with a mountain of detailed rules and lots of paperwork that is costly and burdensome, and the compliance costs are naturally passed to consumers in higher product and service prices.

Yes, regulatory programs can benefit citizens, but the costs are seldom transparent, as evidenced by business compliance outlined above. Further, regulatory policies are difficult to measure in fiscal terms, which makes them true stealth taxes. Also, those regulations have the force of law, which grants the "unelected bureaucrat" the means of enforcement—and recourse is often prohibitively expensive.

Regulatory costs are hard to determine, but undeniably significant. At the end of the nineteenth century, government accounted for less than 10 percent of the US economy, and today it accounts for almost half of our economy and a third of the US GDP, and federal regulation shares a lot of responsibility for that growth.[738]

Consider the fact that today there are more than seventy federal regulatory agencies manned by hundreds of thousands of federal bureaucrats (many contractor proxies as well) that issue maybe 3,500 new rules annually to a regulatory code now north of 168,000 pages.[739]

Research on the impact of these government regulations indicates the total annual cost is somewhere between $2–4 trillion, a significant drag on economic growth and a questionable government overreach.[740]

A major problem with the growing mountain of government regulation is the lack of accountability. Regulations are created by unaccountable federal agencies, often with broad aspirational language like "No Child Left Behind," but such programs never adjust to the reality of limited resources, no matter their impact on the regulated businesses, much less the consumers. They have the real potential to have significant negative effects on prices, wages, and jobs.[741]

Yes, regulations can improve air and water quality, highway safety, and much more. But we must ask: When do the costs associated with regulations exceed their benefits, or worse, become counterproductive?[742]

Another problem with the effects of regulation is whether it is taken captive by special interests. After all, various interest groups often convince government agencies and/or Congress to use their coercive power to benefit one group at the expense of broader society. This issue is explored extensively in my book, *The Deeper State*, where we learn about the influence of corporations, special interest think tanks, and rich individuals on our government policies.[743]

No doubt we need some government regulation. However, due to progressives, our lives today are overregulated by big government, and we need to return to where we began, a place where less was better.

What Will Progressives Do to Future Government?

The definition of insanity is doing the same thing over and over again and expecting a different result. Modern progressives are "crazy" because they refuse to learn from their own history.

Twenty-first century progressives will joust with the same problems their nineteenth-century forefathers wrestled with, and they will approach solutions in much the same vein. Their answer is always more big government programs.

Their headline problems, according to progressive leaders, are economic inequality—the few wealthy and the rest less well-to-do, power is concentrated in private hands (monopolies like telecommunication and financial giants)—and the exclusion of minorities.

To help overcome these problems, progressives will seek to create a much larger government safety net beyond the many programs now in place. Specifically, they will seek social insurance programs that guarantee jobs for all with a "livable wage," healthcare, and all the other necessities of life.

They will use big government to force inclusion for all people without regard to immigration status, sexual orientation, race, gender, social standing, and whatever other categories the politically correct progressives dream up next.

The bottom line for twenty-first-century progressives when it comes to government regulation is best captured by Ms. Carol Negro, founder and director of MyLiberty, the Tea Party Patriots of San Mateo County, California. She wrote about the progressive nanny state in *American Thinker.* "Only one thing matters to progressives," she said, "that is growing the central government and its power." She then identified a host of issues progressives defend and then exposes their true goal. Consider a few of those issues below.[744]

> Illegal immigration, like abortion is a cause celebre…and progressives will resist the smallest limitation on the grounds that it might lead to the idea that there are legitimate reasons to control borders.[745]

> They use the same 'logic' with abortion: letting live babies die unattended in broom closets after botched abortions must not be outlawed because it might lead to further limitations of a woman's right to 'choose.'
>
> Progressives offer all sorts of explanations for their bizarre, inefficient, ineffective, illogical, irrational, contradictory, and demonstrably failed theories and policies. But that's just their puppet show; their circuses for public consumption.[746]

"There is one goal, and one goal only for Progressives," explained Ms. Negro. "Government growth and its intrusion into every aspect of our lives. When you understand that, all their apparently idiotic policies make perfect sense."[747]

Of course, the craziest of the progressives is their newest star, Alexandria Ocasio-Cortez, the twenty-nine-year-old socialist, who upset a long-time incumbent to win a seat in the US House of Representatives. AOC, as Ms. Ocasio-Cortez has come to be called, has big progressive plans for government.

She came to Washington on a wave of promises to provide free "Medicare for All [Life]" and free college tuition for all. Once sworn in, she wasted no time calling for her "Green New Deal" (a throwback to FDR's New Deal) to force the quick conversion from fossil fuels to clean green renewable energy. And perhaps her biggest present that showed her socialist colors was a call for the wealthy to pay taxes of at least 70 percent.

What's really scary isn't that people like AOC exist, but that there are so many gullible voters who believed her and her ilk.

Conclusion

Progressives salivate for the time when they will once again control the presidency and the Congress. Then Katie bar the door: Big government will return with a vengeance and our deficit will go into outer space as the government accelerates the production of paper money. But these perils seem beyond the capability of progressives to grasp; it is a clear case of denial of reality as well as of history and common sense. Controlling the government is the key to controlling every aspect of our lives and squashing opposition.

14

Progressivism's Impact on Economy

The problem with socialism is that you eventually run out of other people's money.[748]

—Margaret Thatcher, former British prime minister

Progressives may be big-hearted people, but their economic ideas to spend others' hard-earned money, assisted by the coercive arm of big government, will eventually bankrupt this country. Besides, the surge in socialist-type thinking among the current flock of Democratic Party progressives like those in the House promises to make our near future very troubled, especially if they also take over the presidency and the Senate.

This chapter is a CliffsNotes of sorts on our economy, profiling past progressive manipulation of our nation's financial activities and concluding with progressive plans for our future—perhaps a future more reminiscent of the Soviet Union's failed command economy or the contemporary Venezuelan economic disaster with its 10 million percent inflation, or something like President Franklin D. Roosevelt's

1930's New Deal economy that helped America overcome the Great Depression.

America's Economy

A wise and frugal government…shall restrain men from injuring one another, shall leave them otherwise free to regulate their own pursuits of industry and improvement, and shall not take from the mouth of labor the bread it has earned. This is the sum of good government.[749]

—President Thomas Jefferson, First Inaugural Address,
March 4, 1801

Our founders were mostly frugal men rightly concerned that future generations would abandon common sense and endanger our economy with too much public debt. President Jefferson said as much in a letter to Samuel Kercheval dated June 12, 1816:

I place economy among the first and most important virtues, and public debt as the greatest of dangers to be feared. To preserve our independence, we must not let our rulers load us with perpetual debt. If we run into such debts, we must be taxed in our meat and drink, in our necessities and in our comforts, in our labor and in our amusements.[750]

It will be helpful for some readers to review the institution of the economy before delving into the particulars of progressive economic history and their future plans for our money.

An economy (from Greek οίκος, "household" and νέμομαι, "manage") is the result of the production, distribution or trade, and consumption of goods and services by different agents that come together within the context of culture, values, education, technology, history, social and political structures, legal systems, geography, and the availability of natural resources. Economic agents can be individuals, businesses, organizations, or governments with which we have "economic transactions" by agreeing to the value or price of goods or services, usually in terms of currency.[751]

A market-based economy like we have in the United States is one where goods and services are produced to meet demand and supply among economic agents using some means of exchange such as credit or debit, such as currency. Further, the US has a mixed economy, which refers to a capitalist economy with mostly private ownership of the means of production where the accumulation of capital is the fundamental driving force.

Economic growth is "an increase in the capacity of an economy to produce goods and services, compared from one period to another. Traditionally, aggregate economic growth is measured in terms of gross national product (GNP) or gross domestic product (GDP), although alternative metrics are sometimes used." The US has the world's seventh-highest per capita GDP and has the world-leading industrial sector, with the world's second-largest industrial output.[752]

America is a very blessed nation with an abundance of natural resources, a mature infrastructure, and a highly productive workforce. As a direct result, we have the highest average household and employee income and the fourth-highest median household income in the world.

Now to the condition of our current economy. "First of all the economy itself is really strong," said Commerce Secretary Wilbur Ross in December 2018, who cited as proof statistics about low unemployment and high consumer confidence. But there are worrisome indicators that the future isn't necessarily going to be so rosy, according to Oren Cass, a senior fellow at the Manhattan Institute and author of *The Once and Future Worker: A Vision for the Renewal of Work in America*.[753]

Mr. Cass threw cold water on our celebration over Secretary Ross' pronouncement about our "strong" economy. Cass cited some indicators of trouble ahead. He explained that our Centers for Disease Control and Prevention confirms American life expectancy is declining, a phenomenon not seen since World War I. Further, as our GDP surged in the recent years, the Economic Innovation Group's Distressed Communities Index reports that the most prosperous US zip codes account for the entire net increase in employment, which means the balance of the country has fewer jobs today than in 2007.[754]

Although the current economic metrics point to a boom, the labor market sends a very different signal, albeit somewhat opaque. Specifically, although today's unemployment rate is low, there are more men out of work today than in 2007. Specifically, 19 percent of men between the ages of twenty-five and fifty-four are not working full-time compared to 16.6 percent in 2007, 14.4 percent in 2000, and 13.6 percent in 1989.[755]

It is understandable that we don't tend to talk about labor-market problems with unemployment at or below 4 percent, as it was in late 2018. And even though our deficit-financed tax cuts give us a momentary lift, recession can't be too far ahead, Mr. Cass warns. Thus, there are understandable calls to revitalize the industrial economy by creating better job opportunities, something President Trump pursues and so do progressives.[756]

Yes, everyone wants to create more jobs, but that outcome has a high cost. First, we need to build a pathway in our education system that helps workers prepare for those jobs. Second, we must rebuild our industrial economy—President Trump's goal—that leads to the creation of better job opportunities for those hoped-for better educated workers. Of course, Republican tax cuts alone won't do that, and certainly progressive big-government programs of redistribution of wealth won't, either.

We've seen similar challenges in the past, and progressives jumped on ideologically charged ideas that gave us big government, higher taxes, and a mixed economy. What might the progressives do if they gain control of our government? We'll address that after first reviewing past progressive economic programs.

Past Progressive Economic Accomplishments

Progressives began to enjoy a significant impact on the American economy beginning with Theodore Roosevelt's presidency, which changed government's relationship with big business. Until Roosevelt's presidency, the government gave the titans of industry *carte blanche* to accomplish their goals. However, Roosevelt believed government had the right and responsibility to regulate big business for the interest of the general public. He believed that big business' "existence marked a naturally occurring phase of the country's economic evolution," and he also believed the time had come to arrest its actions for the benefit of the public.[757]

Mr. Roosevelt used his seven years as president to institute numerous progressive reforms that directly impacted our economy. He targeted unscrupulous monopolies with the creation of the Bureau of Corporations and shepherded through at the time the Pure Food and Drug Act as well as the Meat Inspection Act that helped consumers. Even later as an ex-president when he ran as the Progressive Party's presidential candidate, he lobbied for old age pensions, unemployment insurance, and a graduated income tax.[758]

Woodrow Wilson, a Democrat, won the 1912 presidential election in part because the newly minted Progressive Party's candidate and former president Theodore Roosevelt split the vote with the Republican candidate, William Howard Taft. Once in office, Wilson showed his progressive colors as well in terms of programs that had a significant impact on our economy.

Mr. Wilson, known as the "professor president" because of his six professorships before becoming governor of New Jersey and then quickly winning the presidency, was very much an economic reformist. He introduced the Underwood-Simmons Bill (Revenue Act of 1913 that imposed the federal income tax after the ratification of the Sixteenth Amendment), created the Federal Reserve Act, the Federal Trade Commission Act, and the Clayton Anti-Trust Act—all tools to further

Wilson's goal of taking away power from large corporations and banks, a long-time progressive agenda item.

Years after Wilson left the presidency (1921) and in the wake of the nation's economic implosion, Franklin D. Roosevelt (FDR) took the helm as president (1933), promising more progressive, big-government actions to lift the country out of the Great Depression. He quickly pushed for the National Industrial Recovery Act, which regulated industry and protected the workers' right to organize, a clear progressive favoring act. But at the same time, he cut government spending, which runs counter to progressive views.[759]

A real push to show his progressive colors only came when FDR felt populist pressure from three famous leftists with big followings. First, among the threesome was Father Charles Coughlin, a Canadian-American Roman Catholic priest based in Detroit, Michigan, and a popular radio show host, who used his National Union for Social Justice's 8.5 million members to demand labor rights, easy credit, and the nationalization of banks and industries.[760]

The second progressive of note was Louisiana's Senator Huey P. Long Jr., nicknamed "The Kingfish," who led his five million-member Share Our Wealth Society to pressure FDR by advocating the seizure of private fortunes and then distributing those funds to American families through the issuance of checks. FDR initially didn't embrace Long's message, and besides, the president cut government spending—which Senator Long reacted to by accusing the president of selling out to the wealthy titans at the time: J. P. Morgan (big banker) and John D. Rockefeller (oil industry business magnate).[761]

Dr. Francis Everett Townsend, a California medical physician, the third progressive of note, created the Townsend Clubs that boasted two million members, and he used that influence on behalf of aging Americans to demand that FDR create a federal grant of $200 per month for every senior citizen, which influenced FDR in his decision to establish the Social Security system.[762]

FDR did feel the pressure, but only after Coughlin, Long, and

Townsend threatened to create a third party to run against him did the president take action. FDR caved to the pressure, as evidenced by a statement written to Harold Ickes, FDR's secretary of the interior: "I must move further to the left."[763]

Soon after his reelection, FDR showed evidence of a shift to the left. In April 1935, he signed the Emergency Relief Appropriation Act, and that summer the pro-labor Wagner Act, officially known as the National Labor Relations Act. Those actions were capped in August 1935, when FDR increased taxes for the wealthy and created Social Security, along with unemployment insurance and aid to low-income families and the physically handicapped.[764]

FDR's radical shift to a progressive agenda was almost blunted by the Supreme Court, however. At first the high court struck down the National Industrial Recovery Act and almost struck down Social Security before FDR, with encouragement from progressives, came up with the idea of packing the high court with more justices who would be pro-New Deal. Then our so-called independent judiciary backed down under FDR's court packing scheme, ensuring his progressive New Deal wealth transfer measures survived.[765]

Just how did such progressive programs created by administrations over the past century impact our economy? Herbert Hovenkamp, a professor at the University of Pennsylvania Law School and the Wharton School, provided a surprising answer to the question. He wrote an outstanding article, "Appraising the Progressive State," for the *Iowa Law Review,* which isn't necessarily a defense of progressivism; rather, it dissects the advantages and disadvantages of the ideology for our economy.[766]

The most eye-opening part of Hovenkamp's article is his assessment of our economy under twentieth-century progressive administrations—Theoedore Roosevelt, Woodrow Wilson, Franklin Roosevelt, John Kennedy, Lyndon Johnson, Jimmy Carter, Bill Clinton, and Barack Obama. Surprisingly, Hovenkamp's analysis shows that the economy during progressive (Democratic Party)-led governments performed marginally better than economies during conservative, Republican-run administrations.

Professor Hovenkamp explained why he believes progressive economic policies worked better than Republican-run programs. He said that during FDR's administration, for example, there was an increased reliance on science and expertise to make policy, what Hovenkamp said was a process that insulated government decision-making from direct citizen control. As James Landis, the former chairman of the Securities and Exchange Commission (1934–1937) said, it is essential that complex economic policy issues be decided "by those best equipped for the task." That is a progressive view that dates back to the father of early American progressivism, German philosopher Georg Wilhelm Friedrich Hegel (1770–1831) and one that reflected the views of progressive leaders like Roosevelt, Wilson, and others up to the present. [767]

No doubt managing an economy is complex and policies must adjust to the times. We need people in government who understand such issues to help guide national policies, something the progressives evidently learned and went about embracing within government.

Professor Hovenkamp explained that transformation—introducing economic advisers to government—began in the early nineteenth century, when the United States was severely underdeveloped. At that time, government intervention was necessary to spur development, and one mechanism for stimulating development was the use of monopoly grants, tax breaks, and other subsidies. Even Chief Justice John Marshall (1801–1835) encouraged the use of monopoly grants to further a strong national and pro-regulatory interpretation of the Constitution's Commerce Clause to facilitate national development. [768] Once the Industrial Revolution (1870–1916), with the help of monopolies, built up America's infrastructure and fueled our economy, progressives like Roosevelt and Wilson came on the scene to change the economy to better serve everyone, not just the new industrialists. Hovenkamp explained that journalist Henry George at that time asked an important question: Why did America amass so much wealth but produce so much poverty? Of course, as Hovenkamp explained, the wider distribution of the country's wealth became the goal of progressives like Roosevelt and Wilson.

Hovenkamp has plenty of criticism for progressives and their policies, but not when it comes to overall economic performance. The fact is, according to Hovenkamp, twentieth-century progressives understood the need to be flexible. He wrote that:

> ...progressive policy is seldom fixed, but tends to vary with developments in science, economics, demographics, politics, or the pull of interest groups. In the progressive state, most means of production remain privately owned, although with significantly more government intervention than is true of a more classical state. In sum, the underlying principles of the progressive state are more complex and considerably less elegant than those of classicism, libertarianism, or any other theory that employs more categorical, less empirically driven conceptions about the appropriate roles of government and the market.[769]

Hovenkamp explained the root of progressive economic success:

> New Deal economic policy was the first to use a broad combination of taxation and spending policies in order to manage economic growth and distribution. For the most part, New Deal policy makers were writing on a clean slate, and their error rate must be read in that light. Nevertheless, more active management very likely contributed heavily to the smaller size and shorter duration of extreme recessions since that time, including the very large recession of 2007 to 2008. At the same time, the motivations for New Deal management were both economic and political. For example, the Roosevelt administration pumped more money into areas where unemployment was higher and poverty more widespread, but many of these also

happened to be areas that were more likely to swing Democrat. The distribution also reflected the power of individual members of Congress, and particularly the Roosevelt administration's favoritism toward the South, where Roosevelt was politically vulnerable. New Deal growth in federal spending contributed significantly to the rise of personal incomes, suggesting overall returns that exceeded outlays, although they were variable. Federally financed public-work projects produced particularly strong returns in the form of improved economic performance at the local level. By contrast, the impact of the National Industrial Recovery Act is ambiguous and difficult to assess. (Overall, however, when one uses microeconomic measures of performance to evaluate the New Deal with 80 years of hindsight, it appears to have succeeded in stimulating both income and durable goods consumption, and reducing mortality and crime rates, although perhaps not private unemployment.)[770]

Professor Hovenkamp performed an analysis using comparative statistics concerning economic performance by the political party occupying the White House. He found what's obvious to most readers today. The Republicans tended to favor smaller government, less regulatory intervention, lower taxes, less regulation of wages and working conditions, and opposed labor unions.

The Democrats who occupied the White House over the past century typically believed very differently than the Republicans—they were far more progressive ideologically than the Republicans. The Democrats tended to support government growth and more regulation, higher taxes, and organized labor, as well as called for greater commitment to wealth redistribution. These differences have become especially pronounced since the 1980s until the most recent 2018 election cycle.

What's especially noteworthy is what Hovenkamp found when he analyzed the economic data points across the presidential administrations from Hoover to Obama.

I'm generally skeptical about statistics, because, as Mark Twain popularized: "There are three kinds of lies: lies, damned lies, and statistics." However, Professor Hovenkamp presents a compelling analysis of the economic data, which is quoted verbatim below. It demonstrates that progressive administrations produced more favorable results than Republican administrations. Draw your own conclusions.

The statistics on basic economic growth are quite stunning. Growth in real GDP per capita per year is not merely higher under Democrat presidents, it is roughly 70% higher. Going back through the administration of Harry Truman, GDP growth increased at a rate of 4.35% under Democrat Presidents as opposed to 2.54% under Republicans. The factual record, based on generally available statistics is reliable, although the authors of the most prominent report comparing administrations' decline to relate the differences to presidential economic policy.

The government has actively kept statistics on GDP since 1929 to 1930, which go back further than Truman and covers all of the Franklin D. Roosevelt presidency and three years of Herbert Hoover's. If one includes these, the differences are even more pronounced, approaching two-to-one. Annual GDP growth during the included three years of Herbert Hoover's presidency (1930 to 1932) was approximately -10%, while during FDR's administration it was around +8.0%. That comparison is unfair, however, because the Hoover administration reflected the worst years of the Great Depression, while the Roosevelt years reflected both the recovery and the rapid growth caused by the lead-up to World War II. As a result, both Hoover's highly negative number and FDR's highly positive one are best considered as outliers.

Other comparisons are noteworthy. For example, average annual GDP growth during the eight years of the presidency of Ronald Reagan, a Republican hero, was no higher (term 1, 3.12%; term 2, 3.89%; average, 3.51%) than growth under Jimmy Carter (3.56%), whom Reagan supporters have vilified. In fact, the only post-War presidents to produce higher numbers were Kennedy/Johnson (shared term, 5.74%), Johnson (4.95%) and Clinton (term 1, 3.53%; term 2, 4.03%; average, 3.78%). Both Presidents George H. W. Bush (2.05%) and George W. Bush (term 1, 2.78%; term 2, .054%; average, 1.42%) also fared much more poorly.

The story on jobs and employment is even more telling. Numbers concerning job creation are more significant than GDP growth to the extent that they reflect the shorter-term effects of presidential administrations and distinctive policies directed at labor and employment. In any event, job creation and GDP growth are strongly correlated, moving almost in tandem since the 1960s. The same thing cannot be said of tax cuts. Considerable evidence suggests that cuts in marginal tax rates have no measurable impact on economic growth. Further, to the extent a correlation exists it is between economic growth and tax cuts at the bottom of the income ladder. There is no measurable correlation between tax cuts to higher earners and job growth. The most likely explanation for this is that tax cuts to employers do little to stimulate job creation but result mainly in more savings. By contrast, tax cuts to lower wage earners enables them to spend more, stimulating growth in the process.

Both real nonfarm wages and labor productivity have increased more quickly under Democrats than under Republicans. Further, Democratic presidents have overseen the creation of roughly twice as many private-sector jobs per year as Republican administrations. During its eight years, the Reagan administration saw a smaller increase in jobs per year (roughly two million) than the Carter administration (roughly 2.55 million). Overall, annual job growth was the best during the administrations of Presidents Clinton, Carter, and Johnson. However, recent job growth in the Obama administration enabled him to finish his presidency with a similar record as well. In any event, the economy produced many more new jobs during the Obama administration (roughly 15 million) than the eight years of the Bush administration (roughly 1.3 million). Household income growth as of January 2013, five years into President Obama's presidency, lagged behind Reagan and Clinton, particularly for older Americans; but it was very far ahead of rates under both Presidents Bush. Overall, these data show that older Americans (above 45), and particularly those without a college education, are lagging behind in income growth in all administrations.

The historical record is much the same on wages, labor unions and collective bargaining. Few areas have served to divide the progressive state from its critics more than attitudes toward labor unions. Progressives began to observe at the beginning of the 20th century that shareholders are unified into a single person by virtue of corporate legal personality, while labor unions are treated as cartels. For them, this fact explained why labor needed to be organized in order to get its fair share. Today, thanks in part to a rising tide of anti-union activity and the growth of right-to-work provisions, labor is receiving an ever declining share of the benefits of increased productivity, and wages in strong right-to-work states are lower than those in the nation as a whole. That fact itself explains a significant portion of the increasing disparity of wealth in the country: wages are growing much more slowly than productivity. The result is that the benefits of increased productivity are accruing mainly to capital.

The historical relationship between marginal tax rates and economic growth also gives little support to the anti-progressive argument for continually reducing taxes of most types. One Congressional Research Service report in 2012 found little to no evidence that higher marginal tax rates impeded economic growth, although lower tax rates on upper income ranges contributed noticeably to uneven wealth distribution. That study concluded that historically 'higher tax rates are associated with slightly higher real per capita GDP growth rates.' Today inequality is at its highest point in a century, and a reversal could be a major boost to growth, both domestically and worldwide.[771]

The professor concludes that "no general empirical case can be made that progressive policy has harmed the United States economy." Then he returns to his opening salvo that economic growth is hardly the sole driver of policy choices, as we saw earlier in the examples of FDR caving into populist pressure to embrace progressive issues.

Hovenkamp admits that the progressive state has its share of imperfections, but done right, it has a superior record of economic performance given its historic concern for political participation and widely distributed economic growth. It does tend to rely heavily on regulatory intervention, which must be constrained. Further, progressives have an unwelcomed proclivity for special-interest control or crony capitalism, which tends to undermine their credibility.

The professor's favorable conclusion regarding past progressive economic policies begs the question whether the current cohort of progressives and their rather radical socialistic proposals are likely to be consistent with the past.

What Are Progressives Likely to Do with Our Economy in the Future?

The year 2020 will host a dogfight among political campaigns over the presidency, with twenty-two Republican and twelve Democrat Senate seats and all House seats up for grabs. It is quite possible that Democratic Party progressives could end up controlling the presidency and both chambers of Congress beginning in January 2021. What then should we expect in terms of economic policies?

Much depends on whether the radical progressives run the election tables in 2020. Consider two possible outcomes should the Democrats toss the Republicans out and take all the reins of government. The options are both progressive in their orientation: moderate progressives and the more radical socialist progressives like freshman congresswoman Alexandria Ocasio-Cortez.

In early 2019, we got a glimpse of the possible impact that outcome might have, should the socialist progressives like Ocasio-Cortez win it all. We saw Ocasio-Cortez announce the Green New Deal, which was quickly endorsed by most Democratic Party candidates for the presidency. Also, shortly after that announcement, on February 14, Amazon announced that it had canceled plans to build a headquarters in New York City and attributed that decision to progressives, who fiercely opposed the marketing giant.

Although the two events were separate, together they send a serious cautionary message to the American public about the radical progressives. The Green New Deal is about growing government and draining the taxpayer. The Amazon project is about capitalism and jobs.

Amazon's spokesperson said about the cancelation: "A number of state and local politicians [such as Ocasio-Cortez] have made it clear that they oppose our presence and will not work with us to build the type of relationships that are required to go forward."[772]

Amazon's decision will cost the greater New York City area as many as forty thousand jobs, a project supported from the start by some local leaders such as progressive New York Mayor Bill De Blasio. However, Ocasio-Cortez, who represents the Fourteenth Congressional District that includes the Bronx and Queens, the epicenter of the canceled Amazon project, celebrated the marketing giant's decision. The progressive darling wrote: "Anything is possible: today was the day a group of dedicated, everyday New Yorkers and their neighbors defeated Amazon's corporate greed, its worker exploitation, and the power of the richest man in the world."[773]

The moderate progressives are far more likely to win than radicals like Ocasio-Cortez because they are indeed pretty popular. This cadre of progressives are like Tony Evers, the new governor of Wisconsin. Evers, a self-identified Wisconsin progressive said his form of progressivism is simple and not radical like that of Ocasio-Cortez. "The people of Wisconsin—they care whether their roads are safe. They care whether they have a good education system. They care about having access to affordable healthcare." That's his form of progressivism, which is about "solving problems that people have."[774]

Like most moderate progressives, Evers favors Medicaid expansion and a $15 minimum wage. He wants to give middle-class families a 10 percent break in their income taxes. He also promised during the campaign to stand up to big business and ensure that average people get a voice in government.[775]

There are plenty of other progressives like Evers, and they enjoy popular support across the nation—which is why Democratic Party politicians are flocking to acquire the progressive label, such as Senators Bernie Sanders (I-VT), Elizabeth Warren (D-MA), Kirsten Gillibrand (D-NY), Kamala Harris (D-CA), and Cory Booker (D-NJ). However, and without exception, these senators openly embrace the progressive label but also radical reforms with real cost implications for our economy: "Medicare for All [Life]," tuition-free public college, a national $15 minimum wage, universal pre-kindergarten, job guarantees, nationwide infrastructure rebuilding, criminal justice reform, Green New Deal, and much more.

Progressives are gaining in popularity because they have tapped into working-class anxieties, much like President Trump's populist appeal. Why? Evidently, faith in capitalism is plummeting, which helps progressives. Specifically, most Millennials (51 percent) reject capitalism, according to a Harvard University poll. They are likely to favor a progressive economy, as outlined in the previous section.[776]

Progressive economist Dean Baker argues that the left needs to be realistic and see that "the market is a tool, it is incredibly malleable." He makes the case that our market economy can be restructured to redistribute wealth downward rather than upward, which enriches primarily the wealthy.[777]

Baker outlines two steps for progressives to restructure capitalism to serve their purposes.

First, he proposes rewriting the rules about wealth distribution. In his book, *Reflections on the Future of the Left*, he suggests ways to wealth distribution, such as imposing a tax on financial transactions to weaken Wall Street's power; changing monetary policies to ensure full employment; shortening the workweek to tighten labor markets; and changing law to make it easier to cut executive salaries.[778]

Second, Baker, a cofounder of the Center for Economic and Policy Research in Washington, DC, recommends ensuring economic security for all. He favors a federal minimum wage of $15 per hour, a universal basic income, and a government program that would guarantee a job for everyone.[779]

The Center for American Progress (CAP) suggests other policies for future progressive government leaders to add to their economic agenda that would offer broader protections for Americans. Evidently, "the polling shows that workers across race support similar views on economic policy issues," said David Madland, the coauthor of a CAP report entitled "The Working-Class Push for Progressive Economic Policies."

"They support a higher minimum wage, higher taxes on the wealthy, and more spending on healthcare and retirement," Madland writes. "There is broad support among workers for progressive economic policy."[780]

That study delineates a number of important and popular progressive programs:

Paid family leave is supported by 73 percent of college-educated workers, 69 percent of the white working class, 72 percent of the black working class and 63 percent of the Hispanic working class.

When it comes to requiring equal pay, 91 percent of college-educated workers, 86 percent of the white working class, 82 percent of the black working class and 85 percent of the Hispanic working class indicate support.

Spending more government money on retirement draws wide support, with 52 percent of college-educated workers, 64 percent of the white working class, 78 percent of the black working class and 72 percent of the Hispanic working class saying they would like to see this.

When it comes to healthcare, 63 percent of college-educated workers, 64 percent of the white working class, 84 percent of the black working class and 77 percent of Hispanic workers agree say the government should increase, and not decrease, spending.

As for higher taxes on the wealthiest Americans, 72 percent of college-educated workers, 74 percent of the white working class, 69 percent of the black working class and 73 percent of Hispanic workers say they believe taxes on those earning more than $250,000 annually should be raised.[781]

Collectively, these so-called moderate progressive economic agenda items could break the bank, unless there is a significant restructuring of our economy. But there is a growing cadre of far-left progressives that, if they find themselves heading the government, could take our economy in even a more radical direction.

The socialist wing of the Democratic Party is especially frightening—just think about Ms. Ocasio-Cortez on steroids. She represents a growing youthful part of the left that is gaining a voice and in time might just have a commanding voice in our government.

Consider a sampling of some of her quotes in addition to those already profiled.

- "Capitalism has not always existed in the world and will not always exist in the world."[782]

- "To me, what socialism means is to guarantee a basic level of dignity. It's asserting the value of saying that the America we want and the America that we are proud of is one in which all children can access a dignified education. It's one in which no person is too poor to have the medicines they need to live."

- "Unemployment is low because everyone has two jobs.... Unemployment is low because people are working 60, 70, 80 hours a week and can barely feed their kids."[783]

- "And so I do think that right now we have this no-holds-barred, Wild West hyper-capitalism. What that means is profit at any cost. Capitalism has not always existed in the world, and it will not always exist in the world. When this country started, we were not a capitalist [nation], we did not operate on a capitalist economy."

- "People often say, how are you gonna pay for it? And I find the question so puzzling because, how do you pay for something that's more affordable? How do you pay for cheaper rent? How do you pay for—you just pay for it."

- "There's no debate as to whether we should continue producing fossil fuels. There's no debate."

- "Once you get to the tippy-tops, on your 10 millionth dollar, sometimes you see tax rates as high as 60% or 70%. That doesn't mean all $10 million are taxed at an extremely high rate. But it means that as you climb up this ladder, you should be contributing more."[784]

We can hope that the Congresswoman is an anomaly. However, the fact is, according to a 2018 Gallup poll, the Democratic Party faithful are more than ever before represented by people who speak favorably (57 percent) about socialism, much like this young congresswoman—and the general population is trending in that direction as well.[785]

President Trump is very much aware of the growing favorable views about socialism. In his 2019 State of the Union address, he said "We are alarmed by new calls to adopt socialism in our country."

He continued: "America was founded on liberty and independence—not government coercion, domination and control. We are born free, and we will stay free. Tonight, we renew our resolve that America will never be a socialist country."[786]

The threat of socialism is real for Mr. Trump, an issue he frequently mentions. He told a Chattanooga, Tennessee, crowd in November 2018: "They [the Democrats] want to impose socialism on our country." Weeks later, the president told another crowd in Tupelo, Mississippi, "I do really want to run against a true socialist because I can't believe that's what this country wants."[787]

Unfortunately, a growing element of the country is attracted to socialism. A Fox News poll found that 36 percent of Americans said it would be a good thing for the country to move to socialism, and the favorable views are especially significant among America's youth. A Gallup poll found that younger Americans have a more positive view of socialism than capitalism.[788]

Seventeen percent of Americans define socialism as government ownership of the means of production, half the number who defined it this way in 1949 when Gallup first asked the question. Most contemporary Americans say socialism connotes equality for everyone, while others say it means the provision of benefits and social services, a modified form of communism. A quarter weren't able to give Gallup an answer.[789]

Do these people really know anything about socialism? According to the Merriam-Webster online dictionary, socialism is defined as a political-economic ideology that advocates the "collective or governmental ownership and administration of the means of production and distribution of goods." That is, government runs everything, an outcome many progressives support.[790]

Likely, the growing support for socialism reflects youthful idealism and a failure to understand its horrible historical record. Check out Nicolas Werth's 1997 book, *The Black Book of Communism: Crimes, Terror, Repression,* and read about socialism's death toll. It is very grim:

Twenty-five million in the former Soviet Union and another sixty-five million under communist China's former dictator, Mao Zedong.[791]

Evidently, the clamor among young Democrats for socialism demonstrates that they are ignorant of history and don't watch the latest news coming out of socialist Venezuela—or worse, they truly hate this country and wish for its downfall.[792]

Modern-day, socialist Venezuela is nothing to envy. It faces seven-figure annual inflation, it suffers a total lack of basic necessities, and the average citizen is on a forced diet because the food supply is critically short. That is tragic, especially given that only a decade ago it was a prosperous nation that still rests on the world's largest energy reserves.

There is a possible explanation for this widespread naiveté regarding socialism. The reader will recall from an earlier chapter on America's education system that I mentioned the favorable advocacy of socialism in our public classrooms. No wonder Millennials, much less younger people, say they would rather live in a socialist country (44 percent) than a capitalist one (42 percent). They were brainwashed by our corrupted public education establishment that pushes social studies curricula tainted by socialist favoring materials put in place by educators reared on a diet overseen by progressive leader John Dewey, who among other twentieth-century influential educators, applauded the former Soviet Union's communist education system.[793]

Don't believe that? Marketwatch hosted the Open Syllabus Project, which tracks books and works assigned to students. It found that Karl Marx's *The Communist Manifesto* ranks at the top of the most frequently assigned texts at American universities.[794] That should not surprise those who consider the philosophical leanings of curriculum developers identified in the education chapter of this volume.

Our "expert" public school curriculum developers fill our common core education curricula with social justice-dominated material; it's a little wonder that, with all that socialistic philosophy, our young people grow up to spout nonsense like "I prefer socialism over capitalism."[795]

Conclusion

America's economy is complex and has changed radically over the nation's history, by reason of the Gilded Age (Industrial Revolution) and the coincidental progressive-led social reformation. Thus, over the past century, and thanks to progressivism's influence, our economy changed in ways that would surprise our founders—frankly, not all in an unfavorable manner. However, what contemporary progressives have in mind for our future economy is off-the-scale frightening and truly radical. Follow the money! Control over the economy brings either life or death to a nation. Progressive plans will not bring life, but it will strengthen their control.

SECTION IV

Introduction: Progressivism's War Against American Exceptionalism

No people can be bound to acknowledge and adore the Invisible Hand which conducts the affairs of men more than those of the United States. Every step by which they have advanced to the character of an independent nation seems to have been distinguished by some token of providential agency.[796]

—George Washington, first inaugural address, April 30, 1789

American "exceptionalism" as originally intended is a term mostly rejected by progressives. It stems from the American Revolution, what one political scientist called "the first new nation" of the modern world and spawned the American ideology of "Americanism," which is based on liberty, equality, individualism, republicanism, democracy, and capitalism.[797]

The concept has a number of potential origins, but what isn't disputed is that the term is a political tool used from the time of Founding Father George Washington to President Donald Trump for both domestic and foreign policy purposes. It rhetorically connects Americans to a shared identity that tracks back to our early years.

John Winthrop was a Puritan preacher and founding governor of the Massachusetts Bay Colony, the first permanent English settlement in America. In 1630, Winthrop may first have conveyed the general concept of exceptionalism in a sermon to encourage his congregation they had a God-given mission in founding the new American colony. Winthrop concluded that sermon with a phrase adapted from Jesus' Sermon on the Mount (Matthew 5–7): "For we must consider that we shall be as a city upon a hill. The eyes of all people are upon us." That perspective, the "city on a hill" image, is characteristic of American exceptionalism even to this day.[798]

That possible origin of the term is rejected by some who argue that Winthrop's thinking at the time was not intended to imply a vision for the new nation. Rather, Winthrop focused on the example the Puritans would provide other colonists and perhaps those that might follow them to the Promised Land.

Another possible origin is attributed to Thomas Paine, a founding revolutionary American figure who published a pamphlet, *Common Sense*, which shared a vision about the new American nation, stating: "We have it in our power to begin the world over again." He opined that the "birthday of a new world is at hand." That statement evidences an exceptionalist's view that encouraged the coming revolution.[799]

Others credit Alexander Hamilton's writing in the "Federalist Papers" as describing America's exceptionalist political experiment. Hamilton wrote:

> It seems to have been reserved to the people of this country, by their conduct and example, to decide the important question, whether societies of men are really capable or not of establishing good government from reflection and choice, or whether they are forever destined to depend for their political constitutions on accident and force.[800]

Even our founding documents reflect principles that suggest America's exceptionalism. Our Declaration of Independence emphasized truths about human equality and rights grounded in biblical doctrine. The Declaration affirmed certain unalienable rights to "life, liberty, and the pursuit of happiness." That statement might be understood as a kind of equality of opportunity, a view President Abraham Lincoln expressed in 1861, "to afford all an unfettered start, and a fair chance in the race of life."[801]

In 1862, President Lincoln used his remarks to Congress about the emancipation of the slaves to call attention to America's exceptional situation. He called America "the last best hope of earth," and then the very next year, the war-time president described America in his Gettysburg Address as a nation "dedicated" to the proposition that "all men are created equal." That's the principle at the heart of America's culture and evidence of her exceptionalism.[802]

Social scientist Seymour Martin Lipset agrees that the roots of the ideology of American exceptionalism traces back to our early founders. He wrote:

> Born out of revolution, the United States is a country organized around an ideology which includes a set of dogmas about the nature of a good society. Americanism, as different people have pointed out, is an 'ism' or ideology in the same way that communism or fascism or liberalism are isms.... The nation's ideology can be described in five words: liberty, egalitarianism, individualism, populism, and laissez-faire. The revolutionary ideology which became the American Creed is liberalism in its eighteenth- and nineteenth-century meanings, as distinct from conservative Toryism, statist communitarianism, mercantilism, and noblesse oblige dominant in monarchical, state-church-formed cultures.[803]

Although there are many similarities between the US and other Western democracies, explained Lipset, the social scientist maintains that, as a result of our revolutionary origins, modern-day America remains "exceptional" and "qualitatively different from all other countries."[804]

America's exceptionalist thinking even traces back to our frontier experience. In 1893, American historian Frederick Jackson Turner said exceptionalist thinking shaped American culture by creating a tendency for western expansion, views that became commonplace in popular textbooks. He wrote about rugged individualism and egalitarianism, great achievements, hard work, idealism, and dedication among self-made men. These ideas shaped culture and identified America globally as an exceptional place.[805]

American exceptionalism can also be traced in part to President Theodore Roosevelt, who said the United States' role in the world included using its power for good. In part, that led to Roosevelt's creation of the Monroe Doctrine to block European colonization of Latin America by expanding our influence through increased military intervention in the Western Hemisphere.

A few short years later, President Woodrow Wilson expressed a similar sentiment with his 1918 "Fourteen Points" speech following the end of the First World War and again when he proposed the League of Nations, which put America squarely in the camp of using our might to promote democracy, international order, and free trade. He viewed American exceptionalism as driving our sense of duty to help the world by ending conflicts such as entering the "Midnight War," the Russian Revolution against the Russian Bolsheviks (Soviets) in July 1918, and without Congress' knowledge and approval.

Another view of the origin of the concept is attributed to Soviet dictator Joseph Stalin, who in 1929 used the label. Evidently, in June 1927, Jay Lovestone, the leader of the Communist Party in America, argued that American strength prevented communist revolution. Meanwhile, Stalin took exception to Lovestone's ideas as "the heresy of American exceptionalism," allegedly another first use of the term.[806]

Historian Deborah Madsen said exceptionalism represents the nation's identity no matter its origin. She wrote:

American exceptionalism permeates every period of American history and is the single most powerful agent in a series of arguments that have been fought down the centuries concerning the identity of America and Americans.[807]

Contemporary American exceptionalism is under attack from progressives, however. This cabal seeks to destroy the concept by disassembling, neutering the basic building blocks of our exceptionalism.

Consider that American exceptionalism represents ideals associated with this country's rich history. Five of those ideals are addressed in this section.

The fact is progressives tend to be fascistic when it comes to some of the ideals that made America exceptional, which President Trump labels as reflective of our country's greatness. Among those ideals progressives attack with vehemence are our individuality, capitalism, liberty, equality, and patriotism.

Each of these is addressed by a chapter that considers the unique nature of that ideal for America as well as its role in keeping America exceptional in the world. Then I examine how progressives responded to each ideal, often with fascistic actions, and suggest how progressives might address each one in the future, especially should they once again acquire the reins of government power.

15

Individualism: An Ideal of American Exceptionalism

The primary safeguard of American individualism is an understanding of it; of faith that it is the most precious possession of American civilization, and a willingness courageously to test every process of national life upon the touchstone of this basic social premise.

—Herbert Hoover, 31st President of the United States[808]

The epitome of American individualism is a former slave who escaped bondage to become the first African-American to attain historic stature. Frederick Douglass, born on a Maryland plantation in 1818, became a fierce defender of individualism when he was just sixteen years old.

Early in his life, Douglass was frequently whipped, and was eventually sent to Baltimore to build ships before fleeing from slavery by traveling to the north to become an antislavery orator and autobiographer of *Narrative of the Life of Frederick Douglass.*[809]

Douglass was a principled man who favored American individualism based on self-reliance and opposed any subordination of individual rights. Even after the Civil War (1861–1865), Douglass asked that former slaves be left to fend for themselves—evidence of his view on individualism.[810]

Douglass' spirit of individualism is embedded in America's DNA, a vital ingredient in what makes America exceptional. It was part of the make-up of our founders and great Americans like Douglass who established this new country based on individual liberty.

President Herbert Hoover (1874–1964) coined the phrase "rugged individualism" to contrast Americans against their European forefathers who were so accustomed to the totalitarianism of Europe.[811] Hoover wrote:

> Individualism has been the primary force of American civilization for three centuries. It is our sort of individualism that has supplied the motivation of America's political, economic, and spiritual institutions in all these years. It has proved its ability to develop its institutions with the changing scene. Our very form of government is the product of the individualism of our people, the demand for an equal opportunity, for a fair chance.[812]

Hoover explained the source of American individualism as an epic expression, the pioneer spirit that emerged as a "response to the challenge of opportunity, to the challenge of nature, to the challenge of life, to the call of the frontier."[813]

American individualism grew without government's help, wrote Hoover. It received its "character from our contacts with the forces of nature on a new continent. It evolved government without official emissaries to show the way; it plowed and sowed two score of great states; it built roads, bridges, railways, cities; it carried forward every attribute of high civilization over a continent."[814]

Hoover saw new frontiers beyond our early twentieth-century challenges and borders, such as the "great continent of science." He offered that individualism "is the only pioneer who will penetrate the [future] frontiers in the quest for new worlds to conquer. The very genius of our institutions has been given to them by the pioneer spirit. Our individualism is rooted in our very nature."[815]

Progressives Attack Individualism

American individualism's critics dispute its importance. French writer de Tocqueville said individualism is about being selfish and self-absorbed. He worried that "the American political religion of equality would lead to a society in which each thought only of himself and individualism decayed into egotism and materialism," according to C. Eric Mount, in his *Review of Religious Research.*[816]

America's "rugged individualism," as explained by Hoover, is certainly epitomized by historic American characters like Davey Crockett (1786–1836), "King of the Wild Frontier," who fought at the Alamo, and Daniel Boone (1734–1820), a pioneer, explorer, and woodsman who fought in the Revolutionary War and is best known for allegedly killing a bear with his bare hands. These are prototypical frontier men, rugged individualists who prevailed in America's wilderness and inspired untold others—not the least of which were American youth who watched portrayals of their adventures in movies and on television.

American sociologist Robin M. Williams Jr. (1914–2006) rejected the notion that American individualism entails a "lone cowboy"—or, like Crockett and Boone, a lone woodsman culture estranged from other groups. Rather, he argued that "American individualism has consisted mainly of a rejection of the state and impatience with restraints upon economic activity; it has not tended to set the autonomous individual in rebellion against his social group."[817] However, that view tends to be the fear expressed by progressives who reject individualism.

Progressives are the most vitriolic of all critics of American individualism because they are so strongly attached to government and state intervention, something sociologist Williams rejects, and obviously so did Hoover.

Not just progressives, but many of America's past enemies hate our individualism. Psychologist Martin Seligman explained the perceived problem with American individualism. "In the past quarter-century," he wrote in his book, *Learned Optimism*, "events occurred that so weakened our commitment to larger entities as to leave us almost naked before the ordinary assaults of life.... Where can one now turn for identity, for purpose, and for hope? When we need spiritual furniture, we look around and see that all the comfortable leather sofas and stuffed chairs have been removed and all that's left to sit on is a small, frail folding chair: the self."[818] Seligman obviously doesn't appreciate the value of the frontiersman, the strength of the individual.

The Center for American Progress (CAP) predictably rejects individualism as well, writing:

> Progressives challenged excessive individualism in social thought and politics, promoted an alternative to laissez-faire economics, and replaced constitutional formalism with a more responsive legal order that expanded American democracy and superseded the economic status quo with a stronger national framework of regulations and social reforms.[819]

Of course, replacing "constitutional formalism" means removing individual rights and replacing them with government controls that superintend affairs for the citizens, and thus the citizens belong to government.

It is as if contemporary progressives really want to remake America more like Europe, and one way to accomplish that feat is to attack American individualism. In part, Americans escaped Europe to find freedom in America, and now progressives, who reject much of our founders' aims and our Constitution, seek to turn the United States into the America of Europe.

We turn to a Pew Research Center poll to illustrate American views about the phenomenon of individualism compared with that of

Europeans. Not surprisingly, Americans far more so than Europeans value individualism.

American values differ from our Western European forefathers and their descendants in an important way, such as individualism as opposed to the role of big government, which are very dissimilar.

A 2012 Pew Research Center poll found that nearly six in ten (58 percent) Americans believe it is more important for everyone (the individual) to be free to pursue their life's goals without interference from government, while 35 percent say it is more important for government to play an active role in society.[820] That difference reflects the ideological divide in America between conservatives and libertarians (traditionalists) and big-government liberals (progressives).

Europeans are mostly wedded to the idea that big government—progressive ideology—is critical to their lives, according to Pew. At least six in ten in Spain (67 percent), France (64 percent), and Germany (62 percent), and more than half (55 percent) in Britain say government should ensure that nobody is in need. No wonder West Europeans embraced the European Union that collapsed borders and grew big government with many institutions and regulations, a reflection of the rejection of individualism in favor of the nanny-state (progressive) mentality.[821]

Not surprisingly, three-quarters of American conservatives and libertarians say the individual should be free to pursue goals without big government interference, while at least half of American liberals (progressives) favor government playing an active role to help the needy.[822]

Older Americans tend to be more concerned about big government than their younger counterparts. About half (47 percent) of younger Americans prioritize the freedom to pursue life's goals without interference from the state, and a similar percentage (46 percent) say it is more important for the government to guarantee that nobody is in need. Meanwhile, six in ten older Americans want to keep government out of their affairs.[823]

Americans typically favor individualism when asked if they agree that "success in life is pretty much determined by forces outside our control." Only a third (36 percent) say they have little control, while most Europeans throw up their hands and admit their success in life is predetermined by forces outside their control (read "socialist-leaning, big government").[824]

The tug-of-war between progressive, anti-individualism, big-government ideology and little government, pro-individualism conservativism and libertarianism is a fight worth engaging in, and there is hope.

Hope for American Individualism

David Davenport, former president of Pepperdine University and a visiting fellow at the Ashbrook Center, and Gordon Lloyd, a senior fellow at Ashbrook and a professor at Pepperdine, jointly wrote about rugged individualism in the *Hoover Digest* to identify reasons for both pessimism and optimism about our future. Clearly, one might be pessimistic about the future of individualism because of the current political climate that undermines this classic ideal. After all, more Americans today seem to be content to let big government do more and more.

We saw this quite clearly in the 2016 presidential campaign, whereby progressive Vermont Senator Bernie Sanders, an avowed socialist, ran on promises of more big-government programs ranging from single-payer health insurance (Medicare for All [Life]) to free college and the redistribution of wealth through higher taxes for the wealthy. Even Democratic Party candidate Hillary Clinton embraced progressivism with her big-government solutions.[825]

We shouldn't blame Democrats alone for the progressive push being forged to big government programs now usurping rugged individualism, however. Recent Republican presidents like George W. Bush pushed for big-government programs like "No Child Left Behind" and the expansion of prescription drug benefits for the aged.

Past progressive big-government programs, whether under Obama,

Bush, or back to the time of Roosevelt's New Deal impacted American thinking about individual liberty—individualism. Americans used to rely on churches and nonprofits to meet public needs, but no longer. Most Americans today almost immediately turn to big government to provide a helping hand, a byproduct of progressivism's cultural influence over the past century. Today, American government is ubiquitous, invading our lives on most fronts from healthcare to dictating the size of our drinks; it seems there is no corner of life where government is hands off, even in our parenting.

Many contemporary parents emulate progressive government's assault on individualism. We call them "helicopter parents" who track their children's every move. Whether it's progressive big government or "helicopter parents," the effect is the same—it undermines the old gold of individualism.

Push-back Progressivism's Assault on Individualism

Herbert Hoover understood the threat posed by progressivism (socialism) to American individualism. He argued:

> Our individualism is no middle ground between autocracy— whether of birth, economic or class origin—and socialism. Socialism of different varieties may have something to recommend it as an intellectual stop-look-and-listen sign, more especially for Old World societies. But it contains only destruction to the forces that make progress in our social system. Nor does salvation come by any device for concentration of power, whether political or economic, for both are equally reversions to Old World autocracy in new garments.[826]

"Salvation will not come to us out of the wreckage of individualism," Hoover argued, and continued:

What we need today is steady devotion to a better, brighter, broader individualism—an individualism that carries increasing responsibility and service to our fellows. Our need is not for a way out but for a way forward. We found our way out three centuries ago when our forefathers left Europe for these shores, to set up here a commonwealth conceived in liberty and dedicated to the development of individuality.[827]

Hoover called out progressivism as a maligned and radical social force:

These men would assume that all reform and human advance must come through government. They have forgotten that progress must come from the steady lift of the individual and that the measure of national idealism and progress is the quality of idealism in the individual. The most trying support of radicalism comes from the timid or dishonest minds that shrink from facing the result of radicalism itself but are devoted to defense of radicalism as proof of a liberal mind. Most theorists who denounce our individualism as a social basis seem to have a passion for ignorance of its constructive ideals.

The primary safeguard of American individualism is an understanding of it; of faith that it is the most precious possession of American civilization, and a willingness courageously to test every process of national life upon the touchstone of this basic social premise.[828]

He continued:

Humanity has a long road to perfection, but we of America can make sure progress if we will preserve our individualism, if we will preserve and stimulate the initiative of our people, if we will build up our insistence and safeguards to equality of opportunity, if we will glorify service as a part of our national character. Progress will march if we hold an abiding faith in the intelligence, the initiative, the character, the courage, and the divine touch in the individual.[829]

Like Hoover, Davenport and Lloyd find reasons to be optimistic about rugged individualism, in part because it survived a century of progressivism. They pose the question: Will individualism enjoy a renaissance in the twenty-first century?

They explain that American individualism thrives in a frontier environment and the twenty-first century offers the Information Age, which could very well produce a revival of individualism, by reason of social media, a new domain. This view clearly reflects what Hoover said about the challenges of science many years ago.

The concept that Davenport and Lloyd explain is "networked individualism" *vis-à-vis* social media because we are able to be alone yet maintain connections through technology. We are able to operate with greater individualism while networking with larger social groups that allow us to develop new hobbies and interests. This new individualism is explained by Lee Rainie and Barry Wellman in *Networked: The New Social Operating System*: "The networked operating system gives people new ways to solve problems and meet social needs. It offers more freedom to individuals...because now they have more room to maneuver and more capacity to act on their own."[830]

Time will tell whether "networked individualism" grants a boost to a modern version of Hoover's rugged individualism. But it is irrefutable that technology gives rise to that possibility. Rainie and Wellman explain: "The Internet allowed users to be both more networked and more assertive as individuals."[831]

Another encouraging sign of a rebirth of individualism is the migration of young people away from large corporations to start-up enterprises. Professor Tomas Chamorro-Premuzic of University College of London confirms this trend:

In the fifteen years I've been teaching MBA [masters of business administration] students, their career plans have changed dramatically. Until the early 2000s they aspired to work in traditional corporate jobs…. In the past few years, however, a new favorite career choice has emerged—working for themselves or launching their own business.[832]

Individualism tends to spark creativity among the networked world. A Cornell University study cited by Davenport and Lloyd found that levels of creativity and innovation are higher among individuals as opposed to collectivist group settings. Although it may not be clear as to how this translates across the broader social sphere, it does promote the case for individualism.

Even immigrants give hope that American individualism may survive progressivism. They come mostly to seek a better life and opportunity. Davenport and Lloyd illustrate this view: "When you take a taxi ride in a major U.S. city, your driver is frequently an immigrant who, if given the chance, will tell you how he is working hard so that his children will enjoy the American dream." But, as Milton Friedman once said, even rugged individualism is threatened by the American welfare state and the emphasis on ethnic identity. Friedman explained that this American spirit is threatened by "multiculturalism, and rugged individualism by a welfare state."[833]

On the education front, more and more Americans are saying no to progressive education in our public schools, a view outlined in Section III of this book. Americans are choosing homeschooling and private education alternatives; a return to the classics is surfacing much like the old version of the Boston Latin School and the common school approach of the past, such as the homeschooling curriculum known as Classical Conversations.[834]

Patriotism also encourages rugged individualism, the topic of a forthcoming chapter in this section. For now, consider that Americans still enjoy our rich heritage as evidenced by a continued interest in our national monuments, participation in the political process, and civics in general.

Don't expect progressives to surrender their fight against American individualism, however. They will continue to try to make it irrelevant, an ideal of the bygone years of America's Old West, or redefine it as "me'ism" selfishness of big corporations and the domain of the wealthy. But that's a false analogy.

The fact is individualism has at its core individual liberty, our rights as outlined in the Bill of Rights. We don't want to return to those places and circumstances our founders fled in order to establish a place free from old Europe's totalitarianism and more recently their love of progressive big government.

American progressives are poised to limit our individual freedoms concerning education, healthcare, religion, speech, and self-determination and place them in the hands of big government. Davenport and Lloyd properly warned:

> As Jefferson said, the world belongs to the living, and each gener-
> ation must work out its own understanding of things. We should
> neither have a blind veneration for the past (Federalist No. 14)
> nor deprive the past of its due veneration, without which govern-
> ment could not maintain its stability (Federalist No. 49). [835]

Progressive calls to sever our individual rights by strengthening big government's power through law, executive power, or judicial overreach is a declaration of war against the founders' checks and balances and separations of power in our Constitution. We must counter this assault.

Sustaining American Individualism

A twentieth-century Nobel Laureate in economics and a social philosopher outlined a system of individualism for future European generations that applies to America as well. Friedrich A. Hayek's 1947 speech, "Individualism True and False," viewed individualism as a social construct with the potential to make life better for all, and it is consistent with biblical Scriptures.[836]

The Center for Individualism modernized Hayek's language, yet his ideas are fully applicable for American audiences today who seek to preserve individualism in our culture.

Hayek's manifesto for individualism begins with "We all want social order." Social order is an objective everyone should seek, he said. Basically, we want to live in harmony, yet we also want to better our circumstances. That's "a desired state," argues the economist.

Hayek explains that we often seek that "desired state" by relying on government through the political process. He warns that an overreliance on government tends to drift "towards the worst forms of state control." At the time of Hayek's speech, World War II had just ended and the world faced a host of state-control alternatives: communism, fascism, National Socialism (like Nazism), and democracy. Today, in America, we are seeing a drift toward socialism and away from democracy, evidently a progressive-inspired drift.

The alternative to these state-control types of governance, explained Hayek, is individualism, which is "a set of general rules that everyone observes without government coercion." The rules, he said, provide an institutional framework wherein selecting how to make a living is left up to each person, because that's "the best opportunity to bring about effective coordination of individual effort."

Dr. Hayek then outlines the general rules of individualism. He explained they emerged over time as people in society collaborate in the marketplace: each person follows his or her own conscience, all property is private, and none of it belongs to the state; all are free to try their best, to see what they can achieve and more.

These general rules of individualism are satisfied by an effective competitive market. Individuals take the risk to find out if the results of their efforts create value for others. Consumer preferences tell producers what then to produce.

When individuals are free to produce as they see fit, they tend to contribute to others and institutionalized charity and government welfare become unnecessary. Individuals become collaborative and give with a focus on their family, community, and small group. This outcome promotes great institutions "on which civilization arises."

A system of individualism doesn't depend on the progressive elites to run it, either. Hayek says individualism has no belief in majority decisions, or the few "wise" men to run things because "no-one knows what's best. Everybody is allowed to try and see what they can do."

The political objective is to limit all coercive and restrictive power to ensure voluntary and spontaneous collaboration, which naturally limits governmental restrictions. Further, individuals don't need a government agent to use coercion to force us to act for the good of society.

Unlike progressivism, individualism doesn't try to make people equal. Rather, it treats them equally by granting everyone the power to decide his or her own course. This was the beauty America's founders built into our Constitution.

Finally, Hayek says, individualism is a humble approach to viewing society. Everyone does his or her best and, as a result, mankind achieves great things.

Conclusion

Individualism is an important ideal associated with American exceptionalism. Progressives seek to destroy this unique ideal and replace it with a European-style, big-government reliance—a nanny-state approach to satisfy our every need. That's contrary to our founders' intent and would undermine our efforts to explore the future frontiers of this world.

16

Capitalism: An Ideal of American Exceptionalism

The inherent vice of capitalism is the unequal sharing of blessings; the inherent virtue of socialism is the equal sharing of
miseries.[837]

—Winston Churchill, World War II British Prime Minister

Capitalism is a critical ideal of American exceptionalism that reflects our
founders' intent for a free and prosperous nation. President George
Washington echoed that view in a 1784 letter to Benjamin Harrison: "A
people…who are possessed of the spirit of commerce, who see and who
will pursue their advantages may achieve almost anything."[838]

Contemporary American progressives wage war against capitalism
in part because they consider it evil and a reflection of man's greediness.
This is especially true among American Millennials, those ages eighteen
through twenty-nine, as evidenced by a 2016 Harvard University survey
that found most Millennials (51 percent) oppose capitalism. Even
worse, a bloomberg.com poll found that nearly half of all Millennials
(44 percent) prefer to live in a socialist country.[839]

No wonder progressive-promoting socialists are attacking capitalism and that rising anger encourages high-profile Democratic Party candidates for the presidency and Congress to embrace that radicalism. In fact, Democrats are almost tripping over one another racing to microphones to embrace socialism, promising that it will provide an aspirational equal and just society, as opposed to "evil" (their word) capitalism's legacy.

The legacy of socialism, not of capitalism, is especially dangerous. Mark Perry, a scholar at the conservative American Enterprise Institute and an economics professor at the University of Michigan, said socialism has a fatal flaw: It fails "to emphasize incentives[;] socialism is a theory inconsistent with human nature and is therefore doomed to fail."[840]

In contrast, proponents of capitalism claim it is a founding principle, the free market where citizens can produce, buy, and sell without government interference. Capitalism brings out the best in men by encouraging hard work, integrity, and a drive to do better.

Obviously, a major fight is brewing between American capitalists and socialism-promoting progressives. However, if there is a superior economic system, then let's collaborate to develop it.

This chapter explores capitalism's record and why progressives are so opposed to the concept. Then we consider what the modern crop of progressive leaders might do to American capitalism if they gain political power.

Capitalism's Record in America

Capitalist and twice presidential candidate Steve Forbes says capitalism has gotten a bad rap from progressives. It "is like a fish that doesn't realize the wonder of the water that surrounds it," he said. "Free markets improve people's lives in ways they take for granted."[841]

Forbes explained capitalism for the layman: "In a true free market, the people who start out with the least have the best chance to move ahead. Why? Because you have a growing economy, which means better jobs are being created."

He continued, "So you start out with a simple job, like a summer job at McDonald's or Wendy's or whatever. You start to learn some basic skills, and as your skills increase, so do your chances to move up in life."[842]

Forbes explained that the federal government's own surveys verify this upward mobility in our capitalist economy. The anticapitalists (progressives) focus on the bottom fifth of the population, however. The gap between them and the wealthiest Americans prompts progressive complaints. Forbes explained "They [progressives] overlook the fact that most of those who start out in the bottom quintile, after a decade or 20 years, have moved way up, many of them to the first or second quintile. As you get skills in a vibrant economy, you move ahead. So for those who start out with very little, the free market is their best friend."[843]

The progressive mindset is one of control over the bottom fifth, all the while trying to convince themselves and others that they are really just providing basic support until the misfortunate are able to care for themselves. The reality is that progressives are stifling the individualism that otherwise would carry the bottom quintile out of their circumstances and up the economic chain.

A good case can be made that progressives are deliberate deceivers in that historically they have been able to keep certain groups ignorant of the root cause of their poverty and lower-class status. They have been successful at this in part because they are also deceived, believing that they have the answers for America when the facts show they are wrong.

Evidence of capitalism's success abounds in spite of some troubled starts. "It's tough to make a business succeed, but Steve Jobs [CEO of Apple, Inc.] was abandoned by his biological parents; Larry Ellison [CEO of Oracle Corporation] was an orphan; and Bill Gates [cofounder of Microsoft] was a middle class kid who dropped out of Harvard. So some of the most unlikely people end up doing extraordinary things," Forbes said.[844]

Let's step back and explore capitalism before considering why progressives label it "evil."

The term "capitalism" was first used in 1850 by French socialist Louis Blanc, who wrote: "What I call 'capitalism' that is to say the appropriation of capital by some to the exclusion of others."[845]

In 1867, anticapitalist Karl Marx described a capitalist in his book, *Capital: A Critique of Political Economy*. Marx said the capitalist's "aim is rather the unceasing movement of profit-making. This boundless drive for enrichment, this passionate chase after value, is common to the capitalist and the miser; but while the miser is merely a capitalist gone mad, the capitalist is a rational miser."[846]

Others, like sociologist Rodney Stark, say:

Capitalism is an economic system wherein privately owned, relatively well-organized and stable firms pursue complex commercial activities within a relatively free (unregulated) market, taking a systematic, long-term approach to investing and reinvesting wealth (directly or indirectly) in productive activities involving a hired workforce and guided by anticipated and actual returns.[847]

Economist Deidre McCloskey defines capitalism as "merely private property and free labor without central planning, regulated by the rule of law and by an ethical consensus." She also said, "Above all modern capitalism encourages innovation."[848]

Brian Grinder, a professor at eastern Washington University, and Dan Cooper, the president of Active Learning Technologies, wrote a series of articles defending capitalism in *Financial History*. They explain:

Capitalism is not a transitory economic state that will eventually be superseded by an economic paradise, nor is it inherently evil. It is a human institution that reflects all the warts and flaws of its creators. Like any human being, it can soar to great heights and sink to unbelievable lows. This is why capitalism needs government regulation and an ethical framework established by society outside of the realm of government to succeed.[849]

The key to capitalism's success, according to Grinder and Cooper, is that it "is able to harness self-interest, with its great potential for evil, and use it for the benefit of mankind. This isn't accomplished by elevating self-interest to a position of prominence or superiority over other virtues, but by ensuring that it works within an ethical system that tempers it."[850]

Grinder and Cooper develop the idea that *homo economicus* ("economic man") must operate in a virtuous economy, not one driven by greed but by self-interest. Economist Deirdre McClosky defines this "virtuous" capitalist society with a list of cardinal characteristics: justice, courage, temperance, and produce; and three biblical virtues: faith, hope, and love.[851]

Similarly, Catholic philosopher Michael Novak has his own set of virtues required to operate a modern capitalist business, including diligence, industriousness, prudence, reliability, fidelity, and courage. Lists of qualities such as those are helpful, but the challenge, according to Grinder and Cooper, is to somehow "salvage the ethical standards offered by religion and find a way to effectively instill them in their [business] organizations." Then the authors remind the reader of some serious capitalist violators of ethical standards that give capitalism a bad name, and rightly earn the progressives' "evil" label.[852]

German carmaker Volkswagen was caught cheating on emissions tests, which cost the company billions of dollars in fines. The American bank Wells Fargo created fraudulent accounts for its customers, which created quite the scandal when it was discovered.

Wells Fargo acknowledged the wrongdoing and started to rebuild its soiled reputation with a public statement of contrition: "We know the value of trust. We were built on it. Back when the country went west for gold, we were the ones who carried it back East. By steam. By horse. By iron horse. Over the years, we built on that trust. We always found the way. Until…we lost it."[853]

That acceptance of guilt, which ran as a television commercial, isn't sufficient, however. Perhaps even the ethics training for its employees won't do much either to restore its reputation. It will take many years of perceived sound, ethical business behavior if ever Wells Fargo is to recoup lost ground.

Grinder and Cooper make an important point about capitalism if it is to function properly. Given the above examples, it must have a strong ethical foundation that balances all the virtues properly.

Admittedly, capitalism is plagued by human failings, which explains the importance of regulation and a sound ethical foundation. But the fact is that, "in all of human history, capitalism is the only economic system that has ever [produced] the expansive growth that lifts people out of poverty, raises their standard of living, and reduces income inequality," said Andy Puzder, author of *The Capitalist Comeback: The Trump Boom and the Left's Plot to Stop It.* Puzder explains how capitalism reflects our founders' commitment to limited government and individual freedom. [854]

Puzder sees President Trump's 2016 win as a rejection of progressivism and, by association, socialism as an economic theory. After all, as Puzder wrote, "Hillary Clinton assured voters she would continue Obama's failed progressive legacy as president." [855] However, the ongoing political war in Washington and the rise of progressive candidates in Congress and a bevy of progressives seeking the 2020 Democratic Party nomination give reason for concern that the war against capitalism is far from over.

Progressive Attacks on Capitalism

Progressives are like primitive men who invented false gods to comfort them in the face of chaotic economic situations like recessions and poverty. They turn to big government to create order because capitalism is inherently chaotic, which makes them very uncomfortable.

The division between capitalists and progressives comes down to a philosophical difference in understanding the social contract. Eighteenth-century French philosopher Jean-Jacque Rousseau argued for a collectivist, progressive view that modern man entered a social contract to form society for mutual safety and betterment by giving up some freedom in exchange for order and security. Relinquishing freedom is replaced by safety and security, which includes the modern welfare state.[856]

British philosopher John Locke argued for a very different interpretation of the social contract, an individualistic understanding—a capitalist view. He argued that government does not bestow rights upon man, but rights are inherently man's by nature. Rather, government's role is to provide citizens with the tools to defend themselves against the tyranny of their fellow men while protecting their rights to life, liberty, and property. Government is not the guarantor of a certain standard of living, either, as progressives like to argue.[857]

Progressives truly believe government is society's agent to undertake the tasks of social justice, entitlement, and wealth redistribution. Further, the state's coercive arm is the "means by which everyone is made to contribute their 'social dues' in the form of either obedience to government regulations or payment of taxes for redistributive purposes," according to Richard M. Ebeling, who writes in "Capitalism 101: 'Progressives' are Enemies of Freedom."[858]

Let there be no misunderstanding about the progressive's political philosophy when it comes to capitalism. Government exists to protect individual rights. Progressives talk about democracy, equality, and social justice, but they intend to enforce that outcome using public policies overseen by elitism, hubris, and authoritarianism. Arguably, one can make the case that progressives will employ a fascistic approach to economic policy.

So how do progressives overcome their insecurity about the chaotic state of capitalism, as outlined at the start of this section? How do they secure government guarantees of secure jobs and income? They take over government with promises to create a welfare "nanny" state by providing a comfortable living for all on an equal basis. These statists will then employ fascistic-like powers to rein in capitalism.

Had progressives been in charge in late-nineteenth-century America, there never would have been an Industrial Revolution; everyone would still be on the farm working the land behind a plow pulled by a team of mules. We've seen similar progressive views evidenced more recently as they clung to old ways in the 1970s and 1980s, objecting to the loss of heavy industry in favor of more service-oriented industries. After all, it was progressives who propped up General Motors to the tune of $11.2 billion and subsidized other failing, old industries.

Warren Meyer, an Arizona businessman, writes in *Forbes* magazine to provide a sure-fire test of whether someone is a progressive. He presents two economic worldviews. The first is a society "where the overall levels of wealth and technology continue to increase, though in a pattern that is dynamic, chaotic, generally unpredictable, and whose rewards are unevenly distributed." The second is a society "where everyone is poorer, but income is generally more evenly distributed and where jobs and pay and industries change only very slowly, and people have good assurances that they will continue to have what they have today, with little downside but also with very little upside."[859]

Progressives will always pick the second "society," explained Meyer, even though it means everyone is poorer and it puts a stop to future improvements. Simply put, progressives want what's in the "bank" today, they want to distribute it equally among all the people, and they want to continue in the same vein for the rest of time.[860]

Meyer says he knows why they always take the socialist worldview in part because that's how they answer public-opinion surveys. Also, he argues, look at the policies progressives endorse. Inevitably, a progressive policy quashes innovation in favor of guaranteed access—certainly those policies that impact economic growth and improvement.

This perspective is really scary. That's what caught Germany in the grips of the Nazi Party (National Socialist Party)—guarantees by the government—healthcare, jobs, housing, education, childcare, and more. Meyer contends that progressives would willingly trade away the promises of capitalism's empowerment of the individual and "would accept a master, would accept impoverishment and stagnation, in order to attain predictability."[861]

Don't believe Meyer? Consider alternatives like Marxism and socialism, which acknowledge mankind's flaws and promise a bright economic future. Proponents of these theories call out capitalism's failure to provide a hope of economic nirvana as a flaw that compels some to conclude that capitalism won't last and must be eventually replaced by a better system.

Marx argued in the Communist Manifesto that capitalism would implode on itself due to fierce competition. He said, "What the bourgeoisie, therefore, produces, above all, is its own grave-diggers."[862] But Marx's revolution eventually backfired.

The red Russians revolted against the monarchists in 1917 and won the opportunity to form the Soviet Union led initially by Vladimir L. Lenin. But instead of spreading across the world to replace capitalism, Marx's promised global communist revolution abruptly ended by reason of President Reagan's leadership and America's capitalistic economic pressure—the real grave-diggers for communism.

Progressives didn't anticipate the quick demise of capitalism as did Marx. Specifically, progressive British economist John Maynard Keynes did predict the end of capitalism and a virtuous outcome. In 1930, Keynes wrote in an essay, "Economic Possibilities for Our Grandchildren": "Assuming no important wars and no important increase in population, the economic problem [capitalism] may be solved, or be at least within sight of solution, within a hundred years."[863]

Keynes anticipated that the attraction of wealth accumulation would diminish with "great changes in the code of morals." That result would come about when we do away with "many of the pseudo moral principles which have gag-ridden us for two hundred years, by which we have exalted the most distasteful of human qualities into the position of the highest virtues—the love of money as a possession—as distinguished from the love."[864]

Economist Robert Nelson argued that Keynes and other progressives trusted that God works "through economic forces and is planning a glorious ending to the world based on the workings of rapidly advancing material productivity." However, Nelson concluded almost a century after Keynes' prediction that virtue would win over love of money "that the faith in the redeeming power of material progress is fading."[865]

Progressives still consider capitalism "evil," but they have yet to find a better alternative. However, that failure has not stopped them from advancing failed socialism as is now occupying America's left as we move closer to the 2020 elections.

What Contemporary Progressives Plan for Twenty-first-Century Capitalism

Capitalism has not always existed in the world and will not always exist in the world.[866]
—Alexandria Ocasio-Cortez, socialist and member of Congress

Democrats are rushing to embrace socialism as an alternative to capitalism. We got a taste of the shift beginning with the surge of support for socialist Senator Bernie Sanders in 2016, but he wasn't alone. In fact, it seems as if today's Democratic Party elite feel they have to apologize for being capitalists. These progressives are acting more like the old socialists, and granting them new power will only lead to the same failed outcomes of the past.

Progressive Democratic Party elite are running away from the benefits of capitalism and toward free college, free cash, free healthcare, guaranteed jobs, and so on. They are saying whatever necessary to keep from alienating their socialist-leaning base.

The coming presidential primary campaign among Democrats appears to be an example of how to one-up each other on every possible progressive, socialist promise, such as guaranteed jobs. "Even our lefty comrades in social democratic Europe don't guarantee jobs for everyone," wrote Kevin Drum, a liberal blogger for the left-wing publication *Mother Jones*. "It would cost a fortune; it would massively disrupt the private labor market; it would almost certainly tank productivity; and it's unlikely in the extreme that the millions of workers in this program could ever be made fully competent at their jobs."[867]

That sounds like something out of Karl Marx's playbook. In fact, Paul Kengor wrote in the *Wall Street Journal* that Marx's communist philosophy "set the stage…for the greatest ideological massacres in history." Marx rebuked capitalism and individual property rights that inspired the likes of Vladimir Lenin, Mao Zedong, North Korea's Kim family, and the Castro brothers, and as a result, many millions of innocents died.[868]

No, we aren't at that point and hopefully never will get to that point in America. However, anticipate that every Democrat running for president in 2020 will be asked to choose between socialism and capitalism. I expect that most will bow to the progressives and openly embrace socialism, which "is just a kinder, gentler version of communism." Alternatively, they will simply rename it—maybe the "New Progressive Economy." Can't you almost hear that announcement on CNN to celebratory cheers?[869]

17

Liberty: An Ideal of American Exceptionalism

Neither the wisest constitution nor the wisest laws will secure the liberty and happiness of a people whose manners are universally corrupt. He therefore is the truest friend to the liberty of his country who tries most to promote its virtue, and who...will not suffer a man to be chosen into any office of power and trust who is not a wise and virtuous man.[870]

—Samuel Adams, American Founding Father

Liberty is a critical ideal of American exceptionalism. Founder Thomas Jefferson called it an "unalienable" right in our Declaration of Independence, but in the past, progressives redefined Jefferson's "liberty"— and should the progressive cabal regain control of all government in 2020, they will further redefine the term to make it far more of a fleeting ideal, thus undercutting American exceptionalism.

The definition of liberty is "the state or condition of people who are able to act and speak freely."[871] It generally means freedom from restraint or control from almost anything, including illegal and harmful activities, but progressives changed our understanding of the word using fascistic tactics to rob those who disagree with them about liberty, which includes our right to speak openly about issues, to publicly evidence deep-seated and especially religious beliefs, to make choices, and more. Although progressives may profess to be democratic in thought, they often act differently when opposed by those with contrary core beliefs.

True liberty is now fleeting. It once meant that Americans had the right to speak what they will, no matter how unpopular, without fear of government reprisal. Liberty used to mean the right to worship according to the dictates of one's faith. Liberty used to mean the right to bear arms in defense of oneself and freedom from government's overreach. Liberty meant the right to be secure in one's home and with one's family, and it once meant the right not to be deprived of life and property without due process. That's all changing, due to progressives.

Our founders enshrined in our founding documents the principles of liberty that gave us great prosperity, safety, and happiness, of which the rest of the world looks upon with envy. Further, our founders established the role of government as to secure our liberty by protecting each individual's rights, and not as a guarantor of a certain standard of living or desired access to various material things, as progressives argue.

Any government intrusion weakens, undermines, and potentially destroys a person's liberty. Yet progressives use the tyranny of big government to usurp our individual liberty.

Liberty is a broad issue that needs examination to fully understand its scope and the context to which it applies within American society and as an ideal of American exceptionalism. For that analysis, I turned to Carl Eric Scott, who wrote an article about the precious gift of liberty entitled "The Five Conceptions of American Liberty" in *National Affairs*.[872]

Even though most Americans champion liberty, not everyone understands the term in the same way, wrote Scott. Rather, he explains the five conceptions of the term and how those various interpretations lead to political dispute, which adds both bitterness and confusion to our political discourse.[873]

"We need to step back and examine the different meanings of liberty and how they have played out in our history and continue to shape our contemporary debates," writes Scott. He begins by summarizing the "five interlocking" liberties, although each is "distinct."[874]

Liberty is understood as the "protection of natural rights," Scott's first liberty. The second is often used as a reference to the self-governance of a local community or group, a conception, as Scott writes, called "classical communitarian liberty."[875]

These definitions of liberty, "natural rights" and "classical communitarian liberty," trace back to our Founding Fathers. They are expressed in our Declaration of Independence and reflect the teachings of seventeenth-century British philosopher John Locke and French historian Alexis de Tocqueville, who described New England community life in the 1830s as typical of "classical communitarian liberty." These views do complement one another, except, according to Scott, when it came to charting America's future government.

When considering our Constitution, the antifederalists opposed ratification because they insisted America remain a "small polis-like republic," as opposed to the vision expressed in the "Federalist Papers" of an extended republic—a powerful, centralized government—to secure our liberty.[876]

Evidently, the antifederalists embraced a Lockean understanding of politics, which stressed "private rights," expressed at the time as a "state of nature." Meanwhile, founders James Madison and Alexander Hamilton embraced Roman republicanism in their "Federalist Papers" by arguing that the colonies embrace government similar to ancient confederacies and their constitutions.[877]

The colonialists who reveled in the first of the two conceptions of liberty, protection of natural rights, took up arms to fight the British over such issues as "no taxation without representation," but the American rebellion was just as much ignited by those early Americans who favored classical-communitarian liberty.[878]

Scott uses a 1840s-era anecdote to illustrate the view of liberty at our founding. A veteran of the 1775 Battle of Concord, Levi Preston, conversed with Mellon Chamberlain, a historian, who asked whether he (Preston) and his fellow Revolutionary War peers were influenced by certain era philosophers. Preston answered that he had "never heard of 'em. We only read the Bible, the Catechism, Watts's Psalms and Hymns, and the Almanack." Then Chamberlain asked why they fought the British. Preston explained simply, "We had always governed ourselves, and we always meant to. They [the British] didn't mean we should."[879]

Evidently, self-rule was the colonialists' true motivation to fight, according to many historians like Chamberlain, and that's evidence of "classical-communitarian liberty."[880]

That concept of liberty and its power, however, diminished somewhat over the coming centuries, as did the importance of the local community. Yet the communitarian view of liberty remains part of the American political tradition among certain groups and localities, which promote "participatory democracy," that is what some progressives call and advocate for, "direct democracy," which albeit is becoming rather rare.[881]

Third, liberty can be understood as referring to economic individualism, or "economic-autonomy liberty." Scott said this understanding of liberty emerged from natural-rights liberty. That conception found currency during the Progressive Era (late nineteenth and early twentieth centuries), because industrializing the economy at the time required government to protect not just private property (the first concept of liberty), but rights associated with business contracts. This right was viewed as philosophically central to liberty, because it was the view at the time that our Constitution guaranteed "that no American government could deprive any person of liberty without due process of law."[882]

That concept of liberty finds that government's primary aim "is to get out of the way of the individual's own shaping of his economic well-being. This will occur through whatever property he obtains by the sweat of his own brow, to use one of Lincoln's favorite biblical (and Locke-evocative) images, and through his buying, selling, and contracting with others," wrote Scott.[883]

Evidently, according to Scott, some libertarians and conservatives then and now gauge their liberty based on the freedom they see in the economic marketplace for the operation of private enterprise. This liberty was challenged by our late-nineteenth-century government leaders because it resists allowances for monopolies in business and the granting of subsidies, protects collective-bargaining agreements, and establishes market-entry barriers. As you will recall, earlier we considered why government used these economic tools in the early nineteenth century to grow the country's infrastructure and economy, but later abandoned the approach because it favored a minority over the welfare of the majority.

Fourth, liberty can refer to the social justice of a national community, what Scott calls "progressive liberty." It emerged as a concept during the Progressive Era as well, and is a byproduct of economic-autonomy liberty, writes Scott. It also reflects progressive ideology that views confidence in science and the regulation of government affairs by the elite (bureaucracy), especially regarding the oversight of complex systems like economies.

Thus, explained Scott, the conception of liberty became associated with "the collective development of that person's society" and came to mean that society must protect the individual against impoverishment in view of industrial contractual arrangements—wage-labor contracts. As Scott asked: The laborer "could not be made a slave, but how would this really matter if his family was likely to suffer life-threatening penury [state of being poor] the moment he left or lost his job?"[884]

Scott indicates the concern at the time was not just for the financial loss, but the risk of being "pressured to conform to the behavior, perhaps even the political and religious behavior, approved of by his employer." This condition is what President Franklin D. Roosevelt labeled "necessitous men" who "are not free men." Thus, the proper goal of society is "social justice," a self-development type of liberty that makes man truly free.[885]

Progressives also viewed "social justice" liberty as opposed to economic-autonomy liberty, which they associated with individualism, the subject of an earlier chapter in this section. Progressives blame economic theories associated with individualism, which they argue may be useful for American frontiersmen of old but not for a modern, industrial-based economy divided into corporations and wage-earners. Therefore, the old view of the rights to contract known to our early founders, as well as the use of property freely, actually undermines their view of social justice liberty because it helps entrench the power of corporations at the expense of the wage-laborers.[886]

Social justice liberty, according to progressives, also required a rethinking of limits placed by our founders on American federalism, especially regarding the regulation of interstate commerce. Progressives argued then and even now that commerce had become truly national in nature and no longer confined to local (community and state) economies and other artificial barriers. Their reinterpretation of social justice liberty gave new freedom to the federal government to regulate what previously was mostly a local/state matter. Government's reach using the Constitution's Commerce Clause (Article I, Section 8, Clause 3) became incredibly powerful and arguably intrusive.

Finally, fifth, liberty can refer to moral individualism, which Scott calls "personal-autonomy liberty." This type of liberty is the one most discussed within the culture and most often interpreted by the courts and enshrined in the Constitution as the "right to privacy."[887]

Personal-autonomy liberty means individuals are free to do whatever they wish, so long as they do not harm others. This concept traces back to the French Revolution's "Declaration of the Rights of Man and Citizen" (*Déclaration des droits de l'homme et du citoyen de 1789*), which states that "liberty consists in the ability to do whatever does not harm another; hence the exercise of the natural rights of each man has no other limits than those which assure to other members of society the enjoyment of the same rights." Further, that declaration says the "limits" must be established by government law that "only has the right to prohibit those actions which are injurious to society." That is the catch for modern progressives who come to believe that certain lifestyles are harmful not just to individuals but to society—relating to issues such as being overweight, uneducated, drug-addicted, sexually deviant, adhering to religious dogmas, and many more. They also feel compelled, because they believe themselves to be society's elite and smartest, to use government to compel adjustments to others' lifestyles—even if that means disregarding the individual's liberty.[888]

Personal-autonomy liberty often pushes against the majority's effort to regulate our lives. This tension is what our founders (especially the antifederalists) anticipated; they addressed the concern in the Bill of Rights as the first ten amendments to our Constitution to protect minorities from the majority's tyranny.

Although well-meaning, John and Abigail Adams illustrated the threat of majority tyranny. The Adams advocated for laws in Massachusetts that penalized a failure to attend church regularly, and in fact the 1780 Massachusetts constitution directed the legislature to force towns to make provision for "public Protestant teachers of piety, religion, and morality." Similarly, across the young nation at the time, other jurisdictions promoted Christianity through the law, which was fine with the majority Christians of the era, but violated the original intention of the founders, who aimed to protect minorities.[889]

The Supreme Court eventually weighed into this issue (tyranny of the majority) affecting individual liberty and juxtaposed it with their interpretation of the Constitution's intentions. Notably, progressive Justice William Brennan opined to a Georgetown University audience in 1985:

> The Constitution on its face is…a blueprint for government.… When one reflects upon the text's preoccupation with the scope of government as well as its shape, however, one comes to understand that what this text is about is the relationship of the individual and the state. The text marks the metes and bounds of official authority and individual autonomy. When one studies the boundary…one gets a sense of the vision of the individual embodied in the Constitution…a sparkling vision of the supremacy of the human dignity of every individual.[890]

Justice Brennan's progressive view of the "living constitution" is that it calls personal autonomy liberty the "liberation dignity." That view is echoed by Justice Anthony Kennedy in the 1991 case of *Planned Parenthood of Southeastern Pennsylvania v. Casey, 505 U.S. 833*, a decision that reaffirmed the infamous 1973 abortion rights high court case of *Roe v. Wade, 410 U.S. 113*, which considered the constitutionality of laws that criminalized or restricted access to abortions.

Justice Kennedy wrote for the majority in *Roe v. Wade*:

> Our law affords constitutional protection to personal decisions relating to marriage, procreation, contraception, family relationships, child rearing, and education.... These matters, involving the most intimate and personal choices a person may make in a lifetime, choices central to personal dignity and autonomy, are central to the liberty protected by the Fourteenth Amendment. At the heart of liberty is the right to define one's own concept of existence, of meaning, of the universe, and of the mystery of human life." Of course this decision denies the humanity, dignity and liberty of the unborn, a tragic mistake for the high court and a blemish on mankind.[891]

Scott believes those interpretations by the high court will eventually lead to the overturning of laws that prohibit polygamy and polyamory (multiple consenting sex partners), and really all laws grounded in what Justice Antonin Scalia, in his 2003 dissent in *Lawrence v. Texas, 539 U.S. 558*, called a "promotion of majoritarian sexual morality."[892]

Personal-autonomy liberty appears to be central to our democratic heritage and ascendant over our history. This is the battleground conception of liberty that is most in dispute today and especially should progressives take the reins of power, because they are true statists and tend to favor tyranny as opposed to true liberty when in power.

Scott argues that each of the above five conceptions of liberty is genuinely American and has been "posed against one another in various ways," and some even combined over time and thus "have shaped our history and will certainly shape our future as well."[893]

What Have Progressives Done to American Liberty?

If freedom of speech is taken away, then dumb and silent we may be led, like sheep to the slaughter.[894]
—George Washington to a group of military officers in 1783

Much of the intellectual conflict in America in the recent past is about liberty, the most prized and abused of the American ideals that distinguish our country as exceptional.

As we've seen from an examination of the various concepts of liberty, each in its own way likely influenced major events in our nation's history: the American Revolution, the Civil War, and the progressive movement's campaign for the American worker, and the influence continues today, albeit as a divisive element in public debate whether it be regarding homosexual marriage, abortion, Obamacare, or some new progressive agenda item in the future.

The battle lines over liberty are clearly drawn. The political right embraces a natural-rights concept of liberty to view the notion that government is a primary threat, much like our founders' natural-rights view that led us to war against the tyranny of the British. Further, big and intrusive government in America has long denied our liberty through expansive social and political initiatives and intrusions into our private lives like Big Brother in English writer George Orwell's book, *1984*, whereby most of the world became a victim of omnipresent government surveillance and propaganda.

Progressives don't necessarily subscribe to the view that our liberty is threatened by the hand of big government, however. No, they tend to believe the danger to liberty comes not as much from government but from powerful private sources like corporations and the wealthy. We saw that in earlier chapters as we explored the history of the Progressive Era, but that view is shared by modern progressives as well who look suspiciously at the alleged abuses of the powerful and their enterprises.

Progressives then and even now like to quote President Theodore Roosevelt, a Republican and later Progressive Party member, who endorsed government's role in constraining liberty to match his politics. Roosevelt said:

> The history of liberty was the history of the limitation of governmental power. This is true as an academic statement of history in the past. It is actually the liberty of some great trust magnate to do that which he is not entitled to do. We propose, on the contrary, to extend governmental power in order to secure the liberty of the oppressed from the oppressor. We stand for the limitation of his liberty not to oppress those who are weaker than himself.[895]

There must be limits to government power, a view coincidentally shared by progressives and many on the right. They argue that liberty— by which they mean Scott's fifth conception, "personal-autonomy liberty"—is infringed upon when the National Security Agency (NSA) spies on us by listening to our telephonic conversations and monitoring our cyberspace interactions (emails) and when Google collects and then sells our personal information to others who then exploit it for financial or nefarious outcomes. However, progressives depart from those of us on the right when applying their view of liberty as a right to access healthcare, education, and food at the expense of others. Further, progressives claim liberty is robbed when private corporations use their deep pockets to dominate the political process that trumps individual voices, the majority. But progressives go beyond these points to bash "personal-autonomy liberty" among those with whom they disagree, especially on contentious social issues such as speech.

Progressives use a variety of tools to counter speech they consider a threat to their liberty, such as "identity politics" on college campuses, in the media, and at other so-called elite centers. Specifically, progressives tend to reject the concept of my right to disagree with them and seldom defend others' right to do so either. The fact is they attack anyone for offending their sacred identities, a fascist approach to civil liberty (speech).

Progressive sensitivities to speech are fueled by an antiliberty movement on the left, within the media and academia that use administrative punishment, intimidation, and in-your-face disruption (protests) to suppress contrary views. Not surprisingly, this movement and their techniques are on full public display across America today and rooted in the writings of Herbert Marcuse, a far-left ideologue who was a disciple of Martin Heidegger, a German Marxist, philosopher, and member of the Nazi (National Socialist) Party.[896]

In 1965, Marcuse outlined his antiliberty strategy that has come to be known as "identity politics," which requires:

> The withdrawal of toleration of speech and assembly from groups and movements which promote aggressive policies, armament, chauvinism, discrimination on the grounds of race and religion, or which oppose the extension of public services, social security, medical care, etc. Moreover, the restoration of freedom of thought may necessitate new and rigid restrictions on teachings and practices in the educational institutions which, by their very methods and concepts, serve to enclose the mind within the established universe of discourse and behavior—thereby precluding a priori a rational evaluation of the alternatives.[897]

Tom G. Palmer, executive vice president for International Programs at the Atlas Network and a senior fellow at the Washington, DC-based Cato Institute, quotes Marcuse in an article, "The Three Most Pressing Threats to Liberty," to illustrate the point. He writes, "Liberating tolerance, then, would mean intolerance against movements from the

Right and toleration of movements from the Left."[898] Thus, anyone who doesn't agree with them "is shouted down, denied platforms, forced into sensitivity reeducation courses, forbidden from speaking, intimidated, mobbed, and even threatened with violence to get them to shut up."[899]

Marcuse's strategy is evidenced by "identity politics" across our higher education system. Remember the University of Missouri professor caught on camera calling to her backers, "Hey, who wants to help me get this reporter out of here? I need some muscle over here!"[900]

This example is what philosopher John Stuart Mill warned is the chief threat to free speech in democracies. It's not the government, Mill said, but the "social tyranny" of one's fellow citizens, like the Missouri professor who illustrates Marcuse's strategy in action.[901]

Unfortunately, there are numerous examples of conservative speakers invited to contemporary college campuses and then shut down by a Marcuse-like identity politics strategy that is weaponized to deny others their liberty and their freedom of speech.

This phenomenon now infecting much of America's academy represents a twisted view of liberty, free speech that declares young students have "the right to non-offensive speech." That's an example of identity politics that carves out an exception to speech, a violation of the First Amendment, trying to prevent expression that is considered offensive to an identifiable group based on race, ethnicity, gender, or sexual identity.[902]

The Marcuse-like strategy isn't just limited to the academy, however. It takes place in the public square, such as on the National Mall in Washington, DC.

In January 2019, we saw another example of identity politics' radical agenda exposed by leftists and their progressive sponsors. Nicholas Sandmann, a sixteen-year-old Covington, Kentucky, Catholic high school student was standing with his classmates near the Lincoln Memorial in Washington, DC, following their participation in the annual March for Life. The boys' crime that day was smiling at their harassers and wearing pro-Trump, bright-red MAGA ("Make America Great Again") hats, which progressives liken to Ku Klux Klan hoods.

A brief video of the boys went viral on social media, which drew immediate harsh criticisms alleging that the boys harassed an older Native American man, Nathan Phillips. But a longer video of the confrontation exonerated the boys, which shows that Phillips, not the boys, walked over, beating a drum in the boys' faces; Sandmann smiled at the aggressor. Further, the Phillips confrontation coincided with harassment of the boys by self-identified "black Hebrew Israelite thugs" who were just yards away yelling racist and homosexual slurs at them: "Child molesting f**gots," "Dirty a*s crackers," "Future school shooters," and "Incest babies."[903]

Once the video hit social media, there was no stopping the attacks from progressives like former Democratic Party Chairman Howard Dean, who described the boys' school as a "hate factory." Jack Morrissey, the producer of Disney's pro-homosexual *Beauty and the Beast*, tweeted about "MAGA kids" going "screaming, hats first into the wood chipper." That tweet was accompanied with an image from the movie *Fargo* that showed blood flying from a wood chipper.[904]

Even a newly sworn-in member of Congress, Representative Ilhan Omar (D-MN), tweeted about the incident. "The boys were protesting a woman's right to choose & yelled 'it's not rape if you enjoy it,'" wrote Omar. *Roll Call* reported that Omar also erroneously wrote that the students "were taunting 5 Black men [the "Hebrew Israelite thugs"] before they surrounded Phillips and led racist chants."[905]

Fox News' Laura Ingraham reported that Covington Catholic High School reopened days after being closed due to the unwanted negative national attention, including death threats that poured in against the students and school. The Covington diocese even received a suspicious package, and meanwhile, there were many incendiary tweets from self-righteous Hollywood celebrities and liberal commentators calling for attacks on—and even the deaths of—the teenagers.[906]

Those who jumped so quickly to condemn the boys evidenced an "identity politics" strategy Marcuse promoted that now has infected much of the left, especially the progressive movement. The Catholic boys from Kentucky were guilty of being white, wearing MAGA hats, and being present on the day of the March for Life, a very public statement about abortion, an issue that rouses the left like few others.

What might progressives do in the future to our concept of liberty should they gain more control over government?

A Very Different Future "Liberty"

Earlier in this volume, we established that the American left, progressives, coopted the Democratic Party's politics. They now have the opportunity to redefine liberty.

Keep in mind that Democrats are quickly shifting position to radical progressive liberty, as evidenced in their behavior after the 2016 presidential election. Those are now in charge of the progressive movement, and that includes the Democratic Party's agenda.

No one really anticipated Alexandria Ocasio-Cortez, a veteran of the Bernie Sanders' presidential campaign, to run and then win a seat in Congress, and then once sworn into office, literally run through the halls of Congress staging protests. Nor did anyone anticipate Rashida Tlaib, who was expelled in 2016 from the Detroit Economic Club for heckling a speech by President Trump, to win her Democratic primary to go on to secure a seat in Congress as well.

Did anyone anticipate the circus the progressive Democrats staged at the Supreme Court Judge Brett Kavanaugh's confirmation hearing? And did anyone predict that Democratic Senator Cory Booker (NJ)— aka "Spartacus"—would release to the public confidential documents about the Kavanaugh case, a move he called an act of "civil disobedience" and a violation of Senate ethics rules?

These things happened among progressive Democrats at the time they were out of power, the Senate minority. What might they do to our country and conservatives' liberty if ever they regain the presidency and both chambers of Congress?

Understand that progressives are more mobilized today than they were even during the Clinton and Obama years. We saw that sort of influence during the Kavanaugh confirmation battle as to how mass movements can throw into doubt a seemingly inevitable nomination. Once progressives rallied with their coconspirator, the #Me-Too movement, to the effort to deliver a knock-out blow to the nomination, it almost derailed Judge Kavanaugh's nomination based purely on empty, nonsubstantiated allegations.

Given this background, now consider that a future progressive president is likely to face much more pressure than President Obama ever did from the hard left, similar to the push in the Kavanaugh situation. It will be ferocious. How might it impact government policy, much less our liberty?

Remember Speaker Nancy Pelosi's "Paygo" policy that required that any bill that increased entitlement spending or decreased revenues had to identify an offset. Count that policy dead should progressives gain power. Paygo will be kicked to the curb by progressives anxious to spend, and they don't believe deficits matter. Already, progressive commentators fuel those flames with articles such as "Stop Trying to be 'Responsible' on the Budget, Democrats" (*Washington Post*)[907] and "Yes, Democrats are the Party of Fiscal Responsibility. But that will (and should) change" (*Vox*).[908]

Do you believe our liberty will be guaranteed by the Supreme Court even if progressives take over the government? Think again, because progressive Democrats may well follow Franklin D. Roosevelt's attempt to pack the Supreme Court in order to reverse contrary judicial decisions. That idea is gaining steam with leftist commentators in leading publications declaring the possibility worthy of debate. After all, Corey Robin writes in the socialist journal *Jacobin*: "Sometimes you have to break the rules to create a more democratic system."[909]

Another recourse for a progressive-majority-ruled government is the concept that is already an aspect of progressivism, the majoritarian-democratic theory of government, which is based on a true majority ruling the electoral process. After all, our Constitution stipulates that the Electoral College (Article II, Section 1, Clause 2) selects the president, not the majority of votes cast, an issue you will recall angered many Democrats in 2016 when Hillary Clinton won the popular vote over Mr. Trump by 2.9 million, as a result of leftists mostly in California and their East Coast allies.

A constitutional amendment is needed to change how we elect a president, but the point here is that progressives believe in centralizing governmental power and would seek such a remedy if they thought it was possible. However, what's clear is that the progressives' real objective is to secure individual liberty through limited government. What might they do?

What progressives did at the state and local levels in the early twentieth century is a possible precursor to what they might try now at the national level. Specifically, at the time, they imposed aspects of direct democracy that brought about changes such as the recall and referendum initiative, which profoundly changed state governments and impacted republican liberty as a consequence. At the national level, that outcome could return to true majority rule, likely threatening the individual liberty of the minority—something our founders tried to guarantee.

Remember that James Madison and other American founders disagreed with progressive ideology when it comes to human nature, a critical issue to consider. Madison wrote in the "Federalist" that the greatest problem for republican forms of government throughout history is majority tyranny. He worried that majorities would use the democratic process to expropriate the wealth of the minority. (Think here about socialist calls to return to very high tax rates for the country's richest.) After all, the ultimate purpose of civil government, says our Declaration of Independence, is to secure each man's natural right to life, liberty, and the pursuit of happiness—not the coerced redistribution of wealth, taking from the rich and giving to the less fortunate.

Of course, time has a way of reversing fortunes. Recall that Theodore Roosevelt, the Republican progressive who publicly disagreed with the founders' bent on protecting minorities and thus promoted government trampling on the minority's liberty in order to help the majority. He came to favor workers' rights over corporations.

Roosevelt wrote at the time to justify his government-favoring actions:

> No sane man who has been familiar with the government of this country for the last twenty years [the period of the Progressive Era] will complain that we have had too much of the rule of the majority. The trouble has been a far different one—that, at many times and in many localities, there have held public office in the States and in the Nation men who have, in fact, served not the whole people but some special class or special interest.[910]

I fully expect that, should progressives take over this country and then through whatever means (courts, legislation, and executive fiat) necessary, the majority will trample over minority liberties on virtually every possible front to include property, religion, privacy, liberty, and more. Yet they will call their actions the liberation of the people.

18

Equality: An Ideal of American Exceptionalism

We hold these truths to be self-evident, that all men are created equal, that they are endowed by their Creator with certain unalienable Rights that among these are Life, Liberty and the pursuit of Happiness.[911]

—Declaration of Independence, 1776

Equality has meant different things over the country's history starting with our founders. The term is often referred to as an ideal associated with American exceptionalism that was skewed over time, thanks in part to progressives—especially against African-Americans—and arguably it will continue to become more radicalized should progressives retake the reins of government.

What Did Our Founders Mean by Equality?

We began this chapter with a quote from the Declaration of Independence that includes the phrase "all men are created equal." What did our founders mean by that phrase then and how has the meaning changed over the centuries?

That phrase meant that all men share a common human nature, period. Founder Thomas Jefferson, a slave owner, did not mean, as some would wish, that all are somehow identical, or equally talented, prudent, intelligent, or even possess the same reasoning powers; nor was Jefferson compelled at the time to release his slaves to celebrate freedom and equality.

Jefferson meant in part that all free, property-owning males are equal. That was a rather exclusive club of individuals at that time and a view understandably not embraced widely today. Further, it is noteworthy that Frederick Douglass, a black man and former slave from Maryland introduced earlier, asked in a speech at the end of the nineteenth century: "Are the great principles of political freedom and natural justice embodied in that Declaration of Independence, extended to us [black Americans]?" Yes, "equality" was officially extended to African-Americans, but that wasn't initially Jefferson's intention.[912]

Jefferson's intended "equality" only applied as outlined above to people "of equal moral worth [propertied individuals] and as such deserve equal treatment under the law," which in eighteenth-century America did not include slaves, women, debtors, and other groups.[913] However, the context implies that, in spite of being a slave owner himself, he meant all men were entitled to equal justice under the law, something our government established. After all, over the past two centuries, the US eradicated most legal discrimination, and therefore all men are substantially equal under the law, no matter their race, ethnicity, gender, and nation of origin.

Jefferson must have known that the equality he wrote about in the Declaration of Independence would lead to inequality of condition, however. He certainly must have anticipated the new country would develop a neo-aristocracy of sorts based on individual talent and virtue, but not necessarily due to inherited wealth and public position.

Jefferson and the other founders also knew from their experience with European monarchies that man's natural rights were at risk, even among allegedly republican forms of government. Those natural rights—their equality—were in fact at risk over time because, too often, government officials grew autocratic, and the government that should protect the people potentially becomes arbitrary whereby the strongest take whatever they want.

Jefferson understood that the rulers should be the servants, not the proprietors (guardians) of the people. Therefore, each citizen must employ his talents and energy to pursue a dream, with great hope for the future. That resulted in unequal outcomes because of different talents and opportunities. That's a view expressed in "Federalist 10," which states, "From the protection of different and unequal faculties of acquiring property, the possession of different degrees and kinds of property immediately results."[914]

Founder James Madison distinguishes between liberty and equality as well. In "Federalist 10," you can't have the first (liberty) without the second (equality). Madison believed that government's role in this equation was to safeguard man's rights to life, liberty, and the acquisition of property—his equality of opportunity.[915]

The founders understood the potential for abuse of equality, because they knew the nature of man and the fact that even democratic majorities can become just as grievous a tyrant as the despots they abandoned in Europe. That's what founder Madison labeled the "tyranny of the majority."

He feared that tyranny might occur through the guise of government taxation. He said that levying taxes "is an act which seems to require the most exact impartiality, yet there is perhaps no legislative act in which greater opportunity and temptation are given to a predominant party [the majority], to trample on the rules of justice. Every shilling with which they overburden the inferior number [minority] is a shilling [British currency] saved to their own pockets."[916]

The threat was the majority, the "unpropertied," would expropriate the wealth of the "propertied" minority and do so disproportionately for

the public (majority's) benefit. The founders rightly feared the temptation for the majority to transfer money from the wealthy few by unequal
levies through taxation to the benefit of the majority.

This threat of majority tyranny was very real in the minds of the
founders, having seen such a situation in Western Massachusetts, one
mentioned earlier. Madison explained that late-eighteenth-century,
debt-swamped farmers fresh from fighting the Revolutionary War
launched what came to be known as Shay's Rebellion, a scheme to seize
the property of others (the wealthy minority), specifically bankers holding their defaulted mortgages. The rebels demanded the equal division
of the bankers' holding, evidence of the tyranny of the majority.[917]

Madison tried to preclude such an unequal outcome with the new
Constitution. He set out at the Constitutional Convention to guard
against that outcome by limiting the powers in Article I, Section 8, of the
Constitution to very specific entities: funds limited to post offices, roads,
courts, and regulating commerce. Further, those powers were divided
among the three branches as to limit the power of any single body.

Others have tried to interpret our founders' view of equality. Richard
D. Brown writes in *Self-Evident Truths* that our Declaration of Independence is a yardstick of sorts to measure government's treatment of equality as the opportunity to prosper and participate in the political process
as well as equally participate within society and the economy. But our
early years were marked by struggles by many disfavored, equality-chal-
lenged constituencies: women, religious groups, and African-Americans,
explained Brown.[918]

Economic equality was a shortfall for those early Americans, however. The founders evidently, according to Brown, refused to accept economic equality for all, what others call "equality of outcomes." Brown
argued that "equality of opportunity" was impossible due to heritable
property, thus economic inequality was established in many cases at
birth.[919]

Luke Mayville provides yet another perspective about our founders' view of equality in his book, *John Adams and the Fear of Ameri-*

can Oligarchy. Mayville indicates the founders tried to institutionalize equality because they feared that the inequality of wealth distribution would produce a version of aristocracy (similar to what Madison said) and thus threaten the young republic much as the British monarchy had. Therefore, Mayville argued the extremes of rich and poor would distort attempts to realize equality in the new republic, which is arguably true today.[920]

Now take a broader view of equality. There are principles of equality that suggest the complexity of the challenge our founders faced in trying to secure it for our young nation. One writer suggests a simple definition: equality "signifies a qualitative relationship between a group of different objects, persons, processes or circumstances."[921]

Consider some of the equality principles.

There is "formal equality," a principle whereby any two persons of equal status must be treated the same. This might be operationalized by a set of rules that dictates the equal treatment of all employees in an organization.[922]

Aristotle argued for the principle of numerical and proportional equality. The idea of numerical equality occurs when the distribution of treatment, a good, is equal numerically, the same quantity of a good per capita. For example, numerical equality in the classroom means that each student receives the same amount of the teacher's time.[923]

Proportional or relative equality occurs when people are treated in relation to their due. The classroom setting applies to this type of equality as well. The teacher's time will not be numerically equal, but proportionally distributed among the students, which could mean teacher attention is skewed to the more able students, as they may be deemed more deserving, as opposed to the teacher favoring the less able, as they are considered more deserving or needy.

There is a principle of moral equality, which means everyone deserves the same dignity and respect. This principle is rooted in the Bible's New Testament, which elevates the equality of human beings before God to a principle. We will explore this in a moment.

There is also the principle of fundamental equality, which means that persons are alike in important, relevant, and specified respects alone, and not that they are all generally the same or can be treated in the same way.

Finally, no review of equality is complete without a consideration of a biblical view of equality. Certainly, biblical equality was considered by our founders, many of whom were known for their Christian faith.

Bible believers like many of our founders have a very clear prescription regarding equality. God states in Genesis 1:27 that all people are created alike in the image of God. They are also made "a little lower than the angels" (Hebrews 2:9, NIV). Therefore every human being deserves our respect and is the object of the love of God.

Jesus said as much in the Gospels. The Lord states in the Gospel of Mark that the greatest commandment is to love and worship God, and the second greatest is "you shall love your neighbor as yourself" (Mark 12:30–31, NIV). That's a clear statement about equality. To Jesus, all people are equal before God.

The Bible does not say that all people are the same, however. Yes, we are equal morally, spiritually, and politically, but our differences are obvious: Some act just and others unjust; there are Jews and Gentiles; women and men; parents and children; rich and poor; intellectually gifted and intellectually challenged. Yet we are all equally made in the image of God.

Some Christians distort true biblical equality by tolerating slavery and racism or by welcoming the wealthy and powerful while neglecting the poor. Other Christians have even made the mistake of teaching a false gospel of wealth and class privilege. They've defended political injustice (even abortion and homosexuality) and corrupt leaders and consumerism.

Equality is a multi-varied term meaning different things to different people, depending on the context. However, it is an ideal that is critical to our society and one abused by progressives, as you will see in the next section.

What Is Progressivism's Record on Equality?

Progressives did a lot of harm to African-Americans beginning with the Progressive Era, which is examined in a study on paternalistic government written by Tiffany Jones Miller, a professor of politics at the University of Dallas. Ms. Miller sheds some startling light on progressives' sense of equality as it applied to black Americans in the late-nineteenth and early-twentieth centuries.[924]

Miller begins with a familiar name, Frederick Douglass, who rightly expressed concern that securing the equality promise for African-American citizens in the post-Civil War era was, by the turn of the nineteenth century, a fleeting notion—and in fact he feared was driving the black man back into slavery.

Douglass viewed equality through the prisms of acquiring property and voting. Unfortunately, some key progressive leaders at the time denied black Americans both property and voting rights, which made a mockery of President Lincoln's Emancipation Proclamation of 1863 and became a black mark on progressive accomplishments.

The former slave, Mr. Douglass, said that without the right to vote, the black man "is the slave of society, and holds his liberty as a privilege, not as a right." It's not that America didn't seek political equality for blacks by adding the Thirteenth (outlawed slavery), Fourteenth (equal protection), and Fifteenth (right to vote) Amendments to the Constitution, but black Americans suffered serious disfranchisement during the Progressive Era.[925]

Historian C. Vann Woodward explained how in the late-nineteenth and early-twentieth century, some Southern states enacted literacy tests, poll taxes, and other restrictions to minimize the black vote, a clear attempt to disfranchise blacks' right to vote (a violation of the Fifteenth Amendment). Consider, as Woodward said, Louisiana's actions in this vein: "In 1896 there were 130,334 blacks registered to vote, by 1904, there were only 1,342."[926]

The disfranchisement of blacks grew to include discriminatory and segregation laws called "Jim Crow Laws" that resulted in "the physical segregation of public schools, public parks and beaches, and public transportation. It was also during this time that drinking fountains, restrooms, and restaurants were segregated, requiring 'blacks' to use separate facilities."[927]

This surge in discrimination, according to historian Axel Schafer, was "the high tide of progressive reform [which] coincided with some of the darkest moments of segregation, discrimination and racial violence."[928]

It was the progressive reformers who led the white-supremacy movement, according to Woodward. The same progressives who championed minimum wages, social insurance, and labor reforms were at the same time promoting policies of segregation for blacks and various "degenerates," the feeble-minded and others.[929]

Worse, race segregation was part of the progressives' ideology at the time. How did this moral framework within progressivism come to deny American blacks and other minorities their constitutionally guaranteed equality?

Progressivism's moral framework traces back to German universities in the post-Civil War era, whereby a group of American social science reformers and economists studied under Georg Wilhelm Friedrich Hegel, the father of progressivism introduced in chapter 1 and the man who wrote, "the state is the divine idea as it exists on earth." Evidently, those Americans who studied under Hegel and his protégés brought the German progressive views about race groups back to the states. The most influential among those Americans was Richard T. Ely, an economist and progressive leader who helped form the American Economic Association and the American Association for Labor Legislation that was to become "the most active and important social insurance lobby in the United States."[931]

Ely and his fellow progressive social scientists were especially influenced by the Germans' emphasis given to ethics: "to the demands of ethics, it is felt, should the entire economic life be made subservient."

The very cornerstone of the progressives' system of "social ethics" was the all-important "ethical ideal."[932]

Ely said the "ethical ideal which animates the new political economy is the most perfect development of all human faculties in each individual, which can be attained [including] all the higher faculties—faculties of love, of knowledge, of aesthetic perception, and the like."[933]

The idea here is that the progressive ideal was to promote the fullest possible ethical development of every human being. Ely said, "Self-development for the sake of others is the aim of social ethics."[934]

What did the progressives' embracement of the German "ethical ideal" mean for America? Specifically, it redefined individual equality to be radically different from that which Douglass and our founders understood and intended.

Ely explained the progressive understanding of the "ethical ideal": "When we speak of freedom as something to be highly prized…[we] do not mean merely freedom from restraint or compulsion." No, according to Ely, "true liberty" is more than freedom to make decisions about one's own life free from government's interference. He said "'true liberty' is 'positive' because it means the expression of positive powers of the individual to 'make the most and best of [himself]' to develop to his full potential for the good of others," as Miller wrote.[935]

The progressive shift from a "negative" to a "positive" conception is quite significant, according to Professor Miller. Ely explained the right and potential to become free in a "positive" sense requires "a long and arduous constructive process," or a "social evolution." To progressives, history is a process of development with increasing actualization of a common nature, a view directly traceable to Hegel.[936]

Now consider what that "positive" conception means for those under the heel of progressives. They believe in societal progress and the individual's contribution to the common good, an obligation and part of moral growth upward.

What that means for the progressive is that human psychology evolves for the people, and so does the purpose of government. Thus, the progressives' "ethical ideal" demands evolution of public policies that seek "improvement" for both the citizen and the government.

This approach reverses the roles of the individual and the state. However, our founders intended individuals to chart their path in life, and government was there to aid in this self-governing manner. Government had to restrict decision-making to only punishing those who infringe upon the rights of others while protecting citizens' freedom—a social contract built into our Constitution.

Progressives deny the individual's "natural rights," however. Rather, as political scientist W. W. Willoughby explained, the state possesses "omnipotent rulership over all matters that arise between itself and the individuals of which it is composed." Thus, accordingly, the government has the right to decide how the individual ought to act without restriction. As Ely wrote, "There is no limit to the right of the state save its ability to do good."[937]

Now we turn to the problem with equal rights according to the progressives' "positive" terms. Progressives at the time believed that different races and classes of people were advancing at profoundly different rates. Therefore, it was appropriate, progressives believed, to treat various people groups differently—to discriminate against some—otherwise, they would become frustrated.

"For a long time in this country," Ely wrote, "we were inclined to regard men as substantially equal, and to suppose that all could live under the same economic and political institutions. It now becomes plain that this is a theory which works disaster, and is, indeed, cruel to those who are in the lower stages, resulting in their exploitation and degradation."[938]

That is very much a Darwinian view—likely part of Ely's curriculum at Heidelberg University, as a result of Hegel's influence—that infected American progressive social science students at that time. Government under this concept of equality would need to decide the stage of development of each race or class of people. Miller concluded: "For the progressives, in short, treating the races unequally was not only not unjust, but was, in fact, a very hallmark of government's commitment to moral progress."[939]

That view justifies governmental discrimination against a class of people, according to progressive thinking at the time. It was a popular view among progressives including Theodore Roosevelt, Senator Albert Beveridge (a historian and Indiana senator, 1862–1927) and Senator Henry Cabot Lodge (historian from Massachusetts, 1850–1924). After all, Beveridge argued from the US Senate floor against withdrawing American forces from the Philippines because it was our obligation to develop the Filipinos because they were ill prepared to rule themselves. He said:

> Self-government is a method of liberty—the highest, simplest, best—but it is acquired only after centuries of study and struggle and experiment and instruction and all the elements of the progress of man. Self-government is no base and common thing to be bestowed on the merely audacious. It is the degree which crowns the graduate of liberty, not the name of liberty's infant class, who have not yet mastered the alphabet of freedom. Savage blood, Oriental blood, Malay blood, Spanish example—are these the elements of self-government?[940]

Professor Miller writes that progressives treated American blacks similarly to Beveridge's treatment of the Filipino "savages." She cites progressive economist John R. Commons, Ely's student and a leading Roosevelt New Deal figure, who complained that after the Civil War, the "Negro" race, "after many thousand years of savagery and two centuries of slavery, was suddenly let loose into the liberty of citizenship and the electoral suffrage."[941]

Progressive leader Commons said granting such equality to "Negros" was foolish. "The suffrage must be earned, not merely conferred," he said. He argued that the black man's right to vote should wait until he acquired sufficient "intelligence, self-control, and capacity for cooperation," determined by "an honest educational test," such as the literacy tests that eliminated most black votes in Louisiana at the turn of the twentieth century.[942]

The progressive view at the time was that blacks had to be prepared to participate in society. "The great lesson already learned," Commons wrote, "is that we must 'begin over again' the preparation of the Negro for citizenship. This time the work will begin at the bottom by educating the Negro for the ballot, instead of beginning at the top by giving him the ballot before he knows what it should do for him."[943]

Elitist progressives advocated educational reforms along with segregation. Edgar Gardner Murphy, a Southern progressive at the time, wrote: "There is a distinct assumption of the Negro's inferiority…but there is also a distinct assumption of the Negro's improvability. It is upon the basis of this double assumption that the South finds its obligation."[944]

The progressives considered some very radical policies to deal with the "Negro's improvability." Charlotte Perkins Gilman wrote in the *American Journal of Sociology* that "all blacks beneath 'a certain grade of citizenship [not defined],' those who were not 'decent, self-supporting, [and] progressive,' should be taken hold of by the state.'" They should be placed to live and work in labor camps until such time as they improve their ability to make better decisions.[945]

Understandably, Frederick Douglass denounced such progressive proposals as reenslavement of blacks. But Gilman disagreed:

> It is no dishonor but an honorable employment from the first, and the rapid means of advancement…. All should belong to it—all, that is, below the grade of efficiency which needs no care. For the children—this is the vital base of the matter—a system of education, the best we have, should guarantee the full-est development possible to each; from the carefully appointed nursery and kindergarten up to the trade school fitting the boy or girl for life; or, if special capacity be shown, for higher education.[946]

Progressive government is thus the agent of moral progress and not obligated to recognize any individual's natural rights—equality—but to set the conditions upon which that individual must reach his fullest potential for the common good. Further, progressive government judges the individual's/group's ability and thus can limit his/their equality/freedom until in the government's view he/they advance sufficiently.

Progressivism, according to Miller, is truly paternalistic and not that different than what George Orwell wrote about in *1984*. Orwell's Big Brother is a symbol of dictators across the globe then like Adolf Hitler and Joseph Stalin, and now like China's Xi Jinping and North Korea's Kim Jong-un. Progressives were and likely still want to be our Big Brother and may well consider "labor camps" for those they consider for full citizenship, not to mention reeducation camps such as those now hosted by the Communist Chinese for the Uyghur Muslim population.[947]

What Might modern Progressives Do to Our Equality?

Past progressives, especially those just discussed, wanted to reenslave American blacks until they met some notional equality standard. Even modern progressives carry on their elitist views about equality, which is far from the intention advanced by our founders in the Constitution.

Consider a couple of contemporary progressives and their actions. Ultra-progressive Bill de Blasio, New York's mayor, said, "Fighting inequality is the mission of our times." That is a scary statement coming from a progressive like Mr. de Blasio, who pledges to raise taxes on high-earners—an effort to redistribute wealth—and push for "equality" in terms of housing, public transportation, and schools. Before de Blasio was mayor, New Yorkers had Michael Bloomberg, another progressive who stands for elitist paternalism. "Big Brother" Bloomberg banned cigarettes in bars and trans fats in restaurants, and tried to ban "big-gulp" sodas at fast food restaurants.[948]

Another New York progressive talks about equality with a forked tongue as well. On the forty-sixth anniversary of the landmark *Roe v. Wade* Supreme Court ruling on abortion, Governor Andrew Cuomo signed a so-called Reproductive Health Act that decriminalizes abortion, authorizes virtually any health provider the right to perform abortions, and provides exceptions to abortion after twenty-four weeks, "late term abortion" when most babies can survive, up to the day of birth.

Cuomo signed the late-term abortion bill to the cheers of crass legislators and said New York is "setting the bar" on women's equality. No, it's lowering the bar on the sanctity of life, which is a virtual death sentence for thousands more Empire State babies every year who could otherwise live outside the womb.[949]

It's also the height of hypocrisy to sign such a death-warrant bill condemning many more innocent babies while claiming, as did Governor Cuomo on another day, that "the death penalty [for terrible violent criminals] is morally indefensible and has no place in the twenty-first century." He promised to advance legislation "to remove the death penalty from state law once and for all."[950]

Elsewhere, it was startling just how far some progressives take the abortion issue. My Virginia governor, Ralph Shearer Northam, a medical physician, went even further than Governor Cuomo. In a January 2019 radio interview, Northam said while discussing proposed abortion legislation similar to what New York passed:

> If a mother is in labor, I can tell you exactly what would happen. The infant would be delivered. The infant would be kept comfortable. The infant would be resuscitated if that's what the mother and the family desired, and then a discussion would ensue between the physicians and the mother.[951]

A "discussion would ensue" implies a decision as to whether to allow the baby to live. That's a description of infanticide, murder of a newborn, and should appall every American, or at least those with a conscience. This reminds me of what progressives did to black Americans as outlined earlier in this chapter—deciding not just when a group or individual is ready to join the rest of us, but in this case, whether to live.

What's clear is that many past and current progressives embraced a bizarre definition for "equality," much like Cuomo and Northam's willingness to label killing innocent, pre-born babies "women's equality," and yet in Cuomo's case, he called for the elimination of the death penalty for violent murderers. Where's the justice? Where's the equality? Where's the sanity?

Oh, I forgot. Equality is only granted by elitist government to those who satisfy the progressives' notional standard. We have much to fear for our equality from a future progressive-run government that redefines acceptable behavior and whether to grant the most innocent life or to reeducate those of us who don't agree with the government's radical agenda.

19

Patriotism: An Ideal of American Exceptionalism

Guard against the impostures of pretended patriotism.
—President George Washington[952]

Patriotism is an ideal associated with American exceptionalism. It is the very glue that holds our diverse population together, which progressives have weakened through their control of public education—especially through the promotion of so-called public schools' "New Civics" curriculum. That is taxpayer-funded radical progressivism that keeps our future generation ignorant of their history and refuses to help them to understand how our government functions and what their obligations are as citizens. Expect this distortion to continue; patriotism will further diminish as progressives seek to replace it with allegiance to a globalist agenda.

What Is American Patriotism?

President Reagan worried that Americans are losing their patriotism, a view the otherwise optimistic former leader expressed in his January 11, 1989, farewell address to the nation. The outgoing president called on the country to embrace "an informed patriotism." He asked: "Are we doing a good-enough job teaching our children what America is and what she represents in the long history of the world?"[953]

Mr. Reagan (1911–2004) noted that his generation was "taught, very directly, what it means to be an American. And we absorbed, almost in the air, a love of country and an appreciation of its institutions." Reagan learned those lessons from his family, in school, and through the popular culture.[954]

The Gipper, a nickname Reagan earned from his movie roles, observed that parents in the late 1980s were no longer sure whether they should teach their children patriotism. He said "Well-grounded patriotism is no longer in style," and the parents' neglect in educating their offspring about patriotism is replaced by distortions of the ideal by the popular culture.[955]

"We've got to teach history based not on what's in fashion but what's important," Mr. Reagan urged parents and educators. "If we forget what we did, we won't know who we are. I'm warning of an eradication of the American memory that could result, ultimately, in an erosion of the American spirit."[956]

"Patriotism" comes from the Latin word *pater*, meaning father, which is simply a full-throated expression of love, pride, and devotion to one's fatherland. It is rooted in what makes a country great, a precious ideal. Catholic Archbishop John Ireland (1838–1918), the first archbishop of Saint Paul, Minnesota, elaborated on the importance of the term when he declared:

The value of patriotism to a people is above gold and precious stones, above commerce and industry, above citadels and warships. Patriotism is the vital spark of national honor; it is the fount of the nation's prosperity, the shield of the nation's safety. Take patriotism away, the nation's soul has fled, bloom and beauty have vanished from the nation's countenance.[957]

American patriotism has a rich history that has much to do with the idea of American exceptionalism, the view that America was a new thing in history, different from all other countries. America was born of ideas reflected in our founding documents—ideas such as that we were created equal, that we have God-given rights, that we have freedom, and more. We are free to pursue happiness, free to worship, free to speak, and free to select our leaders.

American patriotism celebrates those founding ideas with symbols: our tri-color flag, parades, speeches, readings, fireworks, and more. The subject is also very real and personal for some. J. D. Vance wrote in *Hillbilly Elegy* about patriotism in Appalachia:

Mamaw [his grandmother] always had two gods: Jesus Christ and the United States of America. I was no different, and neither was anyone else I knew. I choke up when I hear Lee Greenwood's cheesy anthem 'Proud to Be an American.' When I think today about my life and how genuinely incredible it is—I feel overwhelming appreciation for these United States.[958]

Some come to patriotism late in life and in a unique way. Evidently, the 2008 Democratic Party's presidential nomination persuaded Mrs. Michelle Obama to embrace patriotism. She remarked before the Wisconsin primary in mid February 2008, "For the first time in my adult life, I am really proud of my country, because it feels like hope is finally making a comeback." Evidently, she hadn't been proud of her country prior to that time.[959]

Newsweek's Evan Thomas rhetorically asked about Obama's "proud of my country" statement: "But a lot of voters did and will wonder:

how could someone who graduated from Princeton and Harvard Law School and won a job at a high-paying Chicago law firm—who was in some way a beneficiary of affirmative action—sound so alienated from her country?"[960]

One's view about patriotism usually depends on the country's history and geopolitics. Patriotism in America is seen as an important aspect of our culture, which is rooted in conservative values that include honor, loyalty, and bravery, especially as they related to those serving in our military.

When former President Barack Obama was running for the presidency in 2008, he observed: "When we argue about patriotism, we are arguing about who we are as a country, and more importantly, who we should be."[961] That view was previously echoed by former US Senator George McGovern, the 1972 Democratic Party's presidential candidate who said at the time: "The highest patriotism is…a love of one's country deep enough to call [it] to a higher standard."[962]

Who we "should be" and calling Americans to "a higher standard" regarding patriotism is an issue that draws some difference of opinion, especially in recent years, as we've seen National Football League (NFL) players take a knee or raise a fist during the playing of our national anthem. Some Americans were insulted by the players' actions, whereas others celebrated those acts as being patriotic and representative of standing up for their beliefs.

The silent protest campaign began against a background of alleged police brutality that started with then San Francisco 49ers quarterback Colin Kaepernick. That protest morphed into a silent statement about patriotism, which even drew President Trump into the mix when he referred to any NFL player making a gesture during the "Star-Spangled Banner" as a "son of a bitch" who should be fired.[963]

Some Americans believe that patriotism goes beyond just standing for the anthem and the pledge; it includes protest as well. Evidently, many other NFL players felt similarly to Kaepernick, because in the wake of President Trump's tweeted criticism, more than two hundred NFL players and even some team owners took part in a variety of gestures during the playing of the national anthem before games.[964]

The NFL players' protest found some sympathy among Americans regarding the core of patriotism as well. Self-identified Democrats especially evidenced a significant drop in patriotism in recent years, according to a Gallup poll; it was down from 45 percent in 2016 to 32 percent in 2017. Gallup started tracking patriotism in 2001 when it peaked at 87 percent.[965]

Patriotism appears to be sliding today, especially among Millennials as compared to their parents. An MTV/AP-NORC poll in May 2018 found that Millennials are much more likely to categorize their parents as "patriotic" than their generation. That view was shared by the children's parents as well and echoes President Reagan's caution about "an erosion of the American spirit."[966]

That erosion is confirmed by other polls. A survey by the firm YouGov found that Americans under age thirty-eight are becoming unmoored from the institutions, knowledge, and spirit traditionally associated with patriotism.[967] Specifically, it found that American exceptionalism is on the decline, with almost half (46 percent) of younger Americans no longer believing that "America is the greatest country in the world" and more than a third (38 percent) not agreeing that "America has a history that we should be proud of." One in eight (14 percent) of Millennials agrees that "America was never a great country and it never will be."[968]

Patriotism is a topic of much discussion stretching across America's two-and-a-half-century history. Mark Twain, the nineteenth-century American humorist, once said: "Patriotism means supporting your country all the time and your government when it deserves it." (Taken from BrainyQuotes on April 26, 2019). That's quite insightful and perhaps touches the point of tension within American culture, because as G. K. Chesterton (1874–1936), an English writer and philosopher, said: "My country, right or wrong' is a thing that no patriot would think of saying. It is like saying, 'My mother, drunk or sober.'"[969]

Just maybe Twain and Chesterton understand American patriotism and why it continues to be so divisive today.

Progressives' Impact on American Patriotism

Little doubt most readers already share the view that the terms "progressivism" and "patriotism" are seldom used in the same sentence. Why? Primarily because it is a widely held view that many Americans believe the left, progressives, are "antipatriotic." Patriotism is an ideal more often than not considered a conservative value; it is commonly thought that while conservatives patriotically wave Old Glory freely and boast it on T-shirts, progressives more often seek to burn it.

It will likely surprise conservatives and perhaps not a few liberals that some of our most patriotic symbols such as the Pledge of Allegiance were created by progressives. Remember the firestorm the US 9th Circuit Court of Appeals created in 2002 when it called for the removal of the words "under God" from our pledge? The California-based Appeals Court said the phrase was an endorsement of religion and therefore violated the Establishment Clause of the First Amendment.

The political class at the time, both liberals and conservatives, virtually fell over themselves rushing to condemn the appeals court's decision to strike "under God" from our pledge. President George W. Bush led the way by calling the ruling "ridiculous," and US Senate Majority Leader Trent Lott called the judges "stupid." Quickly, the US Senate voted overwhelmingly (99 to 0) to go on the record opposed to the court's ruling. Then Speaker of the House Dennis Hastert led many House members to the Capitol's steps to pose before television cameras reciting the Pledge of Allegiance and singing "God Bless America."[970]

The 9th Circuit's decision was reversed by the Supreme Court in the case of *Elk Grove Unified School District v. Newdow*, 542 U.S. 1 (2004) as a matter of procedural law, so the high court never actually addressed the constitutional question.[971]

It may surprise some readers that the disputed phrase, "under God," was not even in the original pledge. The pledge was written by Francis Bellamy in 1892, but the words "under God" were added by Congress in 1954, a move to position the United States aside God as opposed to our godless communist enemy, the Soviet Union.[972]

Writer Bellamy's credentials are especially noteworthy. He was a Baptist minister and a leading Christian socialist, ousted from his Boston church for depicting Jesus Christ as a socialist. Evidently, Bellamy believed that "unbridled capitalism, materialism, and individualism betrayed America's promise." He hoped that his pledge would promote a very different moral vision for America, so he included the phrase, "one nation indivisible with liberty and justice for all," which he thought expressed an "egalitarian vision of America, a secular patriotism to help unite a divided nation."[973]

Bellamy wrote the Pledge of Allegiance for *Youth's Companion*, a Boston-based magazine at the time. The magazine hired Bellamy to play host to a national campaign to sell American flags to public schools using the guise of celebrating the four hundredth anniversary of Christopher Columbus's discovery of America.[974]

Youth's Companion's national flag campaign earned the endorsement of the progressive National Education Association as well as President Benjamin Harrison and Congress to become the national ritual observance in schools. Bellamy's pledge was part of the program's flag ceremony, and he hoped the pledge would promote a moral vision to counter the individualism embodied in capitalism and expressed in the culture evident during the Gilded Age.[975]

Another patriotic symbol is the Statue of Liberty, a figure of Libertas, a robed Roman liberty goddess, that was a donation from the French government (it was dedicated in 1886). The statute rests on an island in New York Harbor, New York, displaying a bronze plaque engraved with the poem, "The New Colossus," which includes the famous line: "Give me your tired, your poor/your huddled masses yearning to breathe free." Those words were penned by Emma Lazarus (1849–1887), the daughter of one of the elite founders of New York City's Knickerbocker Club and a well known poet at the time, as well as a supporter of Henry George's socialistic single tax program. Ms. Lazarus even published a sonnet in honor of Mr. George's book *Progress and Poverty*, which helped spark the Progressive Era. Further, Lazarus was a friend of William Morris, a leading British socialist.[976]

Another symbol of American patriotism is the song "America the Beautiful," written in 1893 by Katherine Lee Bates, a professor at Wellesley College, an all-girls institution that includes graduates like Hillary Clinton. Bates' 1911 book, *America the Beautiful and Other Poems*, expressed outrage at US imperialism in the Philippines (the Spanish-American War, 1898). She was not only an antiimperialist but was very much part of the progressive reform circles in Boston, was an ardent feminist, was a women's suffrage proponent, and lived with fellow Wellesley professor Katharine Coman in what was called at the time a "Boston marriage." Ms. Coman was an economist and social activist as well.[977]

Even though some of the most famous symbols of our patriotism are attributable to leftists (progressives), the American educational establishment failed to promote our rich history and especially civics, the study of the rights and duties of American citizenship. Those educators, under the guidance of progressives, ignored the task of nurturing our youth in the nation's rich history and the responsibilities of citizenship.

As noted earlier in this chapter, President Reagan warned that he noticed that for decades young Americans were woefully ignorant of basic American ideals, history, and institutions—the substance of patriotism. In fact, a 2017 poll by the Annenberg Public Policy Center validated that observation by confirming that only one-quarter of young Americans can name all three branches of government, and only slightly more than a third know the importance of the First Amendment.[978]

The Gipper knew the progressive public schools were partly to blame for this outcome, but he didn't let parents off the hook. He used his farewell address to call upon parents to do more to promote patriotism. "All great change in America begins at the dinner table," Reagan said. "So, tomorrow night in the kitchen I hope the talking begins. And children, if your parents haven't been teaching you what it means to be an American, let'em know and nail 'em on it. That would be a very American thing to do."[979]

The former president concluded his farewell address with: "Freedom is never more than one generation away from extinction.... We didn't pass it to our children in the bloodstream. It must be fought for, protected, and handed on for them to do the same."[980]

President Reagan wasn't as tough as he needed to be on our public schools, however. After all, it shouldn't surprise anyone the American educational establishment—which long ago became a captive of the progressive movement, thanks in a large part to John Dewey, the most influential of all modern American educationalists who had the proclivity for socialization and secularism—is one of America's primary means of influencing the public about progressivism. That's not surprising, because, as Christopher Dawson (1889–1970), a British scholar and author of books on cultural history and Christendom, wrote about progressive leader Dewey:

> In his views our purpose for education is not the communication of knowledge but the sharing of social experience, so that the child shall become integrated into the democratic community. He believed that morals were essentially social and pragmatic and that any attempt to subordinate education to transcendent values or dogmas ought to be resisted.[981]

Mr. Dewey harnessed America's public education establishment to progressivism, which teaches something totally alien to what President Reagan advocated about patriotism. A recent major study confirms that reality and the consequence.

In 2017, the National Association of Scholars (NAS) released a very troubling report, "Making Citizens: How American Universities Teach Civics." The five-hundred-plus-page report suggests that "left-leaning professors have transformed the teaching of traditional civics with an emphasis on activism, creating a pipeline of students eager to serve the goals of secular-progressive causes." Instead of teaching our children "the foundations of law, liberty, and self-government," colleges teach them "how to organize protests, occupy buildings, and stage demonstrations."[982]

The NAS is an independent membership association of academics and others focused on sustaining reasoned scholarship and civil debate in America's colleges and universities. The NAS study, "Making Citizens," indicates that progressives within America's higher education world aim to transform the teaching of civics. To what end? To redefine civics as progressive political activism rooted in the radical program of the 1960s' new left.

This repurposing of American higher education seeks above all to make our college-age children into enthusiastic supporters of the progressives' dream of "fundamentally transforming" America. That "transformation" is a page out of the progressive playbook: decarbonizing the economy (Green New Deal), redistributing wealth, halting capitalism (free markets in favor of socialism), expanding government, elevating international "norms" over America's constitution (globalism), and disparaging American history and ideals like patriotism.[983]

"New Civics" seeks transformation through "systemic change" from an "unjust, oppressive society to a society that embodies social justice," states the NAS report. This "transformation" takes place by instructing students that becoming good citizens means being radical activists who place political activism at the center of everything they do in college.[984]

The modus operandi of New Civics is called "service-learning," which means that, instead of classroom time, the student is engaged in vocational training as a community activist.

New Civics' "service-learning" approach doesn't stop with one course. No, its advocates want to build this activist strategy into every college class and subject.

The study's author, Peter Wood, says New Civics is "really a form of anti-civics:

> Civics in the traditional American sense meant learning about how our republic governs itself.... [New Civics] focuses overwhelmingly on turning students into "activists." Its largest preoccupation is getting students to engage in coordinated social action. Sometimes this involves political protest, but most commonly it involves volunteering for projects that promote progressive causes.[985]

Mr. Wood continues:

> New Civics isn't a pedagogical movement that happens to have been captured by political progressives; it is, to the contrary, one more opportunistic extension of progressive activism. The rationale of civil pedagogy is a fig leaf.[986]

Progressives are open about their intent. The NAS states the following:

> [The progressive] Association of American Colleges & Universities' report *A Crucible Moment* (2012)—[is] a touchstone document of the New Civics.... [and] identifies civics education with political activism "to eliminate persistent inequalities, especially those in the United States determined by income and race," and with activism about "growing global economic inequalities, climate change and environmental degradation, lack of access to quality healthcare, economic volatility, and more."[987]

The *Crucible Moment* report, according to the NAS, clearly demonstrates the "conflation of civics and progressive activism [that] reveals the real point of the New Civics. There is no substantive distinction between the New Civics and other progressive takeovers of higher education, such as the diversity and sustainability movements."

> [The] New Civics is hostile to the free market; supports racial preferences in the guise of diversity; supports arbitrary government power in the guise of sustainability; and undermines traditional loyalty to America in the guise of global citizenship. It is no accident that these components of the modern progressive agenda permeate the New Civics. The purpose of the New Civics is to advance progressive politics.[988]

The "Making Citizens" report outlines what civics education ought to address. It begins with a definition. The Greek origin is the ideal of the *cives*, the city, "a particular place with a particular history and particular polity." Civics education therefore is meant to be "an education in citizenship" as well as "the activity of those who shape and make the laws in a polity, who exercise in common the office of self-governance." This education consists of three components: knowledge of the history of your nation and the civilization from which it arose; knowledge of how laws are passed and your role as a citizen in governing your country; and education about virtue, since the virtue of governing yourself and commanding your own passions is a prerequisite for joining in the collective self-governance of a free state. While civics education should make citizens capable of engaging in politics, it should not forward any particular political program.[989]

The fact is progressives use our public education system to brainwash our children and young college-age adults about an erroneous understanding of American history and government. Unfortunately, progressives who run our educational establishment—top to bottom—are succeeding, as evidenced by polling on the topic among young adults, and in time, if not already now, are changing our culture to embrace progressive thoughts about government and certainly about patriotism. Eventually, changing the future generations' understanding about civics makes them vulnerable to the siren call of the progressives.

What Might Progressives Do to Patriotism in the Future?

Expect progressives to keep pressing for the same social programs and especially the abandonment of patriotism (aka national sovereignty) in favor of a globalist allegiance. Globalism is a radical ideology, a humanist religion, a worldwide effort to replace thoughts about national sovereignty (patriotism) with global governance (regional and world government allegiance) and deliver great wealth to the few elite. It is fueled by progressivism and is making rapid headway in the United States, due to the Democratic Party.

That transformational effort begins by redefining patriotism to fit the progressives' agenda and then denigrating the ideal of patriotism as an archaic anti-reason formulation, an effort already well underway, thanks to our coopted educational system and progressive media. Consider some evidence of this metamorphosis.

First, progressives like Katrina vanden Heuvel, the editor-at-large, publisher, and part owner of the progressive magazine, *The Nation*, redefined patriotism to fit the progressive agenda. She wrote that "patriotism means that no citizen is denied these basic rights"—a job; enough food, clothing, and recreation; a decent home; adequate medical care; protection from fears of old age; and a good education. This list reads like the campaign promise mouthed by virtually every Democratic Party candidate for national office.[990]

Second, patriotism as it is known today must be denigrated, the self-appointed job of progressives like constitutional lawyer Floyd Abrams, who writes in *The Nation* to call for Americans to abandon patriotism. "The left has always had a problem with patriotism," writes Abrams. He accuses the "right" of substituting "flag-waving for reason," and then he quotes Adlai Stevenson (1900–1965, an American lawyer, Democratic Party politician, and diplomat who served in federal government and three times sought his party's presidential nomination) who believed that patriotism is the celebration of "the right to hold ideas that are different—the freedom of man to think as he pleases." Stevenson, according to Abrams, knew at the same time that "to strike freedom of the mind with the fist of patriotism" was "an old and ugly subtlety."[991]

Abrams would replace patriotism's "old and ugly" fist with globalism, a worldwide outcome that fits the progressives' ideological agenda. Author Corey Savage agrees and explains that today we face a choice between the forces of globalism and progressivism on one side and "slavery and feudalism" on the other (adherence to national sovereignty, belief in American exceptionalism, patriotic blindness, *et cetera*). Savage says we either "have to hop off the train of globalism and progressivism or stop that train from moving forward." However, he argues that globalism's "technological system cannot be convinced to backtrack from its glorious 'progress.'"[992]

Savage concludes that the materialist force behind globalism and progressivism is technological progress, and the entire progressive social phenomenon that accompanies that modernization push includes a cornucopia of progressive aims—multiculturalism, feminism, expanding government, dissemination of nuclear families, and more.[993]

The choice is stark, according to Savage and Abrams' way of thinking. Progressives are ready to abandon who we are as a nation to embrace a globalist ideology that kicks American sovereignty and our flag-waving, "naïve patriotism" to the curb and jumps on the globalist bandwagon for a promised bright, prosperous future marked by their litany of progressive outcomes. If you want to kill a nation, kill patriotism. If you want kill patriotism, redefine nationalism as a dirty word. If there is no felling of patriotism for a nation, the people will not care and will simply submit to a progressive government control.

Last Word on Progressivism: Mental Illness, "Banality of Evil," and Ushering in the Antichrist

This volume began by stating that "western humanity as we know it is on a downward spiral thanks in part to cultural Marxism—a social and political movement that promotes unreason and irrationality through the guise of various social justice causes. That ideology deliberately deceives and disarms the malleable, unsuspecting masses." Then we found that cultural Marxism is the tool of the contemporary progressive, which is on full display in this book, beginning with an explanation of progressivism's roots, the incessant attacks on our fundamental rights (Bill of Rights), the frontal assaults on critical American institutions (family, education, religion, government, and economy), and, finally, the purposeful undermining of the very ideals (individualism, capitalism, liberty, equality, and patriotism) that made America exceptional.

Unfortunately, the use of cultural Marxism by progressives is succeeding at pushing America rapidly into a transitional phase of postmodern irrelevance. Yes, American society is rapidly morphing, as a result of progressives' incessant attacks that are making this nation a different place from the one it was only a few years ago. America today is becoming, as I wrote earlier, "far more self-focused and narcissistic, while seeking to destroy the last vestiges of true Christianity, moral principles and everything good that once distinguished this country as a very special place among the nations of the world."

The evidence of progressives' success at dismantling traditional Christian values and replacing them with progressive evil is beyond dispute. They've radically changed our culture. Specifically, they are rapidly succeeding at creating widespread, derogatory attitudes toward men, white people, Christians, and heterosexuals. Further, our contemporary culture no longer tolerates criticism of radical feminists (think "#MeToo movement") or any minority, especially Muslims. It embraces socialism (in lieu of capitalism) and celebrates virtually any sexual perversion (LGBQ), legitimizes lies (fake news), and harnesses big government to enforce radical policies.

Recall this sobering quote from the introduction. Russian author Aleksandr Solzhenitsyn wrote about the former Soviet Union in a statement that very much applies to America today: "Men have forgotten God; that's why all this has happened."[994]

Yes, thanks to progressives and in part due to Christians' abandonment of their calling to be salt and light (Matthew 5:13–16), America today is on a rapid downward spiral. God is mostly absent from our public square, and His judgment is certain, which is why God's people must redouble their efforts by seeking spiritual revival in our land, if it's not already too late.

That call to action means we must appreciate not only these dangerous times but also our enemy, both the political and spiritual adversaries.

Earlier we considered the psychological profile of our human enemy, the progressives, especially their view of Christians. They genuinely hate us. Here is the bottom line regarding these people: Many progressives display symptoms of a mental illness and they are associated with evil, although they think they are good. Further, unless they are stopped, they will become Satan's right-hand men, welcoming the Antichrist and inevitably ushering in the end times. It's that serious!

Yes, progressives are in fact mentally ill, according to psychiatrist Dr. Lyle Rossiter, who argues his case in his 2011 book, *The Liberal Mind: The Psychological Causes of Political Madness.* Dr. Rossiter's work on liberals, aka progressives, finds that their mental illness is characterized by their failure to emotionally grow up; they are physically adults who operate with infantile behaviors—in other words, they are "spoiled brats."[995]

Dr. Rossiter's clinical findings include:[996]

1. The laws and moral codes—the rules—that properly govern human conduct arise from, and must be compatible with, the biological, psychological and social nature of man.
2. The liberal agenda's Modern Parental State violates all of the rules that make ordered liberty possible.
3. The modern liberal agenda is a transference neurosis of the modern liberal mind, acted out in the world's economic, social and political theaters.
4. The liberal agenda's Modern Permissive Culture corrupts the foundations of civilized freedom and is destroying America's magnificent political achievements.

Rossiter asks a critical question:

Why would anyone want a political system that restricts personal freedom instead of enhancing it; denounces personal responsibility instead of promoting it; surrenders personal sovereignty instead of honoring it; attacks the philosophical foundations of liberty instead of defending them; encourages government dependency instead of self-reliance; and undermines the character of the people by making them wards of the state?[997]

Dr. Rossiter's study of liberals suggests they suffer from a form of delusional disorder in their thinking. Another medical source indicates that delusional disorder "is a type of serious mental illness called psychotic disorder. People who have it can't tell what's real from what is imagined." The source continues, "Delusions are the main symptom of delusional disorder. They're unshakable beliefs in something that isn't true or based on reality."[998]

Progressives come across as described, demonstrating "delusions of grandeur," which in common parlance means they believe they are better than others, and they definitely believe their delusions are true. Those misconceptions are rooted in progressive ideology traceable to Darwinism and Hegelianism, which is pervasive today especially among progressive luminaries. Yes, they really feel that they are always right (truth is on their side), and their opponents are those with whom they disagree, and who are obviously wrong. You see, you can't disagree with a progressive and still be considered fully human. Further, anyone who disagrees with progressives is automatically marginalized and labeled as racist, crazy, or just plain evil.

Even though progressivism claims to be seeking mankind's best, by constantly seeking progress, it risks becoming the "banality of evil." Arguably, we are much closer to that place than anyone realizes, a view shared by Reverend Dr. Daniel C. Wilburn in his article, "Progressivism and 'The Banality of Evil'—Nazi Adolf Eichmann's Trial."[999]

The origins of the phrase, "banality of evil," can be traced to the trial of Adolf Eichmann, who was charged in 1961 for Nazi war crimes against European Jews. Hannah Arendt, a Zionist German Jew and philosopher, covered the trial for the *New Yorker*. Her article later morphed into a book, *Eichmann in Jerusalem: A Report on the Banality of Evil*, which describes the former Nazi (Eichmann) "as a normal man, unimportant, stupid, uninterested person, an imbecile." Predictably, Arendt was attacked by fellow Jews as anti-Semitic for "normalizing Eichmann."[1000]

The real issue that drew Jewish ire was that Arendt dared to rhetorically ask in her writing: Why didn't the Jews fight the Nazis? She also accused the Jewish leaders of being complicit with the Nazis by turning in other Jews, handing over Jewish property to Aryans, and covering up for the Nazis as fellow Jews were shipped to Holocaust death camps.[1001]

Arendt explained what she meant by the "banality of evil." She wrote:

> ...only good has any depth. Good can be radical; evil can never be radical, it can only be extreme, for it possesses neither depth nor any demonic dimension yet and this is its horror!—it can spread like a fungus over the surface of the earth and lay waste the entire world. *Evil comes from a failure to think.* It defies thought for as soon as thought tries to engage itself with evil and examine the premises and principles from which it originates, it is frustrated because it finds nothing there. That is the banality of evil.[1002] (Emphasis added)

You see, progressives by contrast suffer today from a "banality of idealism [good]" that is just as dangerous as the Germans' "banality of evil." Progressives reject any contrary views, and it is banal because although they claim a moral position—doing good for the downtrodden—they in fact globalize evil as anything that dominates: big business, white people, men, the wealthy, military, Christians, and more. Further, progressives refuse to self-analyze because they share "a pervasive collective moral consciousness," thus anything that isn't progressive is attacked. "This is mindless, banal good," writes Dr. Wilburn.[1003]

Arendt said Eichmann was a simple idiot, not a monster, as the court insisted. He was not the mastermind of the Holocaust. No, the German people allowed the Holocaust because their banal "collective moral consciousness" took over. They knew better, but turned their collective heads in denial.[1004]

So, "good" German people allowed the Holocaust, because as Gandhi said, "Good men do the worst evil." Eichmann was a "good" man.

He testified that he couldn't stand the sight of blood and his only contribution to the Holocaust was that he calculated how many Jews could fit into rail boxcars—a simple bureaucrat's job. How boring![1005]

This is the scary part. The very same banal "collective moral consciousness" that numbed the German people to the genocide of Jews could infect progressives today in America, much like it has to a lesser extent already. Here's why:

This volume outlined the devastation left in the tracks of past progressives, the "banality of good." Consider that legacy.

- Progressives argued that granting former American slaves equality was foolish. Rather, progressives said the black man's right to vote should wait until he acquired sufficient "intelligence, self-control, and capacity for cooperation." A progressive scholar wrote that many black people should be placed under state control in labor camps until they improved their ability to make better decisions.

- Progressives embraced eugenics that led to the forced sterilization of at least sixty thousand citizens and launched the abortion-on-demand movement, murdering at least fifty million babies since *Roe v. Wade* in 1973. The same type of progressive thinking persists today in support of late-term abortion.

- Progressive FDR refused immigration to Jewish refugees fleeing the Holocaust, turning many of them back to certain death. Other European immigrants were turned back owing to the Eugenics Creed, which aimed to protect America's germ plasm from genetic contamination.

- The progressive takeover of the American education dumbed down our population, condemned many to less than their potential, and discarded patriotism.

- Progressives promote homosexuality and so-called gay-marriage, an abomination to God.

- Progressives gave us radical feminism, which severely damaged the American family.
- Progressives like Woodrow Wilson and LBJ led us into needless overseas wars and wasteful foreign commitments.
- Progressives consider capitalism evil and seek socialistic economic policies and use fascistic tools to advance that agenda.
- Progressives grew our federal government to a monstrous size while marginalizing our civil liberties and states' rights, contrary to our founders' design.
- Progressives created a mountain of regulations to govern every aspect of our lives, a Big Brother-type of government that continues to explode even today.
- Progressives oversaw the expansion of our national debt to $21 trillion—and it's still growing.
- Progressives continue to compromise our civil liberties (Bill of Rights).
- Progressives are destroying our most critical institutions, such as our economy, with programs like Obamacare and the Green New Deal.
- Progressives are whittling away at the very ideals that made America exceptional among the nations of the world.

Yes, progressives are guilty of a "banality of good," which is really the very essence of evil. Why? Because in their arrogant way, they really believe they know best and are willing to destroy anyone who disagrees. The rest of us have been stupid, naïve dupes to allow all this to happen. We embarrass our founders.

This evil, driven by progressives' mental illness of delusional disorder, explains the spiritual fight now raging in America. The very survival of our country is truly at stake. Traditional American culture, which once reflected biblical truth, is under spiritual attack and is successfully being crippled at its core.

Besides the devastation outlined above, today American progressive cultural elites celebrate immorality and work in tandem with Satan to dismantle the remaining vestiges of our former greatness and Christian foundation. What can we do?

Christians must resist progressivism's political correctness, relativism, and prejudice—especially toward our faith. We must defend the biblical truth that is embedded in traditional American culture—rights, institutions, and ideals—by recognizing that the roots of these attacks are spiritual. We must engage in spiritual battle as outlined in Ephesians 6.

This fight promises to be terrible and dangerous. Please understand that, thanks to progressives, contemporary American Christians are considered by our mainstream culture to be a monstrous threat and a minority it's okay to despise, marginalize, and vilify for our beliefs. We are the progressives' cultural bogeyman and a threat to be attacked at every turn. In fact, we are approaching a time when our freedoms could be denied, and we will face penalties such as job loss, harassment, loss of freedom of association, and social stigma.

Then again, we've battled these spiritual forces since the time of Adam and Eve. Quite possibly, the current successful progressive assaults are meant to usher in the prophetic end times and the rise of the Antichrist. The evidence abounds.

Yes, progressives may be paving the way for the coming Antichrist. After all, that movement reflects the very essence of the Antichrist identified in the Scriptures: one opposed to God and His purposes. Further, progressives seek not only to destroy Christians, but to put themselves and their government in God's place.

The word "antichrist" (Greek, αντίχριστος, *antichristos*) appears four times in the New Testament (1 John 2:18; 1 John 2:22–23; 1 John 4:2–4; and 2 John 1:7). We read in 1 John 2:18 (NIV): "Dear children, this is the last hour; and as you have heard that the antichrist is coming, even now many antichrists have come. This is how we know it is the last hour."

This verse means that there are Antichrist-like figures already here, those opposed to God who seek man's worship for themselves. Jesus warned in Matthew 24:24 about such false Christs who will try to seduce even the elect. They are lawless (2 Thessalonians 2:3) and are aided by satanic power (John 17:12).

There are many times in history when Antichrist-like leaders appeared to fit the scriptural characteristics. They denied Christ, were lawless (2 Thessalonians 2:3), a deceiver (Matthew 24:24), a blasphemer (Revelation 13:1), a heretic (1 John 4:3; 2 John 7), substituted themselves for Christ (2 Thessalonians 2:4); a beast (Revelation 13:1), held great power (Revelation 13:1), had a worldwide following (Revelation 13:3), worshipped "the dragon" (Revelation 13:4), powerful speakers (Revelation 13:2; Daniel 7:4), problem solvers (Revelation 6:2), military leaders (Daniel 11:3), arrogant (Daniel 8:25), ruthless (Daniel 8:23), persecuted Christians (Matthew 24:21) and claimed to be God.

Yes, history is filled with Antichrist-like leaders. But when might the actual Antichrist come, and is progressivism paving the way?

Eschatologists differ in their opinions as to the exact time of the Antichrist's appearance on the world scene, but he will arrive in time to verify an agreement that appears to provide safety and security for Israel. It is generally agreed that this act begins the final seven-year tribulation period on earth. But that agreement will be broken three and a half years later. At a certain point, he is indwelt by Satan who literally brings hell to the planet.

The Antichrist will reign like Christ for three and a half years. He even goes to Jerusalem, where he is enthusiastically hailed and revered by the Jews. He will rebuild the temple during his rule and sit on the throne of Solomon. During his reign he will convert the rulers of the earth to his cause and persecute Christians (Matthew 24:21). At the end of his time on the throne, Christ will destroy him.

No one knows whether we are at the prophetic end times, however. What's clear from the matters examined in this book is that American progressives have radically changed our country, a nation that is beginning to evidence the prophetic environment at the end times. Progressives have brought us to this point by removing many of the traces of our original Christian influence by changing our rights, our institutions, and our ideals. They raise up Antichrist-like leaders within the political culture to push America into more radical policies and, by association, much of the West into a spiritually dark direction.

No wonder Christians around the world and especially here in America agree with Solzhenitsyn that "men have forgotten God; that's why all this has happened."

Today we are seized by progressives who embrace the "banality of evil" in the name of progress and their "good" intentions, pushing America to irrelevancy and perhaps ushering in the Antichrist and the end times.

It is my hope that every reader will understand the fullness of the threat and the times—mental illness, evil, and spiritual warfare—posed by the progressive ideology. Once equipped with that understanding, Christians must earnestly pray for our country and for our leaders, and then become active in defending our constitutional rights, our critical institutions, and our ideals before it is too late.

Today, fellow Christians, we are much like Queen Esther of the Old Testament (Esther 4:14, NIV) who was admonished by Mordecai her counselor: "For if you remain silent at this time, relief and deliverance for the Jews will arise from another place.... And who knows but that you have come to your royal position for such a time as this?"

NOTES

1. Steven Warren, "'I Stand for The Flag, I Kneel at the Cross': Democratic Party Leader Forced to Resign Over Social Media Posts," *CBN News*, October 16, 2018, http://www1.cbn.com/cbnnews/us/2018/october/i-stand-for-the-flag-i-kneel-at-the-cross-democratic-party-leader-forced-to-resign-over-social-media-posts.

2. Ibid.

3. David Kupelian, "Why Has the Democratic Party Gone Mad?," *Life Site News*, November 20, 2018, https://www.lifesitenews.com/opinion/why-has-the-democratic-party-gone-mad.

4. Cortney O'Brien, "Dem Official Who Said Republicans Should Be Sent to the 'Guillotine' Insists It Was an Inside Joke," *Townhall*, October 16, 2018, https://townhall.com/tipsheet/cortneyobrien/2018/10/16/dem-official-republicans-should-be-sent-to-the-guillotine-n2528742.

5. Chuck Smith, "As in the Days of Noah," Billy Graham Evangelistic Crusade, January 28, 2009, https://billygraham.org/decision-magazine/february-2009/as-in-the-days-of-noah/.

6. Johannes Jacobse, "Solzhenitsyn: Men Have Forgotten God," American Orthodox Institute, July 6, 2011, http://www.aoiusa.org/solzhenitsyn-men-have-forgotten-god/.

7. Constitutionalism, Wikipedia, accessed February 9, 2019, https://en.wikipedia.org/wiki/Constitutionalism.

8. William *Leuchtenburg, "Progressivism and Imperialism: The Progressive Movement and American Foreign Policy, 1898–1916."* The Mississippi Valley Historical Review. *(December 1952). 39 (3): 483–85.*

9. The Gilded Age Summary & Analysis, SHMOOP, accessed February 9, 2019, https://www.shmoop.com/gilded-age/summary.html.

10. Donald G. Zytowski, "Frank Parsons and the Progressive Movement," *The Career Development Quarterly, Vol. 50, September 2001, pp. 57–65.*

11. Thomas Jefferson to John Taylor, 28 May 1816, National Archives, Founders Online, accessed February 9, 2019, https://founders.archives.gov/documents/Jefferson/03-10-02-0053.

12. Abraham Lincoln, "The Gettysburg Address," Abraham Lincoln Online, accessed February 9, 2019, http://www.abrahamlincolnonline.org/lincoln/speeches/gettysburg.htm.

13. Joe Romm, "5 Quotes from Teddy Roosevelt That Exemplify What It Means To Be A Progressive," Think Progress, August 31, 2015, https://thinkprogress.org/5-quotes-from-teddy-roosevelt-that-exemplify-what-it-means-to-be-a-progressive-a23ad0318987/.

14. "Franklin D. Roosevelt Says to Moneyed Interests (EG Bankers) in 1936: 'I Welcome Their Hatred!,'" Open Culture, September 5, 2012, http://www.openculture.com/2012/09/franklin_d_roosevelt_in_1936_government_by_organized_money_is_just_as_dangerous_as_government_by_organized_mob.html.

15. Our Documents: Franklin Roosevelt's Address Announcing the Second New Deal, FDR Library, accessed February 9, 2019, http://docs.fdrlibrary.marist.edu/od2ndst.html.

16. Eisenhower's Farewell Address to the Nation, accessed February 9, 2019, http://mcadams.posc.mu.edu/ike.htm.

17. Clarence Carson, "The Relics of Intervention: 2. Progressivism," Foundation for Economic Education, May 1, 1982, https://fee.org/articles/the-relics-of-intervention-2-progressivism/.

18. Wayne E. Fuller, The Rural Roots of the Progressive Leaders, *Agricultural History*, Vol. 42, No. 1 (Jan., 1968), pp. 1–14, https://www.jstor.org/stable/3740180?seq=1#page_scan_tab_contents.

19. As cited in William A. Schambra and Thomas West, "The Progressive Movement and the Transformation of American Politics," Heritage Foundation, accessed February 9, 2019, https://www.heritage.org/political-process/report/the-progressive-movement-and-the-transformation-american-politics.

20. Mark R. Levin, *Rediscovering Americanism: And the Tyranny of Progressivism*, Theshold Editions, New York, 2017, p. 29.

21. James Madison, *The Federalist No. 51, Independent Journal*, February 6, 1788, https://www.constitution.org/fed/federa51.htm.

22. As cited in Levin, p. 29.

23. John Dewey, *The History of Liberalism, Excerpts from Liberalism and Social Action*, TeachingAmericanHistory.org, accessed February 7, 2019, http://teachingamericanhistory.org/library/document/excerpts-from-liberalism-and-social-action/.

24. "Massachusetts Constitution," 2 Mar. 1780, Handlin 441—72, accessed February 9, 2019, http://press-pubs.uchicago.edu/founders/print_documents/v1ch1s6.html.

25. Charles E. Merriam, *A History of American Political Theory*, MacMillan, London, 1915, p. 311.

26. Cristina Guarneri, *White Paper: Ending the Civil War on Corruption*, Lulu.com, ISBN 1387920456, 9781387920457, p. 171.

27. As cited in William A. Schambra and Thomas West, "The Progressive Movement and the Transformation of American Politics," Heritage Foundation, accessed February 9, 2019, https://www.heritage.org/political-process/report/the-progressive-movement-and-the-transformation-american-politics.

28. Henry Woodward Hulbert, "Political Science and Christian Missions," *The Thinker: A Review of World-Wide Christian Thought*, Vol. VI, The Christian Literature Co., New York, 1894, p.62.

29. John A. Marini and Ken Masugi, editors, *The Progressive Revolution in Politics and Political Science*, Rowman & Littlefield, 2005, p. 229.

30. "Signers of the Constitution Gunning Bedford Jonathan," Course Hero, Liberty University, accessed February 9, 2019, https://www.coursehero.com/file/p7bbver/Signers-of-the-Constitution-Gunning-Bedford-Jonathan-Dayton-James-Madison-and/.

31. Charles E. Merriam, *A History of American Political Theory*, The MacMillan Company, New York, 1915, p.314.

32. Theodore Roosevelt, "Expansion and Peace," Published in *Independent*, December 21, 1899, accessed February 9, 2019, https://www.bartleby.com/58/2.html.

33. John B. Judis, *The Folly of Empire: What George W. Bush Could Learn from Theodore Roosevelt*, Simon and Schuster, 2010, p. 63.

34. "The Federalist Papers : No. 57," The Avalon Project, The Yale Law School, accessed February 9, 2019, http://avalon.law.yale.edu/18th_century/fed57.asp.

35. Levin, p. 38.

36. Ibid, p. 59.

37. Ibid, p. 60.

38. Thomas G. West, *Vindicating the Founders: Race, Sex, Class, and Justice in the Origins of America*, Rowman & Littlefield, 2000, p. 74.

39. Ronald J. Pestritto and Thomas G. West, editors, *Modern America and the Legacy of the Founding*, Lexington Books, 2007, p. 178.

40. John Dewey, *The Later Works, 1925–1953: 1935–1937*, SIU Press, 1987, p. 15.

41. John Dewey, *The Middle Works of John Dewey, 1899–1924: Journal Articles, Book Reviews*, SIU Press, 2008, p. xi.

42. Eva Brems, *Human Rights: Universality and Diversity*, Martinus Nijhoff Publishers, 2001, p. 76.

43. "The Impact of Enlightenment in Europe," The Beginning of Revolutionary Thinking, U.S. History, accessed February 9, 2019, http://www.ushistory.org/us/7a.asp.

44. Jone Johnson Lewis, "Progressivism Defined: Roots and Goals," ThoughtCo., February 28, 2018, https://www.thoughtco.com/progressivism-definition-4135899.

45. "God Is Dead," Wikipedia, accessed February 9, 2019, https://en.wikipedia.org/wiki/God_is_dead.

46. Ibid.

47. Christopher Burkett, "Remaking the World: Progressivism and American Foreign Policy," The Heritage Foundation, September 24, 2013, http://www.heritage.org/political-process/report/remaking-the-world-progressivism-and-american-foreign-policy.

48. Ibid.

49. Ibid.

50. Guarneri, op. cit., p. 64.

51. Ibid, p. 91.

52. Ibid, p. 165.

53. Ibid, p. 92.

54. Ibid.

55. "The Impact of Enlightenment in Europe," op. cit.

56. Janell Broyles, *The Triangle Shirtwaist Factory Fire of 1911*, The Rosen Publishing Group, Inc., 2003.

57. "Jane Addams," *Wikipedia*, accessed February 9, 2019, https://en.wikipedia.org/wiki/Jane_Addams.

58. Debra Michals, editor, "Alice Paul," National Women's History Museum, 2015, https://www.womenshistory.org/education-resources/biographies/alice-paul.

59. Ibid.

60. Ibid.

61. Ibid.

62. "Nineteenth Amendment to the United States Constitution," Wikipedia, accessed February 9, 2019, https://en.wikipedia.org/wiki/Nineteenth_Amendment_to_the_United_States_Constitution.

63. Michals, op. cit.

64. Marxism and the Battle Over Education, The Internationalist, 2nd Edition, January 2008, https://www.marxists.org/history/etol/newspape/internationalist/Internationalist-SS-2008-Jan-OptV5.pdf.

65. Benjamin F. Wright, *Five Public Philosophies of Walter Lippmann*, University of Texas Press, 2015, p. 36.

66. "The Reform Advocate: Frank O. Lowden," Governor of Illinois, *The Reform Advocate: America's Jewish Journal*, Volume 52, September 2, 1916, p. 113.

67. "Progressivism in the United States," Wikipedia, accessed February 9, 2019, https://en.wikipedia.org/wiki/Progressivism_in_the_United_States.

68. Ibid.

69. "Progressivism in the White House," US History II, OER Services, accessed February 9, 2019, https://courses.lumenlearning.com/suny-ushistory2os2xmaster/chapter/progressivism-in-the-white-house/.

70. Martin Luther, "Letter from Birmingham Jail (1963)," SHMOOP, accessed February 9, 2019, https://www.shmoop.com/historical-texts/letter-from-birmingham-jail/interconnectedness-motif.html.

71. Herbert Hovenkamp, "Appraising the Progressive State," *Iowa Law Review*, Mar. 2017, p. 1063+. *Academic OneFile*, ttp://link.galegroup.com/apps/doc/A491092525/AONE?u=wash92852&sid=AONE&xid=ac0ca22d.

72. "Roosevelt's Progressivism," Boundless US History, Lumen, accessed February 9, 2019, https://courses.lumenlearning.com/boundless-ushistory/chapter/roosevelts-progressivism/.

73. "Coal Strike of 1902," *Wikipedia*, accessed February 9, 2019, https://en.wikipedia.org/wiki/Coal_strike_of_1902.

74. "Presidency of Theodore Roosevelt," Wikipedia, accessed February 9, 2019, https://en.wikipedia.org/wiki/Presidency_of_Theodore_Roosevelt.

75. "Interstate Commerce Commission," Wikipedia, accessed February 9, 2019, https://en.wikipedia.org/wiki/Interstate_Commerce_Commission.

76. Ronald J. Pestritto, *Woodrow Wilson and the Roots of Modern Liberalism*, Rowman & Littlefield Publishers, 2005, p. 256.

77. Jr. Burns, *Our Dying Republic*, Xulon Press, 2011, p. 28.

78. Ibid.

79. "League of Nations," Wikipedia, accessed February 10, 2019, https://en.wikipedia.org/wiki/League_of_Nations.

80. "Woodrow Wilson's Living Constitution," Progressing America, August 20, 2011, http://progressingamerica.blogspot.com/2011/08/woodrow-wilsons-living-constitution.html.

81. Burkett, op. cit.

82. "Progressivism Part II: FDR and the Supreme Court," Freedomworks, accessed February 10, 2019, https://www.freedomworks.org/content/progressivism-part-ii-fdr-and-supreme-court.

83. Ibid.

84. Jerry Dunleavy, "2020 Democrats Heed AOC Call to 'Pack' the Supreme Court and Force America to the Left," *Washington Examiner*, March 20, 2019, https://www.washingtonexaminer.com/news/2020-democrats-heed-aoc-call-to-pack-the-supreme-court-and-force-america-to-the-left.

85. "Roosevelt Announces 'Court-packing' Plan," History, accessed February 8, 2019, https://www.history.com/this-day-in-history/roosevelt-announces-court-packing-plan.

86. Thomas G. West and William A. Schambra, "The Progressive Movement and the Transformation of American Politics," First Principles Series Report #12, Political Thought, July 18, 2007, accessed in The Progressives and the Constitution, The New Anti-Federalist, http://www.anti-federalism.com/2014/08/the-progessives-and-constitution.html.

87. FDR's First Inaugural Address, History Matters, accessed February 8, 2019, http://historymatters.gmu.edu/d/5057.

88. Glenn Beck, *Liars: How Progressives Exploit Our Fears for Power and Control*, Simon & Schuster, Inc., New York, NY, 2016, p.10.

89. Hovenkamp, op. cit.

90. "eugenics," *Merriam-Webster*, accessed February 19, 2019, https://www.merriam-webster.com/dictionary/eugenics.

91. "Charles Davenport and the Eugenics Record Office," Controlling Heredity, accessed February 19, 2019, https://library.missouri.edu/exhibits/eugenics/davenport.htm.

92. Trevor Burrus, "How States Sterilized 60,000 Americans—And Got Away with It," Foundation for Economic Education, January 28, 2016, https://fee.org/articles/how-states-got-away-with-sterilizing-60-000-americans/.

93. Lutz Kaelber, "Eugenics: Compulsory Sterilization in 50 American States," presentation at 2012 Social Science History Association, accessed February 10, 2019, https://www.uvm.edu/~lkaelber/eugenics/.

94. "Master Race," Wikipedia, accessed February 24, 2019, https://en.wikipedia.org/wiki/Master_race.

95. Trevor Burrus, How States Sterilized 60,000 Americans—And Got Away with It, Foundation for Economic Education, January 28, 2016, https://fee.org/articles/how-states-got-away-with-sterilizing-60-000-americans/.

96. Ibid.

97. Ibid.

98. Ibid.

99. Ibid.

100. Rafael Medoff, "Distorting America's Response to the Holocaust," The David S. Wyman Institute for Holocaust Studies, accessed February 24, 2019, www.WymanInstitute.org.

101. Ibid.

102. Ibid.

103. Ibid.

104. Ibid.

105. Rafael Medoff, E-Mail, Reference. "Distorting America's Response to the Holocaust," October 25, 2018.

106. Samuel Adams, quotation, Meme, accessed February 10, 2019, https://

me.me/i/if-men-of-wisdom-and-knowledge-of-moderation-and-temperance-4872024.

107. Daniel Patrick Moynihan, "Daniel Patrick Moynihan: Culture or Politics?," *The Imaginative Conservative*, accessed February 10, 2019, https://theimaginativeconservative.org/2011/12/moynihan-culture-or-politics.html.

108. "What is Marxism?, Philosophy, All About, accessed February 10, 2019, https://www.allaboutphilosophy.org/what-is-marxism-faq.htm.

109. Beck, op cit., p.3.

110. Sammy Kayes, "Principles of a Modern Progressive Movement," *The Progressive Times*, January 23, 2017, https://medium.com/tptimes/principles-of-a-modern-progressive-movement-a2c3f9e5d25a.

111. Ibid.

112. Zachary Davies Boren, "Major Study Finds That the U.S. Is an Oligarchy," *Business Insider*, April 2014, https://www.businessinsider.com/major-study-finds-that-the-us-is-an-oligarchy-2014-4.

113. Kayes, op. cit.

114. Ibid.

115. Thomas Jefferson, quote, accessed February 10, 2019, https://www.brainyquote.com/quotes/thomas_jefferson_135362.

116. "Yes, Democrats Are Now the Party of Open Borders," *Investors' Business Daily*, July 19, 2018, https://www.investors.com/politics/editorials/illegal-immigration-democrats-open-borders/.

117. Ibid.

118. Ibid.

119. Paul Bois, "How Many Americans Live in 'Sanctuary Cities'? The Numbers Are Stunning," *The Daily Wire*, May 11, 2018, https://www.dailywire.com/news/30522/how-many-americans-live-sanctuary-cities-numbers-paul-bois.

120. Jessica Kent, "NYC Mayor Announces Plan to Guarantee Health Coverage for All Residents," Healthpayer Intelligence, January 14, 2019, https://healthpayerintelligence.com/news/nyc-mayor-announces-plan-to-guarantee-health-coverage-for-all-residents.

121. Micol Lucchi ,"This Is How Switzerland's Direct Democracy Works," World Economic Forum, July 31, 2017, https://www.weforum.org/agenda/2017/07/switzerland-direct-democracy-explained/.

122. "The Freedom of Information Act (FOIA)," Memorandum for Heads of Executive Departments and Agencies, Office of the Attorney General, Washington, DC, March 19, 2009, https://www.justice.gov/sites/default/files/ag/legacy/2009/06/24/foia-memo-march2009.pdf.

123. "Government Transparency," CATO Institute, 2017, accessed February 10, 2019, https://www.cato.org/cato-handbook-policymakers/cato-handbook-policy-makers-8th-edition-2017/government-transparency.

124. Bob Unruh, "Conservatives Fight Back Against Social-Media Bias," *WND*, May 2, 2018, https://www.wnd.com/2018/05/conservatives-fight-back-against-social-media-bias/#6KTHYt48TbxlZYkC.99.

125. Curt Levey, "Google Isn't to Blame for Anti-Conservative Bias," The Daily Caller, December 14, 2018, https://dailycaller.com/2018/12/14/levey-google-bias.

126. Ibid.

127. Charlie Nash, "Google CEO Sundar Pichai Claims Employees Can't Manipulate Algorithms and Aren't Biased," *Breitbar*, December 11, 2018, https://www.breitbart.com/tech/2018/12/11/google-ceo-sundar-pichai-claims-employees-cant-manipulate-algorithms-and-arent-biased/.

128. Ryan Gallagher, "Google Plans to Launch Censored Search Engine in Cina, Leaked Documents Reveal," The *Intercept*, August 1, 2018, https://theintercept.com/2018/08/01/google-china-search-engine-censorship/.

129. Nicole Russell, "Black Lives Matter Violence Undermines Its Credibility," *The Federalist*, July 12, 2016, http://thefederalist.com/2016/07/12/black-lives-matters-violence-undermines-its-credibility/.

130. Ibid.

131. Tony Perkins, "The Southern Poverty Law Center and Violent Bullying," Family Research Council, accessed February 10, 2019, https://www.frc.org/op-eds/the-southern-poverty-law-center-and-violent-bullying.

132. Paul Bedard, "Southern Poverty Law Center Website Triggered FRC Shooting," *Washington Examiner*, February 6, 2013, https://www.washingtonexaminer.com/southern-poverty-law-center-website-triggered-frc-shooting.

133. Pete Kasperowicz, "Susan Rice, Who Msled on Benghazi, Warns Trump against 'False Statements,'" *Washington Examiner*, March 22, 2017, https://www.washingtonexaminer.com/susan-rice-who-misled-on-benghazi-warns-trump-against-false-statements.

134. Kathy Gannon, "5 Freed from Gitmo in Exchange for Bergdahl Join Taliban's Political Office in Qatar," *The Associated Press*, October 30, 2018, https://www.militarytimes.com/news/your-military/2018/10/30/5-freed-from-gitmo-in-exchange-for-bergdahl-join-insurgents-in-qatar-taliban-says/.

135. Jon Greenberg, "Donald Trump Says Iran Got $150 Billion and $1.8 Billion in Cash. That's Half True," Politifact, April 27, 2018, https://www.politifact.com/truth-o-meter/statements/2018/apr/27/donald-trump/donald-trump-iran-150-billion-and-18-billion-c/.

136. Rod Dreher, "The Limits of Progressive Solidarity," *The American Conservative*, July 10, 2018, https://www.theamericanconservative.com/dreher/limits-of-progressive-solidarity/.

137. Dan Siskin, "Intersectional Politics and Progressive Solidarity," A Medium Corporation, June 27, 2017, https://medium.com/@dan.sisken/intersectional-politics-and-progressive-solidarity-af8bcf596920.

138. Emmanuel Saez, "Striking It Richer: The Evolution of Top Incomes in the United States" (Updated with 2012 preliminary estimates), U.S. Berkeley, September 3, 2013, https://eml.berkeley.edu/~saez/saez-UStopincomes-2012.pdf.

139. Elizabeth Warren, *This Fight Is Our Fight*, Metropolitan Books, 2017, pp. 4–5.

140. Eric Bradner, "Progressives Reject 'Phony Moderation' at Netroots Nation, Setting Tone for 2020 Primary," CNN, August 5, 2018, https://www.cnn.com/2018/08/05/politics/netroots-nation-progressives-democratic-direction-2020/index.html.

141. Amie Parnes and Justin Sink. "Obama Fills Out His Progressive Agenda: Push on Wages, Gun Control, Climate and Immigration." *The Hill*, February 13, 2013, p. 1.

142. Tom Head, "The American Gay Rights Movement," ThoughtCo., February 7, 2019, https://www.thoughtco.com/american-gay-rights-movement-721309.

143. NHE Fact Sheet, CMS.GOV, accessed February 10, 2019, https://www.cms.gov/research-statistics-data-and-systems/statistics-trends-and-reports/nationalhealthexpenddata/nhe-fact-sheet.html.

144. Parnes, op. cit.

145. Daniel Weintraub, "A Culture of Coverage," Fox & Hounds, September 13, 2013, http://www.foxandhoundsdaily.com/2013/09/culture-coverage/.

146. Theo Anderson, "Progressives Are the New Silent Majority," Billmoyers.com, January 19, 2017, https://billmoyers.com/story/progressives-new-silent-majority/.

147. Patrick Gleason, "Long Before The $32 Trillion Price Tag, Bernie Sanders' Home State Exposed High Cost Of Single Payer," *Forbes*, August 31, 2018, https://www.forbes.com/sites/patrickgleason/2018/08/31/long-before-the-32-trillion-price-tag-bernie-sanders-home-state-exposed-high-cost-of-single-payer/#2bf04a7456f7.

148. "Progressivism in the United States, cite Note 79," Wikipedia, accessed February 10, 2019, https://en.wikipedia.org/wiki/Progressivism_in_the_United_States#cite_note-79.

149. Gleason, op. cit.

150. "15 Reasons Raising Minimum Wage Is Bad," Republican Reader, accessed February 10, 2019, http://www.republicanreader.com/15-reasons-raising-minimum-wage-is-bad/.

151. Ryan J. Suto, "7 Goals for Progressive Millennials," Fair Observer, May 3, 2016, https://www.fairobserver.com/region/north_america/7-goals-for-progressive-millennials-88438/.

152. As cited in Thomas Burke, "Bottom-Up Government," *American Thinker*, July 13, 2013, https://www.americanthinker.com/articles/2013/07/bottom-up_government.html.

153. Ibid.

154. Carl Eric Scott, "Late-Republican Times? A Long-Term View," *National Review*, February 26, 2015, https://www.nationalreview.com/postmodern-conservative/late-republican-times-long-term-view-carl-eric-scott/.

155. Burke, op. cit.

156. Noah C. Rothman, "The Fatalist Conceit: Progressives Can't Remodel the Country through Politics—And It's Making Them Miserable." *Commentary*, May 2018, p. 15+.

157. Mike Lillis, "Obama on Gun Control: 'This Time Is Different,'" *The Hill*, February 13, 2013, https://thehill.com/homenews/administration/282721-obama-on-gun-reform-this-time-is-different.

158. Tom Embury-Dennis, "Knife and Gun Crime Rockets across England and Wales—As Police Numbers Hit Historic Lows," Independent (UK), January 25, 2018, https://www.independent.co.uk/news/uk/crime/knife-gun-crime-stats-latest-england-wales-rise-increase-a8177161.html.

159. Ember, Sydney, and Astead W. Herndon. "How Shuttering ICE Went from Fringe to Platform." *New York Times*, 30 June 2018, p. A11(L).

160. Julie Moreau, "GOP Reintroduces Bill Pitting Religious Freedom against Gay Marriage," *NBC News*, March 12, 2018, https://www.nbcnews.com/feature/nbc-out/gop-reintroduces-bill-pitting-religious-freedom-against-gay-marriage-n855836.

161. "Kamala Harris Says Race, Gender Issues 'About American Identity' as 2020 Hopefuls Pitch Progressives." *CNN Wire*, August 4, 2018.

162. Ibid.

163. Anderson, op. cit.

164. Timothy Noah, "How the Liberal Wish List Could Bite Democrats," *Politico*, October 15, 2018, https://www.politico.com/story/2018/10/14/liberals-midterms-democrats-845905.

165. Ibid.

166. "Schatz Leads 32 Members of Congress in Introducing Legislation to End Student Debt Crisis," Brian Schatz, U.S. Senator Hawaii, March 22, 2018, https://www.schatz.senate.gov/press-releases/schatz-leads-32-members-of-congress-in-introducing-legislation-to-end-student-debt-crisis.

167. Ella Nilsenella, "Exclusive: Sen. Brian Schatz's Ambitious New Plan for Debt-free College, Explained 'Shame on all of us for running on this without fixing it,'"Vox.com, March 20, 2018, https://www.vox.com/policy-and-politics/2018/3/20/17124080/brian-schatz-debt-free-college-plan-senate.

168. Katie Hill, "45% of Americans Pay No Federal Income Tax," *Market Watch*, April 18, 2016, https://www.marketwatch.com/story/45-of-americans-pay-no-federal-income-tax-2016-02-24.

169. Ibid.

170. Rothman, op. cit.

171. Maria L. Smith, "The Charity Band-Aid," *The Harvard Crimson*, April 5, 2013, https://www.thecrimson.com/article/2013/4/5/charities-government-institutions/.

172. Ibid.

173. Bernie Sanders, "We Are Facing a National and Planetary Crisis," *The Progressive*, December 6, 2018, https://progressive.org/magazine/we-are-facing-a-national-and-planetary-crisis-bernie-sanders/.

174. Ibid.

175. Daniel J. Weiss, "State of the Union: More Investments in Clean Energy, Less Carbon Pollution," Center for American Progress, February 13, 2013, https://www.americanprogress.org/issues/green/news/2013/02/13/53267/state-of-the-union-more-investments-in-clean-energy-less-carbon-pollution/.

176. "Scientific Consensus: Earth's Climate Is Warming," Global Climate Change, NASA, accessed February 10, 2019, https://climate.nasa.gov/scientific-consensus/.

177. Anderson, op. cit.

178. Matt Viser, "Just a lot of alarmism Trumps skepticism of climate science is echoed across GOP," *Washington Post*, December 2, 2018, https://www.washingtonpost.com/politics/just-a-lot-of-alarmism-trumps-skepticism-of-climate-science-is-echoed-across-gop/2018/12/02/f6ee9ca6-f4de-11e8-bc79-68604ed88993_story.html?utm_term=.abb52b12c808.

179. Ibid.

180. Danielle Kurtzleben, "Rep. Alexandria Ocasio-Cortez Releases Green New Deal Outline," *NPR*, February 7, 2019, https://www.npr.org/2019/02/07/691997301/rep-alexandria-ocasio-cortez-releases-green-new-deal-outline.

181. Ibid.

182. Ibid.

183. Elizabeth Harrington, "Study: Green New Deal Would Cost Up to $94 Trillion," *Washington Free Beacon*, February 25, 2019, https://freebeacon.com/issues/study-green-new-deal-would-cost-up-to-94-trillion/.

184. Ibid.

185. Ibid.

186. Lukas Mikelionis, " 2020 Democrats Jump to Endorse Green New Deal Despite Spending Hundreds of Thousands on Air Travel—Including Private Jets," *Fox News*, February 9, 2019, https://www.foxnews.com/politics/2020-democrats-jump-to-endorse-green-new-deal-despite-spending-hundreds-of-thousands-on-air-travel-including-private-jets.

187. Harrington, op. cit.

188. Ibid.

189. Anthony Adragna and Zack Colman, "'It's crazy. It's loony.'—
Republicans Giddy as Democrats Champion Green New Deal,"
Politico, February 9, 2019, https://www.politico.com/story/2019/02/09/
gop-sees-political-advantage-in-green-new-deal-1160725.

190. Ibid.

191. Noah, op. cit.

192. Ibid.

193. Ibid.

194. Rothman, op. cit.

195. Jeffrey M. Jones, "Americans Hold Record Liberal Views on Most Moral
Issues," Gallup, May 11, 2017, https://news.gallup.com/poll/210542/
americans-hold-record-liberal-views-moral-issues.aspx.

196. Rothman, op. cit.

197. Ibid.

198. Ibid.

199. Martin Gilens and Benjamin I. Page, "Testing Theories of American
Politics: Elites, Interest Groups, and Average Citizens," *Perspectives on
Politics*, Vol. 12/No. 3, September 2014, https://scholar.princeton.edu/
sites/default/files/mgilens/files/gilens_and_page_2014_-testing_theories_
of_american_politics.doc.pdf.

200. Ibid.

201. Eric Levitzaug, "The Radical Left's Agenda Is More Popular Than the
Mainstream GOP's, *New York Magazine*, August 2, 2018, http://nymag.
com/intelligencer/2018/08/the-radical-lefts-agenda-is-more-popular-than-
the-gops.html.

202. Z. Rizvi, A. Kapczynski and A. Kesselheim, "A simple way
for the government to curb inflated drug prices," *Washington
Post*, May 12, 2016, https://www.washingtonpost.com/
opinions/a-simple-way-for-the-government-to-curb-inflated-drug-
prices/2016/05/12/ed89c9b4-16fc-11e6-aa55-670cabef46e0_story.
html?noredirect=on&utm_term=.5304bdf963ef.

203. Ibid.

204. "Polling the Left Agenda," Data for Progress, accessed February 10, 2019,
https://www.dataforprogress.org/polling-the-left-agenda/.

205. Ibid.

206. Levitzaug, op. cit.

207. Helaine Olen, "Memo to Democrats: The Progressive Economic Agenda Is Popular," *Washington Post*, April 17, 2018, https://www.washingtonpost. com/blogs/plum-line/wp/2018/04/17/memo-to-democrats-the-progressive-economic-agenda-is-popular/?noredirect=on&utm_term=. e1a9b8df33f2.

208. Ibid.

209. Ibid.

210. "Progressives Reject 'Phony Moderation' at Netroots Nation, Setting Tone for 2020 Primary," *CNN Wire*, 5 Aug. 2018.

211. Ibid.

212. Ibid.

213. Ibid.

214. "Socialists Have Officially Taken over the Democratic Party," *Investors' Business Daily*, August 13, 2018, https://www.investors.com/politics/ editorials/socialists-have-officially-taken-over-the-democratic-party/.

215. "Progressives Reject 'Phony Moderation' at Netroots Nation, Setting Tone for 2020 Primary," op. cit.

216. Ibid.

217. "Kamala Harris Says Race, Gender Issues 'about American Identity' as 2020 Hopefuls Pitch Progressives," op cit.

218. Ibid.

219. Ibid.

220. Ibid.

221. Ibid.

222. "Progressive Groups Are Organizing to Protect the Gains of the Last Few Years," *Proud Parenting*, November 25, 2016, http://www.proudparenting. com/2016/11/progressive-groups-organizing-protect-gains-last-years/.

223. Kate Mather and Cindy Chang, "LAPD Will Not Help Deport Immigrants under Trump, Chief Says," *Los Angeles Times*, NOV 14, 2016, https://www.latimes.com/local/lanow/la-me-ln-los-angeles-police-immigration-20161114-story.html.

224. Tal Axelrod, "Trump: I respect Roberts but 'everybody knows' 9th Circuit 'totally out of control,'" *The Hill*,

November 22, 2018, https://thehill.com/homenews/
administration/417981-trump-i-have-a-lot-of-respect-for-john-roberts.

225. Ibid.

226. "Exit Polls," Election 2016, CNN, November 23, 2016, https://www.cnn.
com/election/2016/results/exit-polls.

227. "Nearly Six-in-Ten Current Federal Judges Were Appointed by
Democratic Presidents," Pew Research Center, July 16, 2018, http://
www.pewresearch.org/fact-tank/2018/07/16/with-another-supreme-
court-pick-trump-is-leaving-his-mark-on-higher-federal-courts/
ft_18-07-13_judgespresident_sharebyparty/.

228. Lauren Carroll and Allison Graves "Nominate Someone from His List of
Justices to Replace Antonin Scalia," Politifact, January 16th, 2017, https://
www.politifact.com/truth-o-meter/promises/trumpometer/promise/1360/
nominate-someone-his-list-justices-replace-antonin/.

229. "Roosevelt Announces 'Court-packing' Plan," History, accessed
February 10, 2019, https://www.history.com/this-day-in-history/
roosevelt-announces-court-packing-plan.

230. "Progressive Causes Rally Together after Donald Trump's Election."
The Report, *U.S. News & World Report*, November 25, 2016. *Academic
OneFile*, http://link.galegroup.com/apps/doc/A489551295/AONE?u=was
h92852&sid=AONE&xid=ab7a6f43.

231. Asma Kalid, "As More Democrats Embrace 'Progressive' Label, It May
Not Mean What It Used To," *NPR*, October 29, 2018, https://www.npr.
org/2018/10/29/659665970/as-more-democrats-embrace-progressive-
label-it-may-not-mean-what-it-used-to

232. "Progressive Causes Rally Together after Donald Trump's Election," op. cit.

233. Sahil Kapur, "Democrats Learn a Big Lesson for 2020 Vote
About Taking on Trump," *Bloomberg*, November 26, 2018,
https://www.bloomberg.com/news/articles/2018-11-26/
democrats-learn-a-big-lesson-for-2020-vote-about-taking-on-trump.

234. "Progressive Causes Rally Together after Donald Trump's Election," op. cit.

235. Ibid.

236. Ibid.

237. Michael Sainato, "A Progressive Tide," *The Progressive*, October 1, 2018,
https://progressive.org/magazine/a-progressive-tide/.

238. Jonathan Martin and Alexander Burns, "Democrats Capture Control of House; G.O.P. Holds Senate," *New York Times,* November 6, 2018, https://www.nytimes.com/2018/11/06/us/politics/midterm-elections-results.html.

239. Julia Conley, "All That We Love Is On the Line": Progressive Coalition Offers Moral Case and Action Plan to Win Medicare for All," Common Dreams, November 30, 2018, https://www.commondreams.org/news/2018/11/30/all-we-love-line-progressive-coalition-offers-moral-case-and-action-plan-win.

240. Ibid.

241. "Tucker: Enforcing Our Existing Immigration Laws Is Now 'Tantamount to a Hate Crime,'" *Fox News*, January 26, 2018, http://insider.foxnews.com/2018/01/26/tucker-carlson-monologue-trump-immigration-proposal-criticism-left-democrats.

242. John Chynoweth Burnham, "Psychiatry, Psychology and the Progressive Movement," *American Quarterly*, Vol. 12, No. 4, Winter, 1960, p. 457.

243. Ibid., p. 458.

244. Ibid.

245. Ibid.

246. Ibid., p. 459.

247. Ibid., p. 465.

248. Peter Berkowitz, "Progressivism as Religion: Dworkin's Flawed Belief," *Real Clear Politics*, October 6, 2013, https://www.realclearpolitics.com/articles/2013/10/06/progressivism_as_religion_dworkins_flawed_belief-2.html.

249. Ibid.

250. Ibid.

251. Ibid.

252. Ibid.

253. Ibid.

254. Ibid.

255. Ibid.

256. Ibid.

257. Ibid.

258. Ibid.

259. Ibid.

260. Burhham, op. cit.

261. "A Response to Modern Progressivism: A. C. Dixon, 'The Bible at the Center of the Modern University' (1920)," The Peoria Project, accessed February 10, 2019, https://peoriaproject.com/progressivism/the-bible-at-the-center-of-the-modern-university/.

262. Ibid.

263. Ibid.

264. Ibid.

265. Ibid.

266. Ibid.

267. H. James Birx, "Nietzsche & Evolution," *Philosophy Now*, accessed February 10, 2019, https://philosophynow.org/issues/29/Nietzsche_and_Evolution.

268. Ibid.

269. Ibid.

270. Ibid.

271. Ibid.

272. Ibid.

273. Ibid.

274. Andy Sochor, "Progressivism," PlainBibleTeaching, January 18, 2017, http://www.plainbibleteaching.com/2017/01/18/progressivism/.

275. Roger Wolsey, "16 Ways Progressive Christians Interpret the Bible," *Patheos*, January 21, 2014, https://www.patheos.com/blogs/rogerwolsey/2014/01/16-ways-progressive-christians-interpret-the-bible/.

276. Ibid.

277. Ibid.

278. Ibid.

279. Morris M., "9 Surprisingly Progressive Moments in the Bible," listverse.com, May 9, 2013, http://listverse.com/2013/05/09/9-surprisingly-progressive-moments-in-the-bible/.

280. Ibid.

281. Ibid.

282. Kyle Cupp, "What Progressives Fundamentally Don't Get about Traditional Christians," *The Week*, July 23, 2014, https://theweek.com/articles/445113/what-progressives-fundamentally-dont-about-traditional-christians.

283. Ibid.

284. Ibid.

285. Morris M., op. cit.

286. Ibid.

287. Ibid.

288. Ibid.

289. Justin Steckbauer, "Biblical Christianity vs. Progressive Ideology: A Threat to Western Christianity," The Christian Post, July 7, 2018, https://www.christianpost.com/voice/biblical-christianity-vs-progressive-ideology-threat-western-christianity.html.

290. Ibid.

291. Ibid.

292. "Samuel Adams," Brainy Quote, accessed February 15, 2019, https://www.brainyquote.com/quotes/samuel_adams_401706.

293. Tom Head, "Why Is the Bill of Rights Important?," ThoughtCo., April 2, 2018, https://www.thoughtco.com/why-is-the-bill-of-rights-important-721408.

294. Ibid.

295. "How Many Grievances Are Listed in the Declaration of Independence?," Answers.com, accessed February 15, 2019, http://www.answers.com/Q/How_many_grievances_are_listed_in_the_Declaration_of_Independence.

296. "Preamble to the Bill of Rights," Drexel University, accessed February 10, 2019, https://drexel.edu/ogcr/resources/constitution/amendments/preamble/.

297. "Second Bill of Rights," Wikipedia, accessed February 10, 2019, https://en.wikipedia.org/wiki/Second_Bill_of_Rights.

298. Ibid.

299 "First Amendment—U.S. Constitution," FindLaw, accessed February 10, 2019, https://constitution.findlaw.com/amendment1.html.

300. Tom Head, "The First Amendment: Text, Origins, and Meaning," ThoughtCo., January 30, 2018, https://www.thoughtco.com/the-first-amendment-p2-721185.

301. Ibid.

302. Ibid.

303. Ibid.

304. Ibid.

305. Ibid.

306. Ibid.

307. "Schenck v. United States," *Encyclopedia Britannica*, accessed February 10, 2019, https://www.britannica.com/event/Schenck-v-United-States.

308. Ibid.

309. "Schenck v. United States, Wikipedia, accessed February 10, 2019, https://www.britannica.com/event/Schenck-v-United-States.

310. "New York Times v. United States *(1971)*," Bill of Rights Institute, accessed February 10, 2019, https://billofrightsinstitute.org/educate/educator-resources/lessons-plans/landmark-supreme-court-cases-elessons/new-york-times-v-united-states-1971/.

311. Ibid.

312. Ibid.

313. "Daniel Ellsberg," *Wikipedia*, accessed February 10, 2019, https://en.wikipedia.org/wiki/Daniel_Ellsberg.

314. "Texas v. Johnson," Wikipedia, accessed February 10, 2019, https://en.wikipedia.org/wiki/Texas_v._Johnson.

315. Scott Bomboy, "Survey: High School Students, Teachers Differ on the First Amendment," National Constitution Center, December 6, 2018, https://constitutioncenter.org/blog/survey-high-school-students-teachers-differ-on-the-first-amendment.

316. Ibid.

317. Ibid.

318. "From George Washington to the Members of the New Jerusalem Church of Baltimore, 27 January 1793," Founders Online, accessed February 10, 2019, https://founders.archives.gov/documents/Washington/05-12-02-0027.

319. John S. Baker Jr., "Wall of Separation," The First Amendment Encyclopedia, accessed February 20, 2019, https://mtsu.edu/first-amendment/article/886/wall-of-separation.

320. America's Most Biblically-Hostile U. S. President, Wallbuilders, accessed February 10, 2018, https://wallbuilders.com/americas-biblically-hostile-u-s-president/.

321. Todd Starnes, "Government Hostility to Religion Spiked under Obama, New Report Finds," *Fox News*,

June 29, 2017, https://www.foxnews.com/opinion/
government-hostility-to-religion-spiked-under-obama-new-report-finds.

322. Ibid.

323. Ibid.

324. Bill Lueders, "'Shut Up, Already!' The New Battle Over Campus
Free Speech," *The Progressive*, August 1, 2017, https://progressive.org/
magazine/%E2%80%98shut-up-already-%E2%80%99-the-new-battle-
over-campus-free-speech/.

325. Ibid.

326. Ibid.

327. Ibid.

328. "Progressives' Anti-free Speech Itch," *Washingtonpost.com*, 13 Feb. 2016.

329. George F. Will, "Progressives Anti-free Speech Itch, *Washington Post*,
February 12, 2016, https://www.washingtonpost.com/opinions/
progressives-anti-free-speech-itch/2016/02/12/387c1522-d0e8-11e5-b2bc-
988409ee911b_story.html?utm_term=.36ae7d08ae77.

330. "Progressives' Anti-Free speech itch," op. cit.

331. Ibid.

332. Ibid.

333. "Second Amendment," Legal Information Institute, Cornell Law School,
accessed on February 10, 2019, https://www.law.cornell.edu/wex/
second_amendment.

334. Christopher Woolf, "The Origins of the Second Amendment,"
PRI, November 17, 2017, https://www.pri.org/stories/2017-11-17/
origins-second-amendment.

335. Ibid.

336. Ibid.

337. Ibid.

338. Chad Brooks, "The Second Amendment and the Right to Bear Arms,"
LiveScience, June 28, 2017, https://www.livescience.com/26485-second-
amendment.html.

339. "Second Amendment," History, accessed February 11, 2019, https://www.
history.com/topics/united-states-constitution/2nd-amendment.

340. Ibid.

341. Ibid.

342. Ibid.

343. Ibid.

344. Ibid.

345. Ibid.

346. Woolf, op cit.

347. Brooks, op. cit.

348. Ibid.

349. Ibid.

350. Ibid.

351. "Second Amendment," op. cit.

352. Ibid.

353. Brooks, op. cit.

354. "Second Amendment," op. cit.

355. Ibid.

356. Brooks, op. cit.

357. Ibid.

358. "Second Amendment," op. cit.

359. Ibid.

360. Patrick Krey, "Progressives Love Guns." *The New American*, 1 Apr. 2013, p. 40. *Academic OneFile*, http://link.galegroup.com/apps/doc/ A326854321/AONE?u=wash92852&sid=AONE&xid=e953ccea.

361. David Schultz, "The Left and Guns: How I Learned to Stop Worrying and Love the Second Amendment," *International Policy Digest*, March 2, 2018, https://intpolicydigest.org/2018/03/02/ left-guns-learned-stop-worrying-love-second-amendment/.

362. Dean Weingarten, "Gun Control Is in Progressivism's DNA," Ammoland Inc., December 9, 2017, https://www.ammoland.com/2017/12/ gun-control-is-in-progressivisms-dna/#axzz5aQDfZ9EO.

363. Ibid.

364. Christina Wilke, "Obama State of the Union Speech Demands Vote on Gun Control Bills," *Huffington Post*, February 13, 2013, https://www. huffingtonpost.com/2013/02/12/obama-state-of-the-union_n_2647639. html.

365. Ibid.

366. Glenn Kessler, "The NRA's False Claim That Hillary Clinton Doesn't Believe Americans Can Keep Guns at Home," *Washington Post*, August

15, 2016, https://www.washingtonpost.com/news/fact-checker/
wp/2016/08/15/the-nras-false-claim-that-hillary-clinton-doesnt-
believe-americans-can-keep-guns-at-home/?noredirect=on&utm_
term=.2e3aba28e5c9.

367. "So They're Not Coming for Our Guns, Eh? We Call BS," *States News Service*, March 30, 2018, http://link.galegroup.com/apps/doc/ A560905545/AONE?u=wash92852&sid=AONE&xid=69f5d8ef.

368. Ibid.

369. Ibid.

370. "Progressives Should Oppose Gun Control." *UWIRE Text*, 9 Sept. 2016, p. 1, http://link.galegroup.com/apps/doc/A462935400/AONE?u=wash92 852&sid=AONE&xid=772962f0.

371. Ibid.

372. "Fourth Amendment," Legal Information Institute, accessed February 20, 2019, https://www.law.cornell.edu/constitution/fourth_amendment.

373. Carolyn N. Long, "The Origins of the Fourth Amendment," *Insights on Law & Society* 11.2, American Bar Society, May 2011.

374. "The History Behind the 4th Amendment," Swindle Law Group, March 2013, accessed February 11, 2019, http://www.swindlelaw.com/2013/03/ the-history-behind-the-4th-amendment/.

375. Ibid.

376. Ibid.

377. Ibid.

378. Ibid.

379. Ibid.

380. Ibid.

381. Long, op. cit., p. 27.

382. Ibid.

383. "Your 4th Amendment Rights," Judicial Learning Center, accessed February 11, 2019, https://judiciallearningcenter.org/ your-4th-amendment-rights/.

384. "Selection of Supreme Court Cases Involving the Fourth Amendment and the Body," Americanbar.org, accessed February 11, 2019, https://www. americanbar.org/content/dam/aba/images/public_education/presentations/ BodySearchCases_List.docx.

385. Ibid.

386. "Olmstead v. United States," *Wikipedia*, accessed February 11, 2019, https://en.wikipedia.org/wiki/Olmstead_v._United_States.

387. Ibid.

388. "Your 4th Amendment Rights," op. cit.

389. "Selection of Supreme Court Cases Involving the Fourth Amendment and the Body," op. cit.

390. Kevin Bleyer, "The Unseen Threat to the Fourth Amendment Is the Fourth Amendment Itself," *The Daily Beast*, January 4, 2014, https://www.thedailybeast.com/the-unseen-threat-to-the-fourth-amendment-is-the-fourth-amendment-itself.

391. Paul Larkin, "The Fourth Amendment and New Technologies," Heritage Foundation, September 19, 2013, https://www.heritage.org/report/the-fourth-amendment-and-new-technologies.

392. Ibid.

393. "Edward Snowden, Whistle-Blower," Editorial, *New York Times*, January 1, 2014, https://www.nytimes.com/2014/01/02/opinion/edward-snowden-whistle-blower.html.

394. Norman Solomon, "Obama's Willing Executioners of the Fourth Amendment," RootsAction, July 25, 2013, https://rootsaction.org/news-a-views/669-obamas-willing-executioners-of-the-fourth-amendment.

395. "NSA Surveillance," Bernie Sanders U.S. Senate Vermont, January 14, 2014, https://www.sanders.senate.gov/newsroom/recent-business/nsa-surveillance.

396. "Benjamin Franklin on the Trade-off between Essential Liberty and Temporary Safety" (1775), Online Liberty of Liberty, accessed February 11, 2019, https://oll.libertyfund.org/quotes/484.

397. Jonathan DuHamel, "Has the Fourth Amendment been repealed?," ADI, September 13, 2013, https://arizonadailyindependent.com/2013/09/03/has-the-fourth-amendment-been-repealed/.

398. "Fifth Amendment," Legal Information Institute, Cornell Law School, accessed February 11, 2019, https://www.law.cornell.edu/constitution/fifth_amendment.

399. "Pleading the Fifth: Five Notorious Times People Refused to Give Answers," *The Guardian*, February 4, 2016, https://www.theguardian.com/law/2016/feb/04/fifth-amendment-martin-shkreli-michaele-tareq-salahi.

400. Tom Head, "The Fifth Amendment: Text, Origins, and Meaning," ThoughtCo., January 26, 2018, https://www.thoughtco.com/the-fifth-amendment-721516.

401. *Digest of Justinian*, Book 48, Title 2, Note 7, as translated in Scott, the Civil Law (1931), XVII.

402. Ibid.

403. "Green v. United States," Findlaw, accessed February 12, 2019, https://caselaw.findlaw.com/us-supreme-court/355/184.html.

404. Paul Cassell and Kate Stith, "The Fifth Amendment Criminal Procedure Clauses," *Common Interpretation*, accessed February 12, 2019, https://constitutioncenter.org/interactive-constitution/amendments/amendment-v/the-fifth-amendment-criminal-procedure-clauses/clause/6.

405. Ibid.

406. Roger A. Fairfax and John C. Harrison, "The Fifth Amendment Due Process Clause," *Common Interpretation*, accessed February 12, 2019, https://constitutioncenter.org/interactive-constitution/amendments/amendment-v/the-fifth-amendment-due-process-clause-fairfax-and-harrison/clause/19.

407. Richard A. Epstein and Eduardo M. Penalver, "The Fifth Amendment Takings Clause," *Common Interpretation*, accessed February 12, 2019, https://constitutioncenter.org/interactive-constitution/amendments/amendment-v/fifth-amendment-takings-clause-richard-a-epstein-and-eduardo-penalver/clause/4.

408. "Armstrong v. United States, 364 U.S. 40 (1960)," *Justia*, accessed February 12, 2019, https://supreme.justia.com/cases/federal/us/364/40/.

409. Brian P. Smentkowski, "Fifth Amendment," *Encyclopedia Britannica*, accessed February 12, 2019, https://www.britannica.com/topic/Fifth-Amendment.

410. "What Progressives Would Do To the Bill Of Rights if They Could Get Away with It," New York Families, accessed February 12, 2019, https://www.newyorkfamilies.org/what-progressives-would-do-to-the-bill-of-rights-if-they-could-get-away-with-it/.

411. Wendy Kaminer, "Progressives against Due Process," *Spiked*, November 26, 2018, https://www.spiked-online.com/2018/11/26/progressives-against-due-process/.

412. Ibid.

413. Ibid.

414. Ibid.

415. Nancy Pelsoi, "Pelosi Statement on Trump Administration's Plan to Roll Back Title IX Protections," Nancy Pelsoi Speaker of the House, August 30, 2018, https://www.speaker.gov/newsroom/83018/.

416. Bradford Richardson, "Title IX Order on Campus 'Harassment' Violates Rights, Free Speech Advocates Say," *Washington Times*, May 1, 2016, https://www.washingtontimes.com/news/2016/may/1/title-ix-harassment-order-seen-as-free-speech-thre/.

417. "Democrats Attack 3 of the 10 Amendments in the Bill of Rights," *Investors' Business Daily*, June 27, 2016, https://www.investors.com/politics/editorials/democrats-now-attack-3-of-the-10-bill-of-rights/.

418. Senator Joe Manchin, *MSNBC*, June 16, 2016, https://twitter.com/Morning_Joe/status/743407937079521280?ref_src=twsrc%5Etfw.

419. "Sixth Amendment," Legal Information Institute, Cornell Law School, accessed February 12, 2019, https://www.law.cornell.edu/constitution/sixth_amendment.

420. Keith Findley, "The Presumption of Innocence Exists in Theory, Not Reality," Washington Post, January 19, 2006, https://www.washingtonpost.com/news/in-theory/wp/2016/01/19/the-presumption-of-innocence-exists-in-theory-not-reality/?noredirect=on&utm_term=.d1859e718212.

421. Ibid.

422. Ibid.

423. Ibid.

424. As cited in Ellis Washington, "Progressives' 6th Amendment," *WND*, March 22, 2013, https://www.wnd.com/2013/03/progressives-6th-amendment/#MEufo3oLEcjRQlx0.99.

425. Marci Hamilton, Michael McConnell et al, "Clauses of the First Amendment," *Common Interpretation*, accessed February 12, 2019, https://constitutioncenter.org/interactive-constitution/amendments/.

426. Ibid.

427. Ibid.

428. Ibid.

429. "Legal History: Origins of the Public Trial," Vol 35, Issue 2, *Indiana Law Journal*, p. 252. http://www.shestokas.com/wp-content/uploads/2014/11/Legal-History-Origins-of-the-Public-Trial.pdf.

430. Ibid.

431. Ibid, p.256.

432. Clay S. Conrad, "Jury Nullification: The Evolution of a Doctrine," CATO Institute, December 5, 2013, p. 4.

433. Hamilton, op. cit.

434. Craig Trainer, "Antonin Scalia, Defender of the Rights of the Accused," *Weekly Standard*, September 24, 2018. https://www.weeklystandard.com/craig-trainor/antonin-scalia-defender-of-the-rights-of-the-accused.

435. Brian P. Smentkowski, "Sixth Amendment," *Encyclopedia Britannica*, accessed February 12, 2019, https://www.britannica.com/topic/Sixth-Amendment.

436. "Sixth Amendment Court Cases—Confrontation Clause," Revolutionary War and Beyond, accessed February 12, 2019, http://www.revolutionary-war-and-beyond.com/sixth-amendment-court-cases-confrontation-clause.html.

437. Ibid.

438. "The Trial of Sir Walter Raleigh," Quimbee, accessed February 12, 2019, https://www.quimbee.com/cases/the-trial-of-sir-walter-raleigh.

439. Ibid.

440. Hamilton, op. cit.

441. Ibid.

442. Ibid.

443. Ibid.

444. "Is the Presumption of Innocence in the Constitution?," LawInfo, December 12, 2017, https://blog.lawinfo.com/2017/12/12/is-the-presumption-of-innocence-in-the-constitution/.

445. "Coffin v. United States," CaraSearch, accessed February 12, 2019, https://casetext.com/case/coffin-v-united-states.

446. Ellis Washington, "Progressives' 6th Amendment," *WND*, March 22, 2013, https://www.wnd.com/2013/03/progressives-6th-amendment/print/.

447. Thomas Jipping, "Losing the Presumption of Innocence," Heritage

Foundation, September 28, 2018, https://www.heritage.org/courts/commentary/losing-the-presumption-innocence.

448. Robert Laurie, "Democrats Ditch 'Presumption of Innocence' in Favor of 'the Ends Justify the Means,'" *Townhall*, September 26, 2018, https://townhall.com/columnists/robertlaurie/2018/09/26/democrats-ditch-presumption-of-innocence-in-favor-of-the-ends-justify-the-means-n2522496.

449. Ibid.

450. Al Weaver, "Schumer: 'No Presumption of Innocence or Guilt' ahead of Kavanaugh Testimony," *Washington Examiner*, September 25, 2018, https://www.washingtonexaminer.com/news/congress/schumer-no-presumption-of-innocence-or-guilt-ahead-of-kavanaugh-testimony.

451. Ibid.

452. Isaac N. Cohen and Amy L. Wax, "Presumed Innocent No More." *Academic Questions*, Vol. 30, no. 3, 2017, p. 352+. *Academic OneFile*, http://link.galegroup.com/apps/doc/A501863213/AONE?u=wash92852&sid=AONE&xid=2ebcdc83.

453. "Tenth Amendment," Legal Information Institute, Cornell Law School, accessed February 12, 2019, https://www.law.cornell.edu/constitution/tenth_amendment.

454. "McCulloch v. Maryland, 17 U.S. 316 (1819), *Justia*, accessed February 12, 2019, https://supreme.justia.com/cases/federal/us/17/316/.

455. Gail Ablow, "Federalism, Explained: Is Progressive Federalism an Oxymoron?," *Salon*, April 2, 2017, https://www.salon.com/2017/04/02/federalism-explained-is-progressive-federalism-an-oxymoron_partner/.

456. Ibid.

457. Robert Longley, "Federalism and the United States Constitution," ThoughtCo., April 20, 2018, https://www.thoughtco.com/federalism-and-the-united-states-constitution-105418.

458. Ibid.

459. Ibid.

460. Longley, op. cit.

461. Ibid.

462. Ibid.

463. Ibid.

464. Ibid.

465. Ablow, op. cit.

466. Roger Pilon, "The United States as a Post-Constitutional Republic." *inFOCUS*, Fall 2018, p. 3+, http://link.galegroup.com/apps/doc/A560416001/AONE?u=wash92852&sid=AONE&xid=7fe9311b.

467. Ibid.

468. Ibid.

469. Ibid.

470. Ibid.

471. Ibid.

472. Ibid.

473. "Did Nancy Pelosi Say Obamacare Must Be Passed to 'Find Out What Is in It'?" *Snopes*, accessed February 12, 2019, https://www.snopes.com/fact-check/pelosi-healthcare-pass-the-bill-to-see-what-is-in-it/.

474. Ablow, op. cit.

475. Ibid.

476. Damon Root, "Will Liberals Learn to Love the 10th Amendment?" *Reason*, March 2017, https://reason.com/archives/2017/02/04/will-liberals-learn-to-love-th.

477. Ibid.

478. Ibid.

479. "Abraham Lincoln," Brainy Quote, accessed February 12, 2019, https://www.brainyquote.com/quotes/abraham_lincoln_101160.

480. Girija Shinde, "The Undeniable Reasons Why Family Is Important," AptParenting, March 21, 2018, https://aptparenting.com/why-is-family-important.

481. "2010 Census Summary File 1," 2010 Census of Population and Housing, Technical Documentation, SF1/10-4 (RV), issued September 2012, accessed February 13, 2019, p. B-6, https://www.census.gov/prod/cen2010/doc/sf1.pdf#page=504.

482. Andreas Kostenberger, "The Bible's Teaching on Marriage and Family," Family Research Council, accessed February 21, 2019, https://www.frc.org/brochure/the-bibles-teaching-on-marriage-and-family.

483. "Abraham Maslow," Wikipedia, accessed February 21, 2019, https://en.wikipedia.org/wiki/Abraham_Maslow.

484. Jonah Goldberg, "Why Family Structure Is So Important," *Chicago Tribune*, October 28, 2015, https://www.chicagotribune.com/news/opinion/commentary/ct-traditional-families-marriage-20151028-column.html.

485. Ibid.

486. Ibid.

487. Courtney G. Joslin, "The Evolution of the American Family," *Human Rights*, 00468185, Summer2009, Vol. 36, Issue 3.

488. Ibid.

489. Ibid.

490. Ibid.

491. Ibid.

492. "Miscegenation," Bing.com, accessed February 13, 2019, https://www.bing.com/search?q=miscegenation&form=EDGHPT&qs=PF&cvid=25a80af0f1594f66a90167986bb27705&cc=US&setlang=en-US.

493. "The Emancipation Proclamation," National Archives, accessed February 14, 2019, https://www.archives.gov/exhibits/featured-documents/emancipation-proclamation.

494. Joslin, op. cit.

495. Ibid.

496. Murray N. Rothbard, "The Progressive Era and the Family," Mises Institute, June 30, 2003, https://mises.org/library/progressive-era-and-family.

497. Ibid.

498. Ibid.

499. Ibid.

500. Catherine A. Paul, "The Progressive Era," Social Welfare History Project, accessed February 14, 2019, https://socialwelfare.library.vcu.edu/eras/civil-war-reconstruction/progressive-era/.

501. Ibid.

502. Rothbard, op. cit.

503. Paul Kleppner, The Third Electoral System, 1853–1892: Parties. Voters. and Political Culture, Chapel Hill: University of North Carolina Press, 1979, p. 222.

504. Ibid.

505. Rothbard, op. cit.

506. Paul, op. cit.

507. Rothbard, op. cit.

508. Ibid.

509. Ibid.

510. Ibid.

511. Ibid.

512. Ibid.

513. Ibid.

514. Ibid.

515. Ibid.

516. Ibid.

517. "Key Facts about Births to Unmarried Women," Child Trends, accessed February 14, 2019, https://www.childtrends.org/indicators/ births-to-unmarried-women.

518. William Bennett, "Stronger Families, Stronger Societies," *New York Times*, April 24, 2012, https://www.nytimes.com/roomfordebate/2012/04/24/ are-family-values-outdated/stronger-families-stronger-societies.

519. Ibid.

520. "Unmarried and Single Americans Week: Sept. 17–23, 2017," Release Number CB17-TPS.62, Census Bureau, August 14, 2017, https://www. census.gov/newsroom/facts-for-features/2017/single-americans-week.html.

521. Max Kutner, "The Number of People on Food Stamps Is Falling. Here's Why," *Newsweek* , July 22, 2017, https://www.newsweek.com/ people-food-stamps-snap-decline-participation-640500.

522. "*Obergefell v. Hodges*," Wikipedia, accessed February 14, 2019, https:// en.wikipedia.org/wiki/Obergefell_v._Hodges.

523. "The Family Issue as Key to the Growth of the Right," The Network of Spiritual Progressives, accessed February 14, 2019, https:// spiritualprogressives.org/visionary-strategies/family-friendly-policies/ the-family-issue-as-key-to-the-growth-of-the-right/.

524. Katherine Gallagher Robbins and Shawn Fremstad, "4 Progressive Policies that Make Families Stronger," Center for American Progress, October 25, 2016, https://www.americanprogress.org/issues/poverty/

reports/2016/10/25/225731/4-progressive-policies-that-make-families-
stronger/.

525. Ibid.

526. Shawn Fremstad, "How Progressive Policies Can Strengthen Marriage
and Family," IFS Studies, February 10, 2015, https://ifstudies.org/blog/
how-progressive-policies-can-strengthen-marriage-and-family-life/.

527. Ibid.

528. Ibid.

529. Ibid.

530. Jeff Stein, "Does Bernie Sanders' Health Plan Cost $33 Trillion or Save $2
Trillion?," *Washington Post*, July 31, 2018, https://www.washingtonpost.
com/business/economy/does-bernie-sanderss-health-plan-cost-33-
trillion--or-save-2-trillion/2018/07/31/d178b14e-9432-11e8-a679-
b09212fb69c2_story.html?utm_term=.d95a6fa8f72d.

531. David Weigel, "Democrats Plan to Hold Hearings on Medicare for
All," *Washington Post*, January 3, 2019, https://www.washingtonpost.
com/powerpost/democrats-plan-to-hold-hearings-on-medicare-for-
all/2019/01/03/7051eccc-0f6c-11e9-84fc-d58c33d6c8c7_story.
html?utm_term=.78aa5cb4f13c.

532. Shawn Fremstad, "How Progressive Policies Can Strengthen
Marriage and Family Life," Institute of Family Studies,
accessed February 16, 2019, https://ifstudies.org/blog/
how-progressive-policies-can-strengthen-marriage-and-family-life/.

533. Calvin Freiberger, "Democrats take control of House, immediately
introduce bill to fund abortions worldwide," *Lifesite News*, January 3,
2019, https://www.lifesitenews.com/news/democrats-seek-to-undo-trump-
ban-on-foreign-abortion-funding-with-budget-bi.

534. Richard Mitchell quotes, AZ Quotes, accessed February 16, 2019, https://
www.azquotes.com/author/20900-Richard_Mitchell.

535. Andrew Bernstein, "Heroes and Villains in American
Education," The Objective Standard, August 13, 2018,
https://www.theobjectivestandard.com/2018/08/
heroes-and-villains-in-american-education/?add-to-cart=113670.

536. Nadia Pflaum, "Trump: U.S. Spends More than 'Almost Any Other
Major Country' on Education," Politifact, September 21, 2016, https://

www.politifact.com/ohio/statements/2016/sep/21/donald-trump/
trump-us-spends-more-almost-any-other-major-countr/.

537. Bernstein, op. cit.

538. Ibid.

539. Elizabeth Youmans, "The Role of the Bible in Early American Education,"
Darrow Miller and Friends, June 22, 2017, http://darrowmillerandfriends.
com/2017/06/22/bible-role-early-american-education/.

540. Ibid.

541. Ibid.

542. Ibid.

543. Ibid.

544. "Boston Latin School," Wikipedia, accessed February 14, 2019, https://
en.wikipedia.org/wiki/Boston_Latin_School.

545. Youmans, op cit.

546. Ibid.

547. Ibid.

548. As cited in Bernstein, op. cit.

549. Ibid.

550. Youmans, op cit.

551. Ibid.

552. Andrew Bernstein, "Heroes and Villains in American Education,"
The Objective Standard, 13.3 (Fall 2018), p.14+, http://www.
theobjectivestandard.com/.

553. Ibid.

554. Ibid.

555. Ibid.

556. Ibid.

557. Ibid.

558. Ibid.

559. Ibid.

560. Ibid.

561. Ibid.

562. Ibid.

563. Ibid.

564. Ibid.

565. Ibid.
566. Ibid.
567. Ibid.
568. Ibid.
569. Ibid.
570. Ibid.
571. Ibid.
572. Ibid.
573. Ibid.
574. Ibid.
575. Ibid.
576. Ibid.
577. Ibid.
578. Ibid.
579. Ibid.
580. Ibid.
581. Ibid.
582. Ibid.
583. Ibid.
584. As cited in Bernstein, "Mortimer J. Adler: American Philosopher and Educator," *Encyclopedia Britannica*, June 24, 2018, www.britannica.com/biography/Mortimer-J-Adler.
585. As cited in Bernstein, Eunice Fuller Barnard, "A Teacher's Teacher Tells What Education Is," *New York Times*, March 21, 1937, 5, quoted in Ravitch, Left Back, 304.
586. As cited in Bernstein, Dewey quoted in Ravitch, *Left Back*, 304.
587. As cited in Bernstein, Rudolf Flesch, *Why Johnny Can't Read*, New York: Harper & Row, 1955, p. 10.
588. Andrew Bernstein, "Heroes and Villains in American Education," op. cit.
589. Ibid.
590. As cited in Bernstein, Martin Gross, *The Conspiracy of Ignorance*, New York: HarperCollins, 1999, p. 78.
591. As cited in Bernstein, Leonard Peikoff, "The American School: Why Johnny Can't Think," in Ayn Rand, *The Voice of Reason: Essays in Objectivist Thought*, New York: Penguin Books, 1989, p. 217.

592. As cited in Bernstein, Ravitch, *Left Back*, pp. 354–55.

593. As cited in Bernstein, Gross, *Conspiracy of Ignorance*, p. 81.

594. Ibid.

595. Ibid., p. 107.

596. Ibid., pp. 115–16.

597. As cited in Bernstein, Annie Holmquist, "High School Reading Lists: 1922 vs. Today," www.theimaginativeconservative.org/2018/05/high-school-reading-lists1922-today-annie-holmquist.html.

598. As cited in Bernstein, Quoted in Gross, *Conspiracy of Ignorance*, pp. 187–88.

599. Bernstein, op. cit.

600. Lisette Partelow et al, "7 Great Education Policy Ideas for Progressives in 2018," Center for American Progress, March 28, 2018, https://www.americanprogress.org/issues/education-k-12/reports/2018/03/28/448156/7-great-education-policy-ideas-progressives-2018/.

601. Ibid.

602. Ibid.

603. Ibid.

604. "Teacher Salaries in America," Niche, accessed February 22, 2019, https://www.niche.com/blog/teacher-salaries-in-america/.

605. Ibid.

606. Ibid.

607. "Elizabeth Warren on Education," On the Issues, accessed February 14, 2019, http://www.ontheissues.org/Social/Elizabeth_Warren_Education.htm.

608. Mona Charen, "Unwarranted: Elizabeth Warren's Flawed Idea," *Real Clear Politics*, February 21, 2019, https://www.realclearpolitics.com/articles/2019/02/21/unwarranted_elizabeth_warrens_flawed_idea_139533.html.

609. Ibid.

610. "It's Time to Make College Tuition Free and Debt Free," Bernie, accessed February 14, 2019, https://berniesanders.com/issues/its-time-to-make-college-tuition-free-and-debt-free/.

611. Ibid.

612. "Grammar School," *Encyclopedia Britannica*, accessed February 22, 2019, https://www.britannica.com/topic/grammar-school-British-education.

613. David Kynaston, Modernity Britain: A Shake of the Dice 1959–62, Bloomsbury, 2014, pp.179–182.

614. As cited in "Eleven-Plus," Wikipedia, accessed February 14, 2019, https://en.wikipedia.org/wiki/Eleven-plus.

615. As cited in Bernstein, Mitchell, *Graves of Academe*, p. 69.

616. Ibid.

617. As cited in Bernstein, Arthur Bestor, *Educational Wastelands: The Retreat from Learning in Our Public Schools,* Urbana: University of Illinois Press, 1953, p. 101.

618. As cited in Bernstein, Gross, *Conspiracy of Ignorance*, p. 115.

619. Brian D. Ray, "Homeschooling Growing: Multiple Data Points Show Increase 2012 to 2016 and Later," NHERI, April 20, 2018, https://www.nheri.org/homeschool-population-size-growing/.

620. "Robert Kennedy," Brainy Quote, accessed February 15, 2019, https://www.brainyquote.com/quotes/robert_kennedy_400532.

621. William A. Schambra and Thomas West, "The Progressive Movement and the Transformation of American Politics," Heritage Foundation, July 18, 2007 , https://www.heritage.org/political-process/report/the-progressive-movement-and-the-transformation-american-politics.

622. Eric Schansberg, "Family, Religion and the American Republic," *Journal of Interdisciplinary Studies*, Vol. 30, No. 1–2, 2018, p. 78+, http://link.galegroup.com/apps/doc/A567326538/AONE?u=wash92852&sid=AONE&xid=999ff9a0.

623. "Opinion: Millennials Stray from Religion, Value More Progressive Ideals." *UWIRE Text*, 4 Sept. 2018, p. 1, http://link.galegroup.com/apps/doc/A552917810/AONE?u=wash92852&sid=AONE&xid=f1cd6113.

624. Ibid.

625. "Gen Z and Morality: What Teens Believe (So Far)," Barna, October 9, 2018, ttps://www.barna.com/research/gen-z-morality/.

626. Ibid.

627. Ibid.

628. Ibid.

629. Peter Berkowitz, "The Tyranny of Secular Faith: Progressivism Marches

Relentlessly toward Its Destination: The One True Secular Kingdom."
Hoover Digest, no. 1, 2016, p. 111+, http://link.galegroup.com/apps/doc/
A444819112/AONE?u=wash92852&sid=AONE&xid=189999c2.

630. Ibid.
631. Ibid.
632. Ibid.
633. Ibid.
634. Ibid.
635. Bruce Abramson, "The Decline—and Fall?—of Religious Freedom
in America," *Mosaic*, August 3, 2015, https://mosaicmagazine.com/
essay/2015/08/the-decline-and-fall-of-religious-freedom-in-america/.
636. Ibid.
637. Berkowitz, op. cit.
638. Abramson, op. cit.
639. Ibid.
640. Ibid.
641. Ibid.
642. Ibid.
643. Ibid.
644. Ibid.
645. Ibid.
646. Ibid.
647. Ibid.
648. Ibid.
649. Ibid.
650. Ibid.
651. Ibid.
652. Ibid.
653. Ibid.
654. Ibid.
655. Ibid.
656. Ibid.
657. Ibid.
658. Ibid.
659. Ibid.

660. Ibid.

661. Ibid.

662. David Siders, "'You Don't Just Get to Say That You're Progressive': The Left Moves to Defend Its Brand," Politico, December 9, 2018, https://www.politico.com/story/2018/12/09/progressives-democrats-2020-election-1049959.

663. Roger Taylor, "Progressivism Takes Its Place among the Major Religions," *American Thinker*, August 31, 2018, https://www.americanthinker.com/articles/2018/08/progressivism_takes_its_place_among_the_major_religions.html.

664. James Madison, "Government," Brainy Quote, accessed February 16, 2019, https://www.brainyquote.com/topics/government.

665. "Transcript of Federalist Papers, No. 10 & No. 51," ourdocuments.gov, accessed February 16, 2019, https://www.ourdocuments.gov/print_friendly.php?flash=false&page=transcript&doc=10&title=Transcript+of+Federalist+Papers%2C+No.+10+%26amp%3B+No.+51+.

666. "Alexis de Tocqueville," Wikiquote, accessed February 16, 2019, https://en.wikiquote.org/wiki/Alexis_de_Tocqueville.

667. Thomas Jefferson, Sesquicentenary, Wordpress.com, May 15, 2012, https://sesquicentenary.wordpress.com/2012/05/15/i-consider-the-foundation-of-the-constitution-as-laid-on-this-ground-that-all-powers-not-delegated-to-the-united-states-by-the-constitution-nor-prohibited-by-it-to-the-states-are-reserve/.

668. Ralph Ketcham, *James Madison: A Biography*, University of Virginia Press, 1990, p. 320.

669. Cited in Gil Richard Musolf, "*Dominion and Resistance: The Political Theory of John Dewey,*" *Radical Interactionism in the Rise*, edited by Lonnie Athens and Norman Denzin, Emerald Group Publishing, October 28, 2013, p. 108.

670. Alonzo L. Hamby, "Progressivism: A Century of Change and Rebirth," in *Progressivism and the New Democracy*, ed. Sidney M. Milkis and Jerome M. Mileur, University of Massachusetts Press, 1999.

671. "The U.S. Constitution: A Reader," Hillsdale College Press, 2012, p. 641.

672. Thomas E. Woods, Jr., "33 Questions about American History You're Not Supposed to Ask," Crown Publishing Group, 2007, p. 54.

673. Andrew J. Vinchur, "The Early Years of Industrial and Organizational Psychology," Cambridge University Press, 2018, p. 39.

674. Ilnyun Kim, "From Revolt to Order: The Career of Walter Lippmann's Progressivism, 1913–1914," Seoul National University, accessed February 16, 2019, http://s-space.snu.ac.kr/bitstream/10371/88705/3/7.%20 The%20Career%20of%20Walter%20Lippmann%60s%20 Progressivism%2C%201913-1914.pdf.

675. Schambra and West, op. cit.

676. Erik S. Root, *All Honor to Jefferson?: The Virginia Slavery Debates and the Positive Good Thesis*, Lexington Books, 2008, p. 71.

677. Ronald Pestritto and Taylor Kempema, "The Birth of Direct Democracy: What Progressivism Did to the States," Heritage Foundation, February 25, 2014, https://www.heritage.org/political-process/report/ the-birth-direct-democracy-what-progressivism-did-the-states.

678. Ibid.

679. As cited Pestritto and Kempema, op cit.

680. Ibid.

681. Theodore Roosevelt, "The Right of the People to Rule," American Rhetoric, accessed February 16, 2019, https://www.americanrhetoric.com/ speeches/teddyrooseveltrightpeoplerule.htm.

682. Pestritto and Kempema, op. cit.

683. As cited Pestritto and Kempema, op. cit.

684. "Government Corruption," Now That's Progressive!, accessed February 16, 2019, https://nowthatsprogressive.weebly.com/government-corruption. html.

685. "Think Obama Administration Wasn't Corrupt? Think Again," *Investors Business Daily*, March 21, 2018, https://www.investors.com/politics/ editorials/think-obama-administration-wasnt-corrupt-think-again/.

686. Alex Pappas, "Republicans Examine Accusations of 'Pay to Play' at Clinton Foundation, Amid Plunge in Donations," *Fox News*, December 13, 2018, https://www.foxnews.com/politics/republicans-examine-accusations-of- pay-to-play-at-clinton-foundation-amid-plunge-in-donations.

687. Ibid.

688. "Scandals at State: How Clinton, Kerry Used Office to Enrich Their Families," *Investors' Business Daily*, September

13, 2016, https://www.investors.com/politics/editorials/
scandals-at-state-how-clinton-kerry-used-office-to-enrich-their-families/.

689. Ibid.

690. Ibid.

691. Shane Harris and Nancy A. Youssef, "50 Spies Say ISIS Intelligence Was
Cooked," *The Daily Beast*, September 9, 2015, https://www.thedailybeast.
com/exclusive-50-spies-say-isis-intelligence-was-cooked.

692. Feliks Garcia, "Why Did Hillary Clinton 'What difference does it make?,'"
Independent (UK), July 21, 2016, https://www.independent.co.uk/news/
world/americas/us-elections/hillary-clinton-what-difference-does-it-make-
rnc-2016-benghazi-a7148706.html.

693. Dylan Stableford, "McCabe There Were 25th Amendment Discussions
at DOJ to Remove Trump from Office," *Yahoo News*, February 14, 2019,
https://news.yahoo.com/mccabe-25th-amendment-discussions-doj-
remove-trump-office-140646145.html.

694. Ibid.

695. "Scandals at State: How Clinton, Kerry Used Office to Enrich Their
Families," op. cit.

696. Ibid.

697. Cynthia Roper, "Political Correctness," *Encyclopedia Britannica*,
accessed February 16, 2019, https://www.britannica.com/topic/
political-correctness.

698. "A Little History of 'Politically Correct,'" *Washington Times*, November
15, 2015, https://www.washingtontimes.com/news/2015/nov/15/
editorial-a-little-history-of-politically-correct/.

699. Ibid.

700. Ibid.

701. Ibid.

702. Yascha Mounk, "Americans Strongly Dislike PC Culture," *The Atlantic*,
October 10, 2018, https://www.theatlantic.com/ideas/archive/2018/10/
large-majorities-dislike-political-correctness/572581/.

703. Ibid.

704. Kimberly Amadeo, "Current US Federal Budget Deficit,"
The Balance, January 17, 2019, https://www.thebalance.com/
current-u-s-federal-budget-deficit-3305783.

705. Ibid.

706. Ibid.

707. Ibid.

708. Ibid.

709. Ibid.

710. Ibid.

711. Ibid.

712. Ibid.

713. Lydia DePillis, "US Deficit Rises 17% to the Highest Level Since 2012," CNN, October 16, 2018, https://www.cnn.com/2018/10/15/economy/us-budget-deficit/index.html.

714. Ibid.

715. Ibid.

716. Ibid.

717. Benjy Sarlin, "As the Progressive Push for Big Spending Grows, so Does the Democratic Divide on the Deficit," *NBC News*, August 19, 2018, https://www.nbcnews.comm/politics/congress/progressive-push-big-spending-grows-so-does-democratic-divide-deficit-n901081.

718. Ibid.

719. Ibid.

720. Ibid.

721. Julie Jennings and Jared C. Nagel, "Federal Workforce Statistics Sources: OPM and OMB," Congressional Research Service, January 12, 2018, https://fas.org/sgp/crs/misc/R43590.pdf.

722. "Want Better, Smaller Government? Hire 1 Million More Federal Bureaucrats," *Washington Post*, August 29, 2014, https://www.washingtonpost.com/opinions/want-better-smaller-governmenthire-1-million-more-federal-bureaucrats/2014/08/29/c0bc1480-2c72-11e4-994d-202962a9150c_story.html?utm_term=.5ab06facdcb3.

723. Ibid.

724. John W. York, "Bloated Federal Agencies Have Become the Norm. Here's the Key to Sizing them Down," Heritage Foundation, November 21, 2017, https://www.heritage.org/government-regulation/commentary/bloated-federal-agencies-have-become-the-norm-heres-the-key-sizing.

725. Ibid.

726. Ibid.

727. Ibid.

728. Alan Krinsky, "Why Do Progressives Favor Regulation—and Should We?," *Huffington Post*, February 1, 2011, https://www.huffingtonpost. com/alan-krinsky/why-do-progressives-favor_b_812811.html.

729. "Declaration of Independence," July 4, 1776, http://www.ushistory.org/ declaration/document/.

730. Michael D. Tanner, "Too Many Laws, Too Much Regulation," Cato Institute, March 2, 2016, https://www.cato.org/publications/commentary/ too-many-laws-too-much-regulation.

731. Ibid.

732. Ibid.

733. Krinsky, op. cit.

734. Ronald Bailey, "45 Percent of Americans Say There Is Too Much Government Regulation of Business," Reason, October 12, 2017, https:// reason.com/blog/2017/10/12/45-percent-of-americans-say-there-is-too.

735. Ibid.

736. Ibid.

737. H. Beales, et al., "Government Regulation: The Good, The Bad, and The Ugly," released by the Regulatory Transparency Project of the Federalist Society, June 12, 2017, https://regproject.org/wp-content/uploads/RTP-Regulatory-Process-Working-Group-Paper.pdf.

738. Ibid.

739. Ibid.

740. Ibid.

741. Ibid.

742. Ibid.

743. Ibid.

744. Carol Negro, "What the Progressives Want," *American Thinker*, May 10, 2009, https://www.americanthinker.com/articles/2009/05/what_the_ progressives_want.html#ixzz5cJMmRO4h.

745. Ibid.

746. Ibid.

747. Ibid.

748. Margaret Thatcher, Good Reads, accessed February 16, 2019, https://

www.goodreads.com/quotes/138248-the-problem-with-socialism-is-that-you-eventually-run-out.

749. Steve Straub, "9 Quotes from the Founding Fathers about Economics, Capitalism And Banking," The Federalist Papers, June 10, 2014, https://thefederalistpapers.org/founders/9-quotes-from-the-founding-fathers-about-economics-capitalism-and-banking.

750. Ibid.

751. "Economy," Wikipedia, accessed April 6, 2019, https://en.wikipedia.org/wiki/Economy.

752. James Chen, "Economic Growth," Investopedia, May 24, 2018, https://www.investopedia.com/terms/e/economicgrowth.asp.

753. "America's Economy Is Both Booming and Fading," *Washington Post*, December 4, 2018, https://www.washingtonpost.com/opinions/americas-economy-is-both-booming--and-fading/2018/12/04/758ca1bc-f7fe-11e8-8c9a-860ce2a8148f_story.html?utm_term=.fb6828d75a9e.

754. Ibid.

755. Ibid.

756. Ibid.

757. Sidney Milkis, "Theodore Roosevelt: Impact and Legacy," The Miller Center, accessed February 16, 2019, https://millercenter.org/president/roosevelt/impact-and-legacy.

758. "TR'S Legacy," American Experience, PBS, accessed February 16, 2019, https://www.pbs.org/wgbh/americanexperience/features/tr-legacy/.

759. Peter Beinart, "How Far Will the Left Go?," *The Atlantic*, December 2018, https://www.theatlantic.com/magazine/archive/2018/12/democratic-party-moves-left/573946/.

760. Ibid.

761. Ibid.

762. Ibid.

763. Ibid.

764. Ibid.

765. Ibid.

766. Herbert Hovenkamp, "Appraising the Progressive State," *Iowa Law Review.* 102.3 (Mar. 2017), https://ilr.law.uiowa.edu/print/volume-102-issue-3/appraising-the-progressive-state/.

767. Ibid.

768. Ibid.

769. Ibid.

770. Ibid.

771. Ibid.

772. Andrea Gonzalez-Ramirez, "AOC and Progressive Groups Succeed at Kicking Amazon out of New York," Yahoo, February 14, 2019, https://www.yahoo.com/news/aoc-progressive-groups-succeed-kicking-194500652.html.

773. Ibid.

774. "As More Democrats Embrace 'Progressive' Label, It May Not Mean What It Used To." *Morning Edition*, 29 Oct. 2018, http://link.galegroup.com/apps/doc/A560373156/AONE?u=wash92852&sid=AONE&xid=ecb43d45.

775. Ibid.

776. Ibid.

777. Ibid.

778. Ibid.

779. Ibid.

780. Alex Rowell and David Madland, "The Working-Class Push for Progressive Economic Policies," Center for American Progress, April 17, 2018, https://www.americanprogressaction.org/issues/economy/reports/2018/04/17/169879/working-class-push-progressive-economic-policies/.

781. Helaine Olen, "Memo to Democrats: A Progressive Economic Agenda Is Popular." *Washington Post*, 17 Apr. 2018. World History in Context, http://link.galegroup.com/apps/doc/A535029430/WHIC?u=wash92852&sid=WHIC&xid=cdd4a8ee.

782. Alexandria Ocasio-Cortez, Brainy Quote, accessed February 16, 2019, https://www.brainyquote.com/authors/alexandria_ocasiocortez.

783. Tristan Justice, "7 Staggering Quotes Made by Progressive Democrats' New Star," The Daily Signal, November 06, 2018, https://www.dailysignal.com/2018/11/06/7-staggering-quotes-made-from-progressive-democrats-new-star/.

784. Tanza Laudenback, "Alexandria Ocasio-Cortez Has a Plan

to Tax the Wealthiest Americans 60% to 70%," *Business Insider*, January 13, 2019, https://www.businessinsider.com/us-progressive-taxes-alexandria-ocasio-cortez-tax-plan-2019-1.

785. "Irony Alert! 'Progressive' Democrats Embrace Obsolete Socialism," States News Service, September 18, 2018. Academic OneFile, http://link.galegroup.com/apps/doc/A554750480/AONE?u=wash92852&sid=AONE&xid=1241280c.

786. Zachary B. Wolf, "Trump clearly has a game plan for socialism in 2020," *CNN*, February 9, 2019, https://www.cnn.com/2019/02/08/politics/trump-socialism/index.html.

787. Ibid.

788. Ibid.

789. Frank Newport, "The Meaning of 'Socialism' to Americans Today," Gallup, October 24, 2018, https://news.gallup.com/opinion/polling-matters/243362/meaning-socialism-americans-today.aspx.

790. "Socialism," Merriam-Webster, accessed February 16, 2019, https://www.merriam-webster.com/dictionary/socialism.

791. "The Black Book of Communism," Wikipedia, accessed February 16, 2019, https://en.wikipedia.org/wiki/The_Black_Book_of_Communism.

792. "Irony Alert! 'Progressive' Democrats Embrace Obsolete Socialism," op. cit.

793. Ibid.

794. Tom Bemis, "Karl Marx is the most assigned economist in U.S. college classes," Marketwatch.com, January 31, 2016, https://www.marketwatch.com/story/communist-manifesto-among-top-three-books-assigned-in-college-2016-01-27.

795. "Irony Alert! 'Progressive' Democrats Embrace Obsolete Socialism," op. cit.

796. John P. Warren, "Progressives and American Exceptionalism," Townhall, September 9, 2017, https://townhall.com/columnists/johnpwarren/2017/09/09/progressives-and-american-exceptionalism-n2379203.

797. Edward Grabb, Douglas Baer and James Curtis, "The Origins of American Individualism: Reconsidering the Historical Evidence," *Canadian Journal of Sociology / Cahiers canadiens de sociologie*, Vol. 24, No. 4 (Autumn, 1999), pp. 511–533.

798. John Winthrop, "The City Upon a Hill," The Historic Present, accessed February 16, 2019, https://thehistoricpresent.com/2010/06/28/the-city-upon-a-hill-and-puritan-hubris/.

799. "Thomas Paine publishes Common Sense," History.com, accessed February 16, 2019, https://www.history.com/this-day-in-history/thomas-paine-publishes-common-sense.

800. "General Introduction for the Independent Journal. Hamilton," The Avalon Project, Yale Law School, accessed February 16, 2019, http://avalon.law.yale.edu/18th_century/fed01.asp.

801. *Speeches & Letters of Abraham Lincoln*, 1832–1865, New York: E. P. Dutton, 1907, 176, 182–3.

802. "General Introduction for the Independent Journal. Hamilton," op. cit.

803. Seymour Martin Lipset, *American Exceptionalism: A Double-edged Sword,* New York: W. W. Norton & Company, 1996, p. 31.

804. Edward Grabb, Douglas Baer and James Curtis, *Origins of American Individualism: Reconsidering the Historical Evidence, Canadian Journal of Sociology / Cahiers canadiens de sociologie*, Vol. 24, No. 4, Autumn, 1999, pp. 511–533.

805. Jake Sullivan, "What Donald Trump and Dick Cheney Got Wrong About America," *The Atlantic*, January/February 2019, https://www.theatlantic.com/magazine/archive/2019/01/yes-america-can-still-lead-the-world/576427/.

806. Brian T. *Edwards, Gaonkar, Dilip Parameshwar,* Globalizing American Studies, *University of Chicago Press, 2010, pp. 58–59.*

807. Deborah L. Madsen, *American Exceptionalism,* Edinburgh: Edinburgh University Press, 1998.

808. Herbert Hoover, "The Future of American Individualism," Hoover Institution, February 1, 2017, https://www.hoover.org/research/future-american-individualism.

809. "Frederick Douglass, a Champion of American Individualism." Washingtonpost.com, February 1, 2018, http://link.galegroup.com/apps/doc/A525824108/AONE?u=wash92852&sid=AONE&xid=83dbc690.

810. Ibid.

811. David Davenport and Gordon Lloyd, "Rugged Individualism: Two of the Gravest Threats to This Distinctively American Value: Nanny States and

Helicopter Parents." *Hoover Digest*, 2017, p. 42+, http://link.galegroup.com/apps/doc/A491616114/AONE?u=wash92852&sid=AONE&xid=352cfebc.

812. Herbert Hoover, "The Future of American Individualism," Hoover Institution, February 1, 2017, https://www.hoover.org/research/future-american-individualism.

813. Ibid.

814. Ibid.

815. Ibid.

816. C. Eric Mount, Jr., "American Individualism Reconsidered," Centre College (Review of Religious Research, Vol. 22, No. 4, June 1981).

817. Claude S. Fischer, "Paradoxes of American Individualism," Sociological Forum, Vol. 23, No. 2, June, 2008, pp. 363–372, https://www.jstor.org/stable/20110272, Accessed: 20-01-2019 11:43 UTC.

818. Richard Koch, "Is Individualism Good or Bad?," *Huffington Post*, October 7, 2013, https://www.huffingtonpost.com/richard-koch/is-individualism-good-or-_b_4056305.html.

819. Terry McGarty, "Individualism vs. Neo-Progressivism," The Squirrel's Nest, June 14, 2010, http://terrymcgarty.blogspot.com/2010/06/individualism-vs-neo-progressivism.html.

820. "The American-Western European Values Gap," Pew Research Center, November 17, 2011, http://www.pewglobal.org/2011/11/17/the-american-western-european-values-gap/.

821. Ibid.

822. Ibid.

823. Ibid.

824. Ibid.

825. Ibid.

826. Hoover, op. cit.

827. Ibid.

828. Ibid.

829. Ibid.

830. Davenport, op. cit.

831. Ibid.

832. Ibid.

833. Ibid.

834. The Classical Conversations website states: "Our families thrive using three keys to a great education: Classical, Christian, and Community." https://www.classicalconversations.com/.

835. Ibid.

836. Hunter Hastings, "A 10-Point Manifesto for Individualism," Center for Individualism, October 4, 2017, https://centerforindividualism.org/a-10-point-manifesto-for-individualism/?gclid=EAIaIQobChMIrPS3xo773wIV mITICh3bvA2uEAMYASAAEgJzc_D_BwE.

837. Winston Churchill, "Capitalism," Brainy Quote, accessed February 16, 2019, https://www.brainyquote.com/quotes/winston_churchill_101776?src=t_capitalism.

838. "From George Washington to Benjamin Harrison, 18 January 1784," Founders Online, accessed February 16, 2019, https://founders.archives.gov/GEWN-04-01-02-0039.

839. Brian Grinder and Dan Cooper, "In Defense of Capitalism Part 1: The Problem and a Definition," *Financial History*, Winter 2018, p. 11.

840. "Opinion: Socialism vs Capitalism." UWIRE Text, October 3, 2018, p. 1, http://link.galegroup.com/apps/doc/A556666450/AONE?u=wash92852 &sid=AONE&xid=dd4936b6.

841. "Steve Forbes Touts Virtues of Capitalism." *States News Service*, April 28, 2010, http://link.galegroup.com/apps/doc/A225055334/AONE?u=wash9 2852&sid=AONE&xid=a438c68b.

842. Ibid.

843. Ibid.

844. Ibid.

845. Grinder, op. cit.

846. Ibid.

847. Ibid.

848. Ibid.

849. Brian Grinder and Dan Cooper, "In Defense of Capitalism Part II: The Temporal Nature of Capitalism," *Financial History*, Spring 2018, p. 10.

850. Ibid.

851. Ibid.

852. Ibid.

853. Ibid.

854. Edward Conard, "A Rousing Defense of Capitalism," *Real Clear Politics*, June 9, 2018, https://www.realclearpolitics.com/articles/2018/06/09/a_rousing_defense_of_capitalism_137212.html.

855. Ibid.

856. Richard M. Ebeling, "Capitalism 101: "Progressives" are Enemies of Freedom," *Capitalism Magazine*, April 9, 2016, https://www.capitalismmagazine.com/2016/04/capitalism-101-progressives-are-enemies-of-freedom/.

857. Ibid.

858. Ibid.

859. Warren Meyer, "Are Progressives Too Conservative to Accept Capitalism?, *Forbes*, December 12, 2010, https://www.forbes.com/sites/warrenmeyer/2010/12/10/are-progressives-too-conservative-to-accept-capitalism/#5c8c0c7a282a.

860. Ibid.

861. Ibid.

862. "The Communist Manifesto: Famous Lines Quiz," shmoop.com, accessed February 16, 2019, https://www.shmoop.com/communist-manifesto/famous-lines-quiz.html.

863. John Maynard Keynes, "Economic Possibilities for our Grandchildren," *Essays in Persuasion*, New York: W.W.Borton & Co., 1963, pp. 358–373.

864. Ibid.

865. Ibid.

866. "Alexandria Ocasio-Cortez on Capitalism," Brainy Quote, accessed February 16, 2019, https://www.brainyquote.com/quotes/alexandria_ocasiocortez_926278?src=t_capitalism.

867. Ed Rogers, "The Democrats' Frightening Embrace of Socialism." *Washington Post*, May 7, 2018, http://link.galegroup.com/apps/doc/A537655137/AONE?u=wash92852&sid=AONE&xid=f96753c9.

868. Ibid.

869. Ibid.

870. "The Founders' Unchanging Principles of Liberty, National Center for Constitutional Studies," accessed February 16, 2019, https://nccs.net/blogs/articles/the-founders-unchanging-principles-of-LIBERTY-1.

871. "Liberty," Merriam-Webster, accessed February 16, 2019, https://www.merriam-webster.com/dictionary/liberty.

872. Carl Eric Scott, "The Five Conceptions of American Liberty," *National Affairs*, Summer 2014, https://www.nationalaffairs.com/publications/detail/the-five-conceptions-of-american-LIBERTY.

873. Ibid.

874. Ibid.

875. Ibid.

876. Ibid.

877. Ibid.

878. Ibid.

879. Ibid.

880. Ibid.

881. Ibid.

882. Ibid.

883. Ibid.

884. Ibid.

885. Ibid.

886. Ibid.

887. Ibid.

888. Ibid.

889. Ibid.

890. Ibid.

891. "Planned Parenthood v. Casey, United States Supreme Court, 505 U.S. 833," accessed February 25, 2019, https://web.utk.edu/~scheb/decisions/Casey.htm.

892. "The Supreme Court: Accepting Homosexuality," InfoPlease, accessed February 16, 2019, https://www.infoplease.com/us/supreme-court/supreme-court-accepting-homosexuality.

893. Scott, op. cit.

894. "The Right to Speak Freely: The History of Free Speech," History Cooperative, accessed February 16, 2019, https://historycooperative.org/the-right-to-speak-freely/.

895. "Hear TR's Speech 'The Liberty of the People,'" History Matters, accessed February 16, 2019, http://historymatters.gmu.edu/d/5722/.

896. Tom G. Palmer, "The Three Most Pressing Threats to Liberty," Cato Institute, December 8, 2016, https://fee.org/articles/the-three-most-pressing-threats-to-LIBERTY/.

897. Herbert Marcuse, "Repressive Tolerance," Marcuse.org, accessed February 16, 2019, https://www.marcuse.org/herbert/pubs/60spubs/65repressivetolerance.htm.

898. Palmer, op. cit.

899. Ibid.

900. Ibid.

901. Ibid.

902. John Samples, "Campus Speech and Progressivism," Cato Institute, May 12, 2017, https://www.cato.org/blog/campus-SPEECH-progressivism.

903. Ryan Saavedra, "Nicholas Sandmann's Family Makes Major Move Against Media After Being Smeared," The Daily Wire, January 24, 2019, https://www.dailywire.com/news/42636/nicholas-sandmanns-family-makes-major-move-against-ryan-saavedra?utm_source=cnemail&utm_medium=email&utm_content=012519-news&utm_campaign=position1.

904. Craig Banister, "'Beauty and the Beast' Producer Apologizes for Wishing 'MAGA Kids' 'Into the Woodchipper,'" CNS News, January 22, 2019, https://www.cnsnews.com/blog/craig-bannister/beauty-and-beast-producer-apologizes-wishing-maga-kids-woodchipper.

905. Griffen Connelly, "Covington Catholic Lawyer Adds Rep. Ilhan Omar to 'Libel,' 'Get Sued' List," Roll Call, January 23, 2019, https://www.rollcall.com/news/congress/covington-catholic-lawyer-adds-rep-ilhan-omar-libel-get-sued-list.

906. Saavedra, op. cit.

907. Paul Waldman, "Stop trying to be 'responsible' on the budget, Democrats," Washington Post, June 7, 2018. http://link.galegroup.com/apps/doc/A541755988/AONE?u=wash92852&sid=AONE&xid=ed59d0e1.

908. Michael Schmitt, "Yes, Democrats Are the Party of Fiscal Responsibility. But That Will (and Should) Change," Vox, April 20, 2018, https://www.vox.com/polyarchy/2018/4/20/17262944/democrats-fiscal-responsibility-budget-deficits.

909. Corey Robin, "Democracy Is Norm Erosion," Jacobin,

January 2018, https://www.jacobinmag.com/2018/01/democracy-trump-authoritarianism-levitsky-zillblatt-norms.

910. Ronald Pestritto and Taylor Kempem, "The Birth of Direct Democracy: What Progressivism Did to the States," Heritage Foundation, February 25, 2014, https://www.heritage.org/political-process/report/the-birth-direct-democracy-what-progressivism-did-the-states.

911. "Declaration of Independence: A Transcription," National Archives, accessed February 17, 2019, https://www.archives.gov/founding-docs/declaration-transcript.

912. "The Meaning of Thomas Jefferson's Phrase 'all men are created equal,'" Matt Brundage Publications, accessed February 17, 2019, https://www.mattbrundage.com/publications/jefferson-equality/.

913. As cited in "The meaning of Thomas Jefferson's phrase 'all men are created equal,'" op. cit.

914. The Federalist No. 10, Constitution Society, accessed February 17, 2019, https://www.constitution.org/fed/federa10.htm.

915. Ibid.

916. "Federalist No. 10 (1787)," Bill of Rights Institute, accessed February 17, 2019, https://billofrightsinstitute.org/founding-documents/primary-source-documents/the-federalist-papers/federalist-papers-no-10/.

917. "Shays' Rebellion," Wikipedia, accessed February 17, 2019, https://en.wikipedia.org/wiki/Shays'_Rebellion.

918. Sophia Rosenfeld, "The Egalitarians," *The Nation*, April 5, 2017, https://www.thenation.com/article/the-egalitarians/.

919. Ibid.

920. Ibid.

921. "Equality," Stanford Encyclopedia of Philosophy, accessed February 17, 2019, https://plato.stanford.edu/entries/EQUALity/.

922. Ibid.

923. Ibid.

924. Tiffany Jones Miller, "Progressivism, Race, and the Training Wheels of Freedom," *National Review*, November 14, 2011, https://www.nationalreview.com/2011/11/progressivism-race-and-training-wheels-freedom-tiffany-jones-miller/.

925. Frederick Douglass, "What the Black Man Wants," speech before the

Massachusetts Anti-Slavery Society at Boston (April 1865), H105, American History I, Indiana University, accessed February 16, 2019, http://www.indiana.edu/~kdhist/H105-documents-web/week15/Douglass1865.html.

926. As quoted in Miller, op. cit.

927. "Jim Crow Laws," Legal Dictionary, accessed February 17, 2019, https://legaldictionary.net/jim-crow-laws/.

928. As quoted in Miller, op. cit.

929. Ibid.

930. "Hegel's Philosophy of History," Marxists.org, accessed February 17, 2019, https://www.marxists.org/reference/archive/hegel/works/hi/history4.htm.

931. Ibid.

932. Ibid.

933. Ibid.

934. Ibid.

935. Ibid.

936. Ibid.

937. Ibid.

938. Miller, op. cit.

939. Ibid.

940. As cited in Miller, op. cit.

941. Ibid.

942. Ibid.

943. Ibid.

944. Ibid.

945. Ibid.

946. As cited in Miller, op. cit.

947. Lily Kuo, "China Claims Muslim Detention Camps Are Education Centres," *The Guardian*, September 14, 2018, https://www.theguardian.com/world/2018/sep/14/china-claims-muslim-internment-camps-provide-professional-training Note: Beijing incarcerated 1.1 million Uighurs and Kazakhs in China's northwest for the purpose of reeducation, according to former detainees and other witnesses. The inmates are subjected to political indoctrination and abuse. Of course, Beijing officials with the Bureau of Human Rights Affairs of the State Council Information Office

say the camps are really "professional training centers." However, two former detainees of a reeducation camp said they were forced to learn Mandarin Chinese, sing patriotic songs, and study Chinese Communist party doctrine. They were not taught any vocational skills. Besides, the conditions at the facilities were inhumane such as one former detainee said he was forced to wear "iron clothes," an outfit of metal claws and rods that left him immobile, for twelve hours as punishment for disobeying a guard. Another reported seeing a woman having her feet and hands chained together for four days.

948. David Goodman and William Neuman, "Bill de Blasio Is a Progressive. But Is He Progressive Enough?," *New York Times,* July 26, 2018, https://www.nytimes.com/2018/07/26/nyregion/de-blasio-progressive-mayor-nyc.html.

949. Robert Harding, "'Women's Health Matters': Cuomo, NY Lawmakers OK Abortion Rights Bill," Auburn Publications, January 23, 2019, https://auburnpub.com/blogs/eye_on_ny/women-s-health-matters-cuomo-ny-lawmakers-ok-abortion-rights/article_5e051230-1e97-11e9-b5c5-cb9da113c038.html.

950. Alexandra Desanctis, "The Indefensible Morality of Andrew Cuomo," *National Review*, January 26, 2019, https://www.nationalreview.com/2019/01/andrew-cuomo-new-york-abortion-law/.

951. Virginia Governor Ralph Northam, "Infant would be resuscitated if that's what the mother and the family desired," radio interview on *YouTube*, January 30, 2019, https://youtu.be/SkTopSKo1xs.

952. George Washington, Brainy Quote, accessed February 17,2 2019, https://www.brainyquote.com/quotes/george_washington_382162.

953. John Fund, "Reagan Had Only One Warning in His 1989 Farewell Address," *National Review*, January 13, 2019, https://www.nationalreview.com/2019/01/ronald-reagan-farewell-address-learn-history-love-america/.

954. Ibid.

955. Ibid.

956. Ibid.

957. "Foundation Truths," Wordpress.com, April 6, 2013, https://captainjamesdavis.wordpress.com/2013/04/06/the-duty-and-value-of-patriotism-by-john-ireland-1894/.

958. Paul Jankowski, "Brands and Patriotism: Loving America Seems Un-American," *Forbes*, November 15, 2017, https://www.forbes.com/sites/pauljankowski/2017/11/15/brands-and-patriotism-loving-america-seems-un-american/#5c229eca7c4e.

959. Evan Thomas, "Michelle Obama's 'Proud' Remarks," *Newsweek*, March 12, 2008, https://www.newsweek.com/michelle-obamas-proud-remarks-83559.

960. Ibid.

961. "For Progressive Patriotism," *The Nation*, February 2, 2009, pp. 3–4.

962. Ibid.

963. "Diverse United States Divided on Symbols of Patriotism," *USA Today*, October 8, 2017, https://www.usatoday.com/story/sports/nfl/2017/10/08/diverse-united-states-divided-on-symbols-of-patriotism/106437716/.

964. Ibid.

965. Grace Sparks, "American Patriotism Is Down," *CNN*, July 2, 2018, https://www.cnn.com/2018/07/02/politics/american-proud-poll/index.html.

966. "MTV/AP-NORC: Political Views of Young People and Their Parents' Generation," The Associated Press-NORC Center for Public Affairs Research, accessed February 23, 2019, http://www.apnorc.org/projects/Pages/MTVAP-NORC-Youth-Political-Pulse,-May-2018.aspx.

967. Sparks, op. cit.

968. Ibid.

969. Ibid.

970. Peter Dreier and Dick Flacks, "Patriotism and Progressivism," *Peace Review* 15:4 (2003), pp. 397–404.

971. "Elk Grove Unified School District v. Newdow," Wikipedia, accessed February 17, 2019, https://en.m.wikipedia.org/wiki/Elk_Grove_Unified_School_District_v._Newdow.

972. Dreier, op. cit.

973. Ibid.

974. Ibid.

975. Ibid.

976. Ibid.

977. Ibid.

978. Fund, op. cit.

979. Ibid.

980. Ibid.

981. Alberto M. Piedra, "The Tragedy of American Education: The Role of John Dewey," The Institute of World Politics, February 1, 2018, https://www.iwp.edu/news_publications/detail/the-tragedy-of-american-education-the-role-of-john-dewey.

982. David Randall, "Making Citizens: How American Universities Teach Civics," National Association of Scholars, January 2017, https://www.nas.org/images/documents/NAS_makingCitizens_fullReport.pdf.

983. Ibid., p. 9.

984. Ibid.

985. Ibid., p. 11.

986. Ibid.

987. Ibid., p. 47.

988. Ibid., p. 48.

989. Ibid., p. 51.

990. "What Patriotism?," The Nation, July 15, 1991, https://www.thenation.com/article/what-patriotism/.

991. Ibid.

992. Corey Savage, "Are Globalism and Progressivism Inevitable?, Return of Kings, April 3, 2017, http://www.returnofkings.com/117651/is-globalism-and-progressivism-inevitable.

993. Ibid.

994. As cited in F. R. Johannes Jacobse, "Solzhenitsyn: Men Have Forgotten God," AOIUSA, July 6, 2011, http://www.aoiusa.org/solzhenitsyn-men-have-forgotten-god/.

995. Charles Battig, "Progressivism as a Mental Illness," American Thinker, December 28, 2016, https://www.americanthinker.com/blog/2016/12/progressivism_as_a_mental_illness.html#ixzz5fQi7QKoM.

996. Lyle H. Rossiter, "The Liberal Mind: The Psychological Causes of Political Madness, Liberty Mind, accessed February 14, 2019, http://www.libertymind.com/.

997. Ibid.

998. "Delusions and Delusional Disorder," WebMD, accessed February 14, 2019, https://www.webmd.com/schizophrenia/guide/delusional-disorder#1.

999. Daniel C. Wilburn, "Progressivism and 'The Banality of Evil'—Nazi Adolf Eichmann's Trial," February 14, 2018, http://www.lakelandcommunity.org/2018/02/progressivism-and-the-banality-of-evil-nazi-adolph-eichmanns-trial/.

1000. Ibid.

1001. Ibid.

1002. As cited in Wilburn op. cit.

1003. Ibid.

1004. Ibid.

1005. Ibid.